The
Dictionary of
Cliches

The Dictionary of Cliches

James Rogers

Facts On File Publications
New York, New York ● Oxford, England

The Dictionary of Cliches

Copyright © 1985 by James Rogers

Library of Congress Cataloging in Publication Data

Rogers, James.
   Dictionary of cliches.

   1. English language—Terms and phrases. 2. English
language—Usage—Dictionaries. 3. Proverbs, English.
I. Title.
PE1689.R65   423'.1   82-7392
ISBN 0-8160-1010-2   AACR2

Printed in the United States

Book Design: Patti Eslinger

10 9 8 7 6 5 4

Table of Contents

INTRODUCTION

The cliché has a bad name as an overworked and therefore banal expression. Spoken or written by someone who is not thinking much about what he is saying or writing, it usually upholds that reputation. Among people who do pay attention to their phrasing, however, clichés can serve as the lubricant of language: summing up a point or a situation, easing a transition in thought, adding a seasoning of humor to a discourse. Indeed, with a keen sense of where such a familiar saying comes from and what it means one can give his prose a piquant turn by embroidering a cliché, as the columnist George Will did when he exclaimed over the fact that the fans of the Chicago Cubs support their team "through thin and thin." My aim in this dictionary has been to provide that sense of where the familiar expressions of English come from.

Doubtless as you look through this book you will find sayings that strike you as proverbs. Many of them are. Since proverbs represent the distilled wisdom from decades or centuries of human experience, it is small wonder that many of them become fixtures of the language. If you were to leaf through *The Oxford Dictionary of English Proverbs,* however, you would find more unfamiliar than familiar entries, since time passes many proverbs by or overwork causes them to lose favor. The distinction I have made between proverb and cliché is current use: if a proverb still gets heavy duty in the language, it ranks as a cliché.

I accumulated many of the entries in this book in, of all places, China, when a group from *Scientific American* went there to celebrate the launching of the translated edition of the magazine. My colleagues, wordsmiths all, knew of this project and obligingly fired clichés at me throughout the trip. I doubt that there is an easier way to assemble a list of familiar expressions than to draw on the experience of some 50 well-read people, and I am grateful to them for their help.

J. T. R.
Sugar Loaf, N.Y.

The
Dictionary of
Cliches

A

A-OK. The situation couldn't be better. It's a space-age term, first employed by John A. Powers, who was a spokesman for the National Aeronautics and Space Administration. He first used it in connection with a manned space flight in 1961, to indicate that the mission was going well. The term caught on and has since served to describe many things that seem to be functioning perfectly.

A-1. Topnotch, the best. The term derives from Lloyd's Register of Shipping and was applied to ships in first-class condition. Lloyd's of London insured ships and gave the A-1's favorable rates. As defined in the "Key to the Register," the "character A denotes New ships, or Ships Renewed or Restored. The Stores of Vessels are designated by the figures 1 and 2; 1 signifies that the Vessel is well and sufficiently found."

Abandon Hope, All Ye Who Enter Here. You're going into a dismal, unpromising, no-win situation. The expression comes from Dante's *Inferno* (1300), where it appears as, "All hope abandon, ye who enter here." "Here" was the Inferno, or Hell.

Able to Make Head or Tail of It, Not. It's ambiguous, puzzling, unclear. An animal seen indistinctly could have given rise to the saying, and so could a coin that was worn on both sides or wasn't seen clearly. Thus, Margery Mason in *The Tickler Tickled* (1679): "Their Tale . . . had neither Head nor Taile." (Margery Mason, *spinster, pseud.*, is the singular way this author is listed in library catalogues. What her real name was is not recorded.)

According to Hoyle. Following the rules or the established procedures. Edmond Hoyle, an 18th-century Englishman, was an expert on games. A popular card game at that time was whist, a forerunner of bridge. In 1742 he published a handbook on it: *A Short Treatise on the Game of Whist.* Later he published the rules of other card games, and eventually he was recognized as the leading authority on such games.

Ace in the Hole. A good move, maneuver or argument kept in reserve for use at a strategic time. In stud poker it is an ace that is turned facedown on the table; only the player who holds it knows he has a secret source of unmatchable power.

1

Ace up His Sleeve. A surprise, a hidden weapon. The cardsharp, who depended for his living on winning at cards, was known to slip winning cards (of which the ace is the winningest) up his sleeve, to be pulled out and played when they would do the most good. This particular way of putting the thought probably dates from the 19th century, when cardsharps were rampant, but the thought of concealing something useful up one's sleeve is much older. A poem by William Dunbar in the early 16th century refers to "ane fals cairt in to his sleif."

Achilles' Heel. The one weak spot in an otherwise strong character or position. In Greek mythology Thetis, the leader of the sea nymphs, wanted to make sure that her infant son Achilles would be invulnerable in battle as an adult. She held him by the heel and dipped him into the River Styx, whose water was believed to confer invulnerability, but his heel remained dry because her hand was cupped over it. Achilles died as a result of a wound from an arrow that struck him in that heel.

Aching Void. A yearning or longing. The expression appears, with its meaning unmistakable, in *Olney Hymns,* by the 18th-century English poet William Cowper, who may have originated the thought. The verse reads:
> What peaceful hours I once enjoy'd!
> How sweet their mem'ry still!
> But they have left an aching void,
> The world can never fill.

Acid Test. A severe or crucial trial. In times when gold was in wide circulation, the question often arose as to whether an alleged gold coin or object was genuine. Nitric acid was applied; if the piece was false gold, the acid decomposed it, but if it was genuine, the gold remained intact.

Across the Board. Encompassing everything or everyone, as in "The workers received an across-the-board pay increase." The term arose from the notice board displaying odds in a horse race. A bet across the board means that the fan laying down his money stands to collect something if his horse should win (come in first), place (come in second) or show (finish third). In 1958, *The Listener* showed how the meaning had expanded: "There is a common cliché among labour relations specialists in the United States that it is not the across-the-board wage increase . . . which is decisive."

Actions Speak Louder Than Words. What you do is more significant than what you say. The thought was put almost that way in 1692 by Gersham Bulkeley, in *Will and Doom:* "Actions are more significant than words."

2

Add Insult to Injury. To be notably harsh or unkind to someone (perhaps unwittingly); to (in effect) hit someone when he is down. A version of this notion appeared in Latin almost 2,000 years ago in the fables of Phaedrus. He cited a fable by Aesop in which a bald man swats at a fly that has bitten him, misses the fly and hits himself on the head. The fly remarks, "You wished to kill me for a touch. What will you do to yourself since you have added insult to injury?" In English the idea was picked up as early as 1748, when Edward Moore used it in his play, *The Foundling*: "This is adding Insult to Injuries."

Afraid of His Own Shadow. Excessively timid. It is an old way of characterizing the quickly worried or easily frightened, dating at least to 1513, when Sir Thomas More wrote in *Richard III:* "Who maye lette her to feare her owne shadowe?" In another work, in 1533, he came closer to modern usage: "The Ordinaries afeard of their own shadow."

Alarums and Excursions. Turmoil; threatening activity. The expression served as a stage direction in Elizabethan drama to indicate the need for some sort of feverish action, such as the movement of soldiers across the stage to the accompaniment of martial sounds from the wings or backstage. It turns up now in reference to areas or circumstances where the situation is unstable, as in "the alarums and excursions in the Middle East."

Alas and Alack. Sadly; too bad. Probably the terms were combined originally for reinforcement, since they are similar in meaning. "Alas," which was recorded in print as early as the 13th century, serves to express concern or unhappiness, "alack" (15th century) to express sorrow or regret. They had been combined by the 19th century, as reflected in *The Cruise of the Midge*, by Michael Scott (1834): "Alas and alackaday both the pig and the wig were drowned."

Albatross Around the Neck, An. A burden, particularly one that is difficult to get rid of. The real albatross is a large seabird. The Ancient Mariner in Samuel Taylor Coleridge's long narrative poem of that name (1798) tells how as a young sailor he shot with his crossbow an albatross that had guided his storm-driven ship out of the Antarctic. Trouble then befell the ship; the crew, blaming him for it, hung the dead bird around his neck as a curse:

> "Ah! well a-day! what evil looks
> Had I from old and young!
> Instead of the cross, the Albatross
> About my neck was hung."

All Due Respect, With. You're wrong. The phrase comes under the heading of social lubricant. You are about to attack a position taken by someone, but you don't want to seem insulting or

3

overbelligerent. An early example offered a somewhat different perspective; it is in M. R. Mitford's *Our Village* (1826): "[My greyhound] is sliding her snake-like head into my hand, at once to invite the caress which she likes so well, and to intimate with all due respect that it is time to go home."

All Greek to Me. Incomprehensible or unintelligible, as if spoken or written in a foreign language. The term was in use at least 300 years ago in Shakespear's *Julius Caesar:* the character Casca, who is among the group conspiring to kill Caesar, tells Brutus and Cassius how Caesar thrice refused the crown of emperor. Asked if Cicero said anything at the time (Cicero did, speaking in Greek to prevent passersby from understanding him), Casca replies: "Those that understood him smiled at one another and shook their heads; but for mine own part, it was Greek to me."

All His Worldly Goods. Everything he has (usually in the sense that he has lost them all at once, or is so reduced in circumstances that he can carry all of them at the same time). In Edward Lear's poem, "The Courtship of the Yonghy-Bongy-Bò" (1877) one finds:

> On the coast of Coromandel
> Where the early pumpkins blow,
> In the middle of the woods
> Lived the Yonghy-Bongy-Bò.
> Two old chairs, and half a candle,
> One old jug without a handle—
> These were all his worldly goods.

The phrase was locked into the language long ago in the traditional wedding service. It appeared in the *Book of Common Prayer* in 1548 as: "With al my worldly Goodes I thee endowe."

All Sorts and Conditions of Men. Everybody; no restrictions on inclusion. From "A Prayer for All Conditions of Men" in the *Book of Common Prayer* of the Episcopal Church and the Church of England: "O God, the Creator and Preserver of all mankind, we humbly beseech thee for all sorts and conditions of men; that thou wouldest be pleased to make thy ways known unto them, thy saving health unto all nations." The phrase was in the prayer book at least as early as 1662.

All Things to all Men, Be. Show different attitudes to different people in an effort to please everybody or avoid controversy. The Bible records St. Paul as saying in his First Epistle to the Corinthians (1 Corinthians, 9:22), "To the weak became I as weak, that I might gain the weak: I am made all things to all men, that I might by all means save some."

All Thumbs. Clumsy, awkward at physical tasks. Examples of the expression appear in the 16th century, as in Sir Thomas More's

4

A Treatise on the Passion (1534): "Euery fynger shalbe a thombe, and we shall fumble it vp in hast." In modern English it is: "Every finger shall be a thumb, and we shall fumble it up in haste." An example in the *West Somerset Word-Book*, published in 1886, is "Leave it alone, all thumbs! why thee art as clumsy as a cow handling a musket."

All Wet. Wrong; making an implausible argument. According to the *Dictionary of American Slang*, the expression originated in the United States around 1930. One can suppose that the anonymous author of the phrase had in mind a comparison with the notion that a person who lets himself get all wet and stays that way for any length of time is a little abnormal. An old English expression, "to cover oneself with a wet sack," meant to make vain excuses, to adopt a position that could not be taken seriously; it dates from the 16th century.

All Wool and a Yard Wide. Genuine and of excellent quality. One hears this enough to assume it is an old saw or proverb; in fact it appears to have been mainly a verbal expression. In the 19th century, enough short measure and inferior merchandise reached the market for sellers of the products of textile mills in New England to adopt "all wool and a yard wide" as a claim for their "woolen" fabrics.

All and Sundry. Everybody or everything, "Sundry," which is from the same root as "sunder," refers to individuals, so "all and sundry" is a tautology meaning a group of people or things and every individual or item in it. Sir William Fraser wrote in *Wemyss of Wemyss* (1389) of "there [their] thyngys al and syndry."

All at Sea. Lost; bewildered; confused. A person at sea who has lost his bearings is in such a predicament, and the expression probably derives from the time when taking bearings on celestial bodies was the only way to ascertain a ship's position.

All in a Day's Work. A routine matter; something that can be done without undue difficulty. The expression was common by the 18th century, and its origins are lost. Sir Walter Scott's novel *The Monastery* (1820) has the following passage: "That will cost me a farther ride, . . . but it is all in the day's work."

All in the Same Boat. We're in this together; we all share the same risks. The literal origin is in the perils faced by people at sea, particularly in small boats during ancient times. The figurative meaning, which dominates today, was in print by 1584 in Thomas Hudson's poem *Judith*:

> "Haue ye pain? So likewise pain haue we;
> For in one boat we both imbarked be."

5

All to the Good. Satisfactory; tending toward a desirable outcome. This "good" is, or was, an accounting term referring to a balance on the plus side, a net profit or an excess of assets over liabilities. *The Spectator* in 1889 described a man who was "boasting that he . . . had so much heavier a balance in the bank to the good, in consequence."

All's Fair in Love and War. Anything goes in this situation. "All policy's allowed in war and love" turns up in a 17th-century play, *Love at a Venture,* by Susannah Centlivre. The modern expression appeared in 1850 in *Frank Fairlegh,* a novel by Francis Edward Smedley.

All-Out War. An engagement in which each side is fully extended, using all its resources. "All out" in the sense of total or entire is long-lived. In *The Romans of Partenay* (1475) one finds: "They approached Columbere toun all—out." The concept of all-out war dates from World War II and was recorded retrospectively by A. L. Rowse in his *The Expansion of Elizabethan England* (1955): "Not committing herself to an all-out war. . . ."

Almighty Dollar, The. A reference to the influence of money over people's minds, or to America's pivotal role in international finance. Washington Irving seems to have originated the term in *Wolfert's Roost, Creole Village* (1837): "The almighty dollar, that object of universal devotion throughout our land. . . ." Some 200 years earlier the Elizabethan dramatist Ben Jonson wrote of "almighty gold."

Alpha and Omega. The beginning and the end. Alpha (œua) and omega (œun) are the first and last letters of the Greek alphabet. The term appears several times in the New Testament's Revelation to Saint John, including: "I am Alpha and Omega, the beginning and the ending, saith the Lord. . . ."

Alphabet Soup. A jumble of agencies or concepts known mainly by their initials or acronyms. Alfred E. Smith, who had been the governor of New York and the Democratic nominee for President in 1928, was no great admirer of the New Deal instituted by Franklin D. Roosevelt, the Democrat who succeeded him as governor in 1928 and became President in 1933. When such New Deal agencies as the NRA, TVA, CCC and AAA (National Recovery Administration, Tennessee Valley Authority, Civilian Conservation Corps and Agricultural Adjustment Administration) proliferated in Roosevelt's first term, Smith said the Government was "submerged in a bowl of alphabet soup." There really is such a soup, in which pasta is formed in the shapes of the letters of the alphabet.

American Way, The. Conforming with traditions in the United States. The term was in use by 1885, when the *Century Magazine* advised its readers that "Dynamiting is not the American way."

Ancestral Acres. The place one's family came from (and where one may still be living). The Latin poet Horace wrote in his *Epodes* (about 30 B.C.): "Happy the man who far from schemes of business, like the early generations of mankind, works his ancestral acres, with oxen of his own breeding, from all usury free."

And How. That's for sure. Bayard Taylor, a widely traveled American journalist who became the country's minister to Germany in 1878, saw the origins of this expression in a similar German intensive, *und wie*. H. L. Mencken, in *The American Language*, noted that the phrase has also been traced to the Italian *e come* and the French *et comment*, but he was not persuaded "and how" derived from any of these. Incidentally, Taylor, writing about "and how" in a letter to the American poet Edmund Stedman in 1865, defined it in terms of another expression that is practically a cliché these days: "You'd better believe it."

And I Don't Mean Maybe. Do what I say; I'm not kidding. "Maybe" in the sense of perhaps is a contraction of "it may be" and was in use by the 15th century. Today's cliché arose in the United States around 1920. Its originator is unknown, but by 1927 it was part of the language, as is shown in Clarence Buddington Kelland's *Dance Magic:* "Leach is a bearcat and I don't mean maybe."

And So to Bed. The end of that activity (particularly of a day's affairs). The daily entries in the diary of Samuel Pepys, which he kept from January 1, 1660, to May 31, 1669, often end with this phrase. Pepys wrote the diary in a shorthand code that was not deciphered until 1825.

Ants in His Pants. Excessively restless or eager. Hugh S. Johnson, the colorful former Army general who headed the National Recovery Administration in 1933–1934, may have originated this phrase but certainly made it popular. "Full of beans" and "full of red ants" convey the same idea.

Any Port in a Storm. Whatever refuge one can find or stratagem one can resort to in a time of physical or mental difficulty. It is a sailor's expression that was familiar enough by 1780 to appear in a play by the English writer Elizabeth Inchbald: "Here is a door open, i' faith—any port in a storm, they say."

Apple of Discord. A cause of dispute or rancor. In Greek mythology Eris, the goddess of discord, uninvited to the wedding of Thetis and Peleus, sought revenge: she threw a golden apple on a table, saying it was for "the most beautiful." Hera, Pallas Athene

7

and Aphrodite each laid claim to it. Paris, as judge, awarded it to Aphrodite; Hera and Pallas Athene were displeased and sought vengeance. The trouble they stirred up has been credited with bringing about the fall of Troy. In Roman mythology the contending goddesses were Juno, Minerva and Venus.

Apple of His Eye. A cherished person or object. In old English the eye's pupil was known as the apple because it was thought to be spherical and solid. Since the pupil is a crucial and indispensable portion of the eye, it serves as a symbol of something cherished. An example in the Coverdale Bible of 1535 (Zechariah II, 8) is: "Who so toucheth you, shal touche the aple of his owne eye." The expression also appears in Deuteronomy XXXII, 10 as part of a song spoken by Moses:

> He found him in a desert land,
> and in the howling waste of the wilderness;
> he encircled him, he cared for him,
> he kept him as the apple of his
> eye.

Apple-Pie Order. Shipshape; everything just so, in perfect order. The expression is said to have derived from the French *nappes pliées* (folded tableclothes) and from "cap-a-pie [head-to-foot] order." I have also seen it ascribed to the neatly turreted border often fashioned at the edge of a pie crust. In the end one has to agree with the *Oxford English Dictionary* that the origin of the phrase has not been established.

Arm's Length. A distance deliberately maintained to forestall familiarity or domination. Virginia Woolf wrote of a person who was "pompous and ornate and keeps us at arm's length." In relation to, say, labor negotiations, one is likely to read that "arm's-length bargaining" is going on.

Armed to the Teeth. Fully or even excessively equipped with weapons for a contest. The English statesman Richard Cobden (1804–65) is recorded in his *Speeches on peace, financial reform, colonial reform and other subjects* (1849) as saying: "Is there any reason why we should be armed to the teeth?"

As Every Schoolboy Knows. Elementary; basic knowledge (often used condescendingly or as a put-down). In *On Lord Clive* (1840) Thomas Babington, Lord Macaulay, wrote: "Every schoolboy knows who imprisoned Montezuma, and who strangled Atahualpa." Few schoolboys would know either of those facts today, and probably a great many did not know them in 1840 either. Viscount Melbourne once said of Macaulay: "I wish I was as cocksure of anything as Tom Macaulay is of everything."

As Fate (Luck) Would Have It. That's the way it happened, and it was a fortunate turn of events. *American Speech* recorded the expression in 1928: "As luck would have it, we took another road."

As One Man. In unison; unanimously. In the Old Testament (Judges 20 : 8) it is said that "all the people [of Israel] arose as one man" and "gathered against the city [of Gibeah], united as one man." The men of Gibeah had ravished and killed the concubine of a Levite who had spent the night there.

As the Crow Flies. In a direct line; by the shortest route (usually to distinguish travel by air from travel on the ground). Although the crow is not noted for flying long distances in a straight line, it does go directly to its target of opportunity (such as a cornfield), whereas the human traveler has to follow the twists and turns of the road. Robert Southey was close to the modern expression when in 1800 he wrote in a letter: "About fifteen miles, the crow's road."

At His Fingertips. Readily available. It seems to date from early in this century. An example in the *Strand Magazine* in 1905: "He has at his finger-tips every stroke in the game." Then there is "to his fingertips," meaning through and through, as in: "Alive with science to the finger tips." That appeared in the London *Daily Chronicle* in 1907.

At Loggerheads. Unable to agree. A strange word, loggerheads, seldom encountered now without its "at," although it has several meanings, notably blockhead or stupid person. Among the other meanings are; (1) a metal tool with a long handle and a bulbous end; the bulb was heated in a fire and used to melt pitch or heat liquid; (2) a species of turtle with a large head; the name was also applied to other animals with large heads. One can speculate that people at loggerheads are confronting each other much like heated bulbs or heavy-headed animals, belligerently head to head. The phrase, with its meaning of confrontation, was known in 1680 when Francis Kirkman wrote, in *The English Rogue*: "They frequently quarrell'd about their Sicilian wenches, and indeed . . . they [the wenches] seem . . . to be worth the going to Logger-heads for."

At This (Particular) Point in Time. Now. An orotundity that gained wide currency in the early 1970s. It has now almost passed beyond the cliché stage and is quite likely to be employed sarcastically by someone poking fun at orotundity.

At the Tip of My Tongue. Something I know but can't quite recall. The implication is that the elusive fact will soon be retrieved and then can be spoken. Since the tongue is the output end of the speaking apparatus, the expression must have arisen when someone thought that a name or a fact was practically there if only he or she could dredge it up from memory.

Avoid Like the Plague. Shun rigorously; stay away from something at all costs. It has been three centuries since the plague last devastated the populations of Europe, but it has left its mark in this expression. Thomas Moore, assembling Byron's works in 1835, wrote: "Saint Augustine . . . avoided the school as the plague."

Ax To Grind, Have an. To seek a particular objective; to maneuver to achieve a personal goal. The term is often attributed to Benjamin Franklin, but, in fact, it seems to have originated with Charles Miner in the Wilkes-Barre (Pa.) *Gleaner* in 1811. In this tale a man with ax approached Miner (then a boy) and by flattery persuaded him to sharpen the ax on the grindstone in the family's yard. The boy gave it a good edge but got no thanks; indeed, the school bell rang and the man told the boy to get moving because he was late for school. The tale ends with the adult Miner writing: "When I see a merchant over-polite to his customers, begging them to taste a little brandy and throwing half his goods on the counter—thinks I, that man has an ax to grind."

B

Babble Like a Brook. Chatter enthusiastically and perhaps rather incoherently. Thomas Gray's "Elegy Written in a Country Churchyard" speaks of "the brook that babbles by." The phrase is onomatopoetic, that is, the words as spoken resemble the sound of a running brook. A person chattering aimlessly on sounds somewhat the same.

Babe in the Woods. An innocent; someone in a situation he is too unsophisticated to handle. A popular tale in 16th century England concerns a wealthy man who dies, leaving his property to his very young son and daughter. They are to be taken care of by their uncle until they are old enough to inherit the property, but should they die before that time, the uncle is to inherit. The temptation is too much for the uncle, who hires two men to do away with the children. One of the men can't bring himself to do it, so he murders his partner and leaves the children on their own in the woods. They die, being incapable of taking care of themselves in such a harsh environment, and from then on the uncle suffers one calamity after another. The truth is revealed much later when the surviving hireling is arrested for robbery and tells of the uncle's plot against the children.

Back and Fill. To vacillate or be irresolute. In the days of large-scale commercial sailing, when ships had to work their way up and down river channels to get to and from ports, a technique of navigation was to let the tide move the vessel in the appropriate direction and to help control the ship by backing and filling the sails as necessary, that is, by turning them so that the wind tended to slow the vessel down or to help it move forward. The ship was thus kept away from obstacles, which is what a person seems to be doing when he waffles over what to do or what position to take in an argument.

Back of the Hand, Give Him the. Show contempt or disdain. Shakespeare may have been the first to put this gesture into words. In *Julius Caesar* Brutus asks Casca "what hath chanced to-day, that Caesar looks so sad," and Casca replies, "Why, there was a crown offered him: and being offered him, he put it by with the back of his hand; thus: and then the people fell a-shouting."

11

Back to Square One. Starting over; doing something again because the previous effort has failed. The expression, or the concept, turns up in various games such as hopscotch and board games where one has to return to a place one has already passed. It may also be connected with the practice in England some 50 years ago when a map of a soccer (football) field was printed in radio programs with the field divided into squares so that people listening to a radio broadcast of a game could follow the action better.

Back to the Drawing Board. A redesign is necessary. Some years ago a cartoon by Peter Arno showed a man, presumably the designer, walking away from an airplane that has crashed; he says, "Well, back to the old drawing board." It seems likely that Arno was reflecting an expression already in wide use rather than originating it, since the saying is also familiar in several other English-speaking countries. Eric Partridge has suggested that it originated with aircraft designers in World War II.

Back to the Salt Mine. A return to hard or tedious work, or just one's job after one has had a relaxing interval away from it. The expression has been around since about 1950 and seems to have arisen from the widespread notion in the West that both czarist and Communist Russia sentenced certain prisoners to work in the salt mines in Siberia.

Back to the Wall, Have Your. To be under heavy attack or in a desperate position. One can picture the swordsman of yore backed against a wall; unable to retreat any farther or to maneuver for position, he lashes out at his attackers with renewed vigor, knowing it is his last chance. Although a related expression, "to go to the wall," meaning to succumb in a struggle, can be traced to the 16th century, the sense of fighting with one's back to the wall must be even older.

Back-seat Driver. Someone who gives orders when he or she is not in charge. Today's back-seat driver is most likely to be in the front, alongside the real driver, but in the early days of motoring it was not unusual for the driver (often a chauffeur) to be in the front seat and the passengers in the back seat. I would date the expression to the 1920's. Strangely the brash back-seat driver is quite in contrast with the shy or self-effacing person who, in the much older phrase, "takes a back seat."

Backhanded Compliment. A compliment phrased in such a way as to suggest that it is really a criticism or a deprecation. The phrase is probably derived from the notion of giving the back of one's hand, meaning to show contempt or disdain. Leigh Hunt was close to the thought in 1813, when he wrote (in *The Examiner*) of "a back-handed pat on the cheek."

Bad Blood. Ill feeling between two people or between the people on two sides of an issue. Blood was once regarded as the seat of the emotions, and bad blood meant anger. In Jonathan Swift's *The Battle of the Books* (1697) one finds: "Hot words passed . . . and ill blood was plentifully bred."

Bag and Baggage. Everything; all of it. At one time this was a military term meaning all of an army's portable items, including individual soldiers' possessions. Whereas now the expression is usually employed in the sense of, "clear out, with everything you've got," it once meant an army was departing with honor, without having to surrender anything. An example from 1525 is: "We haue with vs all our bagges and baggages . . . that we haue wonne . . . by armes." An example of the more modern interpretation can be traced to 1620: "To kick this fellow . . . and send him downe stayres with his bag and baggage." The first example is from Lord Berners (*Sir John Froissart*), the second from Thomas Middleton (*The Witch*).

Bag of Bones. Thin or emaciated. Sometimes "skin and bones." Examples include "There, get down stairs, little bag o' bones" in Charles Dickens's *Oliver Twist* (1838) and "I am almost ashamed to punish a bag of skin and bones" in Charles Kingsley's play *The Saint's Tragedy* (1848).

Bag of Tricks. All of one's resources; every expedient at one's command. In the fable of "The Fox and the Cat," as by the Brothers Grimm (and in a slightly different fashion by Aesop), the fox boasts that he is "master of a hundred arts, and have into the bargain a sackful of cunning." (In Aesop he says "a hundred shifts," meaning expedients.) They did not serve the fox well; when dogs chased the fox and cat, the cat reached safety by climbing a tree, but the fox was caught. "Open your sack, Mr. Fox, open your sack," the cat cried, but it was too late.

Baker's Dozen. A little extra; specifically, thirteen. The term is usually traced to an act of the English Parliament in 1266, laying down standards of weight for bread. In order to make certain they were meeting the standard, bakers adopted the practice of giving 13 loaves to vendors for each dozen they bought to sell to consumers.

Balance of Power. The influence to swing an issue in a certain direction or to keep it stable. An early (1579) example of the concept appears in Sir Geoffrey Fenton's *The History of Guicciardini, Conteining the Warres of Italie:* "God hath . . . put into your hands the ballance of power."

Ball Bounces, That's the Way the. You have to be fatalistic; this is how things happen. A variant with the same meaning is "That's the way the cookie crumbles." Both expressions seem to have originated in the United States some 30 years ago. The bouncing ball in many games, particularly football, is notably unpredictable; the player has to deal with whatever bounce he gets.

Ball of Wax, a Whole New. A changed situation. Also "the whole ball of wax," meaning the entire situation. William and Mary Morris in the *Morris Dictionary of Word and Phrase Origins* relate that a correspondent in Kentucky suggests an origin from a practice described in *Coke on Littleton* (1620), a text on English law. The practice dealt with the division of land among the heirs of an estate:

> "Every part of the land by itself is written in a little scrawle and is covered by waxe in the manner of a little ball, so as none may see the scrawle. Then the four [there were four heirs here] balls of waxe are put in a hat to be kept in the hands of an indifferent [impartial] man and then the eldest daughter shall first put her hands into the hat and take a ball of waxe with the scrawle within the ball for her part and then the second sister . . . and so on."

Balm in Gilead. Surcease; something soothing. The balm of Gilead is an evergreen tree with leaves that yield an aromatic substance that used to be made into an unguent or ointment valued for soothing pains or healing wounds. In the Old Testament [Jeremiah 8 : 22] Jeremiah, saying he is passing on the word of the Lord, queries:

> Is there no balm in Gilead?
> Is there no physician there?
> Why then has the health of the
> daughter of my people
> not been restored?

Gilead is a mountainous region east of the Jordan River; once part of Palestine, it is now in Jordan.

Baptism of (by) Fire. A soldier's introduction to battle or any battler's introduction to the fray. The term also once meant martyrdom by fire or the experience of any severe ordeal. *Cassell's Encyclopaedic Dictionary* (1902 supplement) says: "When during the Franco-German war of 1870, Prince Louis Napoleon . . . was first exposed, by direction of his father, Napoleon III, and with his own consent, to the fire of the enemy at Saarbrück, the event was called a 'baptism of fire.'" (The French is *baptême de feu.*)

Bark Up the Wrong Tree. To misdirect one's argument or effort. Hunting raccoons in the 19th century, one had to go out at night (because the animals are nocturnal) and usually took a dog to help find them. The pursued raccoon was likely to take to a tree, and the dog was supposed to lurk at the base of that tree and bark until the hunter arrived. If the dog had the wrong tree, the hunter was unlikely to get his prey. Davy Crockett in *Sketches and Eccentricities* (1833) wrote: "I told him . . . that he reminded me of the meanest thing on God's earth, an old coon dog, barking up the wrong tree."

Barkis is Willin'. I'm ready. Barkis was a character in *David Copperfield*, by Charles Dickens (1850), who sent a message to Clara Peggotty by way of Copperfield that, "Barkis is willin'." Barkis meant he was proposing marriage. The term was soon applied to any kind of willingness.

Bat Out of Hell, Like a. Rapidly. Why a bat would leave hell any faster than you or I, given the opportunity, is not clear. Moreover, the habitual flight of the bat is, as an 18th-century writer put it, an "irregular, uncertain and jerking motion," not symbolic of great speed. One can speculate that the originator of the phrase envisioned the bat as abandoning its habitual motion in favor of a fast, streaking flight should it have the chance to escape from hell.

Bated Breath, With. Eagerly expectant; apprehensive. Bate is a good but underworked verb that means, among other things, to moderate, restrain, reduce the intensity of. To bate one's breath is to soften it, quiet it, or to hold it briefly as one is wont to do in a tense situation. An example from 1859 is in the novel *Adam Bede*, by George Eliot (Marian Evans): "To his dying day he bated his breath a little when he told the story."

Bats in the Belfry. Crazy; a bit weird or nutty. Bats live in belfries, among other secluded places, and since a belfry is usually in the tower of a church, the connection between that lofty place and the human head is easily made. The expression appears to have originated in the United States; a correspondent in *Notes and Queries* wrote that the American author Ambrose Bierce had used it in 1907, but the correspondent did not give the quotation. In *Colonel Todhunter* (1911), R. D. Saunders wrote: "It's a case of bats in the belfry on that one subject."

Batten Down the Hatches. Prepare for trouble. A "hatch" provides the entry to a hold where cargo is stored on a ship; at the approach of a storm at sea the order is given to make the hatches secure. "Batten" has several meanings, among them a strip of wood nailed to the cover of a hatch to help hold it firmly in place. Young seamen were advised in *The Novice's or Young Seaman's Catechism* (1860): "It is sometimes necessary in bad weather to put on the gratings [over the hatches] and nail tarpaulins over them; this is called 'battening down.'"

Battle Royal. A fight with a number of participants; a big fight. (It can be a verbal fight.) The term originated in a specific cockfighting event, an elimination tournament starting with 16. The eight winners in the first round fought in the second, the four winners of which fought in the third round; the two finalists met in the "battle royal." The expression was used in both its senses as early as 1672.

Be Buffaloed, To. To be overwhelmed or thwarted. In most countries a buffalo is a form of ox, but in the United States the word also applies to the bison, a formidable and intimidating animal. The meaning of this American expression was put clearly in the *New York Evening Post* in 1904: "The newspapers were what we used to term in the Southwest 'buffaloed' by the McKinley myth—that is, silenced by the fear of incurring the resentment of a people taught to regard McKinley as a saint."

Be That as It May. Accept that point as given and leave it aside, or at least let's drop it and get on with the discussion; let happen what will happen. In the poem *Rose-Leaves*, by Henry Austin Dobson (1840–1921), one finds:

> Rose kissed me to-day.
> Will she kiss me to-morrow?
> Let it be as it may,
> Rose kissed me to-day.

Be of Good Cheer. Go well; don't worry. The expression appears twice in the New Testament (Matthew 14 : 27 and John 16 : 33), both times as a statement by Jesus. In Matthew, when the disciples see Jesus walking on the sea, they are frightened. He says, "Be of good cheer; it is I; be not afraid." And John records Him as saying, in His last long talk with the disciples, "These things I have spoken unto you, that in me ye might have peace. In the world ye shall have tribulation; but be of good cheer; I have overcome the world."

Be-All and End-All. The dominant factor. In Shakespeare's *Macbeth* the first act describes a plot by Macbeth and his wife to assassinate King Duncan of Scotland so Macbeth can become king. Soliloquizing on this scheme, Macbeth says: "If it were done when 'tis done, then 'twere well it were done quickly: if the assassination could trammel up the consequence, and catch, with his surcease, success; that but this blow might be the be-all and end-all here. . . . "

Bête Noire. An annoyance; a thorn in the side; a bothersome person or problem. The literal translation of the French is "black beast." Its use in French and its transfer intact to English probably reflect ancient superstitions about black animals. One was that the black sheep, an oddity in a herd of sheep, bore the mark of the of the devil. Another, still encountered, is that it is bad luck when a black cat crosses your path.

Bear the Brunt. Take the main load or thrust. "Brunt" can mean a blow or an onslaught, either of which is likely to be sustained, and must be endured, in a battle, including a verbal battle or argument. An early example of the phrase is in Robert Barret's *The Theorike and Practike of Modern Warres* (1598): "The first three, fiue [five] or seuen [seven] rankes . . . do beare the chiefe brunt."

Bear the Burden and the Heat of the Day. Cope with adversity or demanding conditions. It is a biblical expression (Matthew 20 : 12), appearing in Matthew's account of the parable by Jesus of the man who hired laborers for his vineyard. Although he hired them in groups over a period of several hours, he paid them all the same amount of money at the end of the day. The ones who had worked the longest complained, "Thou hast made them equal unto us, which have borne the burden and heat of the day." The employer was unmoved, pointing out that the men had agreed on the wage and that he had chosen to "give unto this last, even as unto thee." Of which Jesus said, "So the last shall be first, and the first last; for many be called, but few chosen."

Beard the Lion In His Den. Take on a dangerous task; take a brave action. In the tale of David and Goliath in the Old Testament book of Samuel, Saul is expressing misgivings, saying to David: "You are not able to go against this Philistine to fight with him; for you are but a youth, and he has been a man of war from his youth." David replies: "Your servant used to keep sheep for his father; and when there came a lion, or a bear, and took a lamb from the flock, I went after him and smote him and delivered it out of his mouth; and if he arose against me, I caught him by his beard, and smote him and killed him." An example of the modern expression is in Sir Walter Scott's *Marmion*: "And dar'st thou then / To beard the lion in his den. . . ."

Beat Around the Bush. To approach an objective indirectly. People hunting birds used to employ beaters to flail at bushes, rousing birds for the hunters to shoot at. In the figurative sense the notion is that if one spends too much time in a roundabout approach, the prize may get away or go to someone else. An early example (1572) by the English author George Gascoigne suggests both meanings: "He bet about the bush, whyles other caught the birds."

Beat Swords into Plowshares. Turn to peaceful activities. In the Old Testament (Isaiah 2 : 4) one reads of Isaiah's vision that "the Lord's house shall be established in the top of the mountains," whereupon: "And he shall judge among the nations, and shall rebuke many people; and they shall beat their swords into

17

plowshares, and their spears into pruninghooks; nation shall not lift up sword against nation, neither shall they learn war any more."

Beat Them All Hollow. To defeat or surpass utterly. One of the meanings of "hollow," dating from the 17th century at least, is thoroughly or completely; it may derive from "wholly." As the *Oxford English Dictionary* says: "The origin of this is obscure, and has excited conjecture since its first appearance in literature." The earliest example (1668) cited by the *OED* is from Stephen Skinner's study of English etymology: "He carried it hollow . . . he carried it wholly."

Beat a Dead Horse. Do something futile; belabor an issue that is no longer of interest. A horseman occasionally applies some form of forceful persuasion to a live horse to get it moving; he might do the same to a dead horse, that is, beat it or flog it in frustration, or perhaps in the belief that it is still alive. Related expressions date at least to the 17th century. In 1887 John Morley, biographer of the English political figure Richard Cobden, wrote: "In parliament he [Cobden] again pressed the necessity of reducing expenditure. Friends warned him that he was flogging a dead horse."

Beat a Hasty Retreat. To depart from a position in adverse circumstances or in defeat. In the days when wars were fought on open fields by massed infantrymen, various signals could be conveyed to the troops by specific types of drumbeats. One of them was for retreat.

Beat the Rap. Avoid a penalty; escape punishment. A rap in the sense of a sharp blow is an old word, probably deriving from the sound made by the blow. In the past century the word has taken on many other meanings, including a criminal charge and a prison sentence. One can see the word evolving in the *Atlantic Monthly* of March, 1865: "He who has the bad taste to meddle with the caprices of believers . . . gets the rap and the orders of dismissal."

Beats the Band. Outdoes anything around. Although this expression has a hint of great age about it, it apparently dates only to about 1900 in the United States, a time when band concerts were popular and bands often played at ceremonial occasions such as the Fourth of July. On such an occasion the band was likely to be the most audible and conspicuous entity around, and any action or performance that outdid the band was remarkable. Geraldine Bonner was picking up on the expression in 1900, when she wrote in *Hard Pan:* "Doesn't that beat the band?"

Beauty is Only Skin Deep. Some desirable or admirable things are nonetheless superficial or transient. "Beauty's but skin-deepe" one is told in *A Select Second Husband for Sir Thomas Overburie's Wife* (1606), by John Davies of Hereford. Another facet of the notion is in William Cobbett's *Advice to Young Men* (1829): "The less favoured part of the sex say, that 'beauty is but skin deep'; . . . but it is very agreeable, though, for all that."

Beauty is in the Eye of the Beholder. You see what your mind is predisposed to see, and what you see is not necessarily evident to others. The concept appears as early as 1756 in Edmund Burke's *A Philosophical Inquiry into the Origin of Our Ideas of the Sublime and Beautiful:* "Beauty is, for the greater part, some quality in bodies acting mechanically upon the human mind by the intervention of the senses." The modern expression appears in Margaret Hungerford's *Molly Bawn* (1878).

Beck and Call, At Your. Immediately available; obediently ready. A "beck" is a silent signal, such as a nod of the head or a motion with the forefinger. The sense is apparent in the Earl of Worcester's *Iulius Cesars Commentaryes* (1470): "It should be ready at a beck." In summoning a servant one might have to resort to a "call" as well as a "beck" if the servant did not see the beck or failed to respond to it.

Bed of Roses. A soft or enviable situation. Christopher Marlowe's poem, "The Passionate Shepherd to His Love" (1593), which opens with the memorable line, "Come live with me and be my Love," continues two stanzas later:
> And I will make thee beds of roses
> And a thousand fragrant posies.

When in 1521 the Spanish conquerors of the Aztecs were torturing the Emperor Cuauhtémoc and the prince of Tlacopán in an effort to find out where the Aztec treasure was, the emperor sought to encourage the prince to persevere by saying, "Am I then, upon a bed of roses?"

Bee in His Bonnet, He Has a. He is a bit daft, particularly on some one subject; he is idiosyncratic about something. Anyone who has had a bee caught in his beekeeper's bonnet or his hair or any kind of headgear knows that the experience will quickly make him act rather daft. An earlier related expression was "to have your head full of bees." In that form the expression appears as early as 1513. In 1681 Samuel Colvil wrote, in his *Mock Poem, or Whiggs Supplication:*
> A Scripturist, thou proves, as he was
> In whose fool Bonnetcase a Bee was.

Beer and Skittles, Not all. Not an unmixed pleasure. Skittles is an old game in which one attempts to knock down nine wooden pins set in a square on a wooden base by pitching or sliding a wooden disk at them. Beer was a natural accompaniment to the pleasant hours spent at the game. In *Pickwick Papers*, by Charles Dickens (1836), Mr. Pickwick is sentenced to prison for breach of promise; he observes that the debtors there seem to have a good time and says to his companion, Sam Weller, "It strikes me, Sam, that imprisonment for debt is scarcely any punishment at all." Weller replies, "Ah, that's just the very thing, sir. *They* don't mind it; it's a regular holiday to them—all porter and skittles." Again, "Life ain't all beer and skittles, and more's the pity." That is from *Trilby*, by George Du Maurier (1894).

Beg the Question. To assume as fact what is in doubt; to adopt as true a proposition you are supposedly trying to prove; to try to avoid an issue. The sense is clear in Gilbert Burnet's discussion (1680) of the life of the Earl of Rochester: "This was to assert or beg the thing in Question." The term was in use at least a century earlier.

Beggars Can't be Choosers. If you're a supplicant, you must take what is offered; you can't dictate terms. An earlier form is "Beggars should be no choosers." In that form it was recorded in 1546 by John Heywood in a book on English proverbs: "Folke saie alwaie, beggers shulde be no choosers."

Beggars Description. It is virtually indescribable. The term derives from the almost unheard-of verb "to beggar," meaning (among other things) to exhaust the resources of, to outdo. In Shakespeare's *Antony and Cleopatra* (1606), Antony's friend Enobarbus is describing at some length the opulent Nile barge in which Cleopatra met Antony—purple perfumed sails, silver oars and so on—and then he says: "For her own person, it beggar'd all description."

Behind the 8-ball. In a difficult or undesirable position. In one version of Kelly pool the balls must be pocketed in numerical order except for the 8, which is to be last. A player who causes another ball to touch the 8 is penalized. If he is supposed to pocket a ball that is behind the 8, he is in a difficult position, since it is unlikely he can pocket his ball without hitting the 8.

Believe It Or Not. It's wondrous but true. The expression was the title of a widely distributed newspaper feature by Robert Ripley (1893–1949). The feature described and illustrated happenings or phenomena that were true but so remarkable they were hard to believe.

Bell the Cat, Who'll? Who has the nerve to take on a dangerous job? Aesop's fable, "The Mice in Council," relates how a group of mice who had lost many members to a vigorous cat that lived in "a large country house" met to decide what to do. A young mouse, "rising and catching the eye of the President," made a proposal: "If the Cat wore around her neck a little bell, every step she took would make it tinkle; then, ever forewarned of her approach, we should have time to reach our holes." The audience reacted with a murmur of applause, but "an old gray Mouse, with a merry twinkle in his eye, now got up, and said that the plan of the last speaker was an admirable one; but he feared it had one drawback; he had not told them who should put the bell around the cat's neck."

Bend Your Ear, Let Me. I'll tell you something; listen to me. The notion of the bent and attentive ear was current in 1586, when the Earl of Leicester wrote in a letter: "I neuer . . . bent my ears to credite a tale that first was tolde mee . . ." He apparently remembered it nonetheless.

Benefit of the Doubt, Give the. Make a favorable decision when you find the evidence unpersuasive or conflicting. As a legal term, the expression means to pronounce a verdict of not guilty when the evidence is conflicting. In 1860 Thomas Inman wrote in *On Myalgia*: "We should more frequently give our patients the 'benefit of our doubts,' and abstain from attempting to cure an inflammation." "Myalgia" is one of those medical terms you never hear now; it meant a muscular pain.

Beside Himself. Angry; severely upset. In the New Testament Book of Acts, the Roman governor Festus, hearing Paul tell King Agrippa his defense against accusations made by the Jews, says: "Paul, thou art beside thyself; much learning doth make thee mad."

Beside the Point. Not relevant; a statement that does not contribute to an argument. The literal term is old enough to date from the time of archers; to be beside the point or mark was to be wide of the target. The figurative meaning is also old; Laurence Minot's *Poems* (1352) contains: "But how has Sir Dauid missed of his merkes." When the "mark" became the "point" is uncertain, but one can hazard a guess that with the development of reasonably accurate guns, the object of one's aim shrank in diameter to become more of a point.

Best Bib and Tucker. One's most fashionable array of clothes. In the 17th century a bib was not only the cloth put under a baby's chin to absorb dribbles but also an item worn over the breast by adults; often it was the top part of an apron. A tucker was an item of woman's clothing; as described by Randle Holme in 1688: "A Pinner or Tucker, is a narrow piece of Cloth . . . which compasseth the top of a Womans Gown about the Neck part." Apparently, it was not until sometime in the 19th century that either a man or woman was said to be in his best bib and tucker if he or she dressed up for a notable occasion.

Best of All Possible Worlds, The. The optimal condition, quite often as it is seen by an optimist like Dr. Pangloss in Voltaire's *Candide* (1759): "In this best of all possible worlds . . . all is for the best." A bit of sport is had with the term in James Branch Cabell's *The Silver Stallion* (1926): "The optimist proclaims that we live in the best of all possible worlds; the pessimist fears this is true."

Best of My Ability, To the. I'll do as well as I can, give my utmost. Once it was "my power," which makes a stronger phrase. In *The History of Arthur of Little Britain* (1530), Lord Berners wrote: "I shall do the best of my power."

Best-laid Schemes, The. Things don't always go right, no matter how carefully they are planned. Usually one need not say any more than, "The best-laid schemes . . ." to convey the thought, although in the most familiar example (*To a Mouse*, by Robert Burns), the line is, "The best-laid schemes o' mice and men gang aft a-gley," meaning they often go wrong. Burns was writing of a mouse's winter home that had been destroyed by a plow:

> But, Mousie, thou are no thy lane
> In proving foresight may be vain:
> The best-laid schemes o' mice and men
> Gang aft a-gley,
> And lea's us nought but grief and pain
> For promised joy.

Bet Your Boots, You Can. It's a sure thing. This expression seems to have originated in the United States, where for cowboys and miners boots were crucial and not to be parted with casually. The periodical *All the Year Round* told its readers in 1868: " . . . to 'bet your boots' is confirmation as strong as holy writ—in the mines, at least."

Better Believe, You'd. No doubt of it; you can be sure. The phrase took on new life in 1973, when relief pitcher Tug McGraw made it a slogan for his New York Mets, who unexpectedly won the National League baseball championship but lost the World Series to Oakland in seven games. Actually, the term is far older. Here is the *Yale Literary Magazine* in 1856: "If I catch your daughter from home, you'd better believe, I'll live in clover."

Better Half, My. One's spouse, usually said by a man referring to his wife. Marriage is viewed as uniting two people into a single entity—a couple—of which each person is half. The person using the phrase could really respect his partner's contribution to the marriage, or could be saying it in a patronizing fashion. In either event, the expression was in use by 1590, when Sir Philip Sidney (in *The Countesse of Pembrokes Arcadia*) has Argalus enter the scene and, "forcing up (the best he could) his feeble voice, My deare, my deare, my better halfe (said he) I finde I must now leave thee."

Better Late Than Never. An excuse for not being on time; also used as a civility by the person who has been kept waiting. The term is found in literature as early as 1200; in Chaucer's *Canterbury Tales* (1410), it turns up as, "bet than nevere is late."

Better Safe Than Sorry. Take it easy; steer clear of obvious risks. It sounds like an ancient proverb, but it apparently dates only from the early 19th century, when it was, "it's better to be sure than sorry." The version with "safe" was in circulation by 1933.

Between You and Me and the Lamppost (Gatepost, Bedpost). In secret; confidentially. Since the object mentioned in all three versions is inanimate, the point is that a remark made by one of the two people present will not be overheard. One of the first recorded uses of the term was by Charles Dickens, in *Nicholas Nickleby* (1839): "And between you and me and the post, sir, it will be a very nice portrait too."   .

Between the Cup and the Lip. Any region where things may go wrong. The full expression is usually, "There's many a slip between the cup and the lip." Erasmus said it in Latin in 1539, and he had probably read a similar and much earlier expression in Greek. Other versions include "the cuppe and the mouth" (1539) and "the challice and the chin" (1580). An ancient legend tells us that Ancaeus, a son of Neptune, cultivated a wine vineyard and was harsh with the slaves who worked it, occasioning one of the slaves to predict that Ancaeus would never get to taste the wine from the coming harvest of grapes. When the first juice was pressed from the grapes, Ancaeus put some in a goblet and called for the slave in order to demonstrate the prophecy was wrong. As Ancaeus raised the goblet to his lips, the slave said, "There's many a slip between cup and lip." Just then another slave came with the news that a wild boar was tearing up the vineyard. Ancaeus dropped the goblet, went to the scene and lost his life when attacked by the boar.

Between the Devil and the Deep Blue Sea. In a difficult and perhaps inextricable position; facing two equally severe dangers. Since the devil is said to preside in hell and, at best, the deep blue sea is uncomfortable, anyone caught between them is indeed in a precarious spot. In the 17th century the position was sometimes expressed as being between "the devil and the dead sea." A classic example of such a predicament appears in Colonel Robert Monro's account of his service with Gustavus Adolphus of Sweden from 1621 to 1632. He describes an engagement in which his party was exposed to fire not only from the enemy but also from their own side because Swedish guns were aimed too low: "I with my partie, did lie on our poste, as betwixt the devill and the deep sea."

Betwixt and Between. Unsettled; neither one thing nor the other. An example from Frederick Marryat's *Newton Forster* (1832) indicates that the expression was in use early in the 19th century:

"He took the lease of a house in a betwixt and between fashionable street."

Bevy of Beauties. A group of (usually young) women. A bevy is a group or company, and as long ago as 1470 one could read (in *Hors, Shepe and Ghoos*): "A beuve of larkes, a beuve of ladyes, a beuve of quayles, a beuve of roos [roe deer]." The alliterative appeal must have been too much for the flatterer who replaced "a bevy of ladies" with "a bevy of beauties."

Beyond the Pale. Outside the bounds of something, such as decency, good behavior or social recognition, often as the result of some action of one's own. The word comes from the Latin *palus*, meaning stake, including the kind that forms part of a fence. Hence "pale" came to have the figurative meaning of boundary. The modern meaning of "beyond the pale" was evident as early as 1654 in Archbishop John Bramhall's *A Just Vindication of the Church of England*: "For we recognize that there is no salvation to be expected ordinarily without the pale of the Church."

Bide Your Time. Wait for a good opportunity. Bide has several meanings, among them to wait for. In this sense it once served in a number of contexts, such as "bide his grace," used in a work published in 1230 and "bide my leisure," seen in a 1611 version of the Bible. Today, however, it appears only in relation to biding one's time, a more restricted use that came into being about 1850, and can be read in Frederick W. Robertson's *Sermons*: "They bide their time and then suddenly present themselves."

Big Cheese. An important or self-important person (usually said sardonically). Some lexicographers have traced the term to the Persian and Urdu word chīz, meaning thing; indeed, the expression "the real chīz" was once heard among Anglo-Indians. It might also have been a play on "chief."

Big For His Britches, Too. Arrogant; swelled-headed; overestimating himself. Britches is a variant of breeches and originally it signified a covering for that part of the body between the waist and the knees; by the 16th century, however, it also meant trousers. In any event, someone who has literally gotten too big for his britches cuts a rather ridiculous figure, as does someone with an exaggerated sense of his importance, which is probably how the parallel came to be drawn. Today's expression was in the language by 1905, when it appeared in H. G. Wells's *Kipp, the Story of a Simple Soul*: "He's getting too big for 'is britches."

Big Honcho. The boss; the most important person (often said jokingly). The word "honcho" has a Spanish ring to it, but actually it comes from the Japanese *hanchō*, meaning the leader of a squad. It is a safe guess that the word found its way into English during or after World War II, when many Americans were exposed to the Japanese military system and Japanese terms.

Big Shot. A person who is, or thinks he is, of considerable importance. In the 19th century the same thought was expressed as "the big gun"; at times it was phrased as "the big noise." "Gun" had become "shot" by about 1930. Now the term is so common it is often written as one word, "bigshot."

Big Spender. A lavish host (who usually is showing off). Often it is "the last of the big spenders." In any case, it seems like a fairly recent construction, reflecting a time when there were both people with lots of money and plenty of things to spend it on, but in fact the thought is quite old. It is echoed in Thomas Bell's *The Survey of Popery* (1596): "After great getters come great spenders."

Bigger They Come, the Harder They Fall, The. Sometimes the mightiest can most easily be brought low; the most formidable opponent is sometimes quite easily defeated. It is almost standard practice for a boxer to say this before a fight in which he is matched against a bigger man, or after the fight if he has won. The concept is embodied in the biblical story of David and Goliath and appeared 2,300 years ago in *The Histories of Herodotus*: "It is the gods' custom to bring low all things of surpassing greatness." Similarly, in Horace's *Odes* one reads:

> It is the lofty pine that by the storm
> Is oftener tossed; towers fall with heavier crash
> Which higher soar.

Bird in the Hand is Worth Two in the Bush, A. Take advantage of what you have; don't press on in the hope that something better will turn up; to have a thing is better than to presume you'll get more of it or find something superior. It is a piece of folk wisdom ancient enough to have appeared in Aesop's fable, "The Hawk and the Nightingale." The hawk had been hunting all day and finally caught a nightingale.

> "Pray let me go," said the Nightingale; "I am such a mite for a stomach like yours. I sing so nicely too. Do let me go, it will do you good to hear me." "Much good it will do to an empty belly," replied the Hawk; "and besides, a little bird that I have is more to me than a great one that has yet to be caught."

Bird's-eye View. An overview; a broad view. It is easy to see how this metaphor arose before the days of airplanes, when only a bird could get a broad view of the landscape. It was a view many artists imagined and tried to depict. The expression was in the language by the 18th century, as in Horace Walpole's *Anecdotes of Painting in England*: "It exhibits an almost bird's-eye view of an extensive country."

Birds of a Feather Flock Together. People of similar views or interests associate with one another. The term is based on the observation that birds in a group on the ground or in flight are often all of the same species; as it was put in an English work of 1545: "Byrdes of on kynde and color flok and flye all-wayes to gether." The figurative sense was in evidence by 1680, as in John Bunyan's *The Life and Death of Mr. Badman:* "They were birds of a feather, . . . they were so well met for wickedness."

Bite Off More Than You Can Chew. To take on a task that is more than you can handle. Its literal meaning probably sprang from watching children ingest large mouthfuls of food they then had trouble chewing. Its figurative meaning seems to have arisen in the United States in the latter part of the 19th century, with the first recorded use of the term appearing in 1878 in J. H. Beadle's *Western Wilds*: "Men, you've bit off more'n you can chew."

Bite the Bullet. Brace yourself for an unpleasant experience; decide to get on with a difficult task. Although one can find other explanations, it seems most plausible that the term originated in battlefield surgery before the days of anesthesia. A surgeon about to operate on a wounded soldier would urge him to bite on a bullet of soft lead to distract him from the pain; at least it would minimize his ability to scream and thus divert the surgeon. Rudyard Kipling reflected the broader meaning in *The Light that Failed* (1890): "Bite on the bullet, old man, and don't let them think you're afraid."

Bite the Dust. To die in a fracas or to suffer a severe setback. Although Homer used the phrase in the *Iliad:* "May his fellow warriors . . . Fall round him to the earth and bite the dust," it was particularly popular in the many tales of skirmishes between white men and Indians in the American West: "And another redskin bit the dust."

Bite the Hand That Feeds You. Be ungrateful; turn against a benefactor. Dogs do it literally sometimes; people do it figuratively. The expression was in use early in the 18th century, as in Joseph Addison's *The Spectator* (1711): "He is so wonderfully unlucky, insomuch that he will bite the Hand that feeds him."

Bitter End, To the. Enduring an affliction or adversity throughout its course, or affirming that one will do so. On this one, you can take your choice, or decide that both sources contributed to the concept. Capt. John Smith, founder of the British colony in Virginia, published *A Sea Grammer* in 1627, in which he said: "A bitter is but the turne of a Cable about the bits [bitts, the stout posts on a ship's deck to which ropes and cables are fastened]. . . . And the Bitters end is that part of the Cable doth stay within boord." In 1867 Adm. William Smyth, in *The Sailor's Word-Book*, wrote: "When a chain or rope is paid out to the bitter end, no more remains to be let go." The other possible source is in the Bible's Book of Proverbs: "But her end is bitter as wormwood, sharp as a two-edged sword."

Bitter with the Sweet, Take the. The good comes with the bad, the pleasant with the unpleasant. The originating thought that some things taste bitter and some sweet can be seen in the *Lambeth Homilies* of the 13th century. John Locke was closer to the modern meaning in *An Essay Concerning Human Understanding* (1690): "A little bitter mingled in our Cup, leaves no relish for the sweet."

Black Book, In My. Out of favor; marked for punishment or retribution. Numerous black books appear in history and many are simply straightforward records or chronicles of events and possessions, but in the reign of Henry VIII, during his campaign against the Catholic Church, one was compiled to report on alleged abuses in the monasteries. An account almost a century later reported: "their lives, which by a Blacke Booke, containing a world of enormities, were represented in no small measure scandalous." In 1595 Edmund Spenser wrote in one of his sonnets: "Al her faultes in thy black booke enroll."

Black Sheep. Someone who stands unfavorably in a group, as in a family; an oddball; a disgrace. Black sheep were traditionally disliked by shepherds because they were worth less than the standard white sheep. By the early 19th century the term was used to describe disfavored and misbehaving people. In *Old Mortality* by Sir Walter Scott (1816), one reads: "The curates . . . know best the black sheep of the flock." The expression is often encountered as, "There are black sheep in every flock."

Blaze a Trail. Lead the way to new ground, or in a new venture. It was and still is the custom to mark trails through woods by chipping a piece of bark from a tree at intervals, particularly at turnings, thus enabling those who come after (or the original people returning) to follow the route. In the broader sense of opening up a new field of endeavor the usage is fairly recent, dating from about 1900. Leon Mead's *Word-coinage* (1902) tells the reader that, "Professor Bréal has blazed the way for future explorers in the wilderness of philology."

Blessing in Disguise. An apparent misfortune that turns out to be useful or pleasurable. The phrase was known in the 18th century; its modern meaning was explicit by a century later, as seen in *Cassell's Magazine* (1873): "Like many similar disasters, this great calamity was in truth only a blessing in disguise."

Blind as a Bat. Not seeing well; obtuse. An odd expression, really, since bats are not blind. Because they function with precision at night, however, and live in dark places, it was probably easy to think of them as blind in the days before anyone knew about their sound-ranging system of guiding themselves. The term was in the language as early as 1588, in John Harvey's *A Discoursive Probleme Concerning Prophesies:* "As blinde as moules, or bats."

Blind Drunk. In an intoxicated stupor. Doubtless a person who is soused can see, but his vision doesn't connect properly with his thought processes, so he seems to be virtually blind. As early as 1622 Jeremy Taylor, known as the water poet, had captured the image:

> For though he be as drunk as any Rat
> He hath but catcht a Foxe, or Whipt the Cat.
> Or some say hee's bewitcht, or scracht, or blinde,
> Which are the fittest tearmes that I can finde.

Blind Leading the Blind, The. The ignorant or inexperienced guiding the ignorant or inexperienced. In the Gospel according to St. Matthew, Christ's disciples tell Him the Pharisees were offended when He reproved them for transgressing God's commandments. He replies: "Let them alone: they be blind leaders of the blind. And if the blind lead the blind, both shall fall into the ditch."

Blood From a Turnip (Stone), No Getting. Some sources are totally unproductive; don't look for help or money in a hopeless place. Frederick Marryat said it (apparently borrowing an expression from folklore) in *Japhet in Search of a Father* (1836): "There's no getting blood out of a turnip."

Blood Is Thicker Than Water. Relatives stick together; one will do more for a relation than for others. A similar expression in German dates from the 12th century, but in English it seems to have been passed on verbally until the early 19th century when it appeared in print, in 1815, in Sir Walter Scott's *Guy Mannering*: "Weel—Blud's thicker than water—she's welcome to the cheeses."

Bloody But Unbowed. Wounded in body or spirit but not defeated. It smacks of ancient battles in which the combatants belabored one another with swords, staffs, cudgels, halberds and other heavy-duty weapons until the blood flowed, but it does not seem to have been a literary term until about a hundred years ago. A poem in William Ernest Henley's *Echoes* (1888) contains the stanza:

> In the fell clutch of circumstance,
> I have not winced nor cried aloud;
> Under the bludgeonings of chance
> My head is bloody, but unbowed.

Blow Hot and Cold. To be inconsistent or uncertain about something. The notion is old enough to have appeared in Aesop's fable, "The Satyr and the Traveller." The satyr, ranging through a forest in winter, comes upon a traveler half starved and very cold, and invites the man to his cave. On their way the Man kept blowing upon his fingers. "Why do you do that?" said the Satyr, who had seen little of the world. "To warm my hands, they are nearly frozen," replied the Man. Arrived at the cave, the Satyr poured out a mess of smoking pottage and laid it before the Traveller, who at once commenced blowing at it with all his might. "What, blowing again!" cried the Satyr. "Is it not hot enough?" "Yes, faith," answered the Man, "it is hot enough in all conscience, and that is just the reason why I blow it." "Be off with you!" said the Satyr in alarm. "I will have no part with a man who can blow hot and cold from the same mouth."

Blow Off Steam. To vent one's anger or frustration, usually in a noisy way. The literal origin of the phrase was a technique periodically used with a steam boiler, namely blowing off some steam when the pressure got too high. The figurative meaning was in print by 1837 in Frederick Marryat's *Snarleyvow; or the Dogfiend:* "The widow . . . sat . . . fuming and blowing off her steam."

Blow Your Own Horn (Trumpet). Boast; extol what one sees as one's own merits. As early as 1576, Abraham Fleming, in *A Panoplie of Epistles,* wrote: "I will . . . sound the trumpet of mine own merits." Shakespeare, in *Much Ado About Nothing,* has Benedick say: "Therefore is it most expedient for the wise . . . to be the trumpet of his own virtues, as I am to myself."

Blow Your Stack. To show sudden anger. Originally the phrase described clearing a smokestack or the stack on a steamship by blowing air up through it. Figuratively it is one of several phrases characterizing an angry outburst: blow a fuse and blow your top are among the others.

Blown To Smithereens. Destroyed. "Smithereens" is a variant of "smithers," a word of obscure origin meaning fragments or atoms. When the expression first appeared in print, toward the middle of the 19th century, it was sometimes "gone to smithers"; it was also split, knocked, or broken into smithereens.

Blue Blood. An aristocrat or aristocratic person. During the centuries when the dark-skinned Moors ruled Spain, members of the old Castilian families were wont to say with pride that their blood had not been contaminated by Moorish or other foreign admixtures. The term they used was *sangre azul,* which probably sprang from the fact that the veins of the fair-skinned are visibly blue.

Blue Funk, In a. In a depressed or gloomy state of mind. Until fairly recently the term meant a state of extreme nervousness, verging on panic. Funk as a noun has several meanings, including a spark, tobacco smoke, and cowering fear. Each meaning seems to have originated from different but similar Dutch, German or Flemish nouns. Just how the shift from fear to gloom occurred is elusive.

29

Bolt From the Blue, A. A complete surprise. A bolt is a thunderbolt and the blue is a clear sky. The two are seldom associated, which makes their rare meeting a surprise and gives rise to the broader simile. Blue, in the sense of clear sky, has been in the language since at least the 17th century and bolt, in the sense of thunderbolt or the related bolt of lightning, since at least the 16th century, but the term "bolt from the blue" does not seem to have appeared in print until early in the 19th century. Thomas Carlyle, in *The French Revolution* (1837) uses it in the modern sense: "Arrestment, sudden really as a bolt out of the Blue, has hit strange victims."

Bone Dry. Very dry; lacking in alcoholic beverages. The image of dry bones in a human grave or of the bones of an animal long dead in the wild is not one frequently encountered these days, so it is quite remarkable that a term deriving from an earlier time should hang on as it does. Actually, dry as a biscuit, dry as a dog, and dry as dust are older still, all appearing in print as early as the 16th century.

Bone of Contention. A topic of dispute. It derives from the common scene of dogs fighting over a bone. It was in the language as a metaphor by the 16th century, as in William Lambarde's *A Perambulation of Kent* (1576): "This was such a bone of dissention between these deere friends." A closely related term, equally old, is "to cast a bone between," meaning to start an argument or create dissension.

Boon Companion. An intimate associate, particularly in conviviality. The English "boon," which evolved from the French *bon*, meaning good, has been in the language for hundreds of years. So has boon companion. *A Medicinable Morall*, by Thomas Drant (1566), says: "He is my bone companion, its he that cheares up me."

Born With a Silver Spoon in His Mouth. He got his wealth by inheritance rather than by working for it. It is an old tradition for godparents to give their godchild a spoon (perhaps more than one) at the time of christening; among the wealthy, it was usually a silver spoon. Sometimes it was a set of 12, each with the figure of a different apostle at the upper end of the handle, hence the term, apostle spoons. Presumably a child receiving silver spoons was from a wealthy family and would not have to worry about money. Cervantes in *Don Quixote* (1615) reminds us that it is not so with everybody: "Every man was not born with a silver spoon in his mouth."

Born Yesterday, I Wasn't. I'm wiser than you may think; I've been around. As is so often the case, the expression was in the spoken language before it appeared in print. Frederick Marryat makes that clear in *Snarleyvow* (1837): "The widow read the letter and tossed it into the fire with a 'Pish! I was not born yesterday, as the saying is.' " An immensely popular play and motion picture a generation ago was Garson Kanin's *Born Yesterday*, about a woman in business who seemed to be the quintessence of naiveté and dumb-blondedness but was, in fact, a person of great native intelligence.

Born and Bred. A native, usually still living in the place, or at least the region, where he or she was born, raised, and imbued with its traditions. When British actress Fanny Kemble married an American, Pierce Butler, and moved to his Georgia estate, she developed a strong aversion to slavery. After she divorced Butler and returned to England, she wrote (in 1863) *Journal of a Residence on a Georgian Plantation in 1838-1839*, in which she describes discussions with her husband about the slaves, saying such talks always put her "into perfect agonies of distress" for the slaves, for herself and for her husband. "But, after all, what can he do? How can he help at all? Moreover, born and bred in America, how should he care or wish to help it?"

Born to the Purple. Having high station or wealth by inheritance; or sometimes playing the role of privilege so well as to seem born to it. At one time the expression was "born in the purple." It dates to the era of the Byzantine emperors, more than a thousand years ago, when children of the reigning emperor were either born in a room hung with purple curtains or wrapped in purple at birth (or both). Hence the word "porphyrogenite," meaning a child born to the imperial family at Constantinople in a room called the Porphyra. Traditionally purple was also the color of the robes and dress of rulers and others of high rank.

Bosom Buddy. An extremely close friend. This is an American alliterative modification of "bosom friend," a concept old enough to have been in the Bible, where Saint John is portrayed as the bosom friend of Jesus. As used here bosom connotes the seat of one's thoughts or feelings. Robert Greene, in *Never Too Late* (1590), says: "There is nothing better than a bosom friend with whom to conferre."

Boston Brahmin. A member of an old New England family, often used disparagingly to suggest someone of aristocratic manner who is out of the mainstream of contemporary life. The brahmins were the highest of the Hindu castes. In 1860, Dr. Oliver Wendell Holmes fixed the American version: "He comes of the Brahmin caste of New England. This is the harmless, inoffensive, untitled aristocracy."

Both Feet On the Ground, Have. Be practical or realistic. Although one supposes people must have said this for centuries as representative of determination and coolness, examples of it in print are scarce until recently. One is Philip Woodruff (a pen name of Philip Mason) in *The Island of Chamba* (1950): "El Hadramauti . . . is a bit of a theorist and H. M. for all his oddity has his feet very firmly on the ground."

Bottom Line, The. The net result; the profit or loss. The bottom line is at the bottom of a financial statement and reveals how the enterprise fared in a particular period in terms of the difference between income and spending. The bottom line has been familiar to accountants for a long time, but it became a cliché only a few years ago. In 1977, Edwin Land of Polaroid fame tried to give the phrase perspective when, replying to an assertion that the worth of a product is reflected only in the bottom line and a comparison between costs of production and income from sales, he said: "The bottom line is in heaven." His reply is reminiscent of economist Lord Keynes' comment on the tendency of his colleagues to refer to "the long run." He said: "In the long run we are all dead."

Bottomless Pit. Something insatiable, often said facetiously to describe someone with a large appetite. This is "pit" in the sense of pitfall or trap. Miles Coverdale's translation of the Bible in 1835 rendered Job 36 : 16 as, "so shall he kepe the [thee] . . . from the bottomlesse pytte that is beneth."

Bottoms Up. We join in a drink, presumably draining our glasses at one tilt. You are likely to hear the words in any convivial group. It means nothing more than that the glass or mug, which starts out with its top up, soon has its bottom up when you drink assiduously.

Bow and Scrape. Behave obsequiously or with great deference. The term refers to the habit, in former times, of the excessively servile to bow while simultaneously scraping a foot backward. It had appeared in print by 1646, in Jeremiah Whitaker's *Uzziah*: "Have you not known some in a low condition, to bow and scrape"?

Bowl of Cherries, Life Is Just a. We're on Easy Street; everything's pleasant. A mystifying phrase on its face, as cherries aren't particularly symbolic of the good life and don't even represent a supreme dining treat compared to several other fruits and sweets. Ethel Merman sang a song with this title in the musical *Scandals* (1931). Today the term is more likely to be used ironically to suggest that life is in fact falling short of the pleasures implied by a bowl of cherries.

Boys Will Be Boys. That's the way it is; there's no help for it. The remark of a parent whose son has been caught breaking windows, upending trash cans, throwing snowballs at car windows and whatever else boys might do. Boys have been boys for a long time, as indicated by similar expressions appearing in print as early as 1589. A few years later (1597) Thomas Deloney, in *A Gentle Craft*, made the indictment more general: "Youth will be youth."

Brain Trust. The main thinkers or policymakers of an organization (sometimes used sardonically to suggest the big thinkers aren't achieving much). John Kieran, a reporter for *The New York Times*, applied the name "brains department" and the "brains trust" to a group of Columbia University professors who helped Franklin D. Roosevelt prepare speeches when he was running for President in 1932. Once elected he had comparable advisers, prompting *Newsweek* to report in September, 1933: "The President's Brain Trust, a little band of intellectuals, sat at the center of action as similar bands have done in revolutions of the past."

Brass Hat. A person in authority; a bigwig. High-ranking officers in many armies wear a lot of gold braid on their hats; apparently the British were the first (in about 1890) to refer somewhat disrespectfully to these dignitaries as "brass hats." Derivative terms are "top brass," "the big brass" and simply, "the brass."

Brass Tacks, Get Down to. Reach the essentials of a matter at hand. This is one of those clichés that remain only in the figurative sense, its literal sense being somewhat obscure. It could have involved the removal of upholstery and exposure of the brass-plated tacks that held the upholstery to the wood frame. Or it could be that stores selling cloth by the yard once measured precise lengths of cloth by using brass-headed tacks embedded in their counters; by getting down to brass tacks, in effect, buyer and seller were establishing the material's length with certainty.

Brazen It Out. Cope with a tight situation by a show of courage (perhaps false). "Brazen" means brassy, and to put on a brassy face in a difficult situation is an old practice. In Hugh Latimer's *Sermons and Remains* (1555) the phrase "to brazen it" makes its first recorded appearance in print, and in Sir William Waller's *The Tragical History of Jetzer* (1679) one can read: "Father Ireland . . . brazened out the Court. . . ."

Break the Ice. To make a social situation easier; to get a conversation started in an interval of awkward silence. Originally it meant to create paths that allowed ships to move through icy waters. By the 17th century, it was used figuratively, as in *The Art of Converse* (1683): "The Ice being thus broken, another will utter her mind on the same matter."

Breathes His Last. Dies. Shakespeare said it, in *Henry VI.* The Earl of Warwick calls for his brother, the Marquess of Montague. The Duke of Somerset says: "Ah, Warwick! Montague hath breathed his last; and to the latest gasp cried out for Warwick, and said 'Commend me to my valiant brother.' "

Bright and Early. Doing something near dawn, or well ahead of the time that might be expected. Early in the day it is sometimes bright, and some folk are inspired to get out and do things. If it is not bright, inspiration comes harder. The term is apparently of U.S.origin and began to appear in print late in the 19th century, as in the *Transactions of the Illinois Agricultural Society* (1871): "Thursday morning, bright and early, we took a ride around the premises."

Bright as a Button. Alert, perky and quick mentally. The origin was probably in the days some centuries ago when buttons were often made of metal and, at least when they were new, were bright and conspicuous. *Yankee Phrases* in 1803 offered a line from a poem by someone identified only as "a Yankee bard": "As bright as a button her eyes."

Bright-eyed and Bushy-tailed. Alert and ready for action. The phrase was heard in the United States about 50 years ago and also became popular in Canada. The squirrel, sitting on its haunches and looking about brightly for food or the approach of trouble, is surely the inspiration for the term.

Bring Home the Bacon. To arrive with something of value—a prize or one's pay. You have a choice of bacon here. It could be the "Dunmow flitch," a side of bacon awarded annually at Dunmow, England to any married couple who swore they had lived together harmoniously during the past year; the custom was recorded as early as 1362. Or the bacon could be the greased pig that once figured so prominently in American fairs; if you caught it, you could take it home.

Brink of Disaster, On the. Close to serious trouble. People have been on the brink of things from time immemorial: the grave, ruin, destruction. Examples of one or another can be found from the 14th century onward. In Shakespeare's *The Life of Timon of Athens*, Timon says, "You witch me in it, surprise me to the brink of tears."

Brown Study, In a. Preoccupied; deep in thought; gloomy. A 16th-century English work entitled, *A Manifest Detection of the Most Vyle and Detestable Use of Dice-play*, tells us: "Lack of company will soon lead a man into a brown study." A meaning of "brown" that is now virtually lost was "gloomy."

Bruit About. Spread a rumor; pass the word. The verb used in this sense appeared as early as 1548 in a book by Nicolas Udall: "The woman did bruit abrode the rumour."

Brute Force, By. Violently and without subtlety. At one time the term denoted an action of nature or other nonhuman agency. More recently it has come to signify human actions in which strength is applied with little or no thought.

34

Bug Out (Off). Both forms mean to leave. Ordinarily bug out is used when one decides to leave a place, often because the situation is unpleasant or dangerous; bug off, on the other hand, is what one says to someone else when the message is "scram" or "go away." Both terms probably derived from the British verb "bugger," which in one of its senses means to leave and is often expressed as "bugger off."

Bull in a China Shop, Like a. Out of place in a situation; dealing too roughly with a delicate problem. It's a vivid simile, even though it is most unlikely that a real bull was loose in a china shop. Since the fine porcelain known as china was not introduced into Europe until the 16th century and was not manufactured there until the 18th century, the notion of a bull in a china shop is fairly recent. An early example is in Frederick Marryat's *Jacob Faithful* (1834): "Whatever it is that smashes, Mrs. T. always swears it was the *most valuable* thing in the room. I'm like a bull in a china shop."

Bull by the Horns, Seize the. Face up to a difficult situation; take action in a crisis. Evidently a metaphor inspired by a form of bullfighting in which the matador tries to tire and weaken the bull in various ways and then seizes it by the horns in an effort to twist it to the ground. James Howell's *Spanish Proverbs* of 1659 includes the entry: "Take a Bull by the horn, and a man by his word." Jonathan Swift came closer to the modern usage in 1711 in *The Conduct of the Allies*: "(As the old Duke of Schomberg expressed it) to engage with France, was to take a Bull by the Horns."

Bum's Rush. Ejection (usually in an undignified way). In bars and saloons of the United States it has long been the practice to tell a person (usually a man) who is badly dressed, badly behaved or seems unlikely to pay that he must leave, and often to accompany the statement with physical action, such as carrying him out the door. The scene is a perennial subject for cartoonists—the ejected bum lies sprawled on his back on the sidewalk while the bartender or bouncer brushes off his hands outside the swinging doors of the saloon.

Burden of Proof. The necessity of demonstrating the truth of an assertion or a charge one has made. The term is a translation of the Latin *onus probandi*, which was a concept in Roman law. It had appeared in English writing by 1593; Richard Hooker uses it in *Of the Lawes of Ecclesiasticall Politie*: "The burden of proving doth rest on them."

Burn Your Bridges Behind You. Cut off your means of retreat; commit yourself to a course of action or argument. Caesar did it literally in order to stiffen the resolve of his troops. The notion was also occasionally expressed as "to burn one's boats."

Burn the Candle at Both Ends. Overwork oneself mentally or physically. It is doubtful that anyone has ever literally burned a candle at both ends, at least not simultaneously; it would be hard to do. However, it is a vivid image for squandering one's resources. In the past, the meaning was resources in the sense of money or property, as in Nathan Bailey's dictionary of English (1730): "The Candle burns at both Ends. Said when Husband and Wife are both Spendthrifts." The expression was known even earlier. Francis Bacon said in *Promus of Formularies and Elegancies* (1592): "To waste that realm as a candle which is lighted at both ends." The modern connotation had appeared by 1857, when Charles Kingsley wrote, in *Two Years Ago*, "By sitting up till two in the morning, and rising again at six . . . Frank Headley burnt the candle of life at both ends."

Burn the Midnight Oil. Stay up late studying or working. The spoken language has probably contained the expression from the time when people first stayed up late working or reading by the light of an oil lamp. By 1635, the term was in print in English, in Francis Quarles's poem *Emblems*: "We spend our midday sweat, our midnight oil; / We tire the night in thought, the day in toil."

Burning Question. A topic that provokes heated discussion. People have talked of burning "anger," "fever," "shame," "thirst" and other things for centuries, but the burning "question" seems to date from about the middle of the 19th century. French and German have closely similar expressions.

Bury the Hatchet. End a dispute; agree to stop fighting. Believe it or not, there is some controversy about this phrase, as an English expression, to "hang up the hatchet," dating from the 14th century, has been cited as meaning the same thing. However, the latter seems to have meant to take a rest, to cease from one's labors, and not to have been related to fighting. So one returns to the American Indians as the source of the term, and there the evidence is strong. The American statesman John Jay wrote, in 1794: "To use an Indian figure, may the hatchet henceforth be buried forever." More than a century earlier, Samuel Sewall wrote: "Meeting with the Sachem [Indian chiefs], they came to an agreement and buried two axes in the ground, which ceremony to them is more significant and binding than all the Articles of Peace, the hatchet being the principal weapon."

Business as Usual. Continuing to do something in the face of difficulty. It is a somewhat hyperbolic phrase, since the business is ordinarily being carried on under circumstances that are not usual—fire, flood, construction or some other difficulty. In a political sense the term is usually ironic, meaning that some official or party is carrying on a policy in the face of clear indications that it ought to be changed.

Busman's Holiday. Time off spent doing the kind of work you're paid for in your job. It is said that in London, in the days when horse-drawn buses plied the streets, an occasional driver who was particularly concerned about the way the horses were being treated would show up on his day off and ride as a passenger to make sure that the man replacing him for the day was taking proper care of the animals. The story is unverifiable. By 1921, however, not long after the era of the horse-drawn bus, The London *Times* was referring to "busman's holiday" as "proverbial."

Busy As a Cat On a Hot Tin Roof. Frantically active because of a particular problem or plight. A cat finding itself on a hot tin roof is likely to move frantically to get off. Another, and equally vivid expression has one as busy as a one-armed paperhanger. John Ray in 1670 described "to go like a cat upon a hot bakestone" as a proverb. *Cat on a Hot Tin Roof* was the title of a play (1955) by Tennessee Williams.

Busy as (Work Like) a Beaver. Feverishly active. The beaver has stood as a symbol of hard work since at least the 18th century, as its prodigious feats of tree-felling, dam-building and den-building came to be understood. In *Specimens of Newspaper Literature*, J. T. Buckingham cites what was apparently a newspaper ad, in 1775: "The very best Negro Woman . . . as brisk as a Bird, and will work like a Beaver."

Butter Up. Flatter; seek a favor by excessive praise. It is a transfer from the homely practice of spreading an oleaginous substance on bread. Earlier examples of the figurative meaning can be cited, but the pleasantest one comes from the *Saturday Review* of July 5, 1884: "The Lord Chief Justice of England made a tour through America and generously buttered the natives."

Butter Wouldn't Melt in Her Mouth. Said of a cold, aloof person, or of one who looks innocent but probably is not. John Heywood, in his *Proverbs* (1546), picks up the expression as well known at the time: "She looketh as butter would not melt in her mouth." The expression has also been put as: "As demure as if butter would not melt in his (her) mouth."

Buxom Wench. A bosomy woman. "Buxom" once had a variety of meanings, including pliant, submissive, obliging, healthy, comely and plump. It survives today only in the sense of well formed and shapely, with perhaps a hint of plumpness.

Buy for a Song. Get something cheaply or without much effort. The saying is first cousin to "sing for your supper." Both imply that paying with a song or some other kind of entertainment is easier than paying with money or work. The thought appears in *Regulus*, a play by John Crowne (1694): "I bought it for a song."

By Leaps and Bounds. Rapidly; at a great rate. It used to be that the same thought was conveyed in "by leaps," but about a hundred years ago that was not enough for some people, who intensified the thought by speaking of "leaps and bounds," which are essentially the same thing. In either case, the original reference is to the method of locomotion of people and many animals trying to cover ground rapidly.

By Word of Mouth. The spread of information informally, without organized advertising or publicity; speech as distinguished from writing. The term began to appear fairly commonly by the time enough people were literate so that there was a way of communicating other than by the spoken word. It was in print by 1553, in Nicholas Udall's play *Ralph Roister Doister*: "A little message vnto hir by worde of mouth."

By a Long Chalk. By a big margin; thoroughly. In British alehouses and other places it was once the practice to keep track of what customers owed by means of chalk marks. Similarly the points in various games were scored with chalk. Anyone who was ahead by a long chalk was way ahead. The practice is older than references to it in literature; the earliest of those seems to have been in Thomas C. Haliburton's *The Clockmaker* (1837–1840): "Your factories down East . . . go ahead on the English a long chalk."

By and Large. On the whole. It slips so easily off the tongue, with hardly a thought given to where it originated. The term is a holdover from the days of sailing ships; it was an instruction to the helmsman and meant, "Steer close to the wind but not so close that the wind may get around to the back of the sails, thus stopping the ship." One of the meanings of "by" is, "in the direction of," and the nautical meaning of "large" is a wind that crosses the ship's course on the beam or quarter, that is, at a right angle. A companion command, likely to be given to a more experienced helmsman, was "full and by," meaning to steer as close to the wind as possible.

By the Book. Strictly according to the rules. One's instincts suggest this must be a recent expression, dating from the time when books with rules, precepts and instructions became widely available. But Juliet says it to Romeo in Shakespeare's *Romeo* *and Juliet* after Romeo has been swept off his feet by her and steals a kiss: "You kiss by the book."

By the Grapevine. By rumor or hearsay. In the American Civil War "a despatch by grape-vine telegraph" meant a piece of information that was highly likely to prove incorrect. People had real telegraph lines by then; the grapevine, by comparison, would be about as poor a means of communication as one could think of, and that is probably the source of the expression.

By the Same Token. For the same reason; in the same vein. This is "token" in a vague application of its meaning as a sign or evidence, enabling the recipient to associate one thing with another. The phrase was in use by the 15th century. Shakespeare has it in *Troilus and Cressida*. Pandarus, Cressida's uncle, is trying to persuade her of the charms of Troilus, one of the sons of the Trojan king. She is interested, but pursues a strategy of playing hard to get and of scoffing at Pandarus's efforts in behalf of Troilus. Leaving her after one such session, Pandarus says he will return with "a token from Troilus." Cressida replies, "By the same token, you are a bawd."

By the Sweat of His Brow. Through his own hard work. One of the punishments God lays on Adam for eating the forbidden fruit in the Garden of Eden is that henceforward he is going to have to work for his living. As it is put in the Book of Genesis: "In the sweat of thy face shalt thou eat bread, till thou return unto the ground." Henry David Thoreau had a riposte in *Walden* (1854): "It is not necessary that a man should earn his living by the sweat of his brow unless he sweats easier than I do."

C

Cakes and Ale. The good life; pleasure. Shakespeare's keen ear for the common phrases of his time caught this one. In *Twelfth Night* Sir Toby Belch, a roistering type, says to the sour and puritanical Malvolio, who comes to calm down a loud party late at night, "Dost thou think, because thou art virtuous, there shall be no more cakes and ale?"

Calamity Howler. A pessimist; someone who persistently predicts that bad things will happen. It is an expression of American origin, well enough known by 1892 to be reflected in the *Congressional Record*: "We had some 'calamity howlers' here in Washington as well as in Kansas." The thought is reminiscent of what Friar Laurence says to Romeo in Shakespeare's *Romeo and Juliet*:
> Romeo, come forth; come forth, thou fearful man:
> Affliction is enamour'd of thy parts,
> And thou art wedded to calamity.

Call His Bluff. Challenge him to carry out a seemingly empty threat or to prove something apparently dubious he has said. The expression comes from card games, notably poker, in which a player tries to make the set of cards he is holding seem better than it is by betting or bidding boldly on it, perhaps deterring an opponent with better cards from pushing what probably would be a winning hand. "Bluff" in this sense may come from the Dutch verb *bluffen*, meaning to boast.

Call a Halt. Discontinue an activity, usually temporarily. The old German military command *Halt machen!*, dating from the 16th century or earlier, was gradually taken over in other languages. In English it was once said as "make halt," a straight translation of the German. The change to the modern version can be seen developing by 1709 in an item from the *London Gazette:* "The Duke of Marlborough commanded an Hault."

Call a Spade a Spade. Speak plainly; avoid euphemism; tell it like it is. The ancient Greeks had a similar expression. As the dramatist Menander put it: "I call a fig a fig, a spade a spade." Plutarch records: "The Macedonians are a rude and clownish people that call a spade a spade." It has been argued that the Greek word did not mean spade and was mistranslated, but in any case the

40

"spade" has served well for a standard of plain speaking, since it is an ancient, simple and universally recognized implement. The other side of the coin is that someone who leans unduly on rotundity or euphemism is likely to be described as "calling a spade an agricultural implement."

Call in Question. Challenge; cast doubt on. In the New Testament Book of Acts the silversmith Demetrius tries to stir up action against Paul for saying of the shrines the silversmiths make to Diana that gods made by hand are not gods. The town clerk quiets the ruckus, pointing out that the silversmiths should take their case to a lawful assembly, "for we are in danger to be called in question for this day's uproar."

Calm Before the Storm. An intimation, when things are uncommonly quiet, that trouble is brewing. The phenomenon of a calm *after* a storm, perhaps only in contrast with the fury of the storm, has been remarked for centuries. A calm before a storm is also often remarked. Thus one can find, as early as 1576, one writer saying, "After a storme commeth a calme," and another saying, "Calm continueth not long without a storm." The transfer of the meteorological observation to crises in human affairs is at least as old.

Came Up (Smelling Like) Roses. Turned out well (usually the suggestion being that whatever it was turned out better than could have been expected). The transfer is from the look and smell of the rose, which most people find memorably pleasant. The cliché seems to be of American origin and fairly recent, but by 1969 it had a wider scope, as one sees in *The Times* of London: "If some disaster hit us, . . . we would have to soldier on, pretending that everything in the column was coming up roses."

Came the Dawn. At last he got the point or idea. The analogy is to light entering a dark scene, as at sunrise. The word dawn is not as old as one might suppose, dating from the late 16th century; before that people spoke of the dawing or the dawning. In the sense of beginning to grasp an idea it was known by 1823, when it appeared in one of Charles Lamb's *Elia* essays: "You could see the first dawn of an idea stealing slowly over his countenance."

Can't Call Your Soul Your Own. To be so much in thrall to or under the influence of a person or an organization as to have lost one's independence. William Stewart was invoking this lament in his *Buik of the Chroniclis of Scotland* (1535): "They skantlie durst say their saull wes thair owin."

Can't Hit the Broad Side of a Barn. His aim, usually in throwing something, is notoriously bad. The term became popular about 60 years ago as a description of baseball pitchers who have trouble getting the ball in the strike zone. Although it still serves primarily in that sense, at times it is also applied to people who are equally wild with firearms.

Can't See Beyond the End of His Nose. He is intellectually near-sighted, unable to think of anything but the immediate problem (and quite likely only a narrow aspect of that). Francis Bacon used the phrase in print (in French) in 1594; James Howell listed it in 1659 as a French proverb: *Il ne regard plus loin que le bout de son nez.*

Cap Set For Him, Has Her. She is seeking to turn a male acquaintance (or a man she has merely seen) into a suitor. Women at one time almost always wore some kind of headdress, even indoors (often a light cap of muslin). If a woman put on a particularly fancy one, it was assumed she was trying to catch a man's eye. Oliver Goldsmith reflected the usage in 1773, in *She Stoops to Conquer*: "Instead of breaking my heart at his indifference, I'll . . . set my cap to some newer fashion, and look out for some less difficult admirer."

Captain of His Soul. In charge of his own destiny. The idea goes back to Aristotle, who said (in *Nicomachean Ethics*): "A man is the origin of his action." Many other writers have sounded the same theme—among them Sir Francis Bacon, Shakespeare and Tennyson—but the present form of the thought was made memorable in a poem by William Ernest Henley in 1888:

> I am the master of my fate;
> I am the captain of my soul.

Captain of Industry. An influential businessman; often as "captains," to encompass a group of the most influential businessmen of a region or country. The plural phrase is the title of a chapter in Thomas Carlyle's *Past and Present* (1843), and he can be credited as the originator of the cliché.

Cardinal Sin. A major offense. Ancient scholars wrote of seven cardinal virtues and seven cardinal (or deadly) sins. The so-called natural virtues were justice, prudence, temperance and fortitude; the theological ones were faith, hope and charity. The seven sins, as listed by Bishop Thomas Ken in 1711, were pride, envy, sloth, intemperance, avarice, ire and lust. Slight variations on Ken's list can be found elsewhere.

Care a Rap For, Don't. Dislike; have no interest in. The "rap" here is a counterfeit halfpenny that circulated in Ireland in the 18th century. The figurative meaning, reflecting the low worth of one's feelings about something, was evident by 1834 in William Ainsworth's *Rookwood:* "For the mare-with-three-legs [the gallows], boys, I care not a rap."

Carry Coals to Newcastle. Do something superfluous. Newcastle is in the heart of the main coal-mining region in England. It would therefore be the last place to which one would want or need to lug coal. The expression was recorded as common in the 16th century by John Heywood, a compiler of familiar English sayings. Thomas Fuller defined the term in 1662: "That is to do what was done before; or to busy one's self in a needless imployment."

Cart Before the Horse, Get (Put) the. To do things in an illogical order; to have one's priorities awry. Many languages have similar ways of describing an illogical action. Cicero said it in Latin; it (or rather a close relative) appeared first in English in 1340, in *Ayenbite of Inwyt* (Remorse of Conscience): "Many religious folk set the plow before the oxen." The modern version was in use by 1520, as reflected in Robert Whitinton's *Vulgaria:* "That techer setteth the carte before the horse that preferreth imitacyon before preceptes."

Cast Aspersions. Make a damaging or maligning charge. To "asperse," which one rarely hears now, meant to sprinkle or bespatter, and the verb served alone to say what "cast aspersions" says now. Thus in 1611 John Speed wrote (in *The History of Great Britaine*) that "Monkish humours haue aspersed other such men with bitter reproaches." But aspersions have been cast for a long time, too—at least since the 18th century.

Cast Pearls Before Swine. Make a foolish or inappropriate gesture; offer something of value to someone who can't appreciate it. Matthew records this as one of Jesus' remarks in the Sermon on the Mount: "Do not give dogs what is holy, and do not throw your pearls before swine, lest they trample them under foot and turn to attack you."

Cast Your Bread Upon the Waters. Take a chance on a useful return by investing money or a resource. Ecclesiastes says, in the Old Testament book bearing that name, "Cast thy bread upon the waters: for thou shalt find it after many days." On its face the expression is somewhat cryptic; it is often interpreted as meaning that one should be generous with one's money or resources without any expectation of gain, although gain may result.

Cast into Outer Darkness. Ostracized; excluded. St. Matthew's account of Jesus healing the centurion's servant has the phrase. Jesus marvels at the centurion's faith and says, "Truly, not even in Israel have I found such faith. I tell you, many will come from east and west and sit at table with Abraham, Isaac and Jacob in the kingdom of heaven, while the sons of the kingdom will be thrown into the outer darkness; there men will weep and gnash their teeth."

Cast the First Stone. Make an accusation to which you are yourself vulnerable; be too quick to criticize. In the New Testament St. John records the story of how the Pharisees brought to Jesus a woman who had been caught in adultery. They pointed out that under the law she should be stoned. Jesus, aware that adultery was a common sin, said: "He that is without sin among you, let him first cast a stone at her." John continues: "And they which heard it, being convicted by their own conscience, went out one by one . . . ."

Cat Got Your Tongue, Has the? Are you unable to speak? Since it is implausible that the household pet would ever get hold of its owner's tongue, one is forced to examine the many other meanings of "cat" for the origin of the term, which appears to have surfaced in the 19th century. Among them is, "cat-o'-nine-tails," a whip, the anticipation of which could paralyze a victim into silence. There is also the medicinal cat (or kat), which acts on the heart and could produce temporary silence as a side effect. Or it might simply be that the household cat's habit of staring quietly at owners and birds suggested an analogy with the suddenly silent person.

Cat's Meow. A nifty idea, thing or person; something remarkable. In the 1920s the same idea was expressed in several catly ways, including "the cat's whiskers" and "the cat's pajamas." Since the cat has the capability of looking enormously pleased, it is likely that all these expressions derived from that appearance of satisfaction.

Cat's Paw. An agent employed or induced to perform a difficult or dangerous task for someone else. Versions of the term appear in many languages and in various fables. The usual version is that a monkey, who wanted to get some chestnuts from the fire where they had been roasting, employed the paw of his friend the cat to pull them out. Whence also the cliché, "pull his chestnuts out of the fire." The tale is centuries old. In the early versions the paw usually belonged to a dog, and there is some suspicion that the cat got into the act by a mistranslation of the Latin *catellus*, meaning puppy or whelp.

Catbird Seat. A position of advantage or prominence. Red Barber, the radio broadcaster of the Brooklyn Dodgers baseball games for many years, made this term popular. He once explained that it was a Southern expression for which he had literally paid by continually raising (with a weak hand) in a game of stud poker until he lost to an opponent with a strong hand who met every raise. According to Barber, the opponent said: "Thanks for all those raises. From the start I was sitting in the catbird seat." The catbird commands a good view from its lofty perch, but then, so do many birds. Why the catbird's vantage point was singled out is beyond explaining.

Catch More Flies with Honey Than with Vinegar, You Can. You're more likely to get what you want by being pleasant than by being harsh. Thomas Fuller had an early version of this thought in the 17th century: "More Flies are taken with a Drop of Honey than with a Tun of Vinegar." Flies flock to sweet things and ignore sour things.

Catch as Catch Can. By any means available. An old game for children, and also a method of wrestling, carried this name. The participants were allowed any grip they could get. In a slightly different form ("Cacche who that cacche might"), the saying dates from the 14th century.

Change of Heart. A reversal of one's opinion or attitude. The term was known to Shakespeare, who absorbed many current familiar expressions. In *Measure for Measure* (1604) the Duke of Vienna, having cast off the friar's disguise that he had adopted to see what was going on in his realm, says to Isabella:

> Come hither, Isabel.
> Your friar is now your prince: as I was then
> Advertising and holy to your business,
> Not changing heart with habit, I am still
> Attorney'd at your service.

Change of Scene. A trip to a different place; a job switch (usually in the sense that one is doing it to refresh oneself or get a new start). The image is left over from the days when it was the practice in the theater to change the scenery frequently. (Note how many changes Shakespeare calls for.) The figurative meaning is old, too, being reflected in a letter by Lady Mary Montagu in 1716: "Everything I see seems to me a change of scene."

Charity Begins at Home. One should look first after oneself and one's family. The thought, but not the expression, appears in St. Paul's first letter to Timothy: "But if any provide not for his own, and specially for those of his own house, he hath denied the faith, and is worse than an infidel." We are close to the modern saying in John Wyclif's *Of Prelates* (1380): "Charite schuld bigyne at hemself." By 1616, in Beaumont and Fletcher's *Wit without Money,* the modern version appears: "Charity and beating begins at home."

Charmed Life, A. He seems always to be lucky, to be unafflicted by the usual difficulties and dangers. Macbeth, in Shakespeare's play (1606), confronts Macduff, who seeks to kill him. Macbeth takes comfort in a prophecy by three witches that no man born of woman can kill him, and says:

I bear a charmed life, which must not yield
To one of woman born. Whereupon Macduff says,
"Macduff was from his mother's womb untimely
ripped." In the ensuing fight he kills Macbeth.

Chase a Rainbow. Pursue an illusion; venture on a fruitless quest. Rainbows are real enough to the eye but unreachable, and people have been aware of that for centuries, but the notion of "chasing rainbows" as a way of describing a futile action seems not to have turned up until about 1904, when newspapers in the United States began using the expression to refer to footless political activities.

Checkered Career. A life of successes and failures (usually with the implication that the failures predominated). From the alternating color pattern of the checkerboard.

Cheek by Jowl. Close; side by side. A "jowl" is a cheek, and indeed until about the beginning of the 17th century the saying was "cheek by cheek," or "cheke by cheke" as it was written then. It appears as "cheke by ioule" in *Sir Clyomon,* published around 1570. Shakespeare has it in *A Midsummer Night's Dream* (1595): "I'll go with thee, cheek by jowl."

Chew Him Out. Upbraid him; bawl him out; reprimand him severely. The picture arises of a drill sergeant having a hard go at a private or a private first class; in giving vent to his fury the sergeant works his mouth in a manner reminiscent of chewing, of eating up his victim. The term seems to have originated in the U.S. Army in World War II.

Chew the Cud. To ruminate; to think something over. From the practice of cows and other ruminant animals, which regurgitate food and chew it for a second time. John Wyclif had a version of the saying in 1382; it was in its modern form by 1547 in a British book of homilies: "Let vs ruminate, and (as it were) chewe the cudde . . ."

Chew the Rag. To chat; also (mainly in Great Britain) to discuss a point, often contentiously. The British meaning seems to have originated in the British Army about 100 years ago. J. B. Patterson says, in *Life in the Ranks* (1885), that the meaning is "Persisting to argue the point, or 'chew the rag,' as it is termed in rank and file phraseology, with some extra intelligent noncommissioned officer." The kind of rag that is being chewed is open to speculation. It may be the "rag" as a piece of cloth, such as a small child is likely to chew on when he is unhappy, or the verb "rag" in its sense of scolding or bullying.

Chicken Out. To lose one's nerve. "Chicken" as a noun, along with "chicken-hearted," have for centuries been applied to people who are timorous, as chickens seem to be except with inferior chickens; the modern phrase turns the noun into a verb. Sir Thomas Stafford had an early example of the image in 1633: "Not finding the Defendants to be Chikins, to be afraid of every cloud or kite."

Chicken in Every Pot, A. Prosperity for all, or at least enough money in every household to put food on the table. Henri IV, who was king of France from 1589 to 1610, is reported to have said, "I want there to be no peasant in my realm so poor that he will not have a chicken in his pot every Sunday."

Chickens Come Home to Roost, The. Things you have said or done wrongly, or problems you have put aside, are likely to return to plague you; you have to deal with the consequences of your actions. Robert Southey apparently coined this simile in *The Curse of Kehama* (1810): "Curses are like young chickens; they always come home to roost."

Child of Nature. An innocent or naive person. William Wordsworth has it, and may have originated it, in "To a Young Lady, Who Had Been Reproached for Taking Long Walks in the Country," which begins:

> Dear Child of Nature, let them rail!
> —There is a nest in a green dale,
> A harbour and a hold;
> Where thou, a Wife and Friend, shalt see
> Thy own delightful days, and be
> A light to young and old.

Child's Play. An extremely easy or simple task. The phrase was familiar enough by about 1385 for Chaucer to put it in the negative, in *The Merchant's Tale:* "It is no childes play to take a wyf withoute avysement [advisement]."

Chilled to the Bone. Made uncomfortably or extremely cold. This is so common a way of exaggerating a feeling of chilliness (anyone really chilled to the bone would be dead) that its origins are lost. Shakespeare was close to it, though, in *Pericles*, where Pericles, Prince of Tyre, who has been shipwrecked, walks ashore on the coast of Pentapolis, encounters three fishermen and asks them for help, saying:

> What I have been I forgot to know;
> But what I am, want teaches me to think on:
> A man throng'd up with cold: my veins are chill,
> And have no more of life than may suffice
> To give my tongue that heat to ask your help. . . .

47

Chinaman's Chance, Not a. No chance at all. In the middle of the 19th century, when gold mining was a fever in California, many Chinese immigrants tried their hand at it. They were disliked and scorned by the American miners, partly because they worked for such low pay. The Chinaman's "chance" was his likelihood of escaping ostracism or worse in the gold camps; it may also have applied to the likelihood that he would be given an opportunity to find much gold.

Chip Off the Old Block, A. A son who is like his father. Once it was "chip of the old block." The "block" was either wood or stone; in either case, a chip would have the same characteristics as the block. In a slightly different form the expression was in print by 1626 in the play *Dick of Devonshire:* "Why may not I be a Chipp of the same blocke out of which you two were cutt?"

Chip on the Shoulder, Have a. To be edgy, snappish, ready to fight. One would suppose a person with a chip on his shoulder would have all he could do to keep it from falling off. Apparently, however, it was once the fashion among boys for one boy to put a chip of something on his shoulder and dare another boy to knock it off. As a newspaper in New York explained it in 1830: "When two churlish boys were determined to fight, a chip would be placed on the shoulder of one and the other demanded to knock it off—at his peril." This origin is also evident in the St. Louis *Daily Pennant* (1840): "Jonathan's blood is 'pretty considerable riz' anyhow, and it wouldn't take so much as knocking a chip off a boy's shoulder to make it a darnationed sight riz-er."

Chips are Down, The. The situation is urgent and we have to deal with it. One suspects that the saying, which derives from games such as poker in which the money being bet is represented by chips, has been around a long time, but it did not appear in print until some 50 years ago. When the chips are down, the bet has been made and the player is committed to win or lose with his hand.

Cite Chapter and Verse. Give one's authority for an assertion. From the ancient and modern practice, by priests and ministers and others expounding the word of God, of naming not only the book of the Bible that provides the basis for the interpretation but also the numbers of the chapter and verse of the book.

Clean Pair of Heels, Show a. Move rapidly; make a fast getaway. The heels are what you see as a person or an animal is escaping, and when they are "clean," they are unencumbered by a pursuer. Once the thought was expressed as a "fair pair of heels"; it appeared thus in *The Anatomie of Abuses*, by Philip Stubbes

48

(1583): "He showes them a faire pair of heeles; and away goeth he."
The heels were clean by 1881, as in *The Chaplain of the Fleet,* by
Sir Walter Besant and James Rice: "Your husband . . . will show
them a clean pair of heels off the Nore."

Clean Slate, A. A new start, made possible by the removal of a
previous record. From the slate blackboards used in schools and
the small slates used earlier by individual pupils, which could be
erased to make way for new writing. The figurative sense is clear
by 1868 in *The Rock Ahead,* by Edmund Yates: "He had passed
the wet sponge over the slate containing any records of his early
life."

Clean as a Hound's Tooth. Exceptionally clean. Often the phrase is
said by or about someone who is certain of his innocence of a
crime that might be laid to him or is certain that the authorities
won't be able to find any evidence to charge him. It's an odd
phrase, since one would have to be doing dental work on a dog to
know if a hound's tooth was notably clean. The idea becomes
clearer when one finds that the saying originally referred to the
whiteness of a hound's tooth. Thus William Williams, in *Mr.
Penrose, The Journal of Penrose, Seaman* (1783): "A smart
Privateer with a bottom as white as a Hound's tooth."

Clean as a Whistle. Neatly and effectively done; pure. At times in
earlier centuries it was "clear as a whistle," and that version
suggests the origin: in order to give a clear tone, a whistle (particularly one made of wood) must be clean. By 1828, in the *Craven
Glossary* compiled by William Carr, the term was being described
as "the proverbial simile."

Clear (Sound) as a Bell. In good voice or health; a trustworthy
proposition. Thus, Thomas Newton in a translation (1565) from
Latin of Lemnius's *Touchstone of Complexions:* "They be people
commonly healthy, and sound as a Bell."

Clear the Air. Remove obstructions or obscurities that have com-
plicated an issue. The literal origin is in what the sun and the wind
do to remove or dissipate clouds after a storm. The figurative
meaning was in use by 1380, when John Wyclif wrote that "winds
of truth should blow away heresies, and clear the airs of holy
church, which is now full troubled."

Clear the Decks. Make ready for action. In preparation for a naval
battle, particularly with a sailing ship, it was the practice when
possible to remove from the usually cluttered decks everything
that was in the way of firing the guns mounted there. The figurative meaning is to remove impediments or to deal with minor
problems in order to be able to focus on a major undertaking.

Climb the Wall. To be so restless, uneasy or distracted as to feel the need for some action or relief, even if the opportunity or the feat may be impossible. This usage is quite recent, but it derives from the days when soldiers really did climb the walls of fortifications. That practice is reflected in one of the lesser-known books of the Old Testament (Joel 2:7): "They shall run like mighty men: they shall climb the wall like men of war; and they shall march every one of his ways, and they shall not break their ranks."

Cloak-and-Dagger Work. Spying, usually in an atmosphere of intrigue and melodrama. A 16th-century Spanish phrase describing the plays of Pedro Calderón and Lope de Vega was *comedias de capa y espada* (comedies of cape and sword), because they were full of fights and adventures, dramas in which an actor wearing a cloak was quite likely to have a sword or dagger concealed under it. Similar plays in English came to be called "cloak-and-sword" plays or "cloak-and-dagger" plays.

Close Call, A. A narrow escape. A term of American origin, dating from the late 19th century. It may have originated in baseball, where a decision made, or called, by an umpire could have gone either way—that is, it was close.

Close Quarters, In. In a confined space; tightly engaged with a foe. This was a naval term, defined by William Falconer in his *Universal Dictionary of the Marine* (1769) as it applied to merchant ships capable of fighting: "Certain strong barriers of wood stretching across a merchant-ship in several places. They are used as a place of retreat, when a ship is boarded by her adversary, and are . . . fitted with . . . loop holes, through which to fire."

Close Shave. A narrow escape. A man who literally shaves too close is likely to cut or scratch his face. Someone who was just missed by a runaway object saw the similarity and coined the phrase long ago. By 1834 it was in use figuratively in the United States, as in Charles A. Davis's *Letters of Jack Downing:* "I did not so much as get my feet wet when the bridge fell, though it was a close shave."

Close on the Heels of. In hot pursuit. The picture is from hunting, as is suggested by John Trapp in one of his many commentaries on the Bible (1646): "The guilt will haunt you at heels, as a bloodhound."

Closing (Shutting) Up Shop. Ending work for the day; terminating one's business. The playwright Thomas Dekker has a character say, in *The Shoemaker's Holiday* (1599): "We may shut vp our shops, and make holiday."

Clothes Make the Man. Appearances count for a lot. A similar expression was current among the ancient Greeks: "The garment makes the man." In the form "apparel makes the man" the idea turned up in England as early as the 16th century. A century later it was sometimes put as "the taylor makes the man."

Cloud Nine, On. Extremely happy; exhilarated at what has happened. You can attribute this to the ninth (of 10) heavens in Dante's *Paradise*, to various classifications of clouds by meteorological organizations (usually in 10 categories) or simply to the notion that to be up on a cloud would be quite blissful, and if it were a cloud with a particular number, it might be your own, at least for the moment. Dante's ninth heaven has something going for it, since it was closest to the divine presence (in the 10th heaven, the empyrean), but the reference seems a bit too esoteric for an expression that became a cliché around 1950.

Cloud No Bigger Than a Man's Hand, A. A premonitory signal of trouble or danger. In the first Book of Kings in the Old Testament, Elijah says to Ahab, whose people have been suffering from drought, that rain is coming. Elijah then goes to the top of Mount Carmel and tells his servant to look toward the sea. The servant says he sees nothing. Told to keep looking, he says after the seventh look, "Behold, a little cloud like a man's hand is rising out of the sea." This was premonitory of a rainstorm, which in that case was welcome, but the little cloud now more often serves as a symbol of approaching trouble.

Cloud-cuckoo Land. A zany or impractical scheme. In Aristophanes' play *The Birds*, it was a city erected in the air by birds. A city in the air is clearly an improbable place.

Clouded Crystal Ball, A. A poor or mistaken view of what is going to happen. An ancient practice of seersayers is to gaze intently at a clear crystal ball, purporting to see future events there. The practice is also known as "scrying." Someone whose predictions were wrong was said to have been looking into "a clouded ball."

Clue, I Haven't a. I'm in the dark; I can't get a handle on this problem. It is now largely forgotten that once the chief meaning of "clue" (or "clew") was a ball of yarn or thread, and that one use of a clue was to lay down a marker that one could follow back out of a cave, a maze or a labyrinth. The idea remains, though, in the current cliché: One has no lead to follow toward the solution of a problem or toward grasping the meaning of something.

Coast is Clear, The. The way is open for a venture, with no obstacles or enemies in sight. Samuel Johnson's definition, in his *Dictionary of the English Language* in 1755, was: "The danger is over, the enemies have marched off." A coast is a place where you would have to expect impediments to landing or departing if you were, say, a smuggler, and you would take care to look for them before proceeding. A military or naval force might take active steps to remove any impediments, and it seems to be this sense in which the idea first began to appear in print, as in John Palsgrave's work of 1530 on the French language: "The kynge intendeth to go to Calays, but we must first clere the costes."

Cock and Bull Story, A. A tale that is not to be believed and probably is not meant to be believed, having been put forth to divert the hearer's or reader's attention from something else. The origin is probably in the ancient fables wherein animals talked; a conversation between a cock and a bull could have taken some bizarre turns. The age of the expression is evident in John Day's play, *Law-trickes or Who Would Have Thought It* (1608): "What a tale of a cock and a bull he told my father."

Cock of the Walk. The dominant or most noticeable figure in a certain place. Among the many meanings of "walk" as a noun is an enclosure for chickens and other domestic fowl. The rooster in such a place is the boss. As it was put in 1688 by Randle Holme, in *The Academy of Armoury:* "The Cocks Walk is the place where he is bred, which usually is a place that no other Cock comes to."

Cold Blood, In. Ruthlessly; without feeling. "Hot blood" has long been symbolic of anger; "cold blood" symbolizes a harmful action done deliberately. By 1608 it was in print, in Sir Francis Vere's *Commentaries:* "A resolution framed in cold blood."

Cold Feet, To Get. To lose one's nerve; to have doubts about taking on an activity. A version of the idea is found in Ben Jonson's *Volpone* (1605): "I am not, as your Lombard proverb saith, cold on my feet; or content to part with my commodities at a cheaper rate than I am accustomed." The modern sense of being (or becoming) cowardly was in use 100 years ago and possibly earlier. Surely in Lombardy and elsewhere the phrase has its origins in the chilling effect of fear.

Cold Heart, A. A person who is aloof and unfeeling. Antony accuses Cleopatra of being so (in Shakespeare's play of 1606) when he thinks she is currying favor with his archenemy Caesar, and says to the queen he has loved; "Cold-hearted toward me?" Cleopatra replies; "Ah, dear, if I be so, from my cold heart let heaven engender hail, and poison it in the source, and the first stone drop in my neck: as it determines, so dissolve my life!"

Cold Turkey. Straightforwardly; abruptly. To "talk turkey," meaning to speak or deal in a businesslike way, was a common saying by the middle of the 19th century. By 1928 the *Daily Express* of London was advising its readers of the intensified form: "She talked cold turkey about sex. 'Cold turkey' means plain truth in America." The term has had other meanings, including (since about 1955) an abrupt ending of a habit such as smoking. This meaning originated with drug addicts suddenly deprived of their drug (as in a treatment program) and was recorded by the *Dictionary of American Slang* in 1960.

Color of His Money, Didn't Like the. Mistrusted him; found something suspicious about him or his proposal. A similar expression, to "see the colour of his money," was current in England by the 18th century; it meant to have a clear idea of what sort of proposition someone was making. Thomas Gordon, in *A Cordial for Low Spirits* (1718), says: "I have never seen the colour of Mr. Baskett's money." Since in a given country one person's money was quite likely to be the same color as another's, to claim to dislike the color in a particular case meant that the person or the proposition seemed to be faulty or tainted.

Come Hell or High Water. Whatever the consequences or obstacles. One's instinct is to lay the saying to a beleaguered general, perhaps a Confederate general in the Civil War. The fact is, the origin is lost. The saying was well known in the United States by 1900.

Come Off It. Stop doing that; give up that idea. The person being addressed has figuratively mounted a high horse or a podium, or has taken up what looks like an indefensible position. To say of someone that he is on a high horse has for at least 200 years been a way of asserting that he is putting on airs or acting arrogantly; "come off it" may have originated as a means of urging such a person to dismount from that horse. In the form of "come off," it was recorded by the *Century Dictionary* in 1889, as "recent slang, U.S."

Come Up for Air. Pause for a rest or to get some essential supply. The analogy is to the kind of extended diving in which one must hold one's breath (as in looking for pearls) or to what whales do periodically. As a cliché in Australia, Canada and the United States, the figurative sense has been around for about 50 years.

Come a Cropper. Suffer a setback or a fall (literal or figurative). In the early 19th century in England the saying "neck and crop" meant bodily, completely; it originated as a description of the route a rider usually took in being tossed off a horse: over the head (i.e., the neck and crop). "To come a cropper" seems in turn to have been derived from the earlier expression.

Come on Like Gangbusters. To arrive or operate in a loud, vigorous, determined way. "Gangbusters," a radio program popular in the United States some 40 years ago, had an opening theme featuring gunfire and the sound of police sirens, suggesting that the police were about to descend on another gang of criminals. That was coming on like gangbusters.

Come to Grief. Fail; encounter misfortune (often with the implication that it was deserved). "Grief" as a bad end, as a way of saying that things didn't come out according to plan, is a figure that began to appear in print in about the middle of the 19th century. A British example of 1862 is: "A People's College . . . was founded at Nottingham, but speedily came to grief."

Comes to the Same Thing. Is no different; reaches the same end. In Robert Browning's poem, "Any Wife to Any Husband" (1842), a dying woman speculates that her faithful husband may forget her and turn to some other woman soon after becoming a widower:

> Re-coin thyself and give it them to spend,—
> It all comes to the same thing at the end,
> Since mine thou wast, mine art and mine shalt be,
> Faithful or faithless, sealing up the sum
> Or lavish of my treasure, thou must come
> Back to the heart's place here I keep for thee!

Conspicuous by His (Its) Absence. Conveying a message of disapproval by failing to attend an event, or of one's worth by not being included. Conspicuousness usually depends on presence, but sometimes absence stands out even more. Tacitus (A.D. 55–117) put the notion clearly in his *Annals:* "The images of the most illustrious families . . . were carried before it [the bier of Julia]. Those of Brutus and Cassius were not displayed; but for that reason they shone with preeminent luster." Today's version was in evidence by 1859, when the statesman John Russell made a speech in London: "Among the defects of the bill, which were numerous, one provision was conspicuous by its presence and another by its absence."

Conspiracy of Silence. An agreement to say nothing about a delicate situation or a disfavored person. Usually the allegation is made by someone who thinks his achievements are unappreciated or are being deliberately neglected by the authorities or experts. The expression was coined, or at least picked up, by the *Pall Mall Gazette* in 1885.

Consummation Devoutly to be Wished (Desired). A hoped-for outcome (often said ironically to express a wish that is not likely to be realized). Hamlet says it in his famous "To be, or not to be" soliloquy: "To die: to sleep; . . . No more; and, by a sleep to say we end; . . . The heartache, and the thousand natural shocks . . . that flesh is heir to, 'tis a consummation . . . devoutly to be wished."

Conventional Wisdom, The. Widely and uncritically accepted ideas. John Kenneth Galbraith put this phrase in the language in *The Affluent Society* (1958), saying that a name was needed for "the ideas which are esteemed at any time for their acceptability" because they are familiar, stable and predictable. "I shall refer to these ideas henceforth as the conventional wisdom."

Cooked His Goose. Did him in; spoiled his plans. There is an old story that the authorities of a medieval town under siege hung a goose from a tower, the goose symbolizing stupidity. The attackers were so irked that they burned the town, thereby literally cooking the real goose and cooking the townspeople's goose in the modern sense. The story appears not to hold up under scholarly research, which finds the phrase to be of 19th-century origin. It first appeared in print (in such a way as to suggest that it was already in the language) in Henry Mayhew's *London Labour and the London Poor* (1851), which tells of popular opposition to the naming of Nicholas Cardinal Wiseman by Pope Pius IX as archbishop of Westminster. According to Mayhew, a chant in the streets at the time was:

> If they come here we'll cook their goose,
> The Pope and Cardinal Wiseman.

Cookie Crumbles, That's the Way the. What happens happens; fate. This overworked image may be turning into a former cliché, but one still hears it, along with references to "the way the ball bounces." The originator is anonymous. One supposes he had in mind the fact that the pattern of disintegration of a cookie as you eat it is not fully predictable. The saying began to catch on about 1950.

Cool It. Calm down. As a command or a piece of advice this term transfers to human interactions the kind of step taken to deal with an overheated thing, such as an automobile engine. As a cliché it has been around since about 1955. Edwin Gilbert's *Hot and Cool* (1953) puts it this way; "Cool it, girl. Nobody's interested." *The New Yorker* in 1948 suggested an origin for the usage: "The bebop people have a language of their own. . . . Their expressions of approval include 'cool.'"

Cool as a Cucumber. Unruffled; serene. The cucumber, like the watermelon, is served in the summer as a symbol of coolness and thus as an antidote to the heat. In its function as a simile it first symbolized coldness or aloofness. The first act of *Cupid's Revenge*, by Beaumont and Fletcher (1615), has the line: "Young Maids were as cold as Cowcumbers." The modern sense is clear in Thomas de Quincey's discussion (1838) of the ancient historian Thucydides, who, he says, "is cool as a cucumber on every act of atrocity."

Coon's Age, A. A long time. Why it means this is difficult to say. Although there are other meanings of "coon," it certainly seems to be the raccoon that is implied here, and that animal's only association with time is its persistence in raiding one's camp supplies or garbage cans. The "coon's age" is of American origin and was in print by 1843 in William T. Thompson's *Major Jones's Courtship:* "Mary soon got over her skare, but the way she's mad at cousin Pete won't wear off for a coon's age."

Corporal's Guard. A small group. In most armies the corporal is the lowest ranking noncommissioned officer, in charge of the smallest group: the squad, consisting of about eight men. From this unit comes the figurative designation of any small group acting in some common purpose as "a corporal's guard." In this sense it goes back some 200 years.

Costs a Pretty Penny. It's expensive. The "pretty penny" goes back to a time when the penny was a significant coin, but even then it wasn't as significant as a shilling or a quarter or any number of other coins, so one has to look to alliteration for the appeal of the saying. Elizabeth Gaskell's *Mary Barton* (1848) picks it up: "This mourning . . . will cost a pretty penny."

Couldn't Care Less, I. I am exaggeratedly indifferent. This way of expressing boredom or lack of concern seems to have originated in England; in 1952 Sydney Moseley called it "a cant post-war phrase current in England." It made its way to Australia and Canada and reached its peak of overwork in the United States some 20 years ago.

Count Your Chickens Before They're Hatched, Don't. Beware of regarding money, a benefit or a triumph as yours until you really have it. The saying is the moral of Aesop's fable about a milkmaid and her pail. She is given a pail of milk by her employer for doing good work, and she knows the doctor will buy it for a shilling. On the way to his house she envisions buying eggs with the shilling; the eggs will hatch into chickens that she can sell for a guinea (21 shillings), with which she can buy a hat and ribbons. Then she spills the milk. Samuel Butler, in *Hudibras* (1664), wrote:

> To swallow gudgeons ere they're catched
> And count their chickens ere they're hatched.

This gudgeon is a fish.

Country Cousin. An unsophisticated visitor in a city, particularly one whose awkward ways are likely to embarrass his hosts. The phrase was well enough known by 1770 to appear in *The Lame Lover*, by Samuel Foote: "Pester'd at table by the odious company of . . . country cousins."

Courage of His Convictions, Have the. Act in keeping with his opinions; translate thought into deed. A French saying, meaning the same thing *(le courage de son opinion)* was in print by 1864, and thereafter the English equivalent (with either "opinions" or "convictions") began to appear frequently. An example (1887) is T. H. Hall Caine's *Life of Coleridge:* "[He] believed in the efficacy of the birch, and had the courage of his convictions."

Cows Come Home, Until the. For a long time. Cows out to pasture faithfully turn up at the barn, or at the gate leading to it, morning and evening to be milked. This old saying (in 1593 it was "till the Cow come home") referred particularly to the morning appearance, since it implied that some activity would go on all night. In 1620 Alexander Cooke put it this way in *Pope Joane:* "Drinking, eating, feasting, and revelling, till the cow come home, as the saying is."

Crack of Dawn, At the. Early; the first thing. This is "crack" from the old German word *Krach,* meaning a loud noise. Since a loud noise is usually also sudden, the "crack of dawn" is the moment when the sun comes up or when the first light appears in the east. The phrase seems to have originated in the United States about 100 years ago. An early and perhaps the first appearance of it was in 1887, in *Outing,* a magazine devoted to recreactional activities: "At 'crack of day,' as the sergeant expressed it, the stir of camp was started by waking up the cook."

Crack the Code. Fathom a puzzle or secret, particularly one that has deliberately been made opaque, as by encryptation. Once this thought was expressed as "crack the nut," in allusion to the difficulty of breaking open a hard nut. In *The Defence of Good Women,* by Sir Thomas Elyot (1545), one finds: "Nowe knacke [crack] me that nut, maister Candidus." You still hear this in "a tough nut to crack," as applied to a problem. The practice of putting military messages in a code was fairly common by the time of the Napoleonic wars and became routine with the advent of radio communication. In World War II the Allied forces put a good deal of effort into breaking the German and Japanese codes, with some notable successes, and the workaday phrase for solving a hard problem became more often "crack the code" than "crack the nut."

Cradled in the Lap of Luxury. Raised in a wealthy family. "Lap" in the sense of an environment of nurture goes back at least to the early 17th century. By 1802 it had been extended to the wealthy family; Maria Edgeworth's *Moral Tales* of that year refers to a person who was "brought up in the lap of luxury."

Crazy (Dumb, Sly) Like a Fox. Smart and resourceful. The fox has been celebrated for centuries as a crafty animal. Its wiles were remarked in the *Trinity College Homilies,* dating from about 1200. S. J. Perelman made one of these phrases (*Crazy Like a Fox*) the title of a book in 1944.

Crazy as a Coot. Addled like a senile person. The coot is any of several species of web-footed swimming and diving bird. (One of them, the bald coot—*Fulica atra*—gave rise to the phrase "bald as a coot," from the broad white plate on its forehead.) References to the "mad coot" are quite old; John Skelton wrote, in *Phyllyp Sparowe* (1529), of "the doterell, that folyshe pek, and also the mad coote, with a balde face to toote." "Coot," as applied to people, once meant stupid; Bartlett's 19th-century *Dictionary of Americanisms* says that, "Coot . . . is often applied by us to a stupid person." One still hears the term "old coot." Probably the frequent correlation between old age and strange behavior, along with what struck some people as zany antics by the avian coot, led to the current cliché, which has the further appeal of being alliterative.

Cream of the Crop, The. The best of any group. Cream being the choicest part of milk, it did not take long to extend the meaning to best in general. Richard Mulcaster wrote in 1521 (in *Positions*) of "the gentlemen, which be the cream of the common." References to the "cream of the market" as the best of what was being offered for sale are almost as old. "Cream of the crop" was probably inevitable because of its alliteration, which has a notable grip on the human mind. The saying has been in vogue for a good many years, but the time and place of its origin are elusive.

Cricket, That's Not. Unfair; unsportsmanlike; against the rules. Although the game of cricket is ancient and its rules are well known in Great Britain and the former British colonies, the saying that to do something irregular or against the rules is "not cricket" seems to have become current only about the beginning of the 20th century. In 1900 the *Westminster Gazette* said editorially: "We should be very much surprised if the Duke really thought that to dissolve [Parliament] would be 'cricket.'" The then-recent origin of the saying is suggested in William de Morgan's *Likely Story* (1911): "It is scarcely fair play now to make a merit of patience—isn't cricket, as folk say nowadays."

Cried All the Way to the Bank. Gloated over an achievement (often unexpected) that brought in a lot of money. It appears in the autobiography of the popular pianist Liberace, published in 1973, and is probably not a great deal older. Indeed, its one-liner and twisted-meaning nature suggest it originated with a radio comedian or a stand-up comic in a nightclub.

Crocodile Tears. False grief; insincere sympathy. Sir John Mandeville wrote in the 14th century of his voyages, adding so many questionable embellishments that for a time to be called "a Mandeville" was to be a teller of tall tales. One of his tales was that in a certain country "ben gret plenty of Cokadrilles. . . . Theise

Serpentes slen [slay] men, and they eten hem wepynge." The legend took hold that crocodiles weep in false grief as they consume their prey. By 1548 Thomas Cooper could write: "A prouerbe, applied unto them, which hating an other man, whom they would destroie, or haue destroied, they will seme to bee sorye for hym."

Cross That Bridge When We Come to It, Let's. Don't deal with a problem until you have to; don't worry unduly in advance. This is a proverb of such ancient lineage that *The Oxford Dictionary of English Proverbs* does not trace its origin, contenting itself with a quotation from Longfellow to the effect that "Don't cross the bridge till you come to it, . . . Is a proverb old, and of excellent wit."

Cross the Rubicon. To commit oneself irrevocably. Caesar did it literally in 49 B.C., the Rubicon being a river that marked the boundary between Italy and Cisalpine Gaul. By taking his troops across, he provoked a civil war with Pompey. By the 17th century the phrase meant any firm commitment in the face of risk, as in John Owen's work on the death of Christ (1643): "The die being cast and Rubicon crossed."

Crown of Glory. A triumph or notable achievement. It is a biblical phrase, from the First Epistle of Peter (5 : 4): "And when the chief Shepherd shall appear, ye shall receive a crown of glory that fadeth not away."

Cry Over Spilled Milk. To lament uselessly or pointlessly. As early as 1659 James Howell was listing "no weeping for shed milk" as a British proverb. The basis of it is that spilled milk cannot be gathered up and put back in the container.

Cry Wolf. Raise a false alarm; exaggerate a danger. It comes from one of the fables of Aesop and many other compilers. As Aesop puts it:

> A mischievous Lad, who was set to mind some Sheep, used, in jest, to cry "Wolf! Wolf!" When the people at work in the neighboring fields came running to the spot he would laugh at them for their pains. One day the Wolf came in reality, and the Boy, this time, called "Wolf! Wolf!" in earnest; but the men, having been so often deceived, disregarded his cries, and the Sheep were left at the mercy of the Wolf.

Crying in the Wilderness. Pleading a cause that seems forlorn now but may improve. The origin is the Bible (Isaiah 40 : 3): "The voice of him that crieth in the wilderness, Prepare ye the way of the Lord, make straight in the desert a highway for our God." Matthew picks it up (3 : 3) recounting that John the

Baptist came to preach in the wilderness of Judea. It was John who was envisioned in Isaiah's prophecy, Matthew says.

Cudgel Your Brains. Try hard to remember something or to think a problem through. Shakespeare has it in *Hamlet*. In the first scene of Act V the two clowns who have come to dig Ophelia's grave are arguing about whether she should receive a Christian burial; as the discussion progresses the first clown asks who builds stronger than a mason or a shipwright or a carpenter. The second clown, after trying, "the gallows-maker," is asked to try again and says he cannot answer. The first clown says: "Cudgel thy brains no more about it, for your dull ass will not mend his pace with beating, and when you are asked this question next, say 'a gravemaker:' the houses that he makes last till doomsday."

Cup of Tea, Not My. A person, activity or proposal that doesn't appeal to you or that you downright dislike. One would suppose this was British and quite old. Indeed, the British had the phrase "dish of tea" in the 17th century, always as something one enjoyed or looked forward to. The negative notion of something one doesn't like seems to be quite recent. Sometimes, but less often, you hear the positive form: "Now, that's my cup of tea."

Curry Favor. Flatter subtly in an effort to gain some end. The saying falls strangely on the eye and ear because you "curry" a horse. Well, it was a horse originally: Fauvel in the 14th-century French tale *Roman de Fauvel.* The horse was a symbol of slyness and cunning; to curry or groom Fauvel (often spelled Favel) was to seek to recruit the service of deceit and duplicity. In 15th-century English it was "cury fauel," the *u* being the old version of *v*, and as time went on and the term spread by word of mouth, "favel" became "favor." By 1510 Alexander Barclay had the transformed version in *The Mirrour of Good Manners:* "Flatter not as do some; With non curry fauor."

Cut From Whole Cloth. A false story or statement. In the 15th-century a whole cloth and a broad cloth were dependably of a certain size, but as time went on some manufacturers or sellers cheated, and the cloth was less than it was intended to be. A statement cut from whole cloth was similarly undependable. In this sense the phrase had appeared by 1823, when Charles Mathews wrote: "Isn't this entire story . . . made out of whole cloth?"

Cut No Ice. Make no impression; fail to sway someone. The phrase originated in the United States some 100 years ago, perhaps taken over from figure skating or perhaps from the practice of cutting ice from rivers and lakes and storing it for summer refrigeration. *Scribner's Magazine* in 1897 had the figurative sense: "And it don't cut no ice with you whether folks call you inconsistent or not."

Cut Off Your Nose to Spite Your Face. Seek revenge for some pain or injury to oneself; a self-defeating action. A similar expression was stated in Latin by Peter of Blois in 1200. By 1788 Peter Grose was defining it in his *Classical Dictionary of the Vulgar Tongue:* "He cut off his nose to be revenged of his face, said of one who, to be revenged of his neighbour, has materially injured himself."

Cut and Dried. Routine; prepared beforehand. Sometimes it is said as "cut and dry," which is what one does with lumber, herbs, tobacco and flowers. The practice with herbs seems to have been the origin of the saying, which appears as early as 1710 in a letter to the Rev. Henry Sacheverell: "Your Sermon was ready Cut and Dry'd." The transferred meaning arises because cut and dried items, however useful they may be, have lost their freshness.

Cut and Run. Leave hastily; get out of a difficult situation quickly, perhaps giving up something valuable in the process. One did it in the days of sailing ships, when the anchor cable was made of hemp. The practice is explained in *The Elements and Practice of Rigging and Seamanship* (1794): "To *cut and run,* to cut the cable and make sail instantly, without waiting to weigh anchor."

Cut and Thrust. The interplay of a battle or debate. The cut-and-thrust sword was designed to do both of the things implied by its name, and the image of the kind of combat in which a swordsman so armed would alternately thrust the point into an opponent or cut his way out from a group of opponents has been transferred to somewhat gentler encounters such as debates. The figurative meaning began to appear early in the 19th century, somewhat past the time when hand-to-hand combat with swords had been displaced by battles with guns.

Cut of his Jib, I Don't Like the. I'm suspicious of him; his looks bother me. The "jib" is a triangular sail, one or more of which was found at the bow of all but the smallest sailing vessels. To the seasoned nautical eye it was often possible to tell the nationality of a ship by the way its jibs looked. By 1823 Robert Southey had picked up the expanded meaning, writing of the likabililty of certain people, "which depends something on the cut of their jib."

Cut the Coat According to the Cloth. Make the project fit the resources available; keep your expenses within your income. John Heywood had it in his book of English proverbs in 1546: "I shall cut my Cote after my cloth."

Cut the Mustard. Do something well, particularly when it is suspected that one's ability may have declined due to age, infirmity or lack of practice. In American slang of the late 19th century "mustard" came to mean not just the condiment but something that was the best of anything. O. Henry's *Cabbages and Kings* in 1894 had this example: "I'm not headlined in the bills, but I'm the mustard in the salad just the same." Mustard grows as a plant, and "cutting the mustard" in the sense of being able (or still able) to do something may have come from that.

Cut to the Quick. Deeply offended. One meaning of "quick" that has largely gone out of use is flesh, and it is the living flesh that is being cut in the image. The metaphor has been in the language since at least the 16th century, as in Sir Thomas More's *Utopia* (1551): "Their tenants . . . whom they poll and shave to the quick, by raising their rents."

D

Damn with Faint Praise. To show by a weakly or ironically favorable remark that one really disapproves. "Faint praise" was a recognized art by 1633, when Phineas Fletcher wrote in *The Purple Island:* "When needs he must, yet faintly then he praises." Alexander Pope had the modern version in his *Epistle to Dr. Arbuthnot* (1734):

> Damn with faint praise, assent with civil leer,
> And, without sneering, teach the rest to sneer.

Dance Attendance On. Act in a servile way; wait on someone obsequiously. It is the kind of "dance" sometimes described as "kicking one's heels," that is, waiting in an antechamber to be admitted to the presence of someone who is in a position to give you orders or from whom you are seeking a favor. John Skelton put it neatly in 1522 in "Why Come Ye Not to Courte?": "And Syr ye must daunce attendance, / And take patient sufferaunce, For my Lords Grace, / Hath now no time or space, / To speke with you as yet."

Dark Horse. A contestant about whom little is known but who (perhaps because of good qualities that have been deliberately concealed) has a good chance to win. The term came from the racetrack (where it still applies) and found its way easily into politics. It was in print by 1831 in *The Young Duke,* written by Benjamin Disraeli, who was at the time a dark horse himself—a young author who stood four times for Parliament before being elected in 1837 and then went on to become prime minister: "A dark horse, which had never been thought of . . . rushed past the grand stand in sweeping triumph."

Dawned on Me. Finally became apparent. Harriet Beecher Stowe put it negatively in *Uncle Tom's Cabin* (1852): "The idea that they had either feelings or rights had never dawned upon her." The "dawn" here, like the premonitory glimmerings of sunrise, is the arrival of light in the mind.

Days Are Numbered, His. Fate is closing in on him; his death is near. It is an extension of a biblical statement. Daniel, interpreting for King Belshazzar the handwriting on the wall (Daniel 5 : 26); says, "This is the interpretation of the thing: MENE; God hath numbered thy kingdom, and finished it."

Dead Letter. A person, project or idea that no longer has much influence. At one time the phrase meant taking a piece of writing absolutely literally, failing to recognize the spirit of it and thereby rendering it ineffective. Paul has the thought in 2 Corinthians 3 : 6, where he writes of his change to God through Christ: "Who also hath made us ministers of the new testament; not of the letter, but of the spirit: for the letter killeth, but the spirit giveth life." The sense of a thing that has lost its usefulness was current by 1663, when it appeared in James Heath's *Flagellum,* a book on Oliver Cromwell: "To which all other dictates and Instructions were useless, and as a dead letter."

Dead and Gone. Noteworthily absent or done for. Tautology has almost as much appeal to the human mind as alliteration, and "dead and gone" as a way of saying a person has died is an example. Still, it conveys a sense of relief or even pleasure that someone or something is out of the picture. Shakespeare has the phrase as a lament for a death. In *Hamlet* Ophelia has been driven mad by the death of her father, Polonius. In her madness she sings a song to the queen:

> He is dead and gone, lady,
> He is dead and gone;
> At his head a grass-green turf,
> At his heels a stone.

Dead as (Deader Than) a Doornail. Wholly unresponsive, or (of ideas) without prospects for success. Of all the ways to emphasize the deadness of something, likening it to a doornail has to be up there among the improbabilities. And what is a "doornail?" Well, that can be answered; it was a nail with a large head, and at one time it was common practice to stud a door with them for decoration or reinforcement. The popularity of the phrase is probably attributable to alliteration. In any event, the expression goes back at least to 1350 in *The Romance of William of Palerne:* "For but ich haue bote of mi bale I am ded as a dorenail." In modern English: "Unless I get relief from my trouble, I am dead as a doornail."

Dead as (Deader Than) a Mackerel. Out of it; finished. "Dead" is an absolute, like "pregnant," and it is as impossible to be deader as it is to be pregnanter. Never mind. We see here two old sayings that seem to have changed partners over the centuries. One was "dead as a herring" and the other was "mute as a mackeral." Samuel Butler had "dead as a herring" in *Hudibras* (1664) and Samuel Foote offered "mute as a mackerel" in *The Minor* (1760).

Dead of Night. The quietest time; a time to execute a maneuver because you can be fairly sure it will be unexpected. This sense appears in Edward Hall's *Chronicle* (1548): "In the dedde of the night . . . he brake up his camp and fled."

Dead to Rights. Irretrievably; without possibility of error; red-handed. One can only speculate which of the many meanings of "right" gave rise to this saying; perhaps it was the one, now dead itself, meaning " completely." The term "sink to rights" was formerly a way of saying a ship had completely sunk; a miscreant caught "dead to rights" is completely caught in some misdeed. The term is apparently of American origin. In 1881 the *City Argus* of San Francisco wrote of a man who "attempted to get into Banker Sather's cash-box—was caught 'dead to rights' and now languishes in the city Bastille."

Death Warmed Over (Up), Like. Looking ill or exhausted. The suggestion is that you look only slightly better than if you were dead. The phrase appeared in the *Soldier's War Slang Dictionary* in 1939. In *Death and the Dancing Footman* (1942), Ngaio Marsh wrote: "I look like death warmed up and what I feel is nobody's business."

Death's Door, At. Gravely injured, ill or enfeebled. In Wyclif's Bible of 1382 the image appears as "the gates of death." It was "death's door" by the 16th century, as in Miles Coverdale's *A Spyrytuall and Moost Precious Pearle* (1550): "To bring unto deaths door, that he may restore unto life again."

Deep Six. In oblivion; discarded. The standard usage is "give him the deep six," probably in a macabre allusion to the practice of digging graves six feet deep or of burying people at sea in six fathoms of water.

Demon Rum. Hard liquor and its unfortunate consequences. The phrase is from Timothy Shay Arthur's *Ten Nights in a Barroom* (1854): " . . . a slave to the Demon Rum." It is an American expression; as H. L. Mencken says, in *The American Language* (1919), the Englishman "never uses *rum* in the generic sense that it has acquired in the United States, and knows nothing of *rum-dumbs*, *rum-dealers*, the *rum-trade*, and the *rum-evil*, or *Demon Rum*."

Den of Thieves. A rascally group; a place where one has to be on one's guard. When Matthew tells how Jesus drove the money changers and others out of the temple, he reports (21 : 13) that Jesus "said unto them, It is written, My house shall be called the house of prayer; but ye have made it a den of thieves."

Devil Incarnate. A particularly evil person. This one goes way back, to the time when religious folk took the devil very seriously, so that to call another person an embodiment of the devil was a grave charge. It was in print by 1395, in John Purvey's *Remonstrances Against Romish Corruption in the Church:* "A sone of perdicioun, and a devil incarnat."

Diamond in the Rough, A. An unpolished or inexperienced person who nonetheless shows promise in some field. A diamond as it comes from the mine needs cutting and polishing, but it is potentially of great value; the expression transferred easily to promising people. John Fletcher, in *A Wife for a Month* (1624), shows the idea developing: "She is very honest, and will be hard to cut as a rough diamond."

Dictates of Conscience. What you feel or are made to feel you ought to do. Archbishop John Bramhall wrote in 1656 of a man who did something "contrary to the dictate of his conscience." Patrick Henry put it, in one of the articles of the Virginia Bill of Rights (1776): "That religion, or the duty which we owe to our Creator, and the manner of discharging it, can be directed only by reason and conviction, not by force or violence; and therefore all men are entitled to the free exercise of religion, according to the dictates of conscience. . . . "

Did a Slow Burn (Boil). Progressed from annoyance to anger. This is a visual image transferred to the spoken language from the sequence of facial expressions made famous in the movies by the comedian Leo Carroll and later by the actor Edgar Kennedy. It dates from the 1930s.

Die in Harness. Keep on working to the end. Horses, oxen, buffalo and other sources of motive power on farms or pulling vehicles have done it. Macbeth uses the term as his pivotal battle with Macduff seems imminent:

> Ring the alarum bell! Blow, wind! Come, wrack!
> At least we'll die with harness on our back.

Die is Cast. The decision has been made. This is the "die" that forms one of a pair of dice; once it has been thrown, the player must abide by the result. The saying is old enough to have been a proverb in Caesar's time (*iacta alia est*). The biographers of Caesar quote him as saying "*Iacta alea esto*" ("Let the die be cast") as he was about to cross the Rubicon to come to grips with Pompey. In *Richard III* (1594) Shakespeare has King Richard say, as he is about to lose his life and crown in battle, "I have set my life upon a cast, and I will stand the hazard of the die."

Ding-dong Battle. An encounter marked by a rapid exchange of thrusts; an intense struggle with the outcome in doubt. "Ding-dong" represents the regular series of sounds given off by a striking clock because a hammer is regularly striking a gong or a coiled wire. The transfer to a fight, in which the blows are exchanged regularly, followed naturally. A first cousin of the modern phrase appeared in 1680 in Thomas Otway's *The History and Fall of Caius Marius:* "They are at it ding dong."

Dirt Cheap. Extremely low priced. Dirt doesn't usually carry a well-known price, and nowadays it isn't always cheap, but the expression is old enough to suggest a time when it may have been free for the taking. "Dirt-cheap, indeed, it was, as well it might." That line appeared in *Blackwell's Magazine* in 1821.

Dirty Dog. Someone judged as despicable or unreliable. Why this association should be hung on dogs rather than cats, cattle or horses is unclear, except that dogs have been common in human households for so long. The saying itself is apparently fairly recent; Sherard Vines offers an example from 1928 in *Humours Unreconciled*: "Who's been calling me a dirty dog, I should like to know"?

Distance Lends Enchantment. You are likely to think more fondly of a remote person, activity or scene than one that is close by. Diogenes Laertius said something like this nearly 1,800 years ago: "The mountains too, at a distance, appear airy masses and smooth, but seen near at hand they are rough." Thomas Campbell in his poem *Pleasures of Hope* (1799) had it thus:
>'Tis distance lends enchantment to the view,
>And robes the mountain in its azure hue.

Distinction Without a Difference, A. A niggle; a foolish or unthinking argument. William Fulke, a tireless (and tiresome) writer of religious tracts, put this expression in print in 1579: "The distinction remaineth without a difference." A "distinction" is supposed to embody a difference; when it amounts to the same thing, it is a point hardly worth making.

Divide and Conquer. Achieve a victory by causing the opponents to quarrel among themselves. It was a political maxim known to and practiced by the Romans (*divide et impera*, meaning divide and rule). Matthew stated it in another way (12 : 25) in quoting Jesus: "Every kingdom divided against itself is brought to desolation; and every city or house divided against itself shall not stand." Bishop Joseph Hall put it in English in his *Meditations* (1605): "For a Prince . . . is a sure Axiome, Diuide and rule."

Divide the Spoils. Take shares of something obtained by crime, war or plunder. Isaiah alludes to the practice (9 : 3): "Thou hast multiplied the nation, and not increased the joy; they joy before thee according to the joy in harvest, and as men rejoice when they divide the spoil."

Do An About-face. Drastically change one's attitude on a question; make a 180-degree turn on an issue. "About face!" is a military command calling on the recipient to put the ball of his right foot behind the heel of his left foot and then to pivot 180 degrees clockwise on his left heel. The thought is expressed differently but precisely in John Strype's *Annals of the Reformation* (1709): "He had been a very zealous protestant, but under Q. Mary came about, and was as hot the other way."

Do It Up Brown. Do something well; do it to one's satisfaction. In England the phrase has had the meaning of deceive or take in. Either way, it carries the implication of doing something thoroughly and probably comes from the roasting of meat, yielding a brown color that is the result of thorough cooking. One can see the term in the making in *Liber Cure Cocorum* (1420): "Lay hur [the goose] to fyre and rost hyr browne."

Do a Good (Bad) Turn. Help (or hinder) someone. When you come to think of it, "turn," in the sense of an act of goodwill or ill will, is almost never encountered without a qualifying word. It was that way even when it first began to appear in English some 600 years ago, as in Chaucer's "Pardoner's Tale" (c. 1386): "Hadde I nat doon a freendes torn to thee?"

Do as I Say, Not as I Do. I'm not practicing what I preach, but you should take the sermon as your guide. A variant is "Watch what I do, not what I say." Both versions are very old. Boccaccio's *Decameron* (1350) offers: "Do as we say, and not as we do." John Heywood's collection of proverbs in 1546 includes: "It is as folk dooe, and not as folk saie."

Do or Die. It's time to act, even if the result is painful or damaging; go all out. The Scottish Text Society records the Scottish writer Robert Lindsay of Pitscottie as putting it in the 16th century: "He knew weill thair was no remedie but ether to do or die." Sir Walter Scott wrote in 1809: "This expression is a kind of common property, being the motto, we believe, of a Scottish family."

Does My Heart Good. Pleases me; relieves a worry. This is "heart" in its meaning as the seat of the emotions. A forerunner of the modern expression, and really a better way of putting the thought, appeared in 1413 in *The Pylgremage of the Sowle:* "The syght . . . gladyd moche my harte."

Dog Eat Dog. A ruthless competition. A much older saying, dating from at least the 16th century, is "dog does not eat dog." When they do, things are really bad, and that thought seems to have given rise to the modern expression.

Dog in the Manger, A. Someone who is not capable of using something or not entitled to use it but is denying the use of it to someone who is. The saying comes from an Aesop fable of the same title, which reads: "A Dog was lying in a Manger full of hay. An Ox, being hungry, came near and was going to eat of the hay.

The Dog, getting up and snarling at him, would not let him touch it. 'Surly creature,' said the Ox, 'you cannot eat the hay yourself, and yet you will let no one else have any.'"

Dog's Life, It's a. A bleak, miserable existence. The dog's life is often not that bad, one supposes, but from the human standpoint it leaves a lot to be desired, and that is where the comparison comes from. Erasmus made it in 1542: "The most parte of folkes calleth it a miserable life, or a dogges life. . . ."

Don't Look a Gift Horse in the Mouth. Take what's given to you without examining it too critically. You tell the age of a horse by looking at its teeth; you would be impolite in doing that if someone gave you a horse. The saying is ancient (a Latin version of it appeared in a work by St. Jerome in A.D. 420) and exists in many languages. An early English version (1510) appears in John Standbridge's *Vulgaria Standbrigi:* "A gyuen hors may not [be] loked in the tethe."

Done to a Turn. Perfect. Meat and poultry used to be (still are, but not so commonly) roasted by fixing them to a spit that rotated steadily over the fire. A proper roasting was "done to a turn." As the English publication, *The Mirror,* put it in 1780: "The beef was done to a turn."

Donkey's Years. A long time. The *Oxford English Dictionary* traces this phrase to a punning play on the pronunciation of "ears" as "years." Another ingredient is the fact that a donkey can live to a great age. The notion of donkey's years as a long time is fairly recent; E. V. Lucas in *The Vermilion Box* (1916) has a character say: "Now for my first bath in what the men call 'Donkey's ears,' meaning years and years."

Dose of His Own Medicine, Give Him a. Treat him the way he has treated you or others. The familiarity of the expression suggests that it is old, but it seems to have become current only toward the end of the 19th century. Paul L. Ford has this passage in *The Honorable Peter Stirling* (1894): "'He snubbed me,' . . . explained Miss DeVoe, smiling slightly at the thought of treating Peter with a dose of his own medicine."

Dot the i's and Cross the t's. Be thorough; pay close attention to detail. A whiff of the schoolroom hangs over this saying: the children bent over their slates and teacher reminding them to finish off tricky letters such as i and t. If so, it was a schoolroom of long ago where the first such reminder was issued, since the ancestor of the statement was in print by 1540 in William Tyndale's *The Obedience of a Christian Man:* "[They] haue . . . so narrowlye loked on my translatyon, that there is not so much as one I therin if it lacke a tytle ouer his hed, but they haue noted it."

Double in Brass. Take on two jobs to increase one's income or scope of action. This is "brass" as a general term for musical instruments such as the trumpet and the trombone. The phrase probably originated in the 19th-century touring shows and circuses of the United States, in which some of the people in the group not only played in the orchestra or band but also performed as actors, singers, comedians, stagehands and so on.

Down and Out. In poor financial, social or physical condition, particularly with respect to the condition one was in previously. It seems likely that the saying came from boxing, as suggested in O. Henry's *Heart of the West* (1904): "Then he delivered the good Saxon knock-out blow . . . and Garcia was down and out."

Down at the Heels. Looking shabby, probably for want of money. For lack of cash a man doesn't have the worn heels of his shoes replaced. Shakespeare has the other side of the equation in *King Lear:* "A good man's fortune may grow out at heels." In 1732 *A Gentleman Instructed* advised its readers: "Sneak into a corner . . . down at heels and out at elbow."

Down in the Dumps. Dispirited; unhappy. This is not "dump" the refuse heap but "dump" in one of its other meanings, now largely obsolete. The meaning of mental haze could fit, and so could the meaning of mournful tune, but the connection has never been squarely made. The expression goes so far back that the connection may never be made. Sir Thomas More had it in *A Dialoge of Comforte Against Tribulation* (1529): "What heapes of heauynesse, hath of late fallen among vs already, with which some of our poore familye bee fallen into suche dumpes."

Down in the Mouth. Glum; dispirited. It's the way one looks when the corners of one's mouth are turned down in disheartenment or disappointment. Bishop Joseph Hall used it in 1649 in one of his many works, this one with a lengthy title that can be abbreviated as *Cases of Conscience:* "The Roman Orator was downe in the mouth; finding himselfe thus cheated by the money-changer."

Draw a Blank. Fail to remember or find something; fail to recognize what someone is driving at. One of the meanings of "blank," now almost forgotten, is a lottery ticket that does not bring a prize. This is the "blank" that one "draws." Washington Irving wrote of "drawing a blank" in 1824 (in *Tales of a Traveller*), so the saying is at least that old.

Draw the Line at. Make a statement about a degree of behavior that one will not tolerate. The "line" is a boundary, as of property, and in "drawing" it figuratively one is marking off one's territory.

The figurative sense was in print in England by 1821 in *The Examiner:* "They know how to draw the line between private and public feeling."

Draw the Long Bow. Exaggerate; stretch a point; tell a tall tale. The longbow was the weapon of Robin Hood and the principal weapon of British soldiers from the medieval times until soldiers had guns. Tall tales were often told of feats with the longbow, as they are today of feats in fishing. (Whence "fish story.") Sir Roger L'Estrange had a version of the longbow idea in 1668: "There came to us several Tradesmen; the first of them a Poor Rogue that made profession of drawing the long Bow."

Dressed (Fit) to Kill. Spiffily turned out; nattily or showily attired (often with the implication that one has somewhat overdone it). "Kill" means no more here than to wow or impress. It is a hyperbolic way of saying one would or might overwhelm someone of the opposite sex by one's good looks, clothes or personality. The expression was in the language by the 18th century, as reflected by Sir Richard Steele in *The Spectator* in 1711: "If they [Handsome People] do not kill at first sight, as the Phrase is, a second Interview disarms them of all their Power." In a letter of 1818 John Keats wrote: "One chap was dressed to kill for the King in Bombastes."

Dressed to the Nines. Nattily turned out. "Nines?" What can they be? Well, no one is sure. Nine is the highest number before the numerals start recycling, and maybe that is it. Another possibility is that "eyne" is an old plural for "eye," and the phrase "to the eyne" meant to the eyes. Anyway, "nine" or "nines" has turned up as a superlative in more than dress. In 1793, "Thou paints old nature to the nines." In 1836, "Praisin' a man's farm to the nines." In 1863, "Being clad in snowy cotton and japanned to the nine."

Drive You Up the Wall. Annoy you severely. A much older saying is "drive to the wall," and at the time that was thought to be the extremity. John Heywood tells it in his collection of English proverbs (1546): "That deede without woords shall driue him to the wall. And further than the wall he can not go." The intensifying notion that one can be so harried as to be driven up the wall is quite modern.

Drop in the Bucket, A. An insignificant amount. Isaiah speaks (40 : 12) of how God "hath measured the waters in the hollow of his hand, and meted out heaven with the span, and comprehended the dust of the earth in a measure, and weighed the mountains in scales, and the hills in a balance." Then he says (40 : 15), "Behold, the nations are as a drop of a bucket, and are counted as the small dust of the balance. . . ."

Drop of a Hat, At the. Acting readily or on some single signal. In the 19th century it was occasionally the practice in the United States to signal the start of a fight or a race by dropping a hat or sweeping it downward while holding it in the hand. The quick response to this signal found its way into the language for any action that begins quickly without much need for prompting.

Drop the Pilot. Dismiss (usually misguidedly) a competent and tested guide or leader. Kaiser Wilhelm II made the term popular in 1890 by dismissing Otto von Bismarck as German chancellor. Bismarck, a key figure in the Prussian and German governments for many years, had been mainly responsible for the unification of Germany. The British journal *Punch* had a cartoon showing the kaiser as captain of a ship dismissing Bismarck, who was wearing the uniform of a ship's pilot.

Drum Out of the Corps. Expel from an organization. Originally it was a military organization; a soldier or sailor who was being expelled from his regiment or corps for misconduct was literally dismissed to the accompaniment of drumbeats to emphasize his disgrace. The broader meaning was at hand by 1766, as in Thomas Amory's *The Life of John Buncle:* "They . . . ought to be drummed out of society."

Drunk as a Skunk. Quite drunk. It is unlikely that anyone has ever seen a drunken skunk; surely the similarity of sound accounts for the popularity of the phrase. "Drunk" has more than its share of similes; G. L. Apperson, a collector of proverbs and phrases, lists 21, including "drunk as a besom," "a boiled owl," "a piper," "a wheelbarrow" and "the Baltic."

Dry as Dust. Spiritless; boring. It is often put as one word because of Dr. Jonas Dryasdust, the imaginary and ponderous "reverend doctor" to whom Sir Walter Scott addressed the prefaces of several of his novels. Isabella Mayo, who wrote under the pen name of Edward Garrett, refers to "dry-as-dust antiquarian stories" in *The House by the Works* (1879).

Duck Soup. An easy task. It's a mysterious expression (since chicken soup and various other varieties are commoner than duck soup), of unknown origin and not more than about 50 years old. Perhaps it comes from "sitting duck," meaning an easy target, since such a duck could readily be transformed into a variety of edibles, including soup.

Dull as Dishwater. Uninspiring, insipid. It was "ditchwater" originally, as Charles Dickens put it in *Our Mutual Friend* (1865): "He'd be sharper than a serpent's tooth, if he wasn't as dull as ditchwater." "Dishwater" turned up a bit earlier in the expression "dead as dishwater."

Durance Vile, In. Oppressive restraint or confinement. The term may be fading out now, but at one time it was a literary staple when you wanted to say somebody was imprisoned. Robert Burns had it in 1799: "A workhouse! . . . In durance vile here must I wake and weep. . . . "

Dutch Treat. An entertainment for which each participant pays his own share. The British and the Dutch were empire-building rivals in the 17th century, and as a result English has a number of un-flattering expressions referring to the Dutch, among them "Dutch courage" (brought on by drink) and "Dutch talent" (depending more on brawn than brains). "Dutch treat," though, originated as American slang in the late 19th century, probably deriving from the thrifty habits of German and Dutch immigrants.

Dutch Uncle. A man who gives tough advice; a severe disciplinarian. *Notes and Queries*, an old and useful British compendium of views on the origins of words and phrases, said in 1853: "In some parts of America, when a person has determined to give another a regular lecture, he will often be heard to say, 'I will talk to him like a Dutch uncle.' " Joseph C. Neal used it earlier in *Charcoal Sketches* (1837): "If you keep cutting didoes, I must talk to you both like a Dutch uncle." An uncle is usually regarded as a benevolent relative, but the Dutch (and Germans, who centuries ago were called the Dutch and still are occasionally) are thought to be sober and severe, even to their nephews and nieces.

Dyed in the Wool. Having deeply ingrained traits. The original meaning of the phrase was wool dyed while it was raw; the dye penetrated more thoroughly and lasted longer than when wool was dyed after being processed. The figurative meaning existed by 1579, in Sir Thomas North's version of *Plutarch's Lives:* "If he had not through institution and education (as it were) died in wool the manners of children."

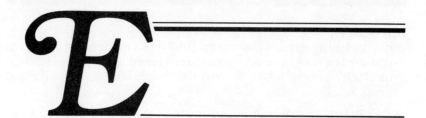

Eager Beaver. Someone who is earnest or overzealous in his work or in pursuit of an objective. The beaver's bent for hard work and persistence is legendary, but can you imagine "industrious beaver"? No, it is the human mind's fascination with rhyme (second only to its fascination with alliteration) that gave rise to and gives currency to "eager beaver." To "work like a beaver" is an 18th-century saying of American origin; the "eager" version seems to be a 20th-century variant that also originated in the United States.

Eager for the Fray. Ready for action (particularly for a competition or a fight). The dramatist Colley Cibber employed it in the early 18th century in *Richard III, altered:*

> Conscience avaunt, Richard's himself again;
> Hark! the shrill trumpet sounds, to horse, away,
> My soul's in arms, and eager for the fray.

Eagle Eye. Sharp vision or percipience; a sharp watch on something. John Prime put it one way in *Faithful & Brief Discourse* (1583): "Eagles eyes haue we till we looke into the sunne." John Keats put it more in the modern way in one of the memorable passages of "On First Looking into Chapman's Homer:"

> Then felt I like some watcher of the skies
> When a new planet swims into his ken;
> Or like stout Cortez when with eagle eyes
> He stared at the Pacific—and all his men
> Looked at each other with a wild surmise—
> Silent, upon a peak in Darien.

Early Bird Catches the Worm, The. The person who gets up, arrives or starts an action first has a better chance than others of achieving an objective. In just this form the expression appeared in 1636 in William Camden's *Remaines of a Greater Worke Concerning Britaine.*

Easier Said Than Done. More difficult to carry out than to contemplate. Sometimes it is "sooner said than done," but now that wording appears oftener in "no sooner said than done," which has quite a different meaning. As "easier" it was in the language by 1483 in the *Vulgaria:* "It is easyer to saye than to do."

Easy Come, Easy Go. What you get with little effort you often lose readily, too. In somewhat different forms ("Lightly come, lightly go"and"Quickly come, quickly go") this idea goes back to the 14th century. Chaucer had it in his Pardoner's Tale" (c.1386): "And lightly as it comth so wol we spende." In the modern form the expression dates from the early 19th century. In 1861 Herbert Spencer wrote that it is "a saying as applicable to knowledge as to wealth."

Easy Pickings. A pushover; a person or thing easily mastered. Probably from the kinds of fruit and vegetable that are easily harvested. The baseball pitcher Christy Mathewson, writing about his art in 1912, said, "Why can the Yankees take game after game from Detroit and be easy pickings for the Cleveland club in most of their games?"

Easy as Pie. A pleasantly uncomplicated task. It can't have to do with the making of pie, which is not easy; surely it derives from the eating of pie, much like the current "piece of cake," which conveys the same thought. In the 19th century "pie" had the meaning in the United States of an easy match, a prize obtained without much effort, as in "Green dogs are pie for him [the raccoon]." This statement appeared in 1895 in the recreational magazine *Outing*, and suggests the ancestry of the more recent "easy as pie."

Eat Crow. Acknowledge a mistake; humble oneself. Crow is not a popular dish, and if one has to abase oneself, eating crow is a way to do it. The expression dates from about 1870 and apparently originated in the United States. The Atlanta *Constitution* told a tale in 1888 about how an American soldier in the War of 1812 bagged a crow while hunting; a British officer who saw the deed complimented the soldier on the shot (an armistice was in force) and asked to see the gun. The soldier handed it to him, whereupon the British officer trained it on the soldier, upbraided him for trespassing and forced him to take a bit of the crow. The officer gave back the gun, and then it was the soldier's turn; he forced the officer to eat the rest of the crow.

Eat Humble Pie. Acknowledge an error; be apologetic; submit to humiliation. It was originally "umble" and really a pie, made out of the "umbles" of the deer, the heart, liver and entrails. (Umbles also came from other animals.) The umbles were a perquisite of the huntsman, who would sometimes eat umble pie while the lord and lady dined on the venison. The word and the umble pie date from at least the 16th century, but "humble pie" as a symbol of apology or submission (and perhaps as a play on the humble station of the people who ate umble pie) does not turn up until the early 19th century. Robert Forby in *Vocabulary of East Anglia* (1825) told his readers that "to make one eat humble pie" was "to make him lower his tone, and be submissive."

Eat Your Hat. What you declare you will do when you are so sure of your position or prediction that the likelihood of really having to eat anything so indigestible is remote. To "bet a hat" is a much older asseveration of positiveness; in *Love's Labour's Lost* Shakespeare has Biron say: "My hat to a halfpenny, Pompey proves the bet Worthy." In *Pickwick Papers* Charles Dickens has Mr. Pickwick ask, when he sees his crowded cell in debtor's prison, if he can live anywhere else; one of his prospective cellmates, a drunken chaplain, says, "Well, if I knew as little of life as that, I'd eat my hat and swallow the buckle."

Eat Your Heart Out. To grieve or worry excessively in a hopeless situation; also what one says to someone in such a situation when one is unsympathetic to him. Sir Thomas Elyot defined it in 1535 a bit differently: "Eate no harte, what does it els signifie, but accombre not thy mynde with thoughtes, ne do not fatigate the [thee] with cares?" The ancient Greeks had an expression (quoted by Plutarch as a "Parable of Pythagoras") that translates as "Eat not the heart." It meant not to consume oneself with troubles or worries, which could be almost as devastating as eating one's heart.

Eating Me Out of House and Home. Consuming or costing more than the supporter can or will sustain. It was once said as "out of house and harbor," as in the *Towneley Plays* of the early 15th century: "Bot were I not more gracyus and rychere befar, I were eten outt of howse and of harbar." When Mistress Quickly in Shakespeare's *Henry IV, Part 2,* is asked why she had Sir John Falstaff arrested, she replied, "He hath eaten me out of house and home; he hath put all my substance into that fat belly of his."

Eating Out of My Hand. Being very cooperative or submissive. It is what tame or at least trusting animals sometimes do, but the broader meaning of a willing or submissive person seems to be fairly recent. Hugh Walpole employs the term in this sense in *Young Enchanted* (1921): "I won a glorious victory and Victoria has eaten out of my hand ever since."

Egg in Your Beer (often phrased as a question beginning "Whaddya want, ——— ?"). Aren't you satisfied with what you've got? Why are you griping? In 1938 *American Speech* took note of the unadorned phrase "egg in your beer" as meaning "an easy job, something for nothing." In 1946 Joseph W. Bishop, Jr., writing in *American Speech* on "American Army speech in the European Theater," said that the version phrased as a question was "an answer to any and all complaints." In 1947 John L. Riordan wrote in the same publication that before the war the phrase had a sexual connotation: "According to the superstition prevailing in certain social strata, the eating of eggs lends one sexual power. The idea is strikingly demonstrated by the bartender's lingo for an order of beer with an egg in it: 'One sexy!' "

Egg on Your Face, To Have. To be embarrassed or chagrined at something one has done or the way one did it; to do something ineptly. The expression originated in the United States some 25 years ago, probably from the fact that someone eating an egg sloppily is likely to wind up with some of it on his face and therefore not looking his best. By 1972 the saying had been picked up in England, as Lord Chalfont reflected in *The Times* of London: "There is something reassuringly changeless about the capacity of the highest military authorities for getting egg on their face."

Eleventh Hour. Late; shortly before an anticipated event. Matthew's parable of the laborers in the vineyard (20 : 1–16) has the men hired at the eleventh hour being paid as much as the ones hired early in the morning, even though the eleventh-hour people worked for only an hour. From this sense of being barely in time to receive some benefit comes the concept of time running out.

Eloquent Silence. Conveying more by saying nothing than by speaking. This oxymoron (a combination of words that normally would not go together because of incongruity) appears as "expressive silence" in James Thomson's "Hymn" (1730). Martin Tupper in *Proverbial Philosophy* (1838) says, discussing discretion: "Well-timed silence hath more eloquence than speech."

Embarrassment of Riches. Too much of a good thing. The phrase, in French (*l'embarras des richesses*), appears in Voltaire's 18th-century play, *Le Droit de seigneur*. It is also (in French) the title of a play by the Abbé d'Allainval in 1726.

End of One's Tether, To Be at the. To have exhausted all the options. It is from the tethered animal, which can go no farther than the end of its rope. Originally the figurative expression meant one should stay within one's limits, as in John Fitzherbert's book, *A Newe Tracte or Treatyse Moost Profytable for All Husbande Men* (1523): "As long as thou eatest within thy tedure, that thou nedest not to begge nor borowe of noo man." The more modern version appeared in 1809 in Benjamin Malkin's *Adventures of Gil Blas:* "At length she got to the end of her tether. . . ."

Enemy Is at the Gate, The. Danger is near. The phrase recalls (and may well date back to) the days of walled cities and fortresses. Rudyard Kipling offered a different version of the thought in his patriotic poem, "For All We have and Are," written in 1914, early in World War I:

For all we have and are,
For all our children's fate,
Stand up and take the war.
The Hun is at the gate!

Enough to Make Him Turn in His Grave. A shocking or disturbing event or idea, particularly one running against the principles of someone now dead. James Payn's *Lost Sir Massingberd* (1864) says: "This holiday-making and mixture of high and low here, are themselves enough to make Sir Massingberd turn in his grave."

Enter the Lists. Take part in a competition or combat. "List" has or once had an astounding number of meanings; this "list" is the fencelike structure that enclosed the area set aside for tilting (trying to unhorse an opponent by means of a lance) in medieval tournaments. Nathaniel Bacon offered the extended meaning in 1647 in his *Historical Discourse of the Uniformity of the Government of England:* "I hold it both needless and fruitless to enter into the Lists, concerning the original of the Saxons."

Entertain High Hopes. Trust for the best. It is a bombastic phrase that usually seems to suggest that the speaker isn't really all that optimistic. Here is Thomas Babington Macaulay, in *The History of England from the Accession of James II* (1849): "Great hopes were entertained at Whitehall that Cornish would appear to have been concerned: but these hopes were disappointed."

Eternal Triangle, The. The social problem of two men in love with one woman or two women with one man. It is "eternal" because it is a story repeated endlessly. The term got locked into the language early in the 20th century, as exemplified by a book review in the London *Daily Chronicle* in 1907: "Mrs. Dudeney's novel . . . deals with the eternal triangle, which, in this case, consists of two men and one woman."

Eternal Verities, The. Enduring principles; something that is supposed to be regarded as important because an authority says it is. John Locke gave the non-sardonic version in Latin in 1681, writing in his *Journal:* "our knowledg of generall things are eternae veritates and depend not upon the existence or accidents of things. . . ."

Even Tenor of Their Way. A calm life or attitude. Sometimes it was put as the "noiseless tenor." The thought is in Thomas Gray's "Elegy Written in a Country Churchyard" (1750):

Far from the madding crowd's ignoble strife,
Their sober wishes never learned to stray;
Along the cool sequestered vale of life
They kept the noiseless tenor of their way.

Ever and Anon. From time to time for an indefinite period. "Anon" here means again, so the term implies a recurrent action. It was well established by the 16th century; Shakespeare has it, and so does Edmund Spenser in *The Faerie Queene* (1590):

> And ever and anon, with rosy red,
> The bashful blood her snowy cheeks did dye.

Every Cloud Has a Silver Lining. There's reason for hope even in the bleakest situation. As an observation the saying is sometimes unsupportable because the clouds are uniformly gray and lowering. Still, as an expression of hope it is old; John Milton had it in *Comus* (1634), wherein a woman lost in a wood takes hope in these words:

> Was I deceived, or did a sable cloud
> Turn forth her silver lining on the night?

Every Inch a King. Whole, complete (of a person); regal in bearing; deserving one's eminence. Sometimes it was "every inch a man," as in Thomas Dekker's *The Shoemaker's Holiday* (1600): "Shoemakers are . . . men euery inch of them, al spirite." It is Shakespeare who has King Lear respond to the Earl of Gloucester in this exchange:

> GLOUCESTER: The trick of that voice I do well remember:
> Is't not the king?
> LEAR: Ay, every inch a king.

Every Man Has His Price. Anyone's opinion or support can be bought; everyone's principles have a limit. The cynicism of this remark suggests that it is recent, a product of a cynical age, but in fact it is quite old. Sir Robert Walpole is quoted in William Coxe's *Memoirs of Walpole* (1798) as having said in 1745: "All those men have their price." In 1761 John Rich wrote in one of his letters: "It is said, but not to the credit of human nature, that every man has his price."

Every Man Jack. All of them (usually men). In the 16th century one of the meanings of "jack" was a common fellow, one of the herd. It is apparently this meaning that gave rise later to "every man jack." Charles Dickens had this exchange in *Barnaby Rudge* (1840):

> "You don't mean to say their old wearers are all dead?"
> "Every one of 'em . . . Every man Jack."

Every Man for Himself. Don't expect help; grab what you can; act on your own. A fuller version, not much heard nowadays, was "Every man for himself, and the devil take the hindmost." Today's version appeared in Chaucer's "Knight's Tale" in c. 1386:

> At the Kynges court, my brother,
> Ech man for hymself, ther is noon oother.

Evil Eye. A look of ill will; a glance thought capable of working harm or laying a curse. In the first sense it is reflected in Matthew's account of the parable of the laborers in the vineyard. When the people who have worked all day reproach the owner for paying the latecomers as much as he paid them, he replies (Matthew 20 : 15); "Is it not lawful for me to do what I will with mine own? Is thine eye evil, because I am good?" In the second sense, the superstition that some people are capable of casting a spell with an evil eye is very old. Virgil has a Latin version of it, referring to an evil eye that bewitched lambs.

Explore Every Avenue. To be (or, more likely, to declare the intention of being) diligent and resourceful in seeking a solution to a problem. The English writer (and member of Parliament) A. P. Herbert (1890–1971) was much preoccupied with British officialese. Once when to "explore every avenue" was proposed in a House of Commons document, he offered as an amendment another cliché: "Leave no stone unturned." The London *Morning Post* in 1936 said the notion of exploring avenues was "invented by the Marquis of Landsdowne when he was Foreign Secretary at the turn of the century" and that since then it has "exercised a mortal fascination over politicians. . . . The exploring of avenues has become one of the main preoccupations of political life."

Eye for (to) the Main Chance, Have an. To look out for one's own interest; to focus on the important objective. John Lyly, who assembled English sayings in the 16th century, has "Let me stand to the main chance" as one of them. In the 17th century Samuel Butler assembled a clutch of clichés in *Hudibras:*

> As the ancients
> Say wisely, have a care o' th' main chance,
> And look before ere you leap;
> For as you sow, ye are like to reap.

Eye for an Eye, An. An exchange of blows or insults; a claim that one is entitled to retaliate for an injury or an insult. In the Old Testament, Exodus 21 is concerned with the judgments that the Lord tells Moses to set before the people of Israel. One of them (21 : 23–25) is: "And if any mischief follow, then thou shalt give life for life, eye for eye, tooth for tooth, hand for hand, foot for foot, burning for burning, wound for wound, stripe for stripe."

Face the Music. To confront or cope with a difficult situation. The music that was being faced, in a situation where courage was required, is now uncertain. It may have been the pit orchestra in a theater; a nervous actor who steeled himself to go on stage would be facing the music (as well as the audience). It may have been the soldier being dismissed from his regiment in disgrace; it was sometimes the practice for the band to play the "Rogue's March" on such an occasion. In any event, the saying was common by 1851. M. Schele de Vere in his book on *Americanisms* (1871) quotes James Fenimore Cooper as saying in 1851: "Rabelais' unpleasant 'quarter' is by our more picturesque people called *facing the music.*" The reference is to a quart d'heure (a quarter of an hour) in which Rabelais found he could not pay his bill at an inn. He brazened his way out of the predicament by accusing the innkeeper of treason against the king, whereupon the frightened host let him go. The episode found its way into French as the *quart d'heure de Rabelais.*

Fact of the Matter (and Matter of Fact). These are both really space-filling phrases now, although they once had (and still have sometimes) the sense that one was getting to the truth or kernel of a subject. This sense is seen in one of the earliest appearances of either phrase, in the *Conferences* of Edmund Campion (1581): "He speaketh of a matter of fact."

Fair Sex, The. Women. It is a bit of gallantry that men have employed since at least 1605, when Cervantes used it in *Don Quixote.* One of Sherlock Holmes' well-known remarks to Dr. Watson is: "Now, Watson, the fair sex is your department."

Fair Shake, A. A reasonable opportunity, usually for an opponent; honorable treatment of an adversary. The phrase is apparently of American origin and probably had to do with the shaking of dice. It was in the language in the broader sense by 1834, when it appeared in *The Life and Writings of Major Jack Downing of Downingville*, by Seba Smith: "Says I, any way that will be a fair shake."

Fair and Square. Straightforward; honest. One can be "fair" in one's dealings, and one can be "square" (in the old sense of honest rather than the modern sense of stodgy), and in putting the words together one has not only an intensifier but also a rhyme. It's been done for a long time; Sir Francis Bacon was writing of "faire, and square" in 1604, and Oliver Cromwell said in one of his letters (1649), "There will clearly be no living for the Portugal unless he . . . do that which is fair and square."

Fair to Middling. Average; tolerable. Both "fair" and "middling" have a remarkable number of meanings, two of which converge: "fair" as moderately good and "middling" as mediocre. Whoever first put them together was doubtless trying to emphasize that a state of health or a performance was no better than average.

Fair-weather Friend. Someone who is loyal only when it involves no trouble for him, who abandons you when you are in difficulty. Alexander Pope, in a letter he wrote in 1736, seemed to touch on both the literal and the figurative meaning: "My Fair-weather friends of the summer are going away for London."

Fall Between Two Stools. To fail or not act because of indecision over two choices (said often of a problem that lands between two people or agencies that might be expected to deal with it). One can imagine a person so absentminded or distracted as to miss each of two nearby seats, landing between them. An old form of the saying is "Between two stools one goes [or falls] to the ground." The Romans had a similar expression. In English it was recognized as familiar by 1390, when it appeared in John Gower's *Confessio Amantis:* "Bot it is seid . . . Betwen two Stoles lyth the fal." In 1536 it appeared in a book of proverbs as "Betwen two stolis, the ars goth to grwnd."

Fall For It. To be deceived or gulled; to be captivated. The term originated in the United States some 60 years ago, perhaps more, and was in print by 1911 in Louis J. Vance's *Cynthia:* "There's only one sensible thing. . . . And I think I can see you falling for it."

Fall From Grace. Lose a high position; fall out of favor. Paul, in his Epistle to the Galatians, says that nothing avails in Christianity "but faith which worketh by love" and that with anything less (5 : 4),"Christ is become of no effect unto you, whosoever are justified by the law; ye are fallen from grace."

Fall Head Over Heels. To be won over or enter an activity so thoroughly as to be almost helpless. The head is normally over the heels, so the term would seem to make more sense as "heels over head," and indeed that is what it was. As early as the 14th century it appeared as "hele ouer hed" in a poem (quoted much later in *Early English Alliterative Poems*). The *Oxford English Dictionary* says the modern version is "a corruption of heels over head." The corruption has been around for a long time, appearing in *Contemplative Man* (1771) as "He gave [him] such a violent involuntary kick in the Face, as drove him Head over Heels." Once one is in a somersault, of course, it is first the head and then the heels that are on top.

Fall by the Wayside. Drop out of a contest or an activity. In the Bible (Matthew 13) one finds Jesus speaking in parables, one about the sower who went forth to sow: "And when he sowed, some seeds fell by the way side, and the fowls came and devoured them up." Jesus then explains the parable: "When any one heareth the word of the kingdom, and understandeth it not, then cometh the wicked one, and catcheth away that which was sown in his heart. This is he which received seed by the way side." Hence the sense of failing to achieve a goal that one set out for.

Fall on Deaf Ears. To be ignored (of a remark or a proposal). Presumably the recipient is not deaf; he simply chooses to act that way. The advice is implicit in Walter Hylton's *Scala Perfeccionis* (1440): "Make deef ere to hem as though you herde hem not."

Fall on Stony Ground. Fail to flourish (said of a statement or an idea that is received coldly or fails to gain acceptance). Like "fall by the wayside," the term comes from Jesus's parable of the sower as recounted in Matthew 13; some of the seeds "fell upon stony places, where they had not much earth; and forthwith they sprung up, because they had no deepness of earth." And Jesus explains (13:20–21): "But he that received the seed into stony places, the same is he that heareth the word, and anon with joy receiveth it; Yet hath he not root in himself, but dureth for a while. . . ."

False Alarm. An unfulfilled warning or expectation. It is often given deliberately as a strategic ploy, as Thomas Nashe suggested in *The Unfortunate Traveller* (1594): "What did I now but one day made a false alarm in the quarter where they lay." The "false alarm" was once a standard military tactic, defined in Charles James's *Military Dictionary* (1802) thus: "False-Alarms, are stratagems of war, frequently made use of to harass an enemy, by keeping them perpetually under arms."

Far Be It From Me. Not something I'm likely to do (sometimes said when just the opposite is true). The saying in its positive sense derives from a passage in the Bible (Job 34 : 10): "Far be it from God, that He should do wickedness."

Far Cry, A. A long distance. the "cry" here is a loud shout, which would not be heard at a distance. Sir Walter Scott put the phrase in print in 1819 in *The Legend of Montrose:* "One of the Campbells replied, 'It is a far cry to Lochow'; a proverbial expression of the tribe, meaning that their ancient hereditary domains lay beyond the reach of an invading enemy."

Far From the Madding Crowd. In a peaceful place; away from turmoil. "Madding," which means acting in a frenzied way, is almost gone from the language now except in references to the "madding crowd." The line is from Thomas Gray's "Elegy Written in a Country Churchyard" (1750), describing "the rude Forefathers of the hamlet" who are buried there:

> Far from the madding crowd's ignoble strife
> Their sober wishes never learn'd to stray;
> Along the cool sequester'd vale of life
> They kept the noiseless tenor of their way.

Thomas Hardy made *Far from the Madding Crowd* the title of one of his novels, published in 1874.

Far and Away. By a large margin. "Far" and "away" both mean well out in front or distant; putting them together makes for emphasis. In the 18th century the same thought was expressed as "far away." The modern term is found by 1883 in *Thirlby Hall*, by William E. Norris: "You are far and away the greatest scoundrel I ever saw."

Fast and Furious. Intense, heated. Robert Burns' *Tam o'Shanter* (1793) has:

> As Tammie glow'red, amazed, and curious,
> The mirth and fun grew fast and furious.

Fat Cat. A wealthy person, usually one whose influence arises from applications of his money or the hope by other people that he will direct some of it toward their cause. H. L. Mencken says in *The American Language* (4th ed.) that the label originated in about 1920 and signified "a rich man willing to make a heavy contribution to a party campaign fund."

Fat is in the Fire, The. Something has happened that will make the action pick up speed or intensity; the damage has been done. Centuries ago the expression meant that an endeavor had failed, probably in analogy to dripping fat that makes the fire blaze up and burn the meat turning on a spit. This is the sense implied by John Heywood in *A Dialogue Conteyning Prouerbes and Epigrammes* (1562): "Than [then] farwell ryches, the fat is in the fyre." The notion that one event is likely to bring on another, perhaps unwelcome, seems to have developed by 1700.

Father Time. The passage of the years, as personified by the cartoonists' staple figure of an old man, bald except for a forelock, carrying a scythe and an hourglass. I wouldn't have thought that the cartoonists' figure was in vogue by the time Shakespeare wrote *The Comedy of Errors* (1594), but Dromio of Syracuse seems to have such a representation in mind as he says, "Marry, sir, by a rule as plain as the bald pate of father Time himself."

Fear or Favor, Without. Impartially. Politician's bombast, sealed into the language by alliteration. Even if it is not said by a politician averring how he will go about his duties, it still carries a suggestion of the pompous, which was implied in this passage in the *Independent Review* (1906): "He [Samuel Johnson] judged authors as if they were criminals in the dock, answerable for every infraction of the rules and regulations laid down by the laws of art, which it was his business to administer without fear or favour."

Feast or Famine. Extremes of success or failure. At one time the saying was "feast or fast," which is a more precise pairing of opposites. One sees it thus in Thomas Fuller's *Gnomologia*, a book on adages, proverbs and sayings (1732): "Is there no Mean, but Fast or Feast?" "Famine" seems to have been a 20th-century substitution.

Feather Your Nest. To provide for one's comfort, usually by laying up money or possessions. *Respublica*, a play of 1553, indicates that the saying was common then: "Now is the time come . . . to feather my nest." Literal nest-feathering is done by many birds to provide softness and warmth for the coming chicks.

Feather in His Cap, A. An honor; a recognition for an achievement; an achievement. It was once a custom in many countries to award a feather to a soldier who had killed an enemy; the feather was worn in the helmet or some other kind of headgear. That is the literal meaning of the term; the figurative meaning of an honor or an achievement was in the language by 1657 in a catalogue of British books: "It's recorded that Solomons Library was the feather in the Plume of his glorious Enjoyments."

Feel It in My Bones. To have a premonition or an intuition about something. In Shakespeare's *Timon of Athens* the Second Lord says, "Lord Timon's mad." The Third Lord replies, "I feel 't upon my bones."

Feel the Pinch. Be affected by some adversity; suffer a hardship or deprivation. Shakespeare is close to this saying when he has King Lear speak of "necessity's sharp pinch" as what he would put up with rather than dismiss half his train and go sojourn with his daughter Goneril. The London *Times* had the modern expression in 1861: "So much money having been spent . . . all classes felt the pinch."

Feet of Clay. A vulnerability; a failing or weakness. The image is from the Book of Daniel (2 : 31–40), in which King Nebuchadnezzar has a dream that Daniel describes and then interprets:

> Thou, O king, sawest, and, behold, a great image. . . . This image's head was of fine gold, his breast and arms of silver, his belly and his thighs of brass. His legs of iron, his feet part of iron and part of clay. Thou sawest till that a stone was cut out without hands, which smote the image upon his feet that were of iron and clay, and brake them to pieces.

The whole image then broke, and the pieces were carried away by the wind. Daniel's interpretation was that Nebuchadnezzar was the head of gold, a king of kings, but that after him would come a series of weaker kingdoms that would finally break up, like the image with feet of clay, and be replaced by the kingdom of God.

Festive Board. A table well supplied with food and drink; a meal at which the people are all in good cheer. Since the 12th century one of the meanings of "board" has been a table, quite often a sizable one, at which people eat; and "festive" derives from "feast." Literary and poetical references to the "festive board" were common; one of the poems of Winthrop M. Praed in 1839 sets a scene "around the festive board." The dining table seems to be called a "board" now only when it is "festive" or "groaning."

Few and Far Between. Rare; infrequent; widely spaced. The saying derives from a poetic device, popular in the 18th century, in which pleasures and visits by angels were thus described. Thomas Campbell has it in *The Pleasure of Hope* (1799):

> Cease, every joy, to glimmer on my mind,
> But leave, oh! leave the light of Hope behind!
> What though my wingèd hours of bliss have been
> Like angel visits, few and far between?

Fiddle While Rome Burns. To display callousness or indifference in the face of calamity; to take up one's time with trifles instead of facing a crisis. Nero was the emperor of Rome from A.D. 54 to 68. In 64 a great fire laid waste much of the city. Many citizens believed he was the instigator of it, believing also that he played his lyre (the fiddle, meaning a member of the violin family, did not appear until about 1500) and recited his own poetry while watching the fire from a tower; Nero blamed the Christians for starting the fire. The story gave rise to the expression, which was in the language by 1649, as in George Daniel's *Trinarchodia:* "Let Nero fiddle out Rome's Obsequies."

Fight Tooth and Nail. Fight fiercely, with all one's resources; cling tenaciously. A Latin proverb expressed this thought as *dentibus et vnguibus.* In the sense of fighting, it appeared in English in 1562 in Ninian Winget's *Certaine Tractates:* "Contending with tuith and naill (as is the prouerb)." In the sense of holding fast, it is equally old, as in Erasmus' *Enchiridion Militis Christiani* (1533):

"Take and holde this with toth and nayle, that to be honour onely which springeth of true vertue."

Fill the Bill. Meet the need; serve the purpose. Of the many meanings of "bill," this is the theatrical one referring to the list of acts being presented. The saying is of American origin and probably originated from the practice of adding an act to fill out a bill. It has also meant to be conspicuous. The first sense, reflecting the modern usage, appears in *Transactions of the Illinois Agricultural Society* in 1860: "Austin Seedling, Dr. W. hopes well from because of its great vigor, but doubts if it fills the bill." The other sense appears in Farmer and Henley's *Slang and Its Analogues* (1891): "To excel in conspicuousness: as a star actor whose name is 'billed' to the exclusion of the rest of the company."

Filled to the Brim. Getting the maximum of satisfaction out of something; exhibiting the utmost. You can't get any more into a container that is thus filled, and the thought easily transfers to other things, as in *The Mikado,* by Gilbert and Sullivan (1885):
>Three little maids from school are we,
>Pert as a schoolgirl well can be,
>Filled to the brim with girlish glee.

Filthy Lucre. Tainted or unacceptable money; dishonorable gain. It is a biblical phrase, coming from Paul's description of the qualities needed in a bishop (Timothy 3 : 5): "Not given to wine, no striker, not greedy of filthy lucre." Paul also has it in his Epistle to Titus 1 : 11, speaking of "vain talkers and deceivers" who among other things are "teaching things which they ought not, for filthy lucre's sake."

Find It in One's Heart. To be disposed or willing to do something (often said with the implication that one is doing a great favor). The earliest use in English is a negative one, in Ralph Robinson's translation of Sir Thomas More's *Utopia* (1551): "They can not fynde in their hertes to loue the author thereof."

Fine Fettle, To Be in. To be in good health, shape or spirits. "Fettle" is, or was, a verb meaning to put in order or arrange. "To be in fine fettle" (also said as "high" or "good") was to be well set up to do something. Occasionally the opposite thought turned up as "poor fettle." A forerunner of the modern term is in Edwin Waugh's *Sketches of Lancashire Life and Localities* (1857), where reference is made to a "Shetland pony in good fettle."

Fine Kettle of Fish, A. A mess; something gone wrong. A kettle of fish was once a conspicuous item at Scottish picnics, as Thomas Newte told his readers in *A Tour in England and Scotland* in 1785: "It is customary for the gentlemen who live near the Tweed to entertain their neighbors and friends with a Fête Champètre, which they call giving 'a kettle of fish.' Tents or marquees are pitched near the flowery bank of a river . . . a fire is kindled, and live salmon thrown into boiling kettles." One can imagine things going wrong, such as a kettle capsizing, giving rise to the ironic expression of a "fine" or "pretty kettle of fish." Henry Fielding has this sense in *Joseph Andrews* (1742): "'Here's a pretty kettle of fish,' cries Mrs. Tow-wouse."

Fine-tooth Comb, A. A figurative tool with which one conducts a thorough search or investigation. Actual combs and files with closely spaced teeth have been around for a long time; the simile is more recent, as in the *Century Magazine* in 1891: "I'll go through this town like a fine-tooth comb but what I'll find him."

Finger Itches To, My. I'm keen to do something. One tends to associate this expression of impatience with the trigger finger, but it is older than the time when triggers were common. Hence it must reflect the eagerness one often feels to get one's hands on something, to act in a situation where one can accomplish something. An early appearance of the phrase is in *Pearl for Princes* (1565): "Is there any thing els that your fyngers itche at, tyll you haue it donne?"

Finger in Every Pie, Have a. To be active in many things (sometimes said sarcastically of someone who is overactive, a busybody). This old saying doubtless originated with kitchen visitors who could not resist testing every pie by sticking in a finger that was then licked off. Bartholomew Harris, in *Parival's Historie of This Iron Age* (1601) wrote: "Lusatia . . . must needs, forsooth, have her Finger in the Pye." Shakespeare uses it in the sense of meddling in *Henry VIII*, where the Duke of Buckingham, speaking of Cardinal Wolsey, says:

> The devil speed him! no man's pie is freed
> From this ambitious finger.

Finishing Touch. The last bit of work on an object or a piece of writing; a polishing stroke. At various times it has been "finishing stroke," "finishing hand" and "finishing touch." As long ago as 1707 it was "stroke" in *Reflexions upon Ridicule*: "A Mind well turn'd, receives the finishing stroke and polish from Science." In 1771 Horace Walpole had it as "touches" in his *Anecdotes of Painting in England:* "We tire of all the painter's art, when it wants these finishing touches."

First Blush, At. On first impression; at first sight. It is not a rush of blood to the cheeks but another meaning of "blush" that now survives only in this expression. That meaning is "glimpse." An early example is in Richard Hakluyt's *The Principall Navigations,*

Voiages and Discoueries of the English Nation (1589): "At the first blush we thought they had been shippes come from France."

First Magnitude, Of the. Prominent; outstanding. Since the 16th century the relative brightness of stars has been described in magnitudes; the brightest stars are of the first magnitude. By extension, the term applies to any prominent person or object, and the extension has been around since at least 1693, when the poet George Stepney put it this way in his translation of Juvenal's eighth Satire:
> Whatever be your Birth, you're sure to be
> A Peer of the First Magnitude, to me.

First Saw the Light of Day. Was born. It is a biographer's clichéd way of recording the birth of a subject. The phrase "light o dai" was in print by 1300. David Hume was close to the biographer's cliché when he wrote, in *Essays and Treatises on Several Subjects* (1752): "As soon as the helpless infant sees the light."

First Water, Of the. Of the highest quality. For centuries diamonds were graded as "first water," "second water," or "third water," the use of "water" in this sense arising from the resemblance of the diamond to water in its clarity and translucence. Only the figurative expression survives now. Theodore E. Hook took note of it in *Sayings and Doings* (1825): "He was certain her family were by no means of 'the first water.'"

First and Foremost. A leading person or point. This is one of those tautologies that speakers of the language seem to love. If you are "first," you are "foremost," and vice versa. The point is driven home by putting them together. The phrase was locked into the language by 1483, as in this example by William Caxton: "And such one is that weneth first and formest that often fyndeth her the last of all." In Henrik Ibsen's *A Doll's House* (1879) there is this exchange:
> HELMER: First and foremost, you are a wife and mother.
> NORA: That I don't believe any more. I believe that first and foremost I am an individual, just as much as you are.

Fish Out of Water, A. A person who is in an unfamiliar or uncomfortable setting; out of one's element. The phrase has been attributed to St. Athanasius, who is said to have used it in A.D. 373 or earlier. The modern usage is clear by 1613, in Samuel Purchas's *Pilgrimage:* "The Arabians out of the desarts are as Fishes out of the Water."

Fish in Troubled Waters, To. To try to take advantage of someone who is perturbed or in difficulty. It comes from the old maxim among fishermen that the fish bite better when the water is turbulent. The broader meaning appeared as early as 1568 in Richard Grafton's *Chronicle of England:* "Their persuasions whiche alwayes desyre your unquietnesse, wherby they may the better fishe in the water when it is troubled."

Fish or Cut Bait. Make a choice; stop procrastinating. Presumably the fellow who loafed in a fishing boat was never very popular, since if he wasn't fishing he could at least be preparing bait for the people who were. Yet the expression seems to be not nearly as ancient as fishing from boats; apparently, it appeared in print for the first time in 1876 in the *Congressional Record,* when Rep. Joseph G. Cannon of Illinois (later the powerful speaker of the House) was quoted as saying: "Now I want you gentlemen on the other side of the House [the Democrats] to 'fish or cut bait' [by voting on a bill to make the silver dollar legal tender]. Gentlemen of the other side, do something positive for once during this session."

Fit as a Fiddle. In fine shape; feeling good. Fiddles are admired for their sound and sometimes for their trim and symmetrical shape. Indeed, to say "his face is made of a fiddle" was once a way of describing someone as charming. Still, fiddles are not known for fitness, and one suspects the allure of alliteration in the origin and perpetuation of the saying, which is quite old. It appeared in 1616 in William Haughton's *Englishmen for My Money:* "This is excellent, i' faith; as fit as a fiddle." At that time "fit" meant appropriate, proper or fitting; its meaning of "in good shape" evolved in the 19th century and transformed the meaning of "fit as a fiddle."

Fits and Starts, By. Intermittently, spasmodically. A "fit" and a "start" are both bursts of activity, implying that before them and after them are periods of relative inactivity. The expression at one time was often put the other way, as in a sentence Bishop John Wilkins wrote in 1640: "The Motion of the earth is always equal and like it self; not by starts and fits." The modern version was known by at least 1620; it appears in one of the sermons by another English bishop, Robert Sanderson.

Fix His Wagon. Deal with an annoyance or a problem that he presents. The thought is of queering something that is important to the other person. Long ago this something was "flints." In *The Clockmaker* (1840) Thomas C. Haliburton wrote: "Their manners are rude. . . . They want their flints fixed for 'em." The "wagon" probably got into the picture as a result of the great westward migrations in the United States a century and more ago, in which the wagon was the main means of transportation.

Flash in the Pan, A. A temporary success or attraction. The "pan" here was the part of the old flintlock musket where you inserted the powder that was ignited by sparks from the flint and thereby set off the charge in the gun that propelled the ball or bullet out of the barrel. Sometimes the powder went off but the gun didn't; that was the flash in the pan. It was defined as follows in the 1810 edition of Charles James's *A New and Enlarged Military Dictionary: "flash in the pan,* an explosion of gunpowder without any communication beyond the touch-hole."

Flat as a Pancake. Singularly flat. The analogy is probably as old as the pancake. It was in print by 1611 in Thomas Middleton's play, *The Roaring Girl:* "Beat all your feathers as flat down as pancakes."

Flattery Will Get You Nowhere. Never mind laying on the persiflage, it will have no effect. In this precise form the saying goes back only to about 1950, but the thought it embodies is old enough to have been expressed in Shakespeare's *Richard II* (1593), where the king says, "He does me double wrong that wounds me with the flatteries of his tongue."

Flesh and Blood. A relative; a living person. The many meanings of this term all derive from a passage in the Bible (Matthew 16 : 17), where Jesus asks his disciples who people say he is. Simon Peter says, "Thou art the Christ, the Son of the living God." Jesus replies, "Blessed art thou, Simon Barjona: for flesh and blood hath not revealed it unto thee, but my Father which is in heaven."

Flip Your Lid. Become irate; lose self-control. In this form the expression is fairly recent, perhaps dating back some 30 years, but the thought is much older. In 1873 Martin F. Mahoney had it in *A Chronicle of the Fermors:* "What wonder if the lid was constantly getting off her temper?"

Floodgates, Open the. Give cause for an outpouring of joy, wrath, tears, affection, grief and so on. The real floodgate is in a dam or a lock and can be opened or closed to control the level of the water, as during a flood. For this reason the extended meaning was first associated with tears, but it soon accommodated a variety of strong emotions. An early example is in Samuel Hieron's *Works* (1607): "It setteth open the very floodgate of Gods wrath."

Flotsam and Jetsam. An accumulation of items of little worth or use; odds and ends. Both words are from maritime law; "flotsam" refers to goods found floating in the sea (usually as a result of a shipwreck) and "jetsam" refers to things thrown overboard for whatever reason. As a reference to odds and ends it was in print by 1884 in *Harper's* magazine "A mania for buying all sorts of flotsam and jetsam."

Flower of Youth. The peak of beauty and fitness. There have been "flower of life," "flower of age" and various other expressions denoting a stage of ripeness, but only "flower of youth" has attained the status of cliché. William Dunbar writes in one of his poems of a man "not in youths flowers." John Dryden, in "Alexander's Feast" (1697), portrays "the god-like hero" sitting on his imperial throne, and:

> The lovely Thais by his side,
> Sate like a blooming Eastern bride
> In flow'r of youth and beauty's pride.

Fly in the Face of. To defy or challenge; to act against the odds. According to the *Oxford English Dictionary*, the original face belonged to a bristling dog, challenging which certainly required a good deal of nerve. The broader meaning turned up as early as 1553 in Thomas Wilson's *The Arte of Rhetorique:* "Let hym have his will, and he will flie in thy face."

Fly in the Ointment. A hitch in one's plans; an obstacle. The phrase is derived from the Bible (Ecclesiastes 10 : 1): "Dead flies cause the ointment of the apothecary to send forth a stinking savor: so doth a little folly him that is in reputation for wisdom and honour."

Fly the Coop. Escape. It is what chickens and other cooped-birds occasionally do, and when, by the middle of the 19th century, "coop" had naturally been extended to mean prison, a prisoner who escaped was said to "fly the coop."

Fly-by-night. An undependable person; one who sets up a business operation, makes some money and departs abruptly. In 1796 Francis Grose defined the expression in *A Classical Dictionary of the Vulgar Tongue* as "an ancient form of reproach to an old woman, signifying that she is a witch." The meaning had broadened by 1823, as in Thomas Love Peacock's *Maid Marian:* "Would you have her married to a wild fly-by-night that accident made an earl and nature a deer-stealer?"

Flying Colors, With. Triumphantly, proudly. The "colors" are the flags or banners borne by a naval ship or a military unit; in victory the colors remain prominently displayed, in defeat they are lowered. John Locke had the figurative meaning in 1692 in *A Letter Concerning Toleration:* "It may . . . bring a Man off with flying Colours."

Foam at the Mouth. Show anger. It is an analogy to the dog with distemper or rabies. Such a dog may behave in an erratic or menacing way. Applied to people it was in the language by 1440, when *Jacob's Well* put it this way: "The man . . . fomyd out at his mowth."

Follow Your Nose. Go straight ahead; continue on. A predecessor, "follow your face," appeared in the poem *Cleanness* in about 1350. Today's version was in print by 1616 in William Haughton's

Englishmen for My Money: "The best way . . . is to follow your nose."

Follow in the Footsteps of. To emulate someone or accept his guidance. The figurative meaning goes back to at least the middle of the 16th-century, when it appeared in *Complaynt of Scotlande* (1549): "You ar obleist to follou the futsteppis of your predecessours in vertu." The 16-century Japanese writer Matsuo Basho had a poignant aphorism in *The Rustic Gate:* "Do not seek to follow in the footsteps of the men of old; seek what they sought."

Food for Thought. Something to ponder; a provocative idea. It is a classic metaphor: food is crucial for the body, and the mind works best when given things to chew on. Robert Southey wrote, in *A Tale of Paraguay* (1825): "A lively tale, and fraught with . . . food for thought."

Fool and His Money Are Soon Parted, A. An ingenuous or dim-witted person is easily persuaded to buy something or invest in something. The fool has been the butt of many gibes, including (1400) "A fooles belle is soon runge;" (1539) "A foles bolt is soon shotte" and in a 1587 work on the Church of England, "A foole and his money is soone parted."

Fool's Gold. An illusion; an object that isn't what it seems to be. Iron pyrites, which have a golden or brassy look, are often found in coal seams and were frequently mistaken for gold. The term has been known since at least 1576, when the explorer Martin Frobisher returned to England with what he thought was "gold minerall." It was pyrite. The *Boston Journal of Chemistry* picked up the term "fool's gold" in 1882 as a name for iron pyrite.

Fool's Paradise. An illusory or insubstantial state of satisfaction. The implication is that only a fool would be unaware that he was being gulled or that his situation was not what it seemed to be. The saying was known by 1462, when it appeared in *The Paston Letters:* "I wold not be in a folis paradyce."

Foot-in-mouth Disease. A capacity for saying the wrong or inappropriate thing. The term is a play on the foot-and-mouth disease of livestock and on the old saying about putting one's foot in one's mouth. Prince Philip of Great Britain coined the word "dontopedology" to express the tendency. Alistair Cooke wrote, in the *Manchester Guardian Weekly* (1970): "President Nixon's latest onset of foot-in-mouth disease unfortunately came just as the American Trial Lawyers' (barristers') Association was about to hold its annual meeting in Miami." The cliché seems to have taken root at about that time.

Footloose and Fancy-free. At liberty, particularly with respect to romantic entanglements. "Footloose" is a word of 19th-century American origin, meaning unhampered and ready to move. "Fancy" here is used in its now largely forgotten sense of being in love. Shakespeare has it in *A Midsummer Night's Dream:*

>And the imperial votaress passed on
>In maiden meditation, fancy-free.

For Better or for Worse. Through thick and thin. It is a phrase from the standard marriage vow. As it is put in the *Book of Common Prayer* of the Church of England and the Episcopal Church, the bride vows to cleave to the groom (and he to her) "for better for worse, for richer for poorer, in sickness and in health . . . till death do us part."

For Crying Out Loud. Oh, for heaven's sake; what you're saying (or doing) is preposterous. The saying is a euphemism (also describable as a minced oath) for "For Christ's sake!" and seems to have been coined, probably in the United States, about 60 years ago.

For Good and All. Definitely; conclusively. It is an odd combination of words that once meant a valid conclusion, a meaning that led to the present sense of finality. People have used it for centuries, as reflected by its appearance in *The Parlament of Byrdes* in the 16th century: "Than desyred all the Byrdes great and smal to mewe the hauke for good and all."

For What It's Worth. Take it at whatever value it has or you think it has. The expression is old. Here is William Langland in *Piers Plowman* (1377): "Take we her wordes at worthe, for here [her] witnesse be trewe."

For the Birds. Worthless; overstated; appealing to the simple-minded. Probably the connotation is that only a birdbrain would go for whatever is being dished out. In J. D. Salinger's *Catcher in the Rye* (1951) Holden Caulfield is quoting and then commenting on a blurb issued by his preparatory school, Pencey Prep: " 'Since 1888 we have been molding boys into splendid, clear-thinking young men.' Strictly for the birds."

For the Life of Me. I can't do it. Considering that life is of such importance to the living, this is what the *Oxford English Dictionary* calls "hyperbolically in trivial use." The hyperbole has been around for a long time; in 1632 William Lithgow, writing of his "travayles," said: "For my life I could neuer attaine to any perfect knowledge thereof."

Forbidden Fruit. Something untouchable or out of bounds. The original forbidden fruit was described by Eve to the serpent in the Garden of Eden (Genesis 3 : 3) "But of the fruit of the tree which is in the midst of the garden, God hath said, Ye shall not eat of it, neither shall ye touch it, lest ye die." The tree was (2 : 17) "the tree of the knowledge of good and evil." The extended meaning was in use by 1663 in James Heath's *Flagellum*, a book on "the life and death, birth and burial" of Oliver Cromwell: "The stealing and tasting of the forbidden fruit of Sovereignty."

Force To Be Reckoned with, A. Something one must take into account because of its strength or influence. The *Manchester Examiner* was close to the saying in 1885, with: "A Ministerial crisis . . . is always . . . a contingency to be reckoned with."

Foregone Conclusion, A. Something already decided; something about which no argument is possible. It is a Shakespearean phrase, perhaps originated by him. In *Othello* the villainous Iago is telling Othello that he has overheard Cassio talking in his sleep about his love for Desdemona, Othello's wife. Othello finds the thought monstrous:

> IAGO: Nay, this was but his dream.
> OTHELLO: But this denoted a foregone conclusion:
> 'Tis a shrewd doubt, though it be but a dream.

Forest for the Trees, Can't See the. Unable to grasp the broad meaning of a situation or the point of an argument because of an excessive attention to details. At one time (and sometimes still) it was "the wood for the trees," and in this form it appeared in John Heywood's collection of English proverbs in 1546.

Forewarned Is Forearmed. Advance knowledge makes for preparedness. The Romans had a similar phrase (*Praemonitus, praemunitus*) and at times the thought has appeared in English as a literal translation of that, an early example being found in *Arden of Feversham* (1592): "Forewarned, forearmed; who threats his enemy, lends him a sword to guard himself withal." In Hill's *Commonplace Book* of 1530 it is: "He that is warned ys half armed."

Forlorn Hope, A. A prospect that's not likely to materialize; a venture with little chance of success. We have a happy linguistic coincidence here. The term comes from *verloren hoop*, a Dutch phrase for the group of picked men chosen to begin an attack. The literal translation is "lost squad [or troop]," reflecting the high risk of the assignment. It was hence easy and natural, by what the *Oxford English Dictionary* calls "word-play or misapprehension of the etymology," for the expression to take on its present meaning in English, which it had done by 1641 in Josias Shute's *Sarah and Hagar:* "If we sin, upon a presumption that we shall conceal either our actions or persons from God, it is a forlorn hope; our iniquities will finde us out."

95

Fortunes of War. The good and bad results of combat; the way the battle goes. William Caxton had it in 1484: "When the toune is taken . . . by fortune of warre."

Forty Winks. A nap. "Wink" for centuries has had as one of its meanings a closing of the eyes for sleep. Shakespeare used it for the permanent sleep, meaning death. The "forty" is another matter; it is a nice, solid number, indicating a substantial amount of activity, and has many biblical connotations, but why exactly it wound up in association with "winks" is a mystery. In any event, the expression was known by 1828, when it appeared in a tale by Pierce Egan describing an "uncommonly big gentleman, told out, taking forty winks."

Fouling His Own Nest. Spoiling his own environment or situation. An old saying in English and other languages is: "It is an ill bird that fouls its own nest." The saying is no longer expressed in this form, but the extended sense of messing up something persists. This sense can be seen as early as 1440 in John Capgrave's *The Life of St. Katharine of Alexandria:* "It is neyther wurshipful ne honest On-to mankeende to foule soo his nest."

Four Corners of the Earth. Far and wide; the remotest regions. In the New Testament revelations of St. John one reads (Revelation 7 : 1): "And after these things I saw four angels standing on the four corners of the earth, holding the four winds of the earth, that the wind should not blow on the earth, nor on the sea, nor on any tree."

Fourth Estate. The newspapers, now more broadly including television, radio and magazines. The British government has for centuries been described as consisting of three estates: the Lords Spiritual, the Lords Temporal and the Commons—or as King, Lords and Commons. It was not unusual to refer to any other influential group as the "fourth estate." Henry Fielding in 1756 wrote of "that very large and powerful body which form the *fourth estate* in this community . . . The Mob." Thomas Carlyle in *Heroes and Hero Worship* (1841) credited the current meaning to the statesman Edmund Burke (1729–1797): "Burke said there were three Estates in Parliament, but, in the Reporters' gallery yonder, there sat a Fourth Estate more important far than them all."

Fraught with Danger (Peril). Perilous; of uncertain outcome. "Fraught," which is a relative of "freight," is a word that has left the language except for expressions such as "fraught with" something bad. Things have been "fraught with difficulties" for a long time, as long as some 400 years anyway, as one sees in *Private Prayers* (1548): "This life of ours is fraught with adversities."

Free and Easy. Loose, relaxed. Martin Lister was using this phrase as long ago as 1699, in his *Journey to Paris:* "In a very free and easie posture."

Free as a Bird. At least temporarily able to do whatever one pleases. People watching birds move through the air must long ago have decided that it was a free and easy life. It's a pity one can't get the bird's opinion, because in fact a bird works pretty hard most of the time getting food, building a nest, defending territory, feeding young, migrating and so on. Still, the bird was symbolic of freedom as long ago as 1533, when John Heywood invoked it in *A Mery Play between the Pardoner and the Frere, the Curate and Neybour Pratte:* "As free As be the byrdes that in the ayre flee."

Fresh as a Daisy. Rested, healthy, in good spirits. It has been "fresh as a daisy," a "buttercup," an "oyster" and probably other things for quite a while. Eaton Barrett had two of them in *The Heroine* (1815): "Forth they walked . . . as fresh as an oyster." And when the heroine asks about "recent blood upon the floor," Dame Ursulina replies: "Recent! Lauk! Sure your ladyship has often read of blood upon floors, and daggers, that looked as fresh as a daisy, at the end of centuries."

Friend at Court, A. Someone who can be helpful in one's dealings with the authorities. People now often think of the court solely as the place with a judge in it, but the saying goes back to the time of absolute monarchs and their courts, or retinues. A forerunner of the present phrase (which itself is some 300 years old) is seen in *The Romaunce of the Rose* (c. 1400): "For freend in court ay better is Than peny in purs."

Friend in Need Is a Friend Indeed, A. Someone who comes to your aid when you're in difficulty is a true friend. Here is the opposite of the fair-weather friend. The thought is old enough to have a Latin version and variants in medieval English going back to 1275. The modern version is close at hand in Richard Whytford's *Werke for Householders* (1530): "A true frende loueth at all tymes and neuer feyleth at nede."

From (Out of) the Frying Pan into the Fire. Moving or being moved from one difficulty to another that is worse. Tertullian had it in Latin some 1,800 years ago. The origin of the phrase is suggested by one of the earliest examples in English, by Sir Thomas More in 1528: "Lepe they lyke a flounder out of a frying-panne into the fyre."

From A to Z. From beginning to end; all the way. To the Greeks it was "from alpha to omega," respectively the first and last letters of the Greek alphabet. In any language it is a natural way of recording an all-inclusive spectrum. Thomas Shelton, writing in 1612 a preface to his translation of *Don Quixote*, said: "Thou needest doe nought else but seeke out a Booke that doth quote them all from the letter A vntill Z."

From Bad to Worse. The situation is deteriorating. You go back to your grammar lessons for this one, recalling that "worse" rather than "badder" is the comparative form of "bad." Otherwise, things would go "from bad to badder." Edmund Spenser was grammatical and more or less rhyming (perhaps in his day it was a closer rhyme than it is to the 20th-century ear) in *The Shepheardes Calendar* (1579):

> Must not the world wend in his common course
> From good to badde, and from badde to worse . . . ?

From Cradle to Grave. Throughout one's life; lifetime coverage. Politicians like this phrase as suggestive of the kind of program they seek to provide for their constituents. Poets like it, too, as in this example in John Dyer's *Grongar Hill* (1726):

> A little rule, a little sway,
> A sunbeam in a winter's day,
> Is all the proud and mighty have
> Between the cradle and the grave.

From Head to Heels. All the way; totally. The prolific William Cowper had the phrase in one of his works in 1781: "So polished and compact from head to heel." A related expression, even older, is "from head to foot," which can be found in print by 1300 and is in *Hamlet*, where Hamlet asks the officers Marcellus and Bernardo if they are armed:

> M. & B. Arm'd, my lord.
> H. From top to toe?
> M. & B. My lord, from head to foot.

From Pillar to Post. From one thing (or place) to another, repetitively. You can find at least two explanations of the origin of this ancient phrase, one that the "pillar" and "post" were part of the fittings in court tennis (a much older and more ornate game than the modern lawn tennis, which is seldom played on lawns now), and the other that it meant from "whipping post" to "pillory." The tennis version seems to have the strongest supporting evidence, even though the phrase was for centuries "from post to pillar." The earliest appearance is in John Lydgate's *The Assembly of Gods* (1420): "Thus fro poost to pylour he was made to daunce."

From Start to Finish. All the way; from beginning to end. Racing contributes this saying, and the earliest recorded example in print concerned crew races. It was in *The Field*, a British publication, in 1868: "A slashing race was rowed from start to finish between the two former [boats]."

From Time Immemorial. Of such long standing as to go beyond living memory. People were saying this in the early 17th century, an example being in William Fulbeck's *Pandectes of the Law of Nations* (1602): "In making title by prescription and continuance of time immemoriall."

From the Bottom of One's Heart. With deep feeling. The speaker may not really feel that profoundly. The phrase has been so overworked that one seems to express more feeling by offering, say, thanks "from the heart." The Church of England's *Book of Common Prayer* had the "bottom" version in 1545: "If one of the parties . . . be content to forgive from the bottom of the heart all that the other hath trespassed against him. . . . "

From the Horse's Mouth. The truth; the straight dope; something from an authoritative or believable source. You can tell the age of a horse accurately by looking at its teeth, which is why one is advised not to "look a gift horse in the mouth." The horse's pairs of permanent teeth appear in succession at definite ages. The lore is old but the expression seems to be of fairly recent (probably 20th-century) origin.

From the Sublime to the Ridiculous. From great to small, success to failure, noble to ignoble (usually rather quickly). As Thomas Paine put it in *The Age of Reason* (1794): "The sublime and the ridiculous are often so nearly related, that it is difficult to class them separately. One step above the sublime makes the ridiculous, and one step above the ridiculous makes the sublime again."

From the Word Go. From the outset; from the start to the end or to the present. This is the "Go!" that starts a race. The saying originated in the United States where in 1838 *Knickerbocker Magazine* showed how to extend the meaning: "You have perjured yourself, from the word 'go'; you have equivocated from Dan to Beersheba." In the biblical reference, Dan is the northernmost and Beersheba the southernmost city of the Holy Land.

Full Head of Steam, with a. Doing something with power, vigor and momentum. It is a term from the days when ships began to be powered by steam. In 1862 *The Times* of London, describing the Civil War naval battle in which the *Merrimac* of the Confederacy rammed and sank the Union ship *Cumberland,* had: "The 'Merrimac' . . . made direct for the 'Cumberland' under a full head of steam." By 1889 Mark Twain was reflecting the extended meaning in *A Yankee at the Court of King Arthur:* "I had got a good head of reserved steam on."

Full Steam Ahead. At top speed; with all the power available. "Full steam" was a technical term describing a steam boiler that had developed its maximum pressure. At full steam a moving vehicle such as a ship or a railroad locomotive would attain maximum speed. A typical statement from the heyday of steam is in William Kingston's *Three Admirals* (1878): "Full steam was put on."

Full and Complete. Thorough. This tautology is a cliché mainly in Congress, where members are forever promising "full and complete" investigations of this or that. The tendency to use two words where one will do is not limited to members of Congress; a forerunner of the cliché turned up in a will lodged in the London Court of Probate in 1417: "This testament is my vole and hole [full and whole] wille."

Funny Money. Money that looks counterfeit or suspicious for some other reason; also currency being manipulated politically. *American Speech* recorded in 1938 that Associated Industries of Nebraska had taken out advertisements against sales-tax tokens of the kind then in use in several other states. "Nebraska needs no spurious coins, which add to the cost of living in sales-tax states," the group said. "*Funny money* buys nothing but increased burdens of government."

Funny as a Crutch. That's a feeble attempt at humor. There's nothing funny about a crutch, and so the saying is a put-down of an essay at humor that is inept or in bad taste. *American Notes and Queries* suggested in 1947 that a book of 1869 by Alonzo F. Hill, *John Smith's Funny Adventures on a Crutch; or, The Remarkable Peregrinations of a One Legged Soldier After the War*, might have been the source. It's hard to believe that a book with such a soggy title would draw much of an audience, but it was popular enough to have been reprinted in the 1890's.

Fur Fly, Make the. Stir things up; cause a fight or an argument. The picture is from what happens, or what one envisions as happening, when two furry animals fight. It can be found as far back as 1663, in Samuel Butler's *Hudibras:*

> I'll make the fur
> Fly 'bout the ears of the old cur.

Gala Occasion, A. A social event special for its fancy dress and spirited entertainment, for its festivity. A bit of repetitiveness here, since "gala" by itself means festivity. The word once stood by itself, as in this example from *The Gentlemen's Magazine* in 1778: "The anniversary of her Majesty's name-day was celebrated at the Russian court with great gala." The society columns of newspapers are the source of the current practice of invariably coupling "gala" with "occasion" or "affair."

Gall and Wormwood. Bitter medicine or experience. "Gall" is bile, the bitter secretion of the liver, and "wormwood" is a medicinal plant with a notably bitter flavor. The expression appears several times in the Old Testament books of Jeremiah and the Lamentations of Jeremiah. For example, Jeremiah 9 : 15: "Therefore thus saith the Lord of hosts, the God of Israel; Behold, I will feed them, even this people, with wormwood, and give them water of gall to drink."

Game Is Worth (Not Worth) the Candle, The. Whatever you're doing is not repaying the time, money or effort you're putting into it. In the days when people played card or dice games by candlelight they sometimes paid a nonplayer to hold the candle so that the light fell on the cards or dice rather than in the eyes of the players. They also had to pay for the candles. When a player was having a run of bad luck, he might well remark that the game, or play, was not worth the price of the candle. An English translation of the *Essays of Montaigne* put it this way in 1603: "The horror of a fall doth more hurt me, then the blow. The play is not worth the candle."

Garden Path, Led Up (Down) the. Deceived, tricked. Sometimes it is simply "led up the garden" and sometimes it is "led her up the garden [path]," suggesting a ploy by an amorous man to lure a young woman to a place where he can attempt to demonstrate his amour. It can happen the other way, too, as indicated by the first recorded appearance of the expression in print, in Ethel Mannin's *Sounding Brass* (1926): "They're cheats, that's wot women are! Lead you up the garden and then go snivellin' around 'cos wot's natcheral 'as 'appened to 'em."

Gather Ye Rosebuds While Ye May. Take advantage of your opportunities; live for the present. The thought has been put by various writers in various ways for a long time. One version is in the Apocrypha, in The Wisdom of Solomon (2 : 8): "Let us crown ourselves with rosebuds, before they be withered." The exact phrase appears in a poem by Robert Herrick in 1648:

> Gather ye rosebuds while ye may,
> Old Time is still a-flying,
> And this same flower that smiles today
> Tomorrow will be dying.

Gay Lothario, A. A debonair fellow; a seducer of women. Lothario was a character in *The Fair Penitent,* a play written by Nicholas Rowe in 1703, and he had a way with women. "Is this that haughty gallant, gay Lothario?" is a line that appears in Act V. The expression is probably being driven out of the language now by the appropriation of "gay," which was once a widely useful word, to mean homosexual almost exclusively.

Gentle Reader. You, as addressed by a courtly author. Readers were constantly addressed in this way until not so long ago; now an author employing the phrase seems (and is probably trying to seem) a bit archaic. The gentle reader has been in print since at least 1542, when Henry Brinklow addressed him in *The Lamentacyon of a Christen agaynst the Cytye of London:* "Iudge thow, gentle reader." Most of the old meanings of "gentle" (noble, excellent, honorable being some of them) are lost and the word survives (in this phrase) as a term of complimentary address.

Get a Handle on It. Find a way of coping with a difficult problem or a hard-to-hold object. My guess is that the originator of this term was a sportswriter or broadcaster describing a football, which is notoriously hard to hold. Most likely he said that the player "couldn't find the handle on it." By 1977 the meaning had expanded beyond sports, as demonstrated in the *Manchester Guardian Weekly:* "It follows that if we could only get a better handle on the arms-building phenomenon, we could do something about it, turn it around."

Get In on the Ground Floor. Be part of the beginning of something. If one is on the ground floor, one has no place to go but up. The expression got its start in U.S. financial activity, as John S. Farmer showed by his definition of it in *Americanisms* (1889): "To be allowed to share in a speculation on the same terms as the original promoters."

Get It Down Pat. Master it; learn how to do it right. "Pat" as an adjective and adverb has several meanings. Here, it means just so, precisely suitable, perhaps from the verb's sense of patting something into shape. In the third act of *Hamlet* a situation arises where Hamlet could kill his uncle the king, who is praying. Hamlet, seeking revenge for the death of his father at the king's hands, says, "Now might I do it pat, now he is praying. . . . " But he decides the time is not ripe ("this is hire and salary, not revenge").

Get Up and Go. Energy, drive, motivation. This thought has been expressed in other ways, including "get up and get," "get up and hustle" and "get up and dust," but "go" has left them all in the dust. You can see the thought developing in John H. Beadle's *The Undeveloped West* (1873): "If you . . . have any 'get up' about you, and can and will work, there's a show for you in rural Nebraska."

Get Your Act Together. Get organized; plan systematically; work coherently. It must be from the theater, reflecting the feelings of an actor who was a bit nervous or thought his performance could be better; but the origin is lost. The expression was in wide use by 1978, when the *Manchester Guardian Weekly* showed how it had expanded beyond the theater: "It [a reform of policy on refugees] merely requires that the administration get its act together. . . . "

Get Your Second Wind. Feel renewed vigor; find that you can continue in a difficult situation. It is a common experience to feel weary and ready to quit after a few minutes of an exercise such as running, swimming or chopping wood, and then to find if you keep at it that the feeling passes and you can continue without much trouble. The phenomenon got the name "second wind," which is almost literally descriptive, long ago. In 1830 Thomas Hood, quoted in an advertisement for the second edition of his book, *The Epping Hunt*, said: "I am much gratified to learn from you [the publisher], that the Epping Hunt has had *such a run,* that it is *quite exhausted,* and that you intend therefore to give the work what might be called 'second wind' by a new impression."

Get a Leg Up On. Make a good or promising start. It comes from mounting a horse or climbing a stile; once you have a leg up, you are on the way to success. Charles Dickens had a variant of the saying in his *Pickwick Papers* (1837): " 'The wall is very low, sir, and your servant will give you a leg up.' "

Get into the Swing of It (Things). Develop a rhythm and momentum in some physical or mental activity. The transfer is from the rhythmic and repetitive motion of the pendulum. Thomas H. Huxley wrote, in *Life and Letters* (1864): "My lectures tire me, for want of practice. I shall soon get into the swing."

Get the Lead Out of Your Feet. Move; pep it up. Usually said as an imperative. Literally to have the weight of lead in the feet or the shoes would make for slow movement or no movement at all. Doubtless the expression started figuratively, with someone who was exasperated by another's slow pace. One can see the image developing in William Jenkyn's *Reformations Remora* (1646): "Shall our Reformation have an heel of lead?"

Get the Sack. Be fired or dismissed. It was once "to get the bag," meaning to leave abruptly and later to be dismissed. Roving workmen carried their tools in a sack or bag, and when the work ended or a workman was dismissed, the worker picked up his sack and moved on. Similar expressions were current in the 16th century, as in *Common Conditions* (1576): "This tinkerly trade, wee geue it the bagge."

Get to the Bottom of It. Find the underlying reason or cause. The "bottom" is usually the beginning, and if you are there, you may be able to tell how the affair began. "Search to the bottom" was in print in 1594, "an examination to the bottom" in 1651. James Monboddo had it as "in order to get at the bottom of this question" in *Of the Origin and Progress of Language* (1773).

Gets His Back (Dander) Up. Becomes irritated, stubborn or angry about something. As "back," the expression most likely came from the cat's habit of arching its back and bristling its fur when confronted by a dog or some other potential enemy. "Dander" is an old word meaning anger; it may have come from the Dutch *donder*, meaning thunder. Seba Smith wrote in *The Letters of Major Jack Downing* (1830): "He was as spunky as thunder, and when a Quaker gets his dander up, it's like a Northwester."

Gets My Goat. Annoys severely. This is one of those widely familiar expressions the origin of which is lost. It began as American slang, apparently early in the 20th century. H. L. Mencken writes in *American Language* (1945) of being told that the saying originated in a practice among certain trainers of horses of soothing a nervous horse by putting a goat in its stall. If someone wanting to see the horse lose a race came and took the goat away, the horse would presumably succumb to an attack of nerves and would not run well. In any event, the first recorded appearance of the expression in print is in Christy Mathewson's *Pitching in a Pinch* (1912): "Then Lobert . . . stopped at third with a mocking smile which would have gotten the late Job's goat."

Ghost of a Chance, Not a. It's hopeless; a lost cause. Among other things, "ghost" means a shadow, an insubstantial thing, and so it serves to intensify the thought that one doesn't stand a chance of succeeding. Here is Thomas Hughes, in *Tom Brown's School*

Days (1857): "Williams hadn't the ghost of a chance with Tom at wrestling."

Gift of the Gods. An inborn talent; a stroke of good fortune. The saying is from the time of the ancient Greeks, who believed in a number of gods, each concerned with a particular aspect of nature or human affairs. Homer, in *The Iliad*, wrote some 2,600 years ago: "If you are very valiant, it is a god, I think, who gave you this gift."

Gild the Lily. To try to improve the appearance of a beautiful object; to make a superfluous gesture. A couple of things that Shakespeare said in one breath, so to speak, in *King John* have been run together here. The king has seized the English throne and has had a second coronation in the hope that it will reinforce his weak position. Lord Salisbury says:

> Therefore, to be possess'd with double pomp,
> To guard a title that was rich before,
> To gild refined gold, to paint the lily,
> To throw a perfume on the violet,
> To smooth the ice, or add another hue
> Unto the rainbow, or with taper-light
> To seek the beauteous eye of heaven to garnish,
> Is wasteful and ridiculous excess.

Gird Up Your Loins. Prepare for action or hard work. The Jews of biblical time usually wore their clothing loose, but in traveling or working or fighting they "girded" (fastened) them with a belt so as to have freer use of their legs. In the figurative sense, the apostle Peter says (Peter 1 : 13): "Wherefore gird up the loins of your mind, be sober, and hope to the end for the grace that is to be brought to you at the revelation of Jesus Christ."

Give (or Cut Off) His Right Arm, He'd. He'll do anything to help; he's exceedingly generous. It is most doubtful that anyone would be *that* generous, so we confront a bit of hyperbole. The earliest use I have found for the saying was in 1942, although I think it is older. That was in *Layoff*, by Robert G. Dean: "He'd cut off his right arm for her, as the saying goes."

Give A Wide Berth To. Avoid; steer clear of. "Berth" is a nautical term with several meanings. As defined in 18th-century British dictionaries, one is: "convenient sea-room for a ship that rides at anchor" (since as it swings on its chain with the wind and tides it can take up a lot of space); the other is: "convenient sea-room, or a fit distance for ships under sail to keep clear, so not to fall foul on one another."

Give Pause. Have or give reason to delay and to reconsider. It sometimes seems that ten percent of this book could be assembled from Shakespeare and one percent from *Hamlet* alone. That is not to say Shakespeare wrote in clichés; his writing is in fact muscular and vivid, and the expressions of his that have remained in the language and may have *become* clichéd owe their long life to those qualities. This particular expression comes from Hamlet's soliloquy, just after he says "ay, there's the rub" to his notion that it might be best to die:

> For in that sleep of death what dreams may come,
> When we have shuffled off this mortal coil,
> Must give us pause . . . .

Give Short Shrift. Make quick work of something; allow little time for something. The word "shrift" and its companion verb "shrive" are almost unused now; they referred to one's confession to a priest. A person condemned to execution was given time for shrift, or at least for collecting his thoughts, and occasionally it was a short time. So it is in *Richard III*, where the Duke of Gloucester (who will become Richard III) has sentenced Lord Hastings to execution. Sir Richard Ratcliff is assigned to see that the deed is done. As Hastings bemoans his fate, Ratcliff says:

> Dispatch, my lord; the duke would be at dinner:
> Make a short shrift; he longs to see your head.

Give You the Shirt Off His Back, He'd. He would do anything for you; he is extremely generous. When you're giving away your shirt, you're down to one of the last things you have. The saying was in print as long ago as 1771, in Tobias Smollett's *The Expedition of Humphry Clinker:* "He would give away the shirt off his back."

Give and Take. An exchange of raillery, insults or blows. Long ago the saying had quite the different meaning of being fair and considerate, of making concessions, as is clear in Fanny Burney's *Evelina* (1778): "Give and Take is fair in all nations." An earlier example, not quite so clear, is in William Horman's *Vulgaria* (1519): "A man must somtyme gyue and somtyme take." The present more limited meaning seems to have become established late in the 19th century.

Give the Go-around. Deflect a claimant or a petitioner; avoid coming to grips with a request. In 1929 *American Speech* took note of the expression, saying that "He gave me the go-around" meant "avoided."

Go (Come) Full Circle. Complete a cycle; recur. Shakespeare again, that originator and recorder of so many familiar expressions. In *King Lear* it involves an interaction between the illegitimate and legitimate sons of the Earl of Gloucester, respectively Edmund and Edgar. Edmund has resorted to several varieties of villainy to make Edgar lose favor with the earl and to do the earl out of his lands and title. In the end, however, affairs turn against Edmund; he and Edgar have a sword fight and Edmund is mortally wounded. He says, "The wheel is come full circle."

Go Against the Grain. To take an action that seems unnatural or illogical. It is hard work when you saw or plane a piece of wood against the "grain," meaning the direction of growth of the tree from which the wood came. By extension, it means to do anything in a way that is unduly difficult or runs against one's instincts. Shakespeare had the extended meaning in *Coriolanus,* where the tribune Sicinius says:

> Say, you chose him
> More after our commandment than as guided
> By your own true affections; and that your minds,
> Preoccupied with what you rather must do
> Than what you should, made you against the grain
> To voice him consul: lay the fault on us.

Go Along for the Ride. Be present (without making a contribution); join an activity for no particular reason. The saying is a product of the automobile age. Apparently in earlier days you took a ride only for a purpose. The saying was current in the United States by 1960, when the *Dictionary of American Slang,* compiled by Harold Wentworth and Stuart Berg Flexner, took note of it and defined it as: "to join in passively, usually for the fun of it, without making an active contribution."

Go Around Robin Hood's Barn. Take (often unnecessarily) a circuitous route; proceed by indirection. Robin Hood, a perhaps legendary figure, has represented since the 14th century the free spirit who robs the rich to pay the poor. He had no barn, since all his activities were outdoors, and so to go around Robin Hood's barn is a labored effort. The phrase is more recent than the legend, having first turned up in print in J. F. Kelley's *Humors of Falconbridge* (1854): "The way some folks have of going round 'Robin Hood's barn' to come at a thing."

Go Bananas. Feel cooped up or driven to distraction; claim one is going out of one's mind because of the situation. How "bananas" got this role is a matter of speculation. Perhaps it was because monkeys and other primates like bananas and the person who feels he is "going bananas" thinks he is being driven to act somewhat like such animals. Here is a passage from *Time* in 1970: "Liza [Minelli] moved into the sheltered, regimented Barbizon Hotel for Women. Liza says: 'I went bananas!'"

Go Climb a Tree. Stop bothering me; your idea (or proposal) is worthless. Oren Arnold wrote in the *Los Angeles Times Sunday Magazine* in 1935 that Americans had become "a trifle disgusted with their one-time penchant for cursing" and were turning to "such puerile phrases" as "go climb a tree."

Go Fry an Egg. Stop bothering me; do something else; you're a nuisance. One would suppose this piece of advice to a pest was fairly new and slangy, but something much like it to mean mind your own business appeared in 1841 in George P. R. James's *The Brigand:* "Fry your eggs, Gandelot, and leave other people to fry theirs."

Go Hat in Hand. Be deferential, humble or cajoling in one's approach to another person. The saying is from the ancient custom of removing the hat or headgear as a gesture of courtesy, respect or salutation. It occasionally is still heard in that sense, but for at least 100 years has tended more often to refer to an attitude of servility or cajolery.

Go Haywire. Go wrong (of a machine); behave in an uncontrolled or even mentally unbalanced way (of a person). Stewart H. Holbrook laid the origin of this expression to Maine logging camps, where workers saved the wire from baled hay and used it for repairing things and for makeshift tools. "A camp that was notoriously poor in its equipment came to be known as a *haywire camp;* and from this usage it spread to mean broken, busted, sick, crazy, no-good and a score of other things, none of them praiseworthy," Holbrook wrote in *Holy Old Mackinaw* (1956). H. L. Mencken, in *The American Language: Supplement I* (1946), was skeptical. "No one," he wrote, "who has ever opened a bale of hay with a hatchet, and had the leaping wire whirl about him and its sharp ends poniard him, will ever have any doubt as to how *to go haywire* originated."

Go It Alone. Do something single-handedly (often after having had or expected help). The 19th-century poet John Godfrey Saxe expressed the thought precisely in *The Game of Life:*
> In battle or business, whatever the game,
> In law or in love, it is ever the same;
> In the struggle for power, or the scramble of pelf,
> Let this be your motto—Rely on yourself!
> For, whether the prize be a ribbon or throne,
> The victor is he who can go it alone!

Go Like the Wind. Move fast. It must have been a whistling wind that gave rise to this analogy for speed. Shakespeare shows that the thought is old. In *A Midsummer Night's Dream* Oberon says to Puck, "About the wood go swifter than the wind. . . ."

Go Off Half-Cocked. To act hastily or with insufficient preparation. The literal meaning of the term goes back to the muskets of
the 18th century; when the hammer was cocked half way, the
firing mechanism was supposed to be locked. If it was faulty, the
gun might go off when it wasn't expected to. The broader meaning is found by 1848 in *The Bigelow Papers*, by James Russell
Lowell: "No, don't go off Half-cock."

Go Scot-free. To get away without payment or penalty. "Scot" is an
ancient word meaning payment, reckoning or tax. The notion of
escaping it appears in the *Charter of 1066* as "Scotfre." In 1531
William Tyndale, writing on the first Epistle of St. John, said:
"The poore synner shulde go Skot fre without oughte at all."

Go Whole Hog. Go all the way; stop at nothing. You have your
choice of two origins. One is that "hog" once meant a shilling, so
that to "go the whole hog" was to splurge. The other derives from
the fact that Moslems had trouble deciding what part of the hog
they could not eat under Muhammad's proscription on eating
pork. William Cowper wrote, in *The Love of the World Reproved;
or Hypocrisy Detected* (1779):

> But for one piece they thought it hard
> From the whole hog to be debar'd;
> And set their wit at work to find
> What joint the prophet had in mind. . . .
> Thus, conscience freed from every clog,
> Mahometans eat up the hog.

Go by the Board. Be lost or finished with. This "board" is the side
of a ship; anything that goes (or is thrown) over the side is lost.
One can see the literal origin in a sentence by John Taylor in
1630: "In this fight their Reare-Admirals Maine Mast was shot by
the boord."

Go for Broke. Go all-out; risk everything. "Broke" in the sense of
penniless or financially ruined has been in the language for 300
years or more, but "go for broke" in the sense of expecting to win
all or lose one's last stake is a gambler's term dating back perhaps 100 years. It also turns up in sports in the sense of giving
one's utmost, win or lose.

Go on the Warpath. Set out to do battle. This is how North American Indians, or white men writing about them, described their
action or route when they went on a warlike expedition. The
transferred meaning was familiar as far away as England by
1888, when the *Pall Mall Gazette* had this headline: "The

Omagh Controversy. Mr. William O'Brien on the War Path."

Go the Route. Stick with a task (usually one in a prescribed format) to the end. The phrase is worked heavily by baseball writers describing a pitcher who lasts for a complete game, and I suspect that such a writer originated it. In the sports pages of the *Chicago Record-Herald,* during the 1913 spring training season, one could read: "This was the first complete battle Cicotte has pitched, and he was watched closely to see if he could go the route." The thought also appears in other contexts, as in Jack Black's *You Can't Win* (1926): "If a Chinese doesn't like you he will keep away from you; if he does like you he will go the route."

Go to His Reward. Die. The statement is often made ironically, implying that the deceased isn't likely to get much of a reward. Thus, Mark Twain, in *Life on the Mississippi* (1883): "He went to his reward, whatever it was, two years ago." Twain may have originated the irony; this passage is the first recorded use of the phrase.

Go to Pot. Deteriorate; disintegrate. The picture is of meat being cut in pieces for the cooking pot, from whence came the meaning of being ruined or destroyed. This meaning, somewhat stronger than today's, was picked up by Nicholas Udall in his *Apophthegmes* (1542): "The riche & welthie of his subjectes went dayly to the potte."

Go to Town. Do something exuberantly or efficiently. In England the saying is hundreds of years old but has a different meaning: to arrive or make one's mark where significant things are happening. In the sense of doing something with gusto it is of American origin, probably dating from the 19th century, when going to town for an outing or a spree was a big day for country folk.

Go to the Dogs. Decline; come to a bad end. At one time (and to a certain extent still) food that was not quite suitable for people to eat was thrown to the dogs. Thomas Cooper had the ancestor of the modern expression in Latin in his *Thesaurus* (1565): "Addicere aliquem canibus" [To bequeath him to the dogs].

God and Mammon. The two (sometimes conflicting) guides of conscience and money-making. *Mammon* was an ancient Aramaic word for riches, and came to symbolize covetousness. In the Bible (Matthew 6 : 24) one is told: "Ye cannot serve God and mammon." From this proscription arose in medieval times the use of "Mammon" as a proper name for the devil of covetousness, as in

Ordynarye of Cristen Men (1502): "A deuyll named Mammona made unto the couetous man vi. commaundementes."

God's Green Earth. Everywhere; a particular plot of ground where something is happening. Belief in a deity carries with it the view that the earth is the stage on which the deity's designs are carried out. Various phrases have expressed the thought over the centuries. An example is in Thomas Stocker's *Ciulle Warres of the Lowe Countries* (1583): "There were but 200 Spaniards laid on Gods deare earth."

Goes Without Saying, It. It's obvious or well known. The ironic thing is that the thing claimed not to need saying is then always said. The French have the same saying (*Cela va sans dire*), which may have been the origin of the English version. The magazine *Literature* gave a typical example of the pattern in 1897: "It goes without saying that the books are not ordinary ones."

Going Around in Circles. Behaving ineffectually; not getting anything accomplished. Perhaps the image is derived from the animals that once (and still in some countries) pumped water or ground grain by walking endlessly in a circle while hitched to a horizontal arm of the machine. At any rate, Patricia Wentworth was picking up the broader meaning by 1942, in *Pursuit of a Parcel*: "He had been rushing around in circles."

Going to Hell in a Handbasket. Indulging in some minor dissipation. The *Dictionary of American Slang* suggests that anything carried in a handbasket has to be small. Actually an older expression is "going to heaven in a handbasket." *Dialect Notes* took account of the saying in 1913, declaring that in Kansas "it means 'to have a sinecure.'" Ten years later the same publication reported that in southwestern Wisconsin the expression meant "to do something easily."

Golden Age. A time when things were better (usually so characterized by later generations rather than by the people who lived through it). Richard Eden caught the thought precisely in *The Decades of the Newe Worlde* (1555): "As wee reade of them whiche in oulde tyme lyued in the golden age."

Golden Mean. The intelligent midpoint. The phrase appears in Horace's *Odes*, written 2,000 years ago: "Whoever cultivates the golden mean avoids both the poverty of a hovel and the envy of a palace."

Gone With the Wind. Evanescent; definitely no longer here. Besides being the title of Margaret Mitchell's only novel and of the enduring motion picture based on the book, the thought and the saying are very old. The 13th-century French poet known only as Rutebeuf had it in *La Complainte Rutebeuf:*

> Friendship is dead:
> They were friends who go with the wind,
> And the wind was blowing at my door.

Good Men and True. Sound folk. It has long been a cliché for the kind of people sought to serve on juries. Nowadays it could as well be "good women and true," but I have never heard it that way. "True" here means reliable. The phrase was current 500 years ago, when William Caxton wrote, in *Fables of Alfonse* (1484): "He is . . . reputed . . . for a good man and trewe." In 1710 Joseph Addison wrote, in *The Tattler*, of "Good Men and true for a Petty Jury."

Good Old (Ole) Boy. A regular fellow; an accepted member of some cohesive group. It is a term from the American South and was defined by *Time* in 1976: "The core of the good ole boy's world is with his buddies, the comfortable, hyperhearty, all-male camaraderie, joshing and drinking and regaling one another with tales of assorted, exaggerated prowess."

Good Samaritan. Someone who helps or stands ready to help a person in trouble. Samaria was the ancient capital of Israel and gave its name to a district of Palestine, whence came Samaritans. It was one of these who figured in the parable told by Jesus to the lawyer who wanted to know, "Who is my neighbour?" The parable (Luke 10 : 30–37) had to do with a man from Jerusalem who was set upon by thieves at Jericho, wounded and left for dead. A priest passed by on the other side, and also a Levite, but "a certain Samaritan" passing by saw the man, bound up his wounds, took him to an inn and provided money for his care. Jesus asks the lawyer, "Which one of these three . . . was neighbour unto him that fell among the thieves?" The lawyer responds that it was the Samaritan, and Jesus says: "Go thou and do likewise."

Good Time Was Had by All, A. It was an enjoyable trip or party. The literary extent of this cliché seldom ranges beyond the diary, the postcard or the bulletins of clubs and societies. What is unusual is the history of the expression. To "have a good time" was a common saying in England in the 16th and 17th centuries. It died out there but was retained by people who had emigrated to America. From there it was reintroduced into England in the 19th century. Stevie Smith, who published a book of verse under the title *A Good Time Was Had by All* in 1937, told Eric Partridge that she took the title from parish magazines, which used the term regularly in reporting on social events in the churches.

Good, Bad or Indifferent. No matter what; to take a person or a thing as he or it comes. The Dutch philosopher Spinoza gave a definition in his *Ethics* (1677): "One and the same thing can at the same time be good, bad, and indifferent, e.g., music is good to the melancholy, bad to those who mourn, and neither good nor bad to the deaf."

Good-for-nothing. An incompentent or lazy person. In 1533 Nicholas Udall recorded this saying in *Floures for Latin Speaking:* "Nequam [worthless] is he that is good for nothynge, but euen a very naughty vnthryfte."

Goods and Chattels. One's possessions. "Chattel" derives from an old French word for cattle, but by the 16th century it had come to mean property and thus to contribute to one of the law's redundancies, since both "goods" and "chattels" mean property. William Lambarde, in *A Perambulation of Kent* (1570), wrote of the "custodie, not of the landes onely, but of the goods and chattels also."

Goody Two-shoes. An excessively good person; a goody-goody. The expression comes from the title of a child's tale, *The History of Little Goody Two-Shoes* (1765), thought to have been written by Oliver Goldsmith for John Newbery, the first publisher of books for children. Goody had one shoe; when she was given a pair of new ones, she ran around showing them to everyone she met, saying, "Two shoes! Two shoes!"

Gordian Knot, Cut the. Deal straightforwardly with a difficult problem, but perhaps by brute force rather than by solving it or meeting the conditions laid down for a solution. Gordius, the king of ancient Phrygia, tied a knot so intricate that no one could untie it. An oracle said that the person who loosened it would rule Asia. Alexander the Great cut it with his sword. In William Fulke's extensive religious tracts of the 16th century one finds (*Heskins Parleament,* 1579): "Hee had found out a sworde to cutt in sunder the Gordian knot."

Got Up Out of the Wrong Side of the Bed. It's a bad day; things aren't going right. It is a homely analogy, suggesting that if you began the day by breaking a habit, things might seem strange or out of sorts all day. Usually it works backward; when things go wrong, you tend to think it has been like that from the start of the day. The thought derives from a time (long ago) when it was believed that the forces of evil prevailed on the left side of the body and that one should not get up from the left side of the bed or put one's left foot on the floor first. Innkeepers sometimes put the left side of the bed against the wall to protect the guest from this hazard. The first recorded use of the saying is in *Marvellous Love*

(1801), which says: "You got up on the wrong side this morning, George."

Grain of Sense, Hasn't a. Is witless, or at least not very smart. John Dryden was picking up this phrase in the 17th century, in his epilogue on Constantine the Great:

> Bold knaves thrive without one grain of sense,
> But good men starve for want of impudence.

Grandstand Play. More for show than substance. It is from the tendency of athletes, and particularly baseball players, to make plays in a flashier way than is really necessary, the object being to gain the attention and perhaps the applause of the spectators sitting in the stands. An earlier expression from the theater embodies the same thought about an actor: "playing to the gallery." The notion of playing to the grandstand is of American origin and was known in the later years of the 19th century, when professional baseball began to make its mark.

Grapes of Wrath. An explosive, dangerous situation resulting from a group's anger or distress over a situation. "Grapes" stand here for any fruit of something planted earlier. Samuel Eliot Morison put it concisely in *The Oxford History of the American People* (1965 edition): "The freedmen were not really free in 1865, nor are most of their descendants free in 1965. Slavery was but one aspect of a race and color problem that is still far from solution here, or anywhere. In America particularly, the grapes of wrath have not yet yielded all their bitter vintage." John Steinbeck made the phrase the title of a novel in 1939, picking it up from Julia Ward Howe's hymn, "The Battle Hymn of the Republic" (1910): "He is trampling out the vintage where the grapes of wrath are stored."

Grasp at Straws. Act in desperation (probably from the image of a drowning person clutching at anything that floats, even something so insubstantial as straws). It is sometimes said as "catch at straws," which is close to the form of the earliest recorded appearance of the thought, in Samuel Richardson's *Clarissa* (1748): "A drowning man will catch at a straw, as the Proverb well says."

Grasp the Nettle. Tackle a difficult or painful task. The nettles are a family of plants with leaf hairs that sting the hand that (usually inadvertently) touches them; to take hold of a nettle deliberately requires an act of courage, which is the source of the figurative meaning. That was the meaning picked up by Sir Spenser St. John in *Hayti* (1884): It was hoped . . . that, grasping the nettle with resolution, he might suffer no evil results."

Gravy Train, Get on the. To obtain money or services without much effort. Real gravy adds a pleasant taste to some basic dish such as meat or potatoes, but you can get along without it. Long ago, in the United States at least, the word took on a transferred meaning of money that came easily or unexpectedly. "Gravy train" implies that a lot of other people are sharing the goodies; it may have originated in railroading as a reference to an easy run. The term seems to have first turned up in print in 1945 in *Lay My Burden Down*, by Benjamin Bodkin: "They is on the gravy train and don't know it. . . ."

Gray Eminence. An influential figure in the background. The original *éminence grise* was François Leclerc du Tremblay, better known as Père Joseph. He was a confidant and adviser of Cardinal Richelieu, who as minister to Louis XIII controlled the government of France in the early 17th century. Many people at the time thought Père Joseph, a Capuchin monk, was an evil influence on the cardinal. At any rate, he was a shadowy figure in the background, which is how the sobriquet arose. Aldous Huxley wrote a book about him, *Grey Eminence* (1941).

Greased Lightning, Like. Exceedingly or unbelievably fast. Since lightning is mighty fast, the notion of "greasing" it adds a touch of hyperbole. The touch had been applied by 1833, when the *Boston, Lincoln and Louth Herald* in England had this sentence: "He spoke as quick as greased lightning."

Great Open Spaces. Undeveloped or unpopulated land of considerable expanse. Doubtless the American West in the 19th century gave rise to the saying, which had become literary by 1924—as in *Leave It to Psmith*, by P. G. Wodehouse: "You will find me somewhere out there in the great open spaces where men are men."

Great Unwashed. The common herd; the lower classes. Shakespeare used "unwashed" in an uncomplimentary sense in *King John*, where he wrote of "another lean unwashed artificer." By 1833 Theodore E. Hook had added the intensifier (in *The Parson's Daughter*): "The 'fat and greasy' and the 'great unwashed' bowed and smiled their best."

Greater Love Hath No Man. You couldn't do more. It is a biblical saying from John 15 : 13: "Greater love hath no man than this, that a man lay down his life for his friends."

Greeks Bearing Gifts, Beware of. Watch out for treachery on the part of certain people who appear to be doing you a kindness. It is from the story of the Trojan horse in Vergil's *Aeneid*. The Greeks, having beseiged Troy for a decade, indicated that they had had enough and would withdraw. They offered the people of Troy a large wooden horse as a gift. Some of the wiser men of Troy urged the people to reject it, saying, "beware the Greeks, even when they bear gifts." But the horse was accepted and brought into the walled city. The Greek soldiers hidden in it killed the guards and set fire to the city.

Green with Envy. Strongly jealous or covetous. People who are unwell are often said to look pale or green; the "pale" is plain enough
to the observer, but the "green" takes a little imagination.
Someone who is deeply envious feels unwell mentally, and this is
apparently why he is said to be green. "Green" is also a Scottish
verb meaning to yearn. The notion of turning green with envy
appears in Charles Reade's *Hard Cash* (1863): "The doctor was
turning almost green with jealousy."

Green-eyed Monster. Jealousy. More from Shakespeare. In
Othello the villainous Iago is trying to make Othello mistrust his
wife, Desdemona. Iago drops hints about her relations with
Cassio, saying among other things:

> O, beware, my lord, of jealousy;
> It is the green-eyed monster, which doth mock
> The meat it feeds on. . . .

The allusion is to cats and tigers and other green-eyed animals,
which toy with their victims before eating them, just as a jealous
lover may both love and hate his beloved if he believes a rival is
gaining her affections.

Grim Reaper. Death. Artists and writers have for centuries been
depicting death as a harvester of souls and bodies; in pictures the
formidable man always carries a scythe as a symbol of his task.
Bishop Thomas Ken offered such a picture in words in
Hymnotheo (1711): "See how Death preys on humane Race; Out
with his Scythe the Tyrant goes, Great Multitudes at once he
mows."

Grin and Bear It. Make the best of a difficult or painful situation,
particularly since there is little or nothing else you can do.
Sometimes it was "grin and abide," but that version is virtually
extinct. Indeed, "grin and bear it" was in print by 1775, in William
Hickey's *Memoirs:* "I recommend you to grin and bear it (an expression used by sailors after a long continuance of bad
weather)."

Grind It Out. Do something with difficulty; perform a tedious task.
It is probably to the gristmill, noisy and slow but perfoming an
important task, that one must look for the source of this expression. The age of the term is also suggested by the fact that Admiral
Nelson used it in 1801, as recorded in his *Dispatches:* "I went on
board Sir Hyde this morning. . . . I ground out something, but
there was not that openness which I should have shown to my
Second in Command."

Grind to a Halt. Stop laboriously. It is the kind of stopping by a ship
when it runs aground, or often by a train or by a machine that has
become clogged. The thought transfers to anything, even such as

a session of the U.S. Senate. Harriet Martineau gave a vivid description of one such halt in *Society in America* (1837): "We went aground—grinding, grinding, till the ship trembled in every timber."

Grist for the Mill. Something I can use. "Grist" has almost lost its once-familiar meaning of grain taken to a mill to be ground. It lingers only in the figurative meaning, which was around by 1655, when it appeared in Thomas Fuller's *The Church-History of Britain:* "And here foreign casuists bring in a bundle of mortal sins, all grist for their own mill."

Grit Your Teeth. Prepare for a strenuous effort or to endure a difficult time. "Gritting" or "grating" one's teeth is what one does literally at such moments, but the suggestion of doing it ahead of time as a preparation is a bit different. That idea was in print by 1887 in Frank R. Stockton's *Borrowed Month:* "I gritted my teeth as I thought what a despicable thing it would be."

Groves of Academe, In the. Associated with a university or a scholarly group. "Academe" was the name of an olive grove near Athens where Plato held forth as a teacher. John Milton gave the phrase a lasting impetus in *Paradise Regained* (1671): "See there the olive grove of Academe, Plato's retirement."

Guiding Light. A mentor or an example in behavior. It is probably a phrase alluding to the beacons that for centuries have aided seamen in knowing where they are or in warning them away from hazards. One is close to this meaning in John Flavel's *Sea-Deliverances* (1691): "The guiding usefulness of it [the sun] to us."

Gum Up the Works. Interfere with or spoil an undertaking, often through incompetence. The saying is left over from the days when the lubrication of machinery was more art than science, and the oil sometimes got so gummy that it interfered with rather than aided the operation of the machine. The *Century Dictionary* put it with some precision in 1889: "To become clogged or stiffened by some gummy substance, as inspissated oil; as, a machine will gum up from disuse."

H

Had Me Stumped. I was unable (at least temporarily) to deal with a problem. The *Oxford English Dictionary* views "stump" in this sense, as being of U.S. origin, probably springing from the difficulty of plowing a field that has not been fully cleared of stumps. By 1833, Seba Smith was using the expression in his writings on "Major Jack Downing": "My Good Old Friend—I'm stumped. I jest got a letter from the Gineral . . . ."

Hair of the Dog That Bit You. A deliberate second experience (usually alcoholic) with something that was a bad first experience. It is ancient folk wisdom that like cures like, so ancient that the idea was expressed in Latin: *Similia similibus curantur.* A specific remedy for a dog bite was hair from the dog that bit you; the hair (often burned first) was applied to the wound. A similar remedy from way back, found in old books of remedies, was that if you drank too much of a certain liquor one night, you should have a small amount of the same stuff the next morning. John Heywood's *Proverbs* had the expression in 1546: "I pray the leat me and my felow haue a heare of the dog that bote us last night."

Half a Loaf is Better Than None. It's better to get part of what you want than none of it. John Heywood's *Proverbs* (1546) had this one:
> Throw no gift at the giver's head;
> Better is half a loaf than no bread.

The thought was put even more sternly in *Naaman the Syrian*, by Daniel Rogers (1642): "He is a foole who counts not halfe a loafe better than no bread, or despiseth the moonshine because the sun is down."

Half a Mind, To Have. To be leaning toward a decision or a course of action. Anybody who really had half a mind probably wouldn't be able to make a decision about anything, but as a figure of speech for wavering a bit, being less than certain, it is vivid. George

Shelvocke gave an example in *A Voyage Round the World* (1726): "They had half a mind to refuse me passage."

Half the Battle, That's. A successful beginning; a promising start; something that contributes significantly toward an objective. Thus, Frederick Marryat in *Valerie* (1849): "Youth . . . is half the battle."

Half-baked Idea. A poorly thought-out notion; a thought or plan that doesn't deserve to be taken seriously. A half-baked pie might be edible, but it would fall short of full satisfaction; the same with an idea. Caroline M. Kirkland applied the concept to a person in *Forest Life* (1842): "It is sometimes a term of reproach with us, in speaking of a silly fellow, that he is not half-baked."

Hammer and Tongs, Go at It (with). Do something furiously, with every resource at one's disposal. The hammer and the tongs were the principal tools of the blacksmith: the tongs to take a piece of hot metal from the fire, the hammer to beat it into shape. This vigorous activity had its figurative analogy by 1708, when it appeared in *The British Apollo:* "I'm now coming at you, with Hammer and Tongs."

Hand Over Fist. Taking something in rapidly (usually money). It's remarkable how many of the stock expressions in the language come from sailing lore. This one started as "hand over hand," which was the way a sailor went up or down the rigging or brought in a line. In this form the expression was familiar in the 18th century and probably earlier. The notion of gathering money in rapidly, with a fistful of coins being stowed away with one hand while the other hand reaches for more, came on (probably in the United States) in the 19th century.

Hand in Glove. On intimate terms; cooperating closely. Once it was "hand and glove." In either version it signifies a close relationship. *The Soddered Citizen* put it this way in 1630:

> Like the hand vnto the glove,
> Y'are ioyn'd, in sweete vnitinge loue.

Hand-to-mouth Existence. An economically precarious way of life; living improvidently. It is an old image of someone who out of need or habit eats food as soon as he gets a hand on it instead of storing any. Alexander Barclay had the image in mind in *The Shyp of Folys* (1509): "Theyr vayne myndes to farther thynges is dull saue on that which from hande to mouth is brought."

Handsome is as Handsome Does. One's actions count for more than one's looks. An ancestor of the saying, described as an "ancient adage" in Anthony Munday's *Sundry Examples* (1580), was: "Goodly is he that goodly dooth." By 1670 John Ray was close to the modern version in *A Collection of English Proverbs:* "He is handsome that handsome doth."

Handwriting on the Wall. A portent or forewarning, usually of something ominous. The Old Testament Book of Daniel tells of an impious feast held by Belshazzar when he became king of Babylonia. During it (5 : 5): "In the same hour came forth fingers of a man's hand, and wrote over against the candlestick upon the plaster of the wall of the king's palace; and the king saw the part of the hand that wrote." Daniel is called in to interpret the message (MENE, MENE, TEKEL, UPHARSIN) and tells the king it means God has numbered the days of his kingdom, and it will be divided between the Medes and the Persians.

Hang Loose. Have a relaxed attitude. Originally (and still) a sports term, the advice is that you will play better if you don't let yourself get tense. Its meaning goes beyond sports, however, as Ellen Willis showed in *The New Yorker* in 1972: "In the meantime, my survival plan is to hang loose. . . ."

Hang by a Thread. Be in a perilous position; be threatened by imminent danger. It is from the story of Damocles in classical mythology. He was a courtier in the reign of Dionysius I of Syracuse in the fifth century B.C., and he was overeffusive in his praise of the ruler's power and happiness. Dionysius wanted to show him that power and happiness are precarious, so he gave Damocles a magnificent banquet. Damocles presumably enjoyed it until he happened to look up; over his head, and aimed at it, was an unsheathed sword suspended by a single hair. The analogy was in English by 1545, in the *Precepts of Cato:* "There are that fayneth it [life] to hange by an heere or a twynned threde."

Hang in Balance. To be undecided; of uncertain outcome. This is the "balance" of fate, by analogy to the ancient two-pan weighing device in which an object of unknown weight was put in one pan and known weights were added to the other until the pans balanced. The concept of a balance of fate dates at least from the 17th century, when it appeared in John Woodall's *The Surgions Mate* (1612): "Men's lives hang in the ballance."

Hang in There. Stick with it, even though the going is tough. Most likely the term is from boxing, for "hanging in there" is what a fighter momentarily getting the worst of it tries to do: cling to the ropes or the arms of his opponent for a respite. The expanded meaning was in evidence by 1971, as this passage from *The Atlantic* shows: "He [Nixon] has a long history of coming from behind, they say, and it would be in his nature to hang in there and fight."

Hanging Fire. Pending, particularly in the sense that something is not happening as soon as expected. It is from the days of muzzle-loading guns, when the charge of powder in the breech sometimes did not explode as quickly as the gunner thought it would; the gun was said to "hang fire."

Happy as a Clam. Quite satisfied with one's situation; feeling carefree. Here is one of those expressions that are mystifying if you think about them instead of just saying them. Who is to know the state of mind of a clam? The picture is clearer when you come upon the old form of the saying: "Happy as a clam dug at high tide." Clams are dug at low tide, so the assumption was that any right-thinking clam would be in the best frame of mind when the tide was high. *Knickerbocker Magazine* was able to say in 1838 that " 'happy as a clam' is an old adage." In Bartlett's *Dictionary of Americanisms* (1848) one finds: " 'Happy as a clam at high tide' is a very common expression in those parts of the coast of New England where clams are found."

Happy-go-lucky. Carefree, unconcerned. This is the only meaning of the phrase today, and it dates from the 19th century. Herman Melville has it in *Moby Dick* (1851): "A happy-go-lucky; neither craven nor valiant." An earlier meaning was haphazard, as luck would have it. It is seen in Edward Arber's *An English Garner* (1699): "The Redcoats cried, 'Shall we fall on in order, or happy-go-lucky?' "

Hard and Fast (Rule). Rigid; fixed. Another nautical term, originally referring to a ship that had run aground or was otherwise on land (as in drydock). In this sense it is found in Admiral William Henry Smyth's *The Sailor's Word-Book* (1867): "Said of a ship on shore." In the sense of something rigid it was around at the same time, being used by J. W. Henley in the House of Commons: "The House has deliberately, after long consideration, determined to have no 'hard and fast line.' "

Hard as Nails. Physically or mentally tough; referring to a person's mental outlook, it usually means that he or she is uncompromising and probably brusque. Charles Dickens had it in *Oliver Twist* (1837), where Fagin asks two of his gang of thieves if they have "been at work this morning." " 'Hard,' replied the Dodger. 'As Nails,' added Charley Bates."

Hat is in the Ring. I'm a candidate. Originally, dating from about 1820, in some places in the United States a man gave or accepted a challenge by throwing his hat in a ring made for boxing or wrestling. The political sense was typified by Theodore Roosevelt when he was running for President (unsuccessfully) in 1912: "My hat's in the ring. The fight is on and I'm stripped to the buff."

Haul Over the Coals. To discipline or upbraid someone. A medieval torture applied to religious heretics (among others) was to pull the victim over hot coals. One of William Fulke's many religious writings (this one dating from 1577) has this passage: "S. Augustine, that knewe best how to fetche an heretike ouer the coles." Today's much milder meaning seems to have developed around the beginning of the 19th century. Maria Edgeworth's *Popular Tales* (1804) has: " 'This is by way of calling me over the coals for being idle, I suppose!' said Sally."

Have No Truck With. Avoid association or dealings. An old meaning of "truck" is trade or barter, and by extension communication or dealings between people. Thus in John Fletcher's *The Chances* (1620): "Hark ye Frederick, What truck betwixt my infant—?" The meaning survives only in today's negative.

Have Your Cake and Eat It, You Can't. You can't have it both ways. Somehow this phrase has been stood on its head, so that it is now illogical; if you have your cake, you can still eat it. The original version was "you cannot eat your cake and have it too," and there logic lies, because if you have eaten it, you no longer have it. John Heywood's *Proverbs* had that version in 1546, and if it was a proverb then, it was already known. As he put it: "Wolde you bothe eate your cake, and haue your cake?"

Have Your Heart in Your Mouth. Be frightened or very anxious. The saying goes back at least to Gaius Petronius, who died in A.D. 66. In his *Satyricon* he said: "My heart was in my mouth."

Have a Bone to Pick. Have a point to argue about, a complaint to settle. In its earliest uses, dating to the 16th century, this expression meant mainly to debate or worry a fine point, as a dog worries a bone. The modern version, which dates to the 19th century, is more suggestive of what happens when there are two dogs and one bone. In British politics to "give one a bone to pick" has meant to get rid of a bothersome opponent or an embarrassing colleague by giving him a lucrative or high-sounding appointment that will effectively remove him from the scene.

Have a Field Day. Have a particularly enjoyable, easy or profitable time. In the 18th and 19th centuries a "field day" was an occasion when troops went onto open grounds for maneuvers or a review. The transferred meaning, still applying to a group activity in a fairly large space, was known by 1848, when it appeared in William Makepeace Thackeray's *The Book of Snobs:* "The mean pomp and ostentation which distinguish our banquets on grand field-days."

Have a Little Nip. Take a drink (usually of whiskey or brandy). This "nip" is apparently from "nipperkin," which long ago was a half-pint of ale and also served sometimes to describe a small quantity of spirits, usually less than a glass. Mrs. Aphra Behn's *Amorous Prince* (1671) has a character who says, " 'Tis something cold, I'le go take a Niperkin of wine."

Have and to Hold, To. To get something you're expected to keep, such as a spouse. The term is standard in marriage ceremonies, as in the *Book of Common Prayer* of the Episcopal Church and the Church of England: "To have and to hold from this day forward, for better for worse, for richer for poorer, in sickness and in health, to love and to cherish, till death us do part."

Head Over Heels. Completely; so fully taken up by something as to be unable to stop or withdraw (as one would be in a somersault). Catullus had the phrase in Latin *(per caputque pedesque)* around 60 B.C. In English it was originally (and more logically, since the head is usually over the heels), "heels over head." An example in 1768 was in Alexander Ross's *Helenore:* "Now by this time the house was heels o'er head." Still, the other version, which the *Oxford English Dictionary* calls "a corruption" of "heels over head," was around just as early, as in *The Contemplative Man* (1771): "He gave [him] such a violent involuntary kick in the Face, as drove him Head over Heels."

Head and Shoulders Above. Far exceeding. The reference is to the measure by which a tall person may tower over a short one. In this sense it appeared in Noah Webster's *American Dictionary* in 1864: "He is head and shoulders above them." Long ago the expression also meant to treat someone or something roughly or violently (probably in reference to seizing a person by the head and shoulders). Thus, in Sir Philip Sidney's *An Apologie for Poetrie* (1581): "All theyr Playes . . . thrust in Clownes by head and shoulders."

Head in the Clouds. Abstracted; absent-minded. It used to be "head in the air," but that apparently didn't convey the notion adequately and the head had to be extended all the way to the clouds. *Trawl* gave a sharp example of the characterization in 1903; "The Laureate crost over the lawn with the dreamy head-in-air gait that was known through five parishes round."

Heads Will Roll. Changes are going to be made in this organization (because things have gone wrong or there is a new boss). Adolf Hitler, harking back to the executions by guillotine during the French Revolution, appears to have coined this phrase, although he was being literal. In 1930 he said: "If our movement is victorious there will be a revolutionary tribunal which will punish the crimes of November 1918 [Germany's surrender in World War I]. Then decapitated heads will roll in the sand." The figurative meaning was in *Time* in 1961: "A.M.C. made it clear, too, that more heads would roll if the workers still failed to get the message."

Heap Coals of Fire on His Head. Return kindness for unkindness, good for evil. St. Paul said, in his letter to the Romans: "If thine enemy hunger, feed him; if he thirst, give him drink; for in so doing thou shalt heap coals of fire on his head." Much the same thing is said in the proverbs of Solomon, appearing in the Old Testament Book of Proverbs, with the addition that if you do those things, "the Lord will reward you." The implication seems to have been that the figurative coals would cause the enemy's heart or attitude to soften.

Hear No Evil. Disregard critical statements or rumors about a person or an organization; think the best. The positive version of the thought is embodied in a Latin phrase, *male audire*. Something like the modern thought appeared in the *Forme of Prayer of the Church of Scotland* in 1584: "If he haue . . . gouerned himselfe in such sorte as the worde of God hath not hearde euill." A legend relating to the Three Wise Monkeys, carved over a door of the Sacred Stable in Nikko, Japan, in the 17th century is: "Hear no evil, see no evil, speak no evil."

Hear a Pin Drop, You Could. The audience is very attentive; things are suddenly quiet after a din. Leigh Hunt may have originated the thought in *The Story of Rimini* (1816): "A pin-drop silence strikes all o'er the place."

Heart and Soul, With. Wholly; engaging all of one's interest or emotions. You do hear "with all my heart" but not often "with all my soul." Putting them together intensifies the statement. Eliza von Booth, who wrote as "Rita," was offering the intensive form in *After Long Grief* (1883): "I saw that you were mine, heart and soul, as ever."

Heart as Big as All Outdoors, A. Extremely generous or compassionate. "All outdoors" has meant everywhere or a great expanse since the early 19th century (mainly in the United States). John Neal wrote in 1825 (in *Brother Jonathan*) of a bear "big as all out o' doors." Probably the reference to hearts of comparable size is comparably old.

Heart of Gold, He Has. He is a kindly and generous man. In *King Henry V* Shakespeare has the king (in disguise) talking with soldiers in his camp, among them Pistol, who, being drawn out on his views of the king, says:

> The king's a bawcock, and a heart of gold,
> A lad of life, an imp of fame;
> Of parents good, of fist most valiant:
> I kiss his dirty shoe, and from heart-string
> I love the lovely bully. What is thy name?

Heart's Content, To One's. To the point of full satisfaction. Shakespeare had some fun with this saying, playing on the two meanings of "content," one with the first syllable accented and one with the second. One place he did so is in *King Henry VI, Part 2*, where the Duke of Suffolk, having married Margaret of Anjou as Henry's surrogate, brings her to the king, who says:

> Her sight did ravish; but her grace in speech,
> Her words y-clad with wisdom's majesty,
> Makes me from wondering fall to weeping joys;
> Such is the fulness of my heart's content.
> Lords, with one cheerful voice welcome my love.

Heart-to-heart Talk. A frank, intimate conversation. The expression seems not to have arrived in print until 1902, when it appeared in *Wolfville Days*, by A. H. Lewis: "He don't own no real business to transact; he's out to have a heart-to-heart interview with the great Southwest."

Heave a Sigh of Relief. Show gratitude that an ordeal is over or has been averted. Heaving usually entails fairly heavy physical work. The heaving of a sigh reflects fairly heavy emotion. The literary convention of heaved sighs dates at least to the 18th century, but the sigh of relief seems to have been recorded later. Matthew Prior's poem, *Answer to Cloe* (1718) has the line: "Heave thou no sigh, nor shed a tear."

Heavens to Betsy. That's astonishing; it's hard to believe. Charles E. Funk chose this expression as the title of one of his books before he attempted to trace its origin, which he was never able to do. One might imagine Betsy to be Elizabeth I, but she was popularly known as Bess, and in any case, the expression seems to have originated in the United States. The earliest printed version apparently is in R. T. Cooke's *Huckleberries from New England Hills* (1892): " 'Heavens to Betsy!' gasped Josiah."

Hell has No Fury Like a Woman Scorned. Beware the anger of a woman who thinks her dignity or worth has been affronted. The line comes from William Congreve's play *The Mourning Bride* (1697):

> Heav'n has no rage, like love to hatred turn'd,
> Nor Hell a fury, like a woman scorned.

Hell is Paved With Good Intentions. It isn't enough to promise good deeds; you must do them. The thought is often expressed as "the road to hell is paved with good intentions." A similar saying, going back to 1574, in *Guevara's Chronicles* by Edward Hellowes, is: "Hell is full of good meanings and wishes." The modern saying was picked up by John Wesley in his *Journal* (1736): "It is a true saying, Hell is paved with good intentions."

Hell to Pay. A reckoning is coming; the consequences will be severe. In 1811 the Duke of Wellington, in one of his dispatches as commander of the forces against Napoleon in the Peninsular War, wrote: "Unless the design has been altered . . . we shall have the Emperor in Spain and hell to pay before much time elapses."

Hell-bent for Election. Moving or acting recklessly, with great speed. People have been "hell-bent" for other things, as *Knickerbocker Magazine* reported in 1835 of a band of Indians, who were "hell-bent on carnage." To be "hell-bent for election" dates from 1840, when Edward Kent was running for governor of Maine. He won, and the event was marked by a song:

> Oh have you heard how old Maine went?
> She went hell-bent for Governor Kent.

Hell-for-leather. Going at top speed, perhaps recklessly. It's the kind of thing Rudyard Kipling would say to describe riding a horse hard and fast. He did say it, and may have coined it, in his "Story of Gadsbys" (1899): "Here, Gaddy, take the note to Bingle and ride hell-for-leather." The "leather" referred to the saddle, bridle and stirrups, which could be expected to take a beating in a hard ride.

Hem and Haw. To indicate uncertainty; to delay or avoid giving a direct response. Both words are representations of the sounds one makes when speaking hesitantly: a clearing of the throat, the "m'm" or "um" or "ah." The expression has over the centuries been rendered as "hum and ha," "hem and hawk" and "hum and haw." In 1469 it appeared in one of the *Paston Letters* as "humys" [hums] and "hays" [ha's or haws]: "He wold have gotyn it aweye by humys and by hays, but I wold not so be answeryd." Gervase Babington, in *A Profitable Exposition of the Lord's Prayer* (1580), wrote: "Wee gape and we yawne, we hem and we hawke."

Here Today and Gone Tomorrow. Transient; unreliable. This way of saying that things are fleeting was well known in the 16th century, when John Calvin wrote of the "prouerbe that man is here to-day and gone to morow."

Here, There and Everywhere. All over; something ubiquitous. In the past the same thought has been expressed also as "here and everywhere" and "here, there, all where." Even the present version is very old, having appeared in Christopher Marlowe's play, *The Tragical History of Dr. Faustus* (1590): "That I may be here and there and everywhere."

Hewers of Wood and Drawers of Water. The people who do the hard, essential work. The Bible tells us (Joshua 9 : 21): "And the princes said, Let them live; but let them be hewers of wood and drawers of water unto all the congregation."

Hide Your Light Under a Bushel. Conceal or disguise your talents. In the original version, which was in the form of advice from Jesus, the meaning was quite the opposite: One should not be modest about one's talents or message. As the Bible puts it (Matthew 5 : 14–15), Jesus says:

> Ye are the light of the world. A city that is set on a hill cannot be hid. Neither do men light a candle, and put it under a bushel [a container], but on a candlestick; and it giveth light unto all that are in the house, Let your light so shine before men, that they may see your good works, and glorify your Father which is in heaven.

Hide nor Hair, Neither. Nothing; invisible. As "in hide and hair," meaning wholly or entirely, the expression goes back to the 14th century, referring to the fact that an animal in hide and hair is all there. An example from Sir James Balfour's *Practicks* (1575) is: "He sall exhibite the samin cattel, in hyde and hair, at ane certane day and place." The negative meaning, apparently more recent, is found in Josiah G. Holland's *The Bay Path* (1857): "I haven't seen hide nor hair of the piece ever since."

High Dudgeon. A state of considerable anger, resentment or ill humor. One meaning of "dudgeon," largely forgotten now, is the hilt of a dagger, and some people think "high dudgeon" derives from the fact that a person in anger might raise his dagger high in preparation to strike. The *Oxford English Dictionary* is unpersuaded, treating the words as separate because "no connexion of sense" has been established. Samuel Butler wrote in *Hudibras* (1663) of a time "when civil dudgeon first grew high." I have always wanted to see or hear of someone in "low dudgeon."

High Horse, Get on a. To act in a superior or arrogant way. In ceremonial processions people of rank were often mounted on horses of unusual height to emphasize their prominence and so they could be seen better. The figurative meaning implies that the "rider" has made his own decision about his rank, that is, he is taking on airs. James Kelly, who published a collection of Scottish proverbs in 1721, had this one: "He is upon his high Horse, Spoken when People fall into a Passion."

High Jinks. Frolic; Revelry. "High jinks" was the name for what people sometimes did at drinking parties in the 17th and 18th century: a throw of the dice determined who should do a stunt for the group or chugalug a goodly quantity of liquor. Sir Walter Scott explained it at some length in *Guy Mannering* (1815):

> On the present occasion . . . the frolicsome company had begun to practise the ancient and now forgotten pastime of *High Jinks*. The game was played in several different ways. Most frequently the dice were thrown by the company, and those upon whom the lot fell were obliged to assume and maintain for a time a certain fictitious character, or to repeat a certain number of fescennine [scurrilous] verses in a particular order. If they departed from the character assigned, or if their memory proved treacherous in the repetition, they incurred forfeits. . . .

High and Dry. Out of it; stranded. The connection is with ships that were cast by storms or pulled onto shore or were put in dry dock. At one time the figurative meaning extended to rarefied or snooty, as in *Barchester Towers,* by Anthony Trollope (1857): "That party which is now scandalously called the high-and-dry church."

High and Mighty. In a position of power or influence; haughty, arrogant, too proud for one's own good. The second meaning is most heard now, said in reference to someone who takes on airs. Long ago the term was a common way of addressing the divinity or a ruler or some other prominent person. The other sense was in use by 1654, when it appeared in Richard Whitlock's *Zootomia*: "Book-learned Physitians, against which they bring in their high and mighty word Experience."

High-water Mark. The maximum point of some event or achievement. When a river or a stream floods, people keep track of the mark left on shores and buildings by the water when it was highest. The Earl of Dudley put the extended meaning neatly in a letter of 1814: "The high-water mark of English faction is very much below the ebb of French violence."

Hill of Beans, Not Worth a. Of little or no value; a trifle. The "bean" as an object of small worth goes way back; Robert of Gloucester had it in his *English Chronicles* in 1297, where he described a message from the king of Germany to King John as altogether "nas wurth a bene." The "hill," which is what beans are sometimes planted on, was added in the United States in the 19th century. It turns up in *My Southern Friends,* by Edmund Kirke (pen name of J. R. Gilmore) in 1863: "I . . . karn't take Preston's note—'taint wuth a hill o' beans."

Hit (Touch) the Spot. Satisfy fully; achieve what is desired. The original "spot" was surely the bull's-eye of a target for archery or firearms. The transfer puts the "spot" in one's mind or digestive tract. Here is *Putnam's Magazine* in 1868: "'I hope that last corjul set you up?' 'Yes, Mr. Plunkitt, it went right to the spot.' "

Hit Below the Belt. To act unfairly or against the rules. The rules of boxing, laid down in 1865 by the Marquess of Queensberry and John G. Chamber, forbade hitting below the belt. The transfer to any kind of unfairness in a contest dates from about that time.

Hit Pay Dirt. Succeed; get rich; find something valuable or useful. The miner was the first to "hit pay dirt," finding gold or silver or some other valuable mineral in the claim he was working. As a symbol of success the idea was in the language by 1884, when the *Century Magazine* had this: "He lives . . . in a style that proves that he has lots of pay dirt somewhere."

Hit or Miss. At random; haphazardly; to do something in awareness that one may succeed or fail. *Lusty Juventus*, by R. Wever (c. 1565) has this line: "I will go seeke them, whether I hyt or mysse." The thought was also put at times as "hittie missie," as in Thomas Wilson's *The Arte of Rhetorique* (1553): "Which shot in the open and plaine fields at all adventures hittie missie."

Hit the Nail on the Head. To say or do something just right; to arrive at the right conclusion. The Romans had a similar saying. In English the thought can be traced to 1508, when John Stanbridge put it in his *Vulgaria:* "Thou hyttest the nayle on the head." To literally hit a nail on the head is something not even the best of hammerers always do.

Hitch Your Wagon to a Star. Aim high; don't pitch your aspirations too low. Ralph Waldo Emerson appears to have originated the expression in his essay on "Civilization" in *Society and Solitude* (1870). The 18th-century poet Edward Young seems to have had the same advice in mind in his *Night Thoughts:* "Too low they build who build beneath the stars."

Hither and Yon. Here and there; back and forth; around and about. In older times the saying was also "here and yonder," which dates from the 15th century. "Hither" means here and "yon" is short for yonder. In 1836 *Tait's Magazine* carried this splendid version: "She swayed hither and yon, and was so coggly that I had fears of a catastrophe on the floor." "Coggly" means shaky.

Hive of Industry. A busy place, particularly a commercial one. It is essentially a tautology, since the beehive is so quintessentially a busy place as to have become a symbol for industriousness. The symbol was in use more than 100 years ago, as one sees in Patrick Barry's *Dockyard Economy and Naval Power* (1863): "A private shipyard is a hive of industry."

Hobson's Choice, A. No choice at all; you take the next item that comes up or you take nothing. This story is laid at the livery-stable of Tobias Hobson, who rented horses in Cambridge, England, at the beginning of the 17th century. He is said to have enforced a rule that the customer had to take the horse nearest the stable door rather than any particular one he might want from the stable. By 1617 Richard Cocks was saying in his *Diary in Japan:* "Once we are put to Hodgsons choise to take such previlegese as they will geve us, or else goe without."

Hog the Limelight. Seek excessively to be the center of attention, the cause of applause. "Limelight," which was generated by heating calcium oxide (the formal name for lime), was the first really effective lighting for the theatrical stage. It was developed for the theater by Thomas Drummond early in the 19th century and so for a time was called "Drummond light." One can assume that the first actor to "hog" it was to be observed soon after the invention.

Hoi Polloi. The common folk; the masses. "Hoi polloi" is a transliteration of the Greek for "the many," and so the usual rendering of the statement as "the hoi polloi" is equivalent to saying "the the many." But John Dryden did it in his *Essay of Dramatic Poesy* (1688): "If by the people you understand the multitude, the *hoi polloi,* 'tis no matter what they think. . . ."

Hoist by His Own Petard. A victim of his own device or plot. A "petard" was a medieval explosive device designed for blowing open gates and barricades. The art of handling gunpowder and fuses was imperfect then, and the petard sometimes went off too soon, blowing up the engineer who set it. In *Hamlet* Shakespeare develops a plot in which the king is arranging to send Hamlet to England with two disloyal college classmates who will be carrying orders to have him killed. Hamlet, telling his mother of the plot, says:

> There's letters seal'd: and my two schoolfellows,
> Whom I will trust as I will adders fanged,
> They bear the mandate; they must sweep my way,
> And marshal me to knavery. Let it work;
> For 'tis the sport to have the engineer
> Hoist with his own petard. . . .

Hold Forth. To declaim or harangue; to talk at length (usually on a particular subject); to present a point of view. In the sense of expounding a creed the phrase is in the Bible (Philippians 2 : 16): "Holding forth the word of life. . . ." The modern sense appears in Narcissus Luttrell's *Brief Historical Relation of State Affairs* (1693): "This week William Penn the quaker held forth at the Bull and Mouth in this citty."

Hold No Brief for. I don't represent him or go along with his argument. In law a "brief" is a statement of the facts in a case and a discussion of what are thought to be the relevant points of law. As long ago as the 17th century to "hold a brief" meant to be retained as counsel in a case. Now the expression, like so many others, is heard only in the negative.

Hold Your Horses. Take it easy; keep calm; don't do anything rash. It is what one had to do with horses when they began to get nervous or excited; by 1844 it had been extended to people, as in the *New Orleans Picayune:* "Oh, hold your horses, Squire. There's no use gettin' riled, no how."

Hold Your Own. Withstand attack or pressure. In 1350 it was "meyntene her [their] owne." The modern thought was put precisely in *The Pilgrimage of Perfection* (1526): "Be neuer ouercome in ony mater, but holde thyne owne."

Hold a Candle to Him, Can't. Can't compare with him. The now unheard positive version was what was done by hired lads called linkboys in the days before street lighting. A "link" was a torch. The boy would walk ahead of his employer, lighting the way with a link or candle. The occupation did not require much skill, and so the negative took on the meaning of someone who was inferior. In 1725 John Byrom published his "Epigram on the Feuds between Handel and Bononcini," with this verse:

> Some say, that Seignior Bononcini
> Compar'd to Handel's a mere Ninny;
> Others aver, to him, that Handel
> Is scarcely fit to hold a candle.

Hold at Bay. Keep a difficult or threatening situation from getting worse. This is "bay" from the old French *abai*, meaning the baying sound hounds make when they are pursuing or have cornered a quarry. In 1530 John Palsgreve, explaining certain French usages, gave one that translated: "Yonder stagge is almost yelden, I here the houndes hold hym at beye."

Hold the Bag. To be left in a foolish position; to be stuck with a responsibility; to be left in the lurch. To "give the bag" once meant, in England at least, to quit a job, and then it came to mean the opposite: to dismiss someone. The held bag was in print by 1793, when Thomas Jefferson used it: "She will leave Spain the bag to hold." In each case the "bag" was probably a figurative bag that was thought to contain something valuable or was expected to have something valuable put in it but turned out to be or to remain empty.

Hold the Fort. Keep things going while I'm away. The literal meaning was to defend a position at all costs, and it appears to have originated with General William Tecumseh Sherman, who signaled "Hold the fort!" to another general from the top of Kennesaw Mountain during a Civil War battle in 1864.

Hole in the Head, I Need It Like a. That's something so undesirable or ridiculous that I most definitely don't want it. The analogy is to a bullet hole, which in the head would most likely be fatal. The expression apparently originated as slang in the United States in the late 1940s.

Hollow Leg, He Has a. There seems to be no end to the amount of liquor or food he can put away. In 1926 *American Speech* said the name "John Hollow Legs" was "hobo lingo" for a hungry man.

Honest Injun. Really; I mean it; it's the truth. The European colonists who tangled repeatedly with the North American Indians from the 16th century until almost the beginning of the 20th were not likely to have had a high opinion of the Indian's veracity, and so the expression has a touch of sarcasm, as if an honest Indian was so rare that he could stand as a symbol for truth. Mark Twain had it in *Tom Sawyer* (1876): "Ben, I'd like to, honest Injun; but. . . ."

Honest as the Day is Long. A consistently reliable person. The implication seems to be that he or she is honest all the time, 24 hours a day. (A similar thought is in the story of a boy who told his grandmother he "didn't have time" to do something; she replied, "You had all the time there was.") The phrase seems to be of fairly recent origin; it was used in print by Richard Shattuck in *The Snark Was a Boojum* (1941).

Honest to Goodness. Really; for sure. An odd combination, since "honesty" is thought to be "good" and "goodness" presumably includes "honesty." The phrase is of American origin, I suspect by a child wanting to assure a parent that he is telling the truth. It became a colloquialism by about 1900. The way the phrase has expanded can be seen in *The Phantom Herd*, by B. M. Bower (a pseudonym of Bertha Sinclair), in 1916: "The real honest-to-goodness twelve-months-in-the-year West."

Hook or By Crook, By. By any means, fair or foul. The most plausible of the many explanations that have been advanced for this phrase is that under the medieval English laws regulating the king's forests people were allowed to pick up wood that had fallen to the ground or cut down such dead branches as could be removed "by hook or by crook," that is, a reaper's hook or a shepherd's crook. The *Oxford English Dictionary* remains skeptical, saying there is no hard evidence for any of the origins that have been proposed and adding that "most of them are at variance with the chronology." The chronology is ancient; the phrase "with hook or with crook" appears in one of John Wyclif's works of 1380.

Hook, Line and Sinker. Everything; all of it. The implication of this image from fishing is that the person who swallows a tale or an idea "hook, line and sinker" is rather gullible, since the tale or idea may not stand up to hard scrutiny. This phrase originated in the United States about the middle of the 19th century, but a much older English phrase ("to swallow a gudgeon") embodied the same idea. A gudgeon is a small fish used for bait. John Lyly in *Euphues* (1579) writes: "You have made both me and Philautus to swallow a Gudgen."

Hope Against Hope. To want something keenly even when the odds against getting or achieving it are enormous. The phrase derives from the Bible (Romans 4 : 18); Saint Paul is writing about Abraham, "Who against hope believed in hope, that he might become the father of many nations, according to that which was spoken."

Hope Springs Eternal. Some people are always optimistic, even in the severest adversity. The line is from Alexander Pope's *Essay on Man* (1733): "Hope springs eternal in the human breast."

Horns of a Dilemma, On the. Faced with a difficult choice in which each of the alternatives is unsatisfactory. A "lemma" is a proposition in argument, and a "dilemma" is an argument confronting an adversary with two or more alternatives, each of which he finds repugnant. In scholastic Latin this was *argumentum cornutum*, a horned argument. Nicholas Udall explained it in his *Apophthegmes* (1548): "Thys forked questyon; which the sophisters call an horned questyon, because that to whether of both partyes a bodye shall make a direct aunswere, he shall renne [run] on the sharpe poyncte of the horne."

Horse Sense. Common sense; shrewdness. The phrase is of 19th-century American origin, probably from someone who depended on his horse and took note of the horse's tendency to do the sensible thing, for example, to avoid situations that might cause a fall. In 1870 the *Nation* wrote of "the new phrase—born in the West, we believe—'horse sense,' which is applied to the intellectual ability of men who exceed others in practical wisdom."

Horse of a Different Color, A. A topic or a plan that represents a change from what one thought was being talked about or considered. Shakespeare offered the companion saying in *Twelfth Night* (1601), where Maria is offered a comment on her plans against

Malvolio and responds: "My purpose is, indeed, a horse of that colour." In 1798 the Philadelphia *Aurora* had a line on President John Adams, to whom the paper referred sarcastically as King John I: "Whether any of them may be induced . . . to enter into the pay of King John I is 'a horse of another color.' " One suspects the image originated in racing, where one might have bet on a horse of a certain color only to find that a horse of another color is winning.

Hot Stuff. A person, idea or activity worthy of unusual attention; the latest thing. It started out in the United States as slang in the 19th century and was known to a writer on the *Kansas City Star & Times* in 1889: " 'Miss Middleton's Lover.' Were there room for two more words in that last line, 'Hot Stuff' might be appropriate."

Hounds of Hell. Fearsome or dangerous people or animals. In Greek mythology Cerberus, fittingly portrayed as grim and frightening, was the three-headed dog that guarded the entrance to hell. The thought that more than one such creature might be abroad was even grimmer. Thus "hounds of hell," as in *The Mirour for Magistrates* (1587): "Iarring [jarring] like two hounds of hell."

Hour of Need. The time when one needs help or succor. Matthew Arnold knew of the expression in 1867, when he wrote "Rugby Chapel":

> Then, in such hour of need
> Of your fainting, dispirited race,
> Ye, like angels, appear,
> Radiant with ardour divine!

How Do You Like Them Apples? What do you think of that (usually in contrast to something else). The term probably originated in a comparison of certain apples with others in a marketplace. By the 1930's it was serving for almost any comparison. In Edward Albee's play, *The American Dream* (1961) Grandma says to Mrs. Barker: "They wanted satisfaction; they wanted their money back." Mrs. Barker responds, "My, my, my." Grandma says: "How do you like *them* apples?"

How Now, Brown Cow. What's up? What next? "Brown cow" is an old (18th century) and obsolete way of referring to a barrel of beer, and it is likely that the saying was originally meant as a suggestion that everybody have another beer in order to prolong a pleasant interlude at the tavern. It perseveres because of its catchy repetition of the "ow" sound. Allan Ramsay, who collected Scottish poems and sayings, said in his play *The Gentle Shepherd* (1725): "The auld anes think it best, With the brown cow to clear their een." The idea of "what next" apparently derives from the question of whether or not to have another beer.

Howling Wilderness. A disordered and frightening place or situation. It is a biblical phrase (Deuteronomy 32 : 10): "He found him in a desert land, and in the waste howling wilderness; he led him about, he instructed him, he kept him as the apple of his eye."

Hub of the Universe. Boston (by its own system of classification). The idea originated with Dr. Oliver Wendell Holmes, who in 1858 (*The Autocrat of the Breakfast-Table*) called his city "the hub of the solar system." *The New Yorker* said in 1948: "Boston hopes to regain its old position as Hub of the Universe by having a World Series between the Braves and the Red Sox."

Hue and Cry. An uproar or to-do over something. In the Middle Ages the *hu e cri* (a Norman-English phrase combining the French *huer* and *cri*, which mean respectively to shout and cry out) was a means of summoning help when one was the victim of a crime or a constable pursuing a criminal. Indeed, one who heard the call and failed to join the chase was subject to punishment.

Huff and Puff. Bluster; show the effects of exertion. Both words represent the sound of heavy breathing, as in anger, threat, exertion or blowing something up. It is in the last sense that the words first appear in print in one of Josuah Sylvester's works (1591): "Thy huff'd, puff'd, painted, curl'd, purl'd wanton Pride."

Hunky Dory. All right, safe, cozy. You can find several explanations for this one, including the fact that a major street in Yokohama, often frequented by American sailors, was Huncho-dori. "Hunk," however, is an old word, derived from the Dutch *honk*, meaning goal. Bartlett's *Dictionary of Americanisms* defined it in 1860: "To be all hunk is to have reached the goal . . . to be all safe." John Farmer's *Americanisms* (1889) had the whole expression, saying: "Both these strange words stand for superlatively good."

I Am Not My Brother's Keeper. I disclaim responsibility. In the biblical story of the brothers Cain and Abel, sons of Adam and Eve, Cain has killed Abel out of jealousy (Genesis 4 : 8–9): "And the Lord said unto Cain, 'Where is Abel thy brother?' And he said, I know not: 'Am I my brother's keeper?' "

I Wouldn't Touch It with a Ten-foot Pole. It's dangerous or disagreeable, and I intend to avoid it. The "ten-foot pole" is not an item ready to hand, and neither is the "barge pole," which figured in a similar expression. Still, they both serve as figures of speech, and so did "tongs." With "tongs" the expression was known by 1639, when John Clarke included it in his *Paroemiologia Anglo-Latino:* "Not to be handled with a paire of tongues." The "ten-foot pole" was in use in the expression by 1758, the "barge pole" by 1877.

Idle Chitchat. Vaporous talk. "Chitchat," formerly two words, is something of a nonsense word, like "tittle-tattle." It was apparently formed (early in the 18th century) because it sounded good and came trippingly off the tongue. Moreover, it seemed to reinforce the notion of idle chat. Before that it was indeed "idle chat." In 1616 someone who has come down in literature only as C. R. wrote *Times' Whistle,* which has this passage: "They will prate till they tire all men with their idle chatt."

If Worse Comes to Worst. If things get really bad. The thought is often put as "if worst comes to worst," which is how it was in *Discovery of the Knights of the Poste* (1597): "If the worst come to the worst, it is but the hiering of a hackney to ryde to London." The first "worst" may have been changed to "worse" by someone thinking of the grammatical progression: bad, worse, worst.

If the Shoe Fits, Wear It. You should acknowledge or accept a remark or a situation that applies to you. Since people aren't too likely to go around trying on odd shoes, the expression is odd. It is also fairly recent, having had for centuries a more logical predecessor, "the cap." "If the cap fits, put it on." That appeared in 1714 in *Molière,* by John Ozell.

Ill Will. Bad or hostile feeling. As "hill wil" in medieval English, the phrase appeared in *Cursor Mundi,* a poem dating from the early 14th century. Closer to the modern version is the wording in *The*

Boke of Duke Huon (1533) by John Berners: "Ye do me greate wronge to owe me youre yll wyll."

Ill-gotten Gains. Something obtained illegally or by trickery. The phrase is part of what was once a proverb: "Ill-gotten gains never prosper." Sometimes it was "evil-gotten," sometimes it was "goods" rather than "gains." In its earliest appearance in English (in William Horman's *Vulgaria* of 1519) it was: "Euyll gotten ryches wyll neuer proue longe."

Imagination Runs Riot. An idea (maybe even a bright one) has been carried too far. Hugh Miller had this expression, and may have originated it, in his *First Impressions of England* (1847): "The sculptor seems to have let his imagination altogether run riot."

Improve Each Shining Hour. Work hard; make the best of your waking hours. One of Isaac Watts' *Divine Songs* (1715) is *Against Idleness and Mischief.* It includes this verse:

> How doth the little busy bee
> Improve each shining hour
> And gather honey all the day
> From every opening flower!

In Full Cry. At a peak of activity, particularly a pursuit. The term is from fox hunting, which as a group activity was popular in England by the 16th century. The meaning had been extended by 1589, when Richard Harvey had the thought in *Plaine Perceuall:* "Will you . . . run upon a Christen body, with full cry and open mouth?"

In His Cups. Drunk. Long ago the phrase meant both drunk and participating in a drinking bout. It appears in one of the Apocryphal books of the Bible (1 Esdras 3 : 22): "And when they are in their cups, they forget their loue both to friends and brethren." The Romans had similar expressions, such as Cicero's "in thy cups, in the midst of thy revels" (*in ipsis tuis immanibus poculis*), suggesting the great age of the association of "cup" (*poculum*) and "carousal."

In His Element. In his most comfortable or favorable environment or situation. Hugh Broughton was close to the modern phrase in one of his letters (1599): "You are in for all day . . . it is your element."

In Hot Water. In trouble. What the original hot water was one cannot say; it may have been the potful that was pitched out the window at an intruder or a bothersome person below, or it may have been the hot water that cannibals were thought to boil their victims in. The Earl of Malmesbury thought it was a modern phrase in 1765, writing in one of his letters: "We are kept, to use the modern phrase, in hot water."

In One Ear and Out the Other. Heard but not remembered. Chaucer had this thought about boring remarks in *Troilus and Criseyde* (c. 1374): "Oon ere it herde, at tothir out it wente."

In Over His Head. Overextended; unable to cope because he has gone farther than his ability will carry him. The analogy is to swimming, including being ducked in the water as scolds and suspected witches once were. Richard Baxter offered the thought in 1653: "That silly women shall be dipt over head in a Gumble-stool for scolding?"

In a Nutshell. Briefly or concisely; encompassed in a small space. Various people have had fun with this idea over the centuries. Pliny said in his *Natural History*, nearly 2,000 years ago, that the *Iliad* had been copied in such a minute script that the entire work could be contained in a walnut shell. In about 1590 Peter Bales in England actually wrote a Bible small enough to go in a walnut shell. And so on. William Freke was closer to the modern meaning in *Select Essays* (1693): "Can we reduce the schoolmen to a Nut-shell?"

In a Pickle. In trouble; in a difficult situation. "Pickle" was originally not the edible that you pull out of a jar but the brine or vinegar the edible was preserved in. Hence, to "be in a pickle" was to be in an uncomfortable environment. John Foxe said in a sermon in 1585: "In this pickle lyeth man by nature, that is, all wee that be Adams children."

In a Pig's Eye. Never; highly unlikely. Whether the originator of this saying meant that a poor idea was something to put in a pig's eye or that it would look bad to a pig's eye is a matter of speculation. As an expression of scorn the expression was picked up in 1872 by Petroleum V. Nasby (David Locke) in one of his satirical newspaper columns: "A poetickal cotashun . . . which . . . wuz,—'Kum wun, kim all, this rock shel fly From its firm base—in a pig's eye.' "

In a Rut. Adhering to a routine (usually with the implication that one could or should get out of it). The figurative meaning must have been in use centuries ago, when ruts in unpaved roads were a commonplace hazards and vehicles were forever getting stuck in them, but it seems first to have appeared in print in Thomas Carlyle's *Essay on Chartism* (1839): "Parliaments, lumbering along in their deep ruts of commonplace."

In a Trice. Quickly; soon. "Trice" as a verb meaning to pull or haul on a rope is almost forgotten now, but it is apparently the source of the noun, which suggests the quick achievement of something by one pull of the rope. At first it was "at a trice," as in *Ipomydon* (1440): "The howndis [hounds] . . . Pluckid down dere all at a tryse." The modern expression is almost as old, turning up in

John Skelton's *Phyllyp Sparowe* (1505):
> To tell you what conceyte
> I had then in a tryce
> The matter were too nyse.

In a Word. Briefly. A bit of hyperbole is usually involved here, since what follows is quite likely to be more than a word. In *The Two Gentlemen of Verona* Shakespeare has Valentine describe Proteus to the Duke of Milan:
> His years but young, but his experience old;
> His head unmellow'd, but his judgement ripe;
> And, in a word, far beyond his worth
> Comes all the praises that I now bestow,
> He is complete in feature and in mind
> With all good grace to grace a gentleman.

In at the Death. Present at the end (usually of something grim or combative). The literal term is from fox hunting, where it dates from at least the 18th century as a way of saying one was present when a party of hunters and hounds ran a fox to ground and killed it. William Windham showed the extended meaning in *Speeches in Parliament* (1800): "For the empty frame of being in at the death."

In the Arms of Morpheus. Asleep and most likely dreaming. The phrase is something of a literary affectation, and those who affect it do not always seem to realize that Morpheus was the god of dreams, the son of the god of sleep. John Lydgate, in *The Assembly of the Gods* (1420), wrote of being carried off: "Anone came in Morpheus & toke me by the sleue [sleeve]."

In the Bag. Success is assured. Although you can hear it asserted that the "bag" here is a shopping bag or a similar object made to carry merchandise, a more plausible origin seems to be the hunter's game bag. When something was in that, you had it for sure. Thus, in the *Book of St. Albans* (1486): "You most take a partrich in yowre bagge."

In the Doghouse. In someone's (often a spouse's) bad graces; being punished, usually by silence or scorn. The figurative doghouse may have arisen from an episode in James M. Barrie's *Peter Pan* (1904), in which Mr. Darling treats Nana, the Newfoundland dog who is the guardian and great favorite of his children, rather badly; the children are offended and go away, and Mr. Darling lives in the dog's house as penance until they return.

In the Groove. Working or playing well. The thought of being "in a groove" as running or working in a fixed channel goes back quite a bit, as when Sir Arthur Helps wrote in 1868 that "his ideas were wont to travel rather in a groove." The current sense seems to have come from the record player in the days when it was called a phonograph and depended solely on a needle running in a groove in the record.

In the Heat of the Battle. At a time of intense excitement, emotion or action. In *The Progresses and Public Processions of Queen Elizabeth*, written almost 200 years ago, John Nichols quotes the Queen as having said in 1588, at the time of the Spanish Armada; "Being resolved, in the midst of the heat of battle, to live amongst you all." A similar expression of cliché status is "in the heat of the moment."

In the Long Run. In the distant future; over the course of a long period of action or development. The allusion is to a race, as between the tortoise and the hare, in which the contestant who leads at the outset may not wind up as the winner. The saying used to be "at the long run," and in that form it served Oliver Cromwell in a speech in 1656: "They [the discontented] must end at the interest of the Cavalier at the long run."

In the Pink. In good health; in tip-top condition. "Pink" has an astonishing number of meanings, one of which is as a general name for the popular garden flower of the genus *Dianthus*. By extension the phrase came to mean the flowering or finest example of something, an object or person at the height of its kind. Since about 1900 it has been limited to health, but earlier it meant excelling in anything—even bad taste—as in this ironical example from G. S. Carey's *Hills of Hybla* (1767):

> Behold her sailing in the pink of taste,
> Trumpt up with powder, frippery and paste.

In the Toils. In the grips of; captured. "Toils," a netlike enclosure for capturing animals, is a noun that serves now only in the cliché. One sees both the literal and the figurative meaning in Aesop's fable *The Lion, The Fox, and the Beasts:* "While I see many hoof marks going in, I see none coming out. It is easier to get into the enemy's toils than out again."

In the Twinkling of an Eye. Very quickly. The phrase is from St. Paul (1 Corinthians 15 : 51–52): "Behold, I shew you a mystery: We shall not all sleep, but we shall all be changed, In a moment, in the twinkling of an eye, at the last trump: for the trumpet shall sound, and the dead shall be raised incorruptible, and we shall be changed."

Independent as a Hog on Ice. Self-assured, cocky. You can come across people in the United States who have never heard this saying, and others who have heard it all their lives. The late Charles E. Funk, who titled one of his books *A Hog on Ice*, could not believe the four-footed animal would be very independent on ice; quite the contrary. He concluded that the "hog" here is the Scottish term (sometimes spelled "hogg") for the heavy stone used in the game of curling. Once it is started down the ice, it is

140

quite independent. Likewise, if it stopped and remained as an obstacle, it would be quite independent. The *Century Dictionary* in 1889, discussing the curling-stone "hog," offered this thought: "Origin obscure; by some identified with hog (i.e., swine), as 'laggard stones that manifest a pig-like indolence,' or, it might be thought, in allusion to the helplessness of a hog on ice, there being in the United States an ironical simile, 'as independent as a hog on ice.' " Funk found that the expression was known in all the northern states from Maine to Illinois and in many southern states (sometimes as "pig" rather than "hog"), but was unfamiliar west of the Mississippi.

Indian Giver. Someone who demands the return of an object he was thought to have offered as a gift; thus, a two-faced person. The Smithsonian Institution, issuing in 1907 a *Handbook of American Indians,* ascribed this saying to "an alleged custom among Indians of expecting an equivalent for a gift or otherwise its return." The term was known by 1764, when Nathaniel Ames put it in a letter: "We Americans well know what is meant by an Indian gift—that is, to make a present but expect more in return than we give."

Inner Man, The. The soul; the seat of one's feelings. Here is another of St. Paul's contributions (Ephesians 3 : 16): "That he [Christ] would grant you, according to the riches of his glory, to be strengthened with might by his Spirit in the inner man. . . ."

Innocent as a Lamb. Naive; free of responsibility. The adult sheep does not turn many people on, but the newborn lamb is seen as cute, vulnerable and innocent. Shakespeare picked up the thought and the phrase in *Henry VI, Part 2,* where the king says: "My lords . . . our kinsman Gloucester is as innocent from meaning treason to our royal person as is the suckling lamb or harmless dove. . . ."

Ins and Outs. The ramifications of a situation or the changes in it; the people in politics who hold office and the ones who don't. The first meaning turned up in 1670 in a memorial by Bishop John Hacket on John Williams, archbishop of York: "Follow their Whimsies and their In and Outs at the Consulto, when the Prince was among them." The second meaning is in one of Lord Chesterfield's letters (1764): "I believe that there will be something patched up between the *ins* and the *outs.*"

Iron Hand in a Velvet Glove. Disguised firmness; a gentle demeanor concealing a resolute personality. Thomas Carlyle wrote in *Latter-Day Pamphlets* (1850): "Soft of speech and manner, yet with an inflexible vigour of command . . . 'iron hand in a velvet glove,' as Napoleon defined it." Napoleon seems to have originated the phrase.

It Never Rains but It Pours. Often, when you've been waiting a long time for something, you get too much of it. One can hear the lament of the farmer and the gardener, who keep hoping for rain and then get a heavy storm that damages their plants. *It Cannot Rain But It Pours* was the title of a work by John Arbuthnot in 1726. An example of the broader meaning was offered by Charles Kingsley in *Yeast* (1848): "It never rains but it pours, and one cannot fall in with a new fact or a new acquaintance but next day twenty fresh things shall spring up as if by magic."

It'll All Come Out in the Wash. We'll find out sooner or later what's going on, and we needn't worry about it now. The literal thought is that dirt on an item of clothing will be dissolved eventually in the washing. An old form of the saying, used by Cervantes in *Don Quixote* (1612), is: "All will away in the bucking." To "buck" cloth or clothing was to steep it in lye as a form of bleaching. Henry Festing Jones, who collaborated with the novelist Samuel Butler, once quoted Butler as saying in 1876: "As my cousin's laundress says, 'It will all come right in the wash.' "

It's Not the Heat, It's the Humidity. The real problem is different from what it seems to be; I'm bothered not by the obvious difficulty but by a related one. Since the weather is a well-worn topic of conversation, this saying was probably in the spoken language long before it appeared in Langdon Mitchell's play, *The New York Idea* (1906): "It's not so much the heat as the humidity."

It's a Dilly. It's something; it's remarkable. This "dilly" comes from the first syllable of "delightful" or "delight" and has a British ring to it. Indeed, its first recorded appearance in print was in *Punch* (1909): "I sent out the ordinary cards . . . with 'Dancing' in one corner of the card, but in the *other* corner was 'Bare feet'. Wasn't it a dilly idea?"

It's the Pits. It's bad or unpleasant; it's the worst. Although the expression isn't very old, having originated in the United States about 10 years ago, the kind of "pit" originally referred to is lost. "Coal pit," "armpit," "automobile racetrack pit" (the scene of hectic, grueling and nerve-wracking action)? Woody Allen wrote in *The New Yorker* in 1977 that "watching TV all day is the pits."

Ivory Tower. A place remote from reality. The term was originated (in French) by the 19th-century French writer Charles Augustin Sainte-Beuve in a poem of 1837, where, referring to Victor Hugo and Alfred de Vigny, he wrote: "Hugo, strong partisan . . . - fought in armor, and held high his banner in the midst of the tumult; he still holds it; and Vigny, more discreet, as if in his tower of ivory, retired before noon."

J

Jaundiced Eye. A prejudiced view. Jaundice, a condition brought on by several diseases, turns various parts of the body yellow (*jaune* is the French word for yellow). Among them may be the eyes. It was once believed that the person looking through such eyes saw everything as yellow. By extension, the jaundiced eye came to mean a prejudiced view, usually rather negative or critical. Bishop Joseph Hall said in 1640, in one of his many religious writings: "Jaundised eies seem to see all objects yellow. . . ." Alexander Pope, in *An Essay on Criticism* (1711), wrote:

> All seems infected that the infected spy,
>
> As all looks yellow to the jaundiced eye.

John Hancock. One's signature. The biggest and boldest signature on the Declaration of Independence was that of John Hancock of Massachusetts. The same significance attaches to "John Henry." That version originated in the American West in the 19th century, but who John Henry was is unknown. In *Western Words* (1981), a collection of cowboy expressions, Ramon Adams writes: "John Henry is what the cowboy calls his signature. He never signs a document, he puts his *John Henry* to it."

Johnny-come-lately. A newcomer; someone inexperienced in the field under discussion. A British expression from the early 19th century is "Johnny Newcome," applied to a sailor newly assigned to a naval ship. Sometimes it was "Johnny Raw." "Johnny-come-lately" is apparently the American version of the same thought and dates from the 19th century. It appeared in *The Adventures of Harry Franco*, by Charles F. Briggs (1839): " 'But it's Johnny Comelately, aint it, you?' said a young mizzen topman."

Jot or Tittle. A minute amount (or nothing, as in the saying "not one jot or tittle"). "Jot" is a variant of the Greek iota, the letter *i*, which was the smallest letter in the Greek alphabet; "tittle" is the dot over the *i*. The phrase appears in the Bible (Matthew 5 : 18), where Jesus says, "For verily I say unto you, Till heaven and earth pass, one jot or one tittle shall in no wise pass from the law, till all be fulfilled."

Jury-rigged. A temporary or makeshift repair. The term comes from the older "jury mast," which was defined as follows in the *Seaman's Grammar* (1627): "A Iury Mast, that is, when a Mast is borne by the boord [lost], with Yards, Roofes, Trees, or what they can, spliced or fished together they make a Iury-mast." "Jury-rigged" was explained in Thomas Newte's *A Tour of England and Scotland in 1785:* "The ship is to be jury-rigged: that is, to have smaller masts, yards, and rigging, than would be required for actual sailing." The source of "jury" here is unknown; it may be the French *jour,* meaning day, so that "jury" would have meant something done for the day.

Keep Up With the Joneses. Try to live in the style of one's neighbors or acquaintances (usually with the implication that the effort is straining or exceeding one's financial or social resources). "Keeping Up with the Joneses" was the title of a comic strip which ran in many United States newspapers from 1913 to 1931. The originator, Arthur R. ("Pop") Momand, based it on his own experiences as a newly married young man making $125 a week and living in Cedarhurst, New York. He originally intended naming the strip "Keeping Up with the Smiths," but changed to the Joneses because it seemed "more euphonious."

Keep Your Eyes Peeled. Be on the lookout or alert. The reference is probably to the apple, orange, potato and so on that are better (or useful only) if they are peeled. A newspaper in the United States (*The Political Examiner* of Shelbyville, Kentucky) was recording the advice as early as 1833, although there it was "keep your eye skinned." In 1853 the *Daily Morning Herald* in St. Louis offered this advice: "Young man! Keep your eye peeled when you are after the women."

Keep Your Fingers Crossed. To hope that something spoken, thought of or put in train will succeed, or that nothing will happen to make it fail; wish me luck. Making the sign of the cross to ward off danger or evil is an old superstition that probably was the origin of this saying, and so one would suppose the saying is quite ancient. It seems, however, to have become popular in England around 1920 and in the United States around 1930.

Keep Your Head Above Water. Stay solvent (barely); avoid disaster. It is the way one avoids drowning, and so it extends readily to the avoidance by struggle of other kinds of disaster, mostly financial. Henry Fielding had it in *The History of the Adventures of Joseph Andrews* (1742): "If I can hold my head above water it is all I can."

Keep Your Powder Dry. Stay prepared for action. In the days when the powder and the ball were loaded into a gun separately, you had to keep your powder dry or the gun would not fire. Oliver Cromwell sealed the expression into the language during his expedition into Ireland in 1649; addressing his troops as they were about to cross a river to begin an attack, he said; "Put your trust in God; but be sure to keep your powder dry."

Keep Your Shirt On. Stay calm; don't get riled. A tendency of a man who thinks he is about to get into a fight is to pull off his coat, and perhaps his shirt, so that he has free use of his arms. Probably this is the source of the expression, which was known by 1854 when it appeared in *The Spirit of the Times*, by George W. Harris: "I say, you durned ash cats, just keep yer shirts on, will ye?"

Keep a Stiff Upper Lip. Remain stoical; maintain one's courage; do not show emotion in an adverse situation. John Neal used it in *Down Easters* (1833): "What's the use of boohooin'? . . . Keep a stiff upper lip; no bones broke—don't I know?" The saying arises from the fact that a prelude to crying is a trembling of the upper lip; the advice is to keep it firm and not to weep. The British have an expression almost as old: "Keep your pecker up." The "pecker" here is an analogy to the beak of a bird.

Keep the Ball Rolling. Take action to sustain a conversation or an activity. The popularity of the phrase in the United States can be traced to the presidential campaign of 1840, when supporters of William Henry Harrison took to rolling big balls in political parades and chanting "keep the [Harrison] ball rolling." The British have an expression, "keep the ball up" or (sometimes) "rolling." It is a figure drawn from what happens in such games as soccer and tennis.

Keep the Pot Boiling. Sustain an activity at a brisk rate. Peter Heylin was between the literal and figurative uses of the saying in 1657, when he wrote: "So poor, that it is hardly able to keep the Pot boiling for a Parsons Dinner." In 1825 John T. Brockett, in *A Glossary of North Country Words*, recorded that the saying was "a common expression among young people, when they are anxious to carry on their gambols with spirit."

Kick In the Seat of the Pants. Admonish; spur somebody to an action he should be performing. Although it is more often a figurative kick than a literal one, Samuel Butler explained both in *Hudibras* (1663):

> But Hudibras gave him a twitch
> As quick as lightning in a breech,
> Just in the place where honour's lodg'd,
> As wise philosophers have judg'd;

Because a kick in that place more
Hurts honour than deep wounds before.

Kick In the Shins. An affront; a setback. The literal "kick" is easy to deliver when you are trying to show your anger at or disapproval of someone's actions or words. To receive one is chastening and humiliating, an experience that provides the basis for the figurative meanings. The same thought was put long ago as "to come over the shins." Thomas Nashe, in a book with a lengthy title that can be abbreviated as *Pasquill and Marforius* (1589), wrote: "To come ouer our shinnes with the same rebuke that hee gaue to Phillip."

Kick Up (Stir Up, Make) a Fuss. Complain; demand action; blow off steam. The *Oxford English Dictionary* suggests that "fuss" may be "echoic" of something sputtering or bubbling, or of a person puffing and blowing. James Beresford put the meaning in *The Miseries of Human Life* (1806): "You have both been making a great fuss about nothing."

Kick Up Your Heels. Show spirit; have a good time. The great irony of this expression is that it used to mean "to die," the phrase, used in that sense, dates from around 1500. The expression now conveying "to die" is "turn up your heels." Then there is the expression "kick your heels," meaning to wait, as in a doctor's office. The cliché probably derives from the action of high-spirited horses and dancing people.

Kick the Bucket. To die. You can choose between two ideas about the origin of this phrase. One is that, in part of England at least, a bucket is not only a pail but also a beam or yoke from which a slaughtered pig was hung by the heels. The other is that the bucket (the pail) has often been the means by which a person bent on suicide carried out his purpose, standing on a bucket, fixing a rope around his neck and then kicking the bucket. In any event, the phrase was known by 1785, when Francis Grose defined it in *A Classical Dictionary of the Vulgar Tongue* as meaning to die.

Kid-Glove Treatment. Extremely gentle handling. The kid glove, made of skin from the kid, or young goat, was once a symbol of elegance and gentility. As wearers of kid gloves were unlikely to engage in roughhousing, the symbol also came to represent delicacy in one's dealings. You can see the idea developing in Henry Hall Dixon's *The Post and the Paddock* (1856): "He was, in fact, a mere kid-glove sportsman."

Kill Two Birds With One Stone. Achieve two objectives with a single effort. It would be remarkable indeed if someone slinging a stone at a bird got one bird, let alone two. Ovid had a similar expression in Latin nearly 2,000 years ago. Related phrases were in English and French literature by the 16th century. Thomas

Hobbes used the modern version in a work on liberty in 1656: "T. H. thinks to kill two birds with one stone, and satisfy two arguments with one answer."

Kill the Fatted Calf. Prepare for a celebration. The phrase comes from the parable related by Jesus of the prodigal son (Luke 15 : 11–32), in which one of a man's two sons ventured "into a far country, and there wasted his substance with riotous living" while the other stayed home and helped his father. When the departed son returned, repentant, the father said to his servants: "And bring hither the fatted calf, and kill it; and let us eat, and be merry: For this my son was dead, and is alive again; he was lost, and is found."

Kill the Goose That Lays the Golden Eggs. Destroy (through greediness) a source of money, or something else of value. The notion springs from a Greek fable about a farmer who owns a goose that lays eggs of gold. He decides that if he kills the goose, he will get all the eggs at once instead of only one at a time. Then he will be rich. The killed goose, of course, lays no more eggs.

King's English. The language, when it is well written or well-spoken. It is an old term, turning up in Shakespeare's *The Merry Wives of Windsor*, but also earlier, sometimes as the "Queene's English." One of the first examples is apparently in Thomas Wilson's *Arte of Rhetorique* (1553): "These fine English clerkes will saih thei speake in their mother tongue, if a manne should charge them for counterfeityng the kinges Englishe."

Kit and Caboodle, The Whole. Everything; the whole lot. Boodle (or buddle) is an old word, and probably evolved from the Dutch *boedel*, possession, meaning a crowd or a bunch; "the whole boodle" was heard as long ago as the early 19th century. Kit is also a time-honored word with many meanings, one of which is a collection of tools or possessions that a person might carry around; "the whole kit" was in use by 1785. Caboodle is essentially a nonsense word, perhaps created by combining "kit and boodle," which once was the wording of the phrase. Stephen Crane's *The Red Badge of Courage* (1895) contains it: "Of course it might happen that the hull kit-and-boodle might start and run, if any big fighting came first-off."

Knee-high to a Grasshopper. Short; young. The phrase was around by 1851, when the *Democratic Review* offered it this way: "You pretend to be my daddies; some of you who are not knee-high to a grasshopper!" Early 19th–century examples include knee-high to a frog, a mosquito, and a toad.

Knock the Spots Off. Win soundly. The spots here are a mystery. One notion maintains they were the spades, clubs, etc., marked on playing cards and sometimes used as targets in pistol shooting. Good shots could knock the spots off. Another idea is that they were facial blemishes or freckles; someone who was roundly trounced in a fight could be said to have had his spots knocked off. The phrase seems to have originated in the United States in the 19th century. It appeared in *Porter's Spirit of the Times*, a Vermont publication, in 1856, in an article on the breeding of Morgan horses: "Addison County leads the van (or 'knocks the spots off,' as we say here in Vermont) and is celebrated over the world for its fine horses."

Know Him From Adam, I Don't. He's a stranger to me. This is the biblical Adam, the first man, who presumably would be unrecognized by anyone today. Charles Dickens used the saying in *The Old Curiousity Shop* (1840): "He called to see my Governor this morning . . . and beyond that I don't know him from Adam."

Know the Ropes. To be familiar with the details of a task or a situation. Old sailing ships had a vast number of ropes to control their sails, and a crewman could not be very effective until he knew which rope did what. This is probably the origin of the phrase. Its first appearance in print seems to have been in Richard Henry Dana's *Two Years before the Mast* (1840): "The captain, who . . . 'knew the ropes,' took the steering oar."

Knows What Side His Bread Is Buttered On. Keeps in mind where his interest lies, where his income comes from. Bread is tastier with butter than without it, and one would take pains to see that at least one side was buttered. The saying is old enough to have been included in John Heywood's *Proverbs* (1546): "I knowe on whiche syde my breade is buttred."

Knuckle Down. To address seriously the business at hand. Most likely it is from the game of marbles, although other notions have been put forward. Dyche and Pardon's *A New General English Dictionary* (1740) defined it as "a particular phrase used by lads at a play called taw, wherein they frequently say *knuckle down to your taw*, or fit your hand exactly in the place where your marble lies."

Knuckle Under. To submit; to acknowledge defeat or another's mastery. At one time the end of a bone at any joint, such as the knee, was called a knuckle. When one went to one's knees, one was knuckling. Indeed, until the 19th century the thought was usually put as "knuckle" or "knuckle down." Perhaps the earliest appearance of the modern term was in Mary E. Braddon's *Mount Royal* (1882): "They must all knuckle under to him."

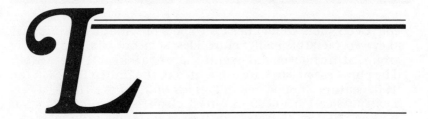

Labor of Love. Something done out of affection or deep interest rather than for money. It is a phrase from Saint Paul (1 Thessalonians 2–3): "We give thanks to God always for you all, making mention of you in our prayers; Remembering without ceasing your work of faith and labour of love, and patience of hope in our Lord Jesus Christ, in the sight of God . . . ."

Lame Duck. An officeholder whose term is expiring and who is not running or cannot run for reelection; particularly one whose successor has already been elected. The British phrase that contains the same words is older than the one in the United States and also has a different meaning: someone who cannot meet his obligations. It came from the early London stock market, which was in Exchange Alley until 1773. A stockbroker who had been cleaned out in the market was known as a lame duck because he "waddled out of the Alley." The American meaning, which dates from about the time of the Civil War, may have been a transfer of the British expression, or it may have derived from hunting: a duck wounded by a hunter is not very effective either as a duck or a hunting trophy.

Land of Milk and Honey. A place or situation full of good things. It is from the episode where the Lord talks to Moses on the mountain, saying (Exodus 3 : 8): "And I am come down to deliver them out of the land of the Egyptians, and to bring them up out of that land unto a good land and a large, unto a land flowing with milk and honey . . . ."

Lap of Luxury, In the. Well off; in a cushy situation. A child sitting in its mother's or father's lap is in a comfortable and comforting position; the image of luxury as a lap was a natural extension, and had been made by 1802, when it appeared in Maria Edgeworth's *Moral Tales*: "Brought up in the lap of luxury."

Last But Not Least. A person or thing that comes at the end of a list or a line but is nonetheless important (or perhaps isn't, but the reciter of the list doesn't want to seem to be slighting the last item). Reciters were using the construction as early as 1580, when John Lyly wrote, in *Euphues and His England*: "Of these three but one can stand me in steede, the last, but not the least."

Last Gasp. The end, or almost the end. The phrase appears in the Apocrypha of the Bible (2 *Maccabees* 7 : 9): "When he was at the last gasp." Shakespeare used it in *King Henry VI (Part 1)*, where La Pucelle (Joan of Arc) says: "Fight till the last gasp; I will be your guard."

Last Laugh, Have the. Score a belated or unexpected triumph; get revenge. It is a most human tendency to laugh in a gloating fashion when one succeeds over someone else; it is an even stronger tendency to find that the tables have turned. In John Ray's *A Collection of English Proverbs* (1742), the thought appears as: "Better the last smile than the first laughter."

Last Legs, On His. Near death or collapse or failure; at the end of his resources. It is an odd way of expressing the thought, and probably springs from the observation that an old and infirm person, or animal, tends to totter. Philip Massinger used it in his play, *The Old Law* (1599): EUGENIA: "My husband goes upon his last hour now." FIRST COURTIER: "On his last legs, I am sure."

Last Resort. The final place to turn for help; the last maneuver. People were saying it by 1672, when Sir William Temple put it thus in an essay on government: "All Government is a Restraint upon Liberty; and under all the Dominion is equally Absolute, where it is in the last Resort."

Last Straw. One thing too much. The picture here is of a horse or a camel being loaded with something that starts out not being burdensome but that as it is added to will at some point overload the beast. In the earliest version it was "feathers on a horse's back"; as Archbishop John Bramhall put it in 1655: "It is the last feather that breaks the horse's back." The camel turns up in Charles Dickens' *Dombey and Son* (1848): "As the last straw breaks the laden camel's back, this piece of underground information crushed the sinking spirits of Mr. Dombey."

Last-Ditch Effort. A struggle made in or a thrust made from one's last line of defense. On a battlefield a ditch is a better place than open ground for taking a defensive stand. King William III of England (r. 1689–1702) is said to have been the originator of the phrase, telling his associates: "I will die in the last ditch." Bishop Gilbert Burnet did not think much of the strategy, saying in *History of His Own Time* (1715): "There was a sure way to see it lost, and that was to fight in the last ditch."

Laugh Out of Court. Cover with scorn or ridicule; show that an argument is worthless. The phrase "out of court" as a means of saying someone's arguments are too poor or trifling to claim serious consideration (as in a court of law) goes back at least to the

151

early 19th century. Adding the thought that the claim is so ridiculous as to be laughable is much more recent. An early example is from the London *Observer* in 1928: "Both American and British opinion is laughing out of court those who monger their scares about the United States Navy."

Laugh Out of the Other Side of Your Mouth. To change from mirth to chagrin, exultation to anger, as a result of a reversal of one's fortunes. Giovanni Torriano, in a work on Italian proverbs in 1666, wrote: "The English say, when one hath conveniently reveng'd ones self on another; Now you can laugh but on one side of your mouth, friend."

Laugh Up Your Sleeve. To be amused or to gloat a bit without giving it away. It was easy to conceal a laugh or a derisive smile in a sleeve when people wore loose and flowing garments, so the expression probably had a literal as well as a figurative meaning in the 16th century, when John Heywood listed it as a proverb—and quite likely earlier. Heywood's version was: "To that I said nought, but laught in my sleeue."

Law and Order. The social condition as most people want it, in which laws exist and are obeyed or enforced. It is a reinforcing phrase, since "law" and "order" go hand in hand although it is possible to have one without the other. Sir T. Wemyss Reid picked up the phrase in his *Life of W. E. Forster* (1881): "To support the Lord-Lieutenant . . . in maintaining law and order in this country [Ireland]."

Law is an Ass, The. Legalism sometimes gets carried to an absurdity. Charles Dickens made this thought prominent in *Oliver Twist* (1838): " 'If the law supposes that,' said Mr. Bumble . . . 'the law is a ass—a idiot.' " Dickens did not originate it, though; it appears in George Chapman's *Revenge for Honour* (1634): "I am ashamed the law is such an ass."

Lay Down the Law. Issue orders; make dogmatic statements. It is often said in irony, since the person referred to is merely blustering. Here is Samuel Foote, in *The Orators* (1762): "I tell thee what, Ephraim, if thee canst but once learn to lay down the law, there's no knowing what thee may'st rise." To "lay down," in the sense of establish or formulate, is an old usage; John Mirk's *Festial*, dating from about 1450, has this passage: "Holy chirche leyth downe songes of melody as Te deum lau. Gloria in excelsis."

Lay It On With a Trowel. Overdo something; apply something (such as flattery) heavily. In *As You Like It* (1598) Shakespeare has Celia say, in response to a remark by Touchstone, "Well said: that was laid on with a trowel."

Lay On, Macduff. Do your damndest. It is what Macbeth says to Macduff when they meet and fight at the end of Shakespeare's *Macbeth:*
I will not yield,
To kiss the ground before young Malcolm's feet,
And to be baited with the rabble's curse.
Though Birnam wood be come to Dunsinane,
And thou opposed, being of no woman born,
Yet I will try the last: before my body
I throw my warlike shield: lay on, Macduff;
And damned be him that first cries 'Hold, enough!'

Lay Your Cards On the Table. Reveal your resources; set out your arguments. In many card games a time comes when a player must put his cards face up on the table to show what he has been holding. Edmund Campion had the extended thought in 1581, when he said, (as recorded in *Conferences Held in the Tower of London with Ed. Campion, Jesuit):* "I would I might be suffered to shewe my cardes."

Lay an Egg. To fail; to do something embarrassing. The "egg" was a duck's in British sports lingo; as early as 1863 it was said of a player who failed to score in cricket that he "achieved a duck's egg." The point being made was the resemblance of an upright egg to a O. In the United States it was "a goose egg." The *New York Times,* describing a baseball game in 1886, said: "The New York players presented the Boston men with nine unpalatable goose eggs in their contest on the Polo Grounds yesterday."

Lead By the Nose. To dominate someone, order him about. It is what one does with various animals, including cattle and bears, by means of a rope tied to a ring passing through the septum of the animal's nose. The thought is in the Bible (Isaiah 37 : 29): "Because thy rage against me, and thy tumult, is come up to mine ears, therefore I will put my hook in thy nose, and my bridle in thy lips, and I will turn thee back by the way by which thou camest." Today's version was well known by the 16th century, an example being in Thomas Lupton's *A Persuasion from Papistry* (1581): "He maye leade them by the noses whiche waye he liste."

Lean and Hungry Look. An appearance of being ready to fight or take action. Julius Caesar, quoted in Plutarch's *Lives,* said something quite like this, referring to Brutus and Cassius: "It is not these well-fed long-haired men that I fear, but the pale and the hungry-looking." Shakespeare picked up the episode in his *Julius Caesar,* where he has Caesar say:
    Let me have men about me that are fat,
    Sleek-headed men, and such as sleep o' nights:
    Yond Cassius has a lean and hungry look;
    He thinks too much: such men are dangerous.

Leave No Stone Unturned. Be thorough in a quest. Legend has it that this was the advice of the oracle of Delphi to Polycrates in 477 B.C., when Polycrates was looking for treasures that the defeated Persian general Mardonius was said to have left in his tent. Latin versions of the saying (*movere omnem lapidum*) were in use by A.D. 1000, and in 1550 Thomas Cramer described the English version as a proverb in his *Defense of the True and Catholike Doctrine of the Sacrament:* "We must turne euery stone (as the prouerbe sayth) to seke out the truthe."

Leave Out in the Cold. Exclude from some activity or place. It probably originated with travelers arriving late at an inn in cold weather and finding they could not get a room. By 1879 T. H. S. Escott was writing in *England:* "The unfortunate traveller . . . often finds himself left out in the cold."

Left Hand Doesn't Know What the Right Hand is Doing, The. One is compartmentalized in one's actions; one is not fully aware of what one is doing. It is a biblical saying (Matthew 6 : 3): "But when thou doest alms, let not thy left hand know what thy right hand doeth."

Left in the Lurch. Left far behind; abandoned, particularly in difficult circumstances. The key word apparently comes from the French *lourche,* a 16th century game said to have resembled backgammon. To be "in the lurch" is in several games a way of saying a player is far behind; in cribbage, for example, a player who has scored only 31 when his opponent has scored 61 is said to be in the lurch. In 1576 Gabriel Harvey wrote in his *Letter-Book:* "Lest he fail in his reckning . . . and so leave himself in the lurch."

Left to His Own Devices. On his own; having to work or calculate his own way out of a predicament. "Device" here means inclination or purpose and is now used only as a plural and hardly at all except in the cliché. That was around by 1870, when Ellen [Mrs. Henry] Wood put it in *Canterbury's Will:* "What would we do, if left to our own devices?"

Leg to Stand On, Doesn't Have a. He is in a weak position or is offering an indefensible argument. The notion of standing on one's own legs as indicating self-sufficiency is quite old; one of the entries of Samuel Pepys in his diary in 1666 was: "I do fear that those two families . . . are quite broken up, and I must now stand upon my own legs." The thought that one might not have a leg to stand on was in the language by 1825, when John Neal put it as follows in *Brother Jonathan:* "As if the Yankee man were determined to leave the . . . brigadier without a leg to stand upon, as a lawyer would say."

Lend an Ear. Listen. Shakespeare, with his keen ear, heard this one, which was apparently common in his time, and put it in Antony's famous speech in *Julius Caesar:*
>Friends, Romans, countrymen, lend me your ears;
>I come to bury Caesar, not to praise him.
>The evil that men do lives after them;
>The good is oft interred with their bones;
>So let it be with Caesar. . . .

Length and Breadth of the Land. Throughout a country or some other definite area. It is a phrase beloved of orators who want a grand way of referring to the country and its people. Doubtless, few of them realize it has been in the language since at least the 13th century. Robert of Gloucester wrote in 1297 of "folk" who had "robbede Wircestressire in lengthe & in brede."

Lesser of Two Evils. The best option when both are difficult or painful. The saying is a modification of an old proverb: "Of two evils choose the less." Chaucer had the thought in *Troilus and Criseyde* (c. 1374): "Of harmes two, the lesse is for to chese."

Let Bygones Be Bygones. Forget the past; start anew. Homer put the thought in *The Iliad* (in Greek): "But we will allow these things to have happened in the past, grieved as we are." By 1546 John Heywood was recording the form as "Let all thyngs past pas." The modern version must have been in use then, too, since Robert of Pitscottie said in his *Chronicles of Scotland* (1577): "Byganes to be byganes."

Let Her Rip. Turn it loose; off you go. The implication seems to be that the ship or the wagon was in a position to go ripping along. In 1859 Bartlett's *Dictionary of Americanisms* said: "A common American slang expression is 'Let her rip!' i.e., let her drive, let her go." In 1853 the *Daily Morning Herald* of St. Louis had this entry: "We've got 'em on the hip, Letter Rip! Letter Rip!"

Let It All Hang Out. Conceal nothing; be freewheeling. The advice dates from some 25 years ago and seems to have originated with blacks in the United States. Quite likely "it" was originally the male sexual organ.

Let Loose (Slip) the Dogs of War. Show no more restraint; start an action in a situation that has been building up to a crisis. One could compile a dictionary of the phrases that Shakespeare originated or made famous; this is apparently one he originated. It is from *Julius Caesar,* where Antony is lamenting the assassination of Caesar and planning action against the conspirators:
>And Caesar's spirit ranging for revenge,
>With Ate by his side come hot from hell,

Shall in these confines with a monarch's voice
Cry 'Havoc,' and let slip the dogs of war;
That this foul deed shall smell above the earth,
With carrion men, groaning for burial.

Let Sleeping Dogs Lie. Leave well enough alone; don't stir up a potentially troublesome affair. It is the watchdog or the dog who is likely to give warning that is literally best left sleeping. Geoffrey Chaucer showed this origin of the thought in *Troilus and Criseyde* (c. 1374): "It is nought good a slepyng hound to wake."

Let Slip Through the Fingers. Lose an opportunity or a chance to catch something. It happens so often, literally, with slippery and not so slippery objects that the transfer to ideas and fugitives was easy and was made a long time ago. You see it in a sermon, "The Vanity of the World," given by Bishop Ezekiel Hopkins in 1668: "All our treasures are like quicksilver, which strangely slips between our fingers when we think we hold it fastest."

Let the Cat Out of the Bag. To reveal something that was supposed to be kept secret. E. Cobham Brewer, who assembled the *Dictionary of Phrase and Fable* more than 100 years ago, explained this one concisely: "It was formerly a trick among country folk to substitute a cat for a suckling pig, and bring it in a bag to market. If any greenhorn chose to 'buy a pig in a poke,' without examination, all very well; but if he opened the sack, 'he let the cat out of the bag,' and the trick was disclosed."

Let the Chips Fall Where They May. Never mind the consequences: speak your mind or do what you think must be done. You can see where the idea came from in a 14th-century proverb: "Hew not too high lest the chips fall in thine eye." Today's advice is to pay attention to the hewing (the task at hand) and not worry about what happens to the chips. Roscoe Conkling, a political boss and U. S. Senator from New York, said in a speech in 1880, "He [President Grant] will hew to the line of right, let the chips fall where they may."

Let's Face It. Accept reality; address ourselves to the problem; accept the challenge. One of the old meanings of "face" is to look at things realistically. Thomas Jefferson wrote in this sense in 1795: "My own quiet required that I should face it [the idea] and examine it." Probably "let us face it" has been in the language equally long, but the current catchphrase seems to have taken hold some 30 years ago, originally in the United States.

Let's Get the Show on the Road. Let's get moving, swing into action. Here is a cliché of American origin that smacks of the circus and the traveling theater group. It dates from around 1910 but seems to have come into overwork during the 1960s.

Lets No Grass Grow Under His Feet. Moves briskly; makes the most of the time or opportunity. It is an exaggerated way of indicating briskness, since one would have to stand in the same place for a long time before the growth of grass would be noticeable; but it is old and has been put in several ways, including "no grass grows under [or on] his heel." That one was used by Nicholas Udall in his *Ralph Roister Doister,* a play of 1553: "There hath growne no grasse on my heele since I went hence." Today's more familiar version appears in Edward Topsell's *The Historie of Foure-footed Beastes* (1607): "The hare . . . leaps away again, and letteth no grass grow under his feet."

Letter Perfect. Just right; as successful as one can be. In the theater an actor or actress who learns a part perfectly is said to have "got it down to the letter." Jerome K. Jerome's *On the Stage* (1885) says: "He would be letter perfect in all by the following Thursday."

Lick Your Chops. Anticipate something eagerly and with pleasure. "Chop" is a descendant of "chap," a word now lost that, until about the end of the 17th century, meant the jaw. Licking the chaps or chops is what many animals do before or after eating. At one time the phrase also signified warming up to play a musical instrument. Thus, from the *Dictionary of Afro-American Slang* (1970): "The tuning up musicians do before a jam session."

Lie Low. Avoid attracting attention; keep out of sight (usually when facing trouble or planning an adventure). It is what one literally does, say, in hunting. Joel Chandler Harris offered the broader meaning in *Uncle Remus* (1880): "All this while Brer Rabbit lay low."

Life and Soul of the Party. Someone whose wit or vibrance enlivens a social occasion. (The phrase is sometimes applied ironically to someone whose sour or leaden behavior has spoiled a social occasion.) You would think "life of the party" would do, and it often does, but intensity is gained by making it "life and soul." That part of the expression is quite old, being found in Benjamin Malkin's translation of *Gil Blas* in 1809: "Ballets incidental to the piece are the very life and soul of the play."

Life of Reilly. The good life; the easy life; living luxuriously without having to work. It is from a song that the vaudevillian Pat Rooney made popular in the 1880s, and "Reilly" was actually "O'Reilly." "Are You the O'Reilly?" was the name of the song, and each verse of the lyrics depicted an aspect of O'Reilly's good life. At the end of each verse Rooney would encourage the audience to sing the chorus:

> Are you the O'Reilly who keeps this hotel?
> Are you the O'Reilly they speak of so well?

Are you the O'Reilly they speak of so highly?
Gor blime me, O'Reilly, you're looking well.

Like It or Lump It. You're going to have to do it (or accept it) anyway, and whether you do it pleasantly or glumly is up to you. You don't hear "lump" as a verb much anymore, but it once meant (among other things) to look sulky or disagreeable. Richard Stanyhurst had that meaning in a work on Ireland in 1577: "They stand lumping and lowring . . . for that they imagine that their evill lucke proceedeth from him." The 19th-century American author John Neal had the current version by 1828 in *Rachel Dyer:* "If you don't like it, you may lump it."

Lion's Share. The greater part of an allotment. The lion that grabbed the biggest share went hunting with other animals in two of Aesop's fables. In one of them his companions were a heifer, a goat and a sheep; at the outset the four agreed to share the catch equally. They caught a stag. The lion divided it in four parts. Aesop continues:

> "Taking the best piece for himself, he said, 'This is mine of course, as I am the Lion'; taking another portion, he added, 'This too is mine by right—the right, if you must know, of the strongest.' Further, putting aside the third piece, 'That's for the most valiant,' said he; 'and as for the remaining part, touch it if you dare.'"

Lips Are Sealed, My. I can't or won't tell you; I am pledged (or have pledged myself) to secrecy. It is hard to picture how one's lips could literally be sealed effectively, so we have here a purely mental image. It had been evoked by 1782, when Fanny Burney included it in *Cecilia:* "I make it quite a principle to seal up my lips from the moment I perceive him." Probably the phrase achieved the status of cliché during the period in 1936 when it was rumored that King Edward VIII of England would abdicate so that he could marry a divorced commoner, Mrs. Wallis Simpson. When the prime minister, Stanley Baldwin, was asked about the situation (his government opposed the marriage and eventually worked out the plan of abdication), his usual reply was, "My lips are sealed."

Little Bird Told Me. I got my information from a source I'm not going to reveal. The origin of the thought, although not quite of the saying, is the Bible (Ecclesiastes 10 : 20): "Curse not the king, no, not in thy thought: and curse not the rich in thy bedchamber: for a bird of the air shall carry the voice, and that which hath wings shall tell the matter." Brian Melbancke was close to the modern form in *Philotimus* (1583): "I had a litle bird, that brought me newes of it."

158

Little Pitchers Have Big Ears. Children hear and understand more than you think they do. The play here is on the resemblance of the ear to the handle of a pitcher. It is an ancient saying, having been recorded by John Heywood in 1546: "Auoyd your children, smal pitchers haue wide eares."

Little Shaver. A small boy. Once "shaver" was a jocose way of saying chap or fellow; thus "old shauer" (1592) and "iollie shauers" (1602). Nowadays the chap or fellow is invariably small. "Little shavers" were around in 1635, too, when Thomas Cranley wrote in *Amanda:* "Thou art . . . not coy . . . to try the courage of so young a shaver."

Live Dangerously. Take risks; be venturesome. Goethe proffered this advice in *Faust* (1808): "Live dangerously and you live right!"

Live and Learn. I'll profit from this mistake. George Gascoigne was offering this advice in 1575 in his play, *The Glasse of Government:* "We live to learne, for so Sainct Paule doth teach."

Live and Let Live. Mind your own affairs and be respectful of those of others. This slogan was carried on the delivery trucks of a grocery store when I was a child (find a grocery store with delivery trucks now), and it mystified me. One had no choice but to live, and one had nothing to do with whether others lived, it seemed to me. The saying still seems to me rather vapid, but it has served for centuries. Gerard de Malynes wrote in *The Ancient Law-Merchant* (1622): "According to the Dutch prouerbe . . . *Leuen ende laeten leuen,* to liue and to let others liue."

Live in Clover. Have it good; be in a happy situation. It is to be in the position of a grazing animal, particularly a cow, confronted with a great (to a cow) delicacy. As Abel Boyer said in his *Compleat French Master* (1699): "Do you think to live in Clover thus all your lifetime?"

Living Doll. An attractive or competent woman. One senses a bit of patronizing here, since a doll is passive and cuddly, so that to apply the term to a girl or woman is to suggest that she may be somewhat short of character or vigor. Sylvia Plath reflected the feeling in *The Applicant* (1966):

> A living doll, everywhere you look.
> It can sew, it can cook,
> It can talk, talk, talk. . . .
> My boy, it's your last resort.
> Will you marry it, marry it, marry it.

Lo and Behold. Would you believe; imagine that. We have here one of those redundancies that works its way into the language and then is seldom recognized as a redundancy. "Lo" and "behold" are

159

both very old words meaning give heed or look there; the *Oxford English Dictionary* gives each as an example of the meaning of the other. Yet the combination of the two is not so old and seems originally to have been facetious, a deliberate redundancy. Thus, Charles Dickens in *David Copperfield* (1850): "What does he do, but, lo, and behold you, he goes into a perfumer's shop."

Lock, Stock and Barrel. The whole thing. The "lock" (firing mechanism), "stock" (handle) and "barrel" constitute the major element of a rifle or gun, and the phrase originally described a whole weapon. In Great Britain, and occasionally in the United States, it was "stock, lock and barrel," as in J. G. Lockhart's biography of Sir Walter Scott (1817): "Like the Highlandman's gun, she wants stock, lock, and barrel, to put her into repair."

Long Last, At. Finally, after prolonged (often enforced) delay. An ancient meaning of "last" as a noun, now lost except in the modern cliché, is continuance or duration. In 1523 John Skelton was writing of "solace at longe last."

Long Shot, A. An attempt that has only a slim chance of succeeding. Doubtless the people who shot arrows with bows talked of "long shots," but the phrase (along with its companion, "not by a long shot," which is now more likely to be heard as "no way") seems to come from gunnery. Certainly the early gunner had less of a chance of making a long shot than the skilled bowman, who would be unlikely even to try one that he knew to be beyond his capability. A. R. Marshall's *Pomes* (1888) has: "So Zippy went in for a long shot."

Long Suit, His. Something he is good at or for which he has strong resources. In card games such as bridge a player who holds a goodly number of, say, spades, has a strong resource, particularly if spades are trump. The transfer to other things was made toward the beginning of the present century, as indicated by Andy Adams in *The Log of a Cowboy* (1903): "Young Pete . . . assured our foreman that the building of bridges was his long suit."

Long and the Short of It, The. In sum; the heart of the matter. If you have told it "long" and told it "short," you have surely told it all. Sometimes it was reversed: "the short and the long of it." Robert Manning of Brunne wrote in his *Langtoft's Chronicle* (1330): "To say longly or schorte, alle [that] arms bare."

Long in the Tooth. Old; aging. Here is the first cousin of "don't look a gift horse in the mouth." As a horse gets older, its gums retract, making the teeth look longer. The longer the teeth, the older the horse. Applied to people, the saying is fairly recent, an early example being in J. C. Snaith's *Love Lane* (1919): "One of the youngest R. A.s [rear admirals] on record, but a bit long in the tooth for the army."

Look Daggers At. Regard angrily; show one's displeasure silently. It is a splendid image for the glare: the sharp points of annoyance emanating from the eyes. The image was put vividly by Philip Massinger and Thomas Dekker in *The Virgin Martir*, a play they published in 1622: "Thine eyes shoot daggers at that man."

Looked Down His Nose. Was scornful or snobbish. It is what the person giving a haughty glance seems to be doing. *American Speech* recorded the expression in 1927, saying that it meant to scorn or despise. I suspect the phrase can be found in English works of the 18th or 19th century, but I have not come across it.

Loose Ends, At. Confronting unfinished affairs or incomplete matters in one's life. It derives from the rope or string with one end (or both ends) flopping ineffectively. John Heywood wrote in 1546 of "some loose or od ende" in life.

Lost Cause. A hopeless quest (usually with the implication that someone is still pursuing it, failing or refusing to realize it is lost). The "cause" here is a matter of (usually keen) interest or (usually burning) concern. Matthew Arnold, writing of Oxford in his *Essays in Criticism* (1865), said: "Whispering from her towers the last enchantments of the Middle Age. . . . Home of lost causes, and forsaken beliefs, and unpopular names, and impossible loyalties!"

Loud and Clear. I hear you well; you're getting your message across. The phrase became universal when mobile radios came into use during World War II; the recipient of a message would often say, as reassurance to the sender, "I hear you loud and clear." Actually, the phrase, as a means of saying one is speaking plainly and vigorously to get a message across, is a good deal older. Lewis Carroll used it in *Through the Looking Glass* (1872), where Humpty Dumpty says:

> I said it very loud and clear;
> I went and shouted in his ear.

Low Man On the Totem Pole. The last in line; the least significant person in an organization, group or activity. The totem pole, constructed by certain American Indian tribes, had a series of carvings of totems (symbols) representing signficant events in the history of the family or tribe. Often the totems were human faces or figures. The notion of the "low man" as the most insignificant was introduced by the radio comedian Fred Allen, writing an introduction to a collection of pieces by the American humorist H. Allen Smith. Allen said: "If Smith were an Indian, he would be low man on any totem pole." Smith thereupon made *Low Man on the Totem Pole* (1941) the title of one of his books.

M

Mad As a Hatter. Demented; zany; fey. The Mad Hatter is a memorable character in Lewis Carroll's *Alice in Wonderland*, but the expression is much older. It is thought to derive from the effect on felt workers of the mercury used in making felt hats; after some years many of them developed a tendency toward severe twitching. As early as 1837 Thomas Haliburton had the expression in *The Clockmaker:* "Sister Sal . . . walked out of the room, as mad as a hatter."

Mad As a Wet Hen. Furious; really upset. Here is a phrase that seems to have its origin more in the imagination than in anything relating to real hens. Although chickens don't go looking for opportunities to get wet, they don't usually go into a flap if they get wet. Probably the originator of the phrase was picturing in his mind's eye how a hen would react to water. Anyway, the periodical *American Speech* recorded the saying in 1946 as having originated in the early 19th century. The example given is "Everybody that was not ax'd was mad as a wet hen."

Mailed Fist. Hard, overpowering force. The hand covered with mail, or links of armor, was part of the equipment of the medieval armored soldier; Shakespeare has a reference (in *Coriolanus*) to "his mail'd hand." The "mailed fist" as a symbol of toughness was employed by Kaiser Wilhelm II of Germany in 1897: "But should any one essay to detract from our just rights or to injure us, then up and at him with your mailed fist."

Maintain the Status Quo. Keep things as they are. *Status quo* is a Latin phrase meaning the existing state of affairs. The plea for maintaining it or avoiding change, at least for the present, was to be found in the *Edinburgh Review* as early as 1833: "The *status quo* was to be maintained in Luxemburg during negotiations respecting that duchy."

Make Ends Meet. To find the wherewithal (usually in difficult circumstances) to keep going; to balance one's income and outgo, at least precariously. The "ends" originally were of the year; the idea was that one would take in, from the beginning of the year to the end, enough money to cover one's expenditures. You see this in earlier versions of the saying that were common in England: "to make both ends [two ends; the two ends] of the year meet." An early example is in Tobias Smollett's *The Adventures of Roderick Random* (1748): "He made shift to make the two ends of the year meet." For many people in those times, particularly farmers, income was irregular and not altogether predictable—thus the uncertainty about making the two ends of the year meet.

Make Hay While the Sun Shines. Act while conditions are favorable. The grass that is going to be used as hay needs to be dried after it is cut; rain is likely to spoil it. The farmer, therefore, sought to cut hay on a day when it seemed likely that the sun would be around for that day and one or two more. John Heywood listed the advice as proverbial in 1546: "When the sunne shyneth make hey."

Make No Bones About It. Speak plainly; take direct action. The phrase is so old that the origin is obscure; it may refer to actual bones in soup or to dice. The absence of bones in soup would make the eating of the soup a straightforward matter. The dice thrower who "made no bones" would avoid the usual chants and invocations urging the dice to come up right and would simply throw them. Nicholas Udall was writing in 1533 (in *Flowers for Latin Speaking*): "I will not shrinke to aduenture it . . . I wyll no bones at it."

Make One's Blood Boil. Is infuriating. It is a picturesque but wholly imaginary image, since at a body temperature even far below the boiling point of blood one would be dead. The image was current in the 17th century, when Thomas Otway included it in *Alcibiades* (1675): "I am impatient, and my blood boyls high."

Make Tracks. Leave hastily; flee. Surely the image is from a fleeing animal, perhaps a rabbit in the snow. The phrase dates from the early 19th century and is of American origin, probably reflecting the fact that in those times many people hunted as a means of subsistence. *The Spirit of 'Seventy-Six* (1827) has this line: "Another made up his mind to bow his neck and make tracks."

Make a Clean Breast of It. Confess; tell all. Here is "breast" as the seat of one's thoughts or feelings. Making it clean by telling the truth goes back at least to the 18th century, when the thought appeared in *The Scots Magazine* (1753): "He pressed him . . . to make a clean breast, and tell him all."

Make a Long Story Short, To. To get to the point quickly; to assert (often wrongly, as it turns out) that one is going to be briefer than one might be. This time-filling claim that one is going to be concise goes back to a Latin expression used by Pacuvius in *Iliona* about 160 B.C.: *Ut multa paucis verba unose obnuntiem.* [To make a long story short, I'll tell you in one word.]

Make a Mountain Out of a Molehill. To turn a minor issue into a major one; to make too much of a trifle. The ancient Greeks said the same thing as "to make an elephant of a fly," and the French say "to make a fly of an elephant." The stretch in size from a "molehill" to a "mountain" is even bigger, which is probably why the English saying got its start. That was at least 400 years ago, as shown by Nicholas Udall in his (to use a much abbreviated title) *Paraphrase of Erasmus* (1548): "The Sophistes of Grece coulde through their copiousness make an Elephant of a flye, and a mountaine of a mollehill."

Make a Virtue of Necessity. To do with good grace (even seeking praise) what you have to do anyway; to turn an awkward situation to advantage. The Romans had a phrase that said the same thing (*facere de necessitate virtutem*). Geoffrey Chaucer was putting the thought in English by c. 1374, in *Troilus and Criseyde:* "Thus maketh vertue of necessite."

Make an Honest Woman of Her. To marry a woman one has seduced. "Honest" here seems to be in the sense of preserving or restoring the woman's reputation for chastity and decorum. As Bishop John Earle put it in his *Micro-cosmographie* (1629): "The best work he [the servingman] does is his marrying, for it makes an honest woman."

Make or Break. To go into something knowing that one is either going to succeed or fail. In England in ancient times it was "make or mar," which dates from the 15th century. Charles Dickens picked up "make or break" in *Barnaby Rudge* (1840): "I always tell my girl to make sure beforehand that she has a good man and true, and the chance will neither make nor break her."

Make the Best of a Bad Bargain. Retrieve what one can from an unfavorable situation. In the view of Samuel Johnson's biographer, James Boswell, the saying was "vulgar." Boswell wrote, in his *Life of Samuel Johnson, LL.D.* (1790): "Mrs. Thrale was all for, according to the vulgar phrase, 'making the best of a bad bargain.' "

Make the Grade. Come up to a standard; achieve a desired result. The railroad locomotive had to do this in climbing a hill (the American locomotive, that is; the British would call the hill "a gradient"). When the locomotive got up the hill, it had achieved its objective. Strangely, the transferred meaning, describing success at anything, is quite recent, an example being in *Publishers Weekly* (1930): "Can the seasonal bookshop make the grade . . . ?"

Makes Your Hair Stand on End. Is a frightening or unnerving experience. The goose pimples that come on when one is startled or frightened raise the hairs near them, as the Bible reminds us (Job 4 : 13–14): "Fear came upon me, and trembling, which made all my bones to shake. Then a spirit passed before my face; the hair of my flesh stood up."

Makes Your Mouth Water. You anticipate something keenly or wish you could have it. Ivan Pavlov, the winner in 1904 of the Nobel Prize in Physiology and Medicine, made his experimental dogs do this; they would naturally salivate at the sight of food, and by ringing a bell before presenting food he made them salivate at the sound of the bell, thereby demonstrating the conditioned reflex. In 1555 Richard Eden, writing on the "Newe Worlde," said: "These craftie foxes [cannibals] . . . beganne to swallowe theyr spettle as their mouthes watered for greediness of theyr prey."

Malice Aforethought, With. Premeditated crime or viciousness; doing someone a deliberate bad turn. It is a term from ancient law, picked up in medieval English from Norman French as *malice purpensé[e]* or *prepense* and later translated, as in one of the statutes adopted in the reign of Charles II: "If any person . . . on purpose and with malice forethought . . . shall. . . . "

Man After My Own Heart, A. Someone who sees things, or a particular issue, the way you do. In the Old Testament (1 Samuel 13 : 13,14) Samuel says to Saul:

> Thou hast done foolishly: thou hast not kept the commandment of the Lord thy God, which he commanded thee: for now would the Lord have established thy kingdom upon Israel for ever.
> But now thy kingdom shall not continue: the Lord hath sought him a man after his own heart, and the Lord hath commanded him to be captain over his people, because thou hast not kept that which the Lord commanded thee.

Man Among Men, A. An outstanding man, one with special qualities. In earlier times it was "man of men," as in Shakespeare's *Antony and Cleopatra.* The queen, smitten by Antony, is talking with her attendant Charmian, who keeps praising Caesar. Cleopatra says:

> By Isis, I will give thee bloody teeth,
> If thou with Caesar paragon again
> My man of men.

Man Bites Dog. News. The saying epitomizes the journalist's view of news versus non-news. It is attributed to John B. Bogart, who was city editor of *The Sun* in New York from 1873 to 1890. He said:

"When a dog bites a man, that is not news, because it happens so often. But if a man bites a dog, that is news."

Man of Few Words, A. A taciturn person; one who says things in a pithy way. Such a person is following the advice given in the Bible (Ecclesiastes 5 : 2): "Be not rash with thy mouth, and let not thine heart be hasty to utter any thing before God: for God is in heaven, and thou upon earth: therefore let thy words be few." Erasmus recorded the saying in *Adagia*, his collection of Latin proverbs, published in 1523.

Manner (Manor) Born, To the. Accustomed to a situation, usually an elegant one; following a habit or custom. In *Hamlet*, Shakespeare has Hamlet explain to Horatio and Marcellus why a flourish of trumpets and the sound of guns has been heard. He says it means the dead king "doth wake tonight and . . . keeps wassail." Horatio asks if it is a custom, and Hamlet replies:

> Ay, marry, is't:
> But to my mind, though I am native here
> And to the manner born, it is a custom
> More honour'd in the breach than the observance.

"Manor" seems to have crept in because of a widespread belief that the saying means born to wealth or luxury, as would be typified by living in a manor house.

Many Are Called But Few Are Chosen. Success is rare. It is from Jesus' parable about the kingdom of heaven (Matthew 22 : 1–14), which relates the tale of the king who summoned a large number of people at random to his son's wedding. One man, arriving without a wedding garment, so angered the king that he instructed his servants to cast the man "into outer darkness," adding, "there will be weeping and gnashing of teeth, for many are called but few are chosen."

Mare's Nest. An illusion or a disappointment. Mares don't make nests, which is why a claim to have discovered one is illusory. Formerly, the phrase "horse nest," was occasionally used, but the mare made the first appearance in Robert Peterson's *Galateo* (1576): "Nor stare in a mans face as if he had spied a mare's nest."

Mark My Words. Remember what I say, because it is in the nature of a prediction. Miles Coverdale's translation of the Bible in 1535 renders the passage in Isaiah with the phrase (Isaiah 28 : 23): "Take hede and heare my voyce, pondre and merck my wordes wel." In the King James version the passage reads: "Give ye ear, and hear my voice; hearken, and hear my speech."

Mark Time. Go through the motions; wait for a further development. It was and is a military command to soldiers doing close-order marching drill. At the command "Mark Time!" they are supposed to stop going forward but to keep their feet moving up and down at the marching pace, so that they are ready to move off again quickly. By extension it came to mean any kind of pause to await developments. Thomas Babington Macaulay showed the extended form in his *Essay on Bacon* (1837): "The human mind accordingly, instead of marching, merely marked time."

Marriage Made in Heaven, A. A seemingly predestined marriage; one that has been particularly successful. This is a modified version of an ancient proverb, which appeared in print as early as 1576 in William Painter's *The Palace of Pleasure*: "True it is, that marriages be don in heauen and performed in earth." A variant was offered in 1578 by Jacques Iver in *A Courtlie Controversie of Cupids Cantles*: "The Prouerbe saith, the first marriages are made in Heauen, and the seconde in Hell."

Matter of Life and Death, A. Vitally important; something crucial. Fortunately, it isn't often that anyone faces a moment when he might live or die depending on what happens or what he does, but the image is vivid enough to apply to many other things. Such matters were being discussed by 1857, when *Chambers's Journal* offered: "These are really a life and death matter to our neighbors."

Meat and Drink to Me. Something important or essential, at least in the view of the individual concerned; a source of great pleasure. You might suppose that "food and drink" would have served equally well, but apparently "meat" took precedence because meat is so widely savored. John Frith, in *A Boke Answering unto M. Mores Lettur* (1533), wrote: "It ys meate and drinke to this childe to plaie."

Meet Your Waterloo. Suffer a severe defeat or setback. It was at Waterloo in Belgium that Napoleon and his forces were soundly defeated in 1815 by British and Prussian forces under the Duke of Wellington and Marshal Blücher. Napoleon had so dominated Europe for more than a decade that the name of this pivotal and memorable battle has remained in the language.

Midas Touch. The apparent ability to make money at anything one does. In Greek mythology, Midas was a legendary king of Phrygia; in return for a kindness, Dionysus gave him the power to turn anything he touched to gold. When Midas found that even his food was turning into gold, he begged to have the favor withdrawn, and Dionysus let him wash it away in the River Pactolus. Richard Lassels gave the figurative meaning in *The Voyage of Italy* (1670): "Braue Raphael, whose only touch of a finger could, Midas like, turne gally pots to gold . . . ."

Might and Main, With. By all means at hand; with all one's strength. In time past, "main" was a common word meaning physical strength. In that sense, it survives only in its association with "might." In one of the Wakefield Plays, dating from the early 15th century, there is the line, "With mayn and might."

Milk of Human Kindness. Compassion; understanding. Shakespeare seems to have originated this figure of speech to describe a "nice guy." In the first act of *Macbeth* Lady Macbeth is ruminating on the ruthless deeds her husband plans in order to become king. She says:

> Glamis thou art, and Cawdor, and shalt be
> What thou art promised: yet do I fear thy nature;
> It is too full o' the milk of human kindness
> To catch the nearest way. . . .

Mills of God (The Gods) Grind Slowly. At some point a sinner will be punished; many decisions or events that are important in one's life take time in coming. Some 1,600 years ago the Greek philosopher Sextus Empiricus wrote: "The mills of the gods grind slowly, but they grind small." One of Longfellow's translations was a 17th-century poem, "Retribution," by Friedrich von Logau:

> Though the mills of God grind slowly, yet they grind exceeding small;
> Though with patience he stands waiting, with exact-
> ness grinds he all.

Millstone Around the Neck, A. A burden; a heavy obligation. The typical millstone was some four feet in diameter, ten inches thick and weighed several hundred pounds; to have it literally around the neck could only have been for the purpose suggested in the Bible (Matthew 18 : 6), where Jesus says: "But whoso shall offend one of these little ones which believe in me, it were better for him that a millstone were hanged about his neck, and that he were drowned in the depth of the sea."

Mince Matters, Not To. To come right to the point; to tell it like it is. To mince matters once meant to make light of something; the term turns up only in the negative form now. One sees it both ways in Shakespeare. In *Othello*, Othello says: "I know, Iago, thy honesty and love doth mince this matter, making it light to Cassio." In *Antony and Cleopatra*, Antony says: "Speak to me home, mince not the general tongue: name Cleopatra as she is called in Rome. . . ."

Mind Over Matter. The triumph of thinking over a physical (often bodily) problem. One sees the thought in a slightly different form in William Paley's *Natural Theology* (1802): "The essential superiority of spirit over matter."

Mind Your Own Business. Tend to your own affairs and don't poke around in mine. This cry of annoyance at what appears to be prying is such a common response that it has been in use for eons. In earlier times, it was said most often as "meddle with your own business," reinforcing the notion that the person addressed is being meddlesome. In this form John Palsgrave set it forth in 1530: "Medyll with the thynge that you have a do."

Mind Your P's and Q's. Take pains; be precise. You can take your pick of several explanations. The most obvious one is that a child learning to read is apt to have trouble distinguishing *p* and *q*, and has to be reminded by the teacher to be careful. But *b* and *d* present a similar difficulty, and one is never warned to watch his *b*'s and *d*'s. Another explanation is that tabs in pubs once indicated *p* (pints) and *q* (quarts); either the publican or the drinker could be admonished to keep them straight. In any event, the saying was well established by 1779, when Hannah Cowley wrote (in *Who's the Dupe?*): "You must mind your P's and Q's with him, I can tell you."

Mind's Eye. The imagination; one's mental picture of something. Shakespeare speaks of it in *Hamlet*, where Hamlet and Horatio are discussing the death of Hamlet's father and his mother's quick remarriage. Hamlet says suddenly: "My father!—methinks I see my father." Horatio says: "O where, my lord?" Hamlet replies: "In my mind's eye, Horatio."

Mine of Information. A knowledgeable person (sometimes said sarcastically of someone who can't come up with information he could be expected to have). The transfer of "mine" from a source of coal or ore to an abundant supply of anything dates way back, and encompasses such figures of speech as "mynes of strength" (1541) and "her memory was a mine" (1819). The *Athenaeum* contained the current phrase in 1905 ("Her book is a mine of valuable information."), but it, too, is probably much older.

Mint of Money, A. A large sum. A mint is a place where coins are made and/or stored. The idea was richly used by Thomas Fuller in *A Church-history of Britain* (1655): "A mass, a mint, a mine of money could easily be advanced to defray the expences thereof."

Misery Loves Company. Difficulty or pain is easier to take if you know you are not alone in the experience. John Ray listed the saying as a proverb in 1670. Among the many Latin maxims written by Publilius Syrus in the first century B.C. was: "It is a consolation to the wretched to have companions in misery."

Miss Is As Good As a Mile, A. Failure is absolute, whether it is by a narrow margin or a wide one. In ancient times the saying was, "An inch in a miss is as good as an ell." (An ell is an obsolete unit of measure that differed in various countries; in England it was 45 inches.) One sees the thought evolving in Thomas Fuller's history of the University of Cambridge (1655): "An hair's breadth fixed by a divine finger shall prove as effectual a separation from danger as a mile's distance." The modern version was known by 1821, when James Fenimore Cooper used it in *The Spy*: "A miss was as good as a mile."

Molasses in January, As Slow As. Sluggish or virtually immobile. I see a cold pantry in the New England of the 18th or 19th century as the inspiration for this saying. Molasses is fairly viscous at best, but cold molasses is almost unpourable. The earliest written record I can find is in *Dialect Notes*, which in 1912 said it was a New Hampshire expression.

Moment of Truth. A crisis point; a time for decision; a severe test. The Spanish have the same phrase (*el momento de la verdad*) with a precise meaning: the moment of the final sword thrust in a bullfight. That is a critical moment for both the bull and the bullfighter, so the expression has transferred easily to critical moments of several kinds. Thus, Iris Bromige in *Enchanted Garden* (1956): "This, thought Fiona, was the moment of truth." Ernest Hemingway recorded the bullfight origin of the term in *Death in the Afternoon* (1932): "The whole end of the bullfight was the final sword thrust, the actual encounter between the man and the animal, what the Spanish call the moment of truth."

Monarch of All He Surveys. A property owner or the person in charge of an enterprise; at least someone who feels in command of a situation. The phrase may have originated with the poet William Cowper, who wrote in "Verses Supposed to Be Written by Alexander Selkirk" (1782): "I am monarch of all I survey, / My right there is none to dispute."

Monday-morning Quarterback. A second-guesser; an expert after the fact. One sees the hand of a sportswriter here, but he seems to be anonymous. He was making a play on the fact that most football games are played on weekends, hence on Monday it is easy to be an expert on how the game's strategy could have been improved. In *What Price Football* (1932) Barry Wood wrote of "a kind of sportswriter known to football players and coaches as a 'Monday morning quarterback'" who, "not content with reporting the game, ...must analyze it."

Money is the Root of All Evil. Greed leads people to crime or trickery. Saint Paul said it (Timothy 6 : 10): "For the love of money is the root of all evil. . . ." George Bernard Shaw offered the opinion (in *Maxims for Revolutionists*) that "lack of money is the root of all evil."

Monkey Business. Foolish or mischievous activity. One assumes the sly, alert, advantage-taking behavior of the monkey gave rise to this notion. It must have been fairly new in 1904, when the

Brooklyn Standard Union saw fit to put it in quotes: "A warning to Russia that England will not tolerate any delay or any 'monkey business' whatsoever."

Month of Sundays. A long time. (It would actually be about seven and a half months, but it is unlikely anyone using the expression has any such precise period in mind.) At one time the thought was expressed as "a week of Sundays," but that apparently was not long enough, and by 1832 Frederick Marryat was writing, in *Newton Forster*: "It may last a month of Sundays."

Moral Victory. A defeat or an inconclusive outcome that, nonetheless, a contender sees as a victory because that side has made a point about a principle. Archibald Alison's *History of Europe* (1832) states the thought clearly: "The loss to the contending parties was nearly equal . . . but all the moral advantages of a victory were on the side . . . of the French."

More Here Than Meets the Eye. This is more significant than it appears. Samuel A. Hammett, who wrote under the pen name Philip Paxton, gave the following version in *A Stray Yankee in Texas* (1853): "There might be more in it than at first met the eye." And actress Tallulah Bankhead is credited with giving the phrase a sharp turn when she dismissed a work by Belgian-born author Maurice Maeterlinck with: "There is less in this than meets the eye."

More Honored in the Breach Than in the Observance. The law or custom is more often ignored or flouted than adhered to. The phrase is from the same passage of *Hamlet* as "to the manner born." Hamlet, responding to Horatio's question about whether it is a custom for the king to indulge in "wassail," says: "It is more honour'd in the breach than the observance."

More Power to You. Good luck; I hope your venture succeeds. The phrase was in use by 1842, when it appeared in Samuel Lover's *Handy Andy*: "'More power to you, Andy,' said the Squire." A variant urging on a drinker is "more power to your elbow," which was a bit of encouragement offered by James Russell Lowell in a letter of 1860.

More Sinned Against Than Sinning. Wronged; less responsible for this regrettable situation than others are. It would be interesting to count up the expressions originated or made famous by Shakespeare. This is from *King Lear*. The Earl of Kent, himself a fugitive from the machinations of Lear's daughters Goneril and Regan, finds Lear (in a similar predicament) half crazed, on a heath during a storm. Lear says: "I am a man more sinn'd against than sinning."

More Than I Bargained For. This goes beyond what I expected (or wanted) when the plan or arrangement was made. The notion of bargaining for something, in the sense of making an arrangement or a deal, is old enough to turn up in Shakespeare. The concept that one could get more than expected was around by 1840, when Frederick Marryat picked it up in *Olla Podrida*: "More wind than we bargained for."

More Than One Way to Skin a Cat, There's. There are various ways of doing this thing. Charles Funk believed the idea sprang from the small child's maneuvers with a limb or a bar, during which the child hangs by his arms, lifts his feet up through them and then either continues on in a somersault or hooks his legs up over the limb. Funk imagined a mother watching this, who saw in it a resemblance to skinning a cat. Of course, the expression could simply have come from the process of removing an animal's pelt. In any case, the saying has existed for more than 150 years.

More in Sorrow Than in Anger. I'm disappointed (or regret) that I must take this action. It is another example from *Hamlet*. Horatio tells Hamlet that for two nights the guards Marcellus and Bernardo saw the ghost of Hamlet's father during their watch, and that on the third night Horatio, too, saw the ghost. Hamlet asks about the ghost's expression. Horatio says: "A countenance more in sorrow than in anger."

More or Less. To a greater or lesser extent; maybe yes and maybe no; it's ambiguous. How often one hears this formula for inexactitude, and how old it is! It goes back to around 1225 in the *Ancren Riwle*, where it appears as "more oder lesse."

More the Merrier, The. Come on in—the activity will be livelier with more people. This is the first half of an old proverb; why the second half has disappeared is a matter for speculation, but perhaps its tone was too antisocial. The proverb, as recorded in 1546 by John Heywood, was: "The mo the merier, we all daie [do] here and see. Ye, but the fewer the better far [said hee]." It also appeared at times as "the more the merrier, the fewer the better cheer."

More's the Pity, The. It's regrettable (sometimes said with tongue in cheek, since the speaker is actually rather pleased that the thing has happened). The straight version was employed in 1797 by R. M. Roche in *Children of the Abbey*: "Poor thing, she is going fast indeed, and the more's the pity, for she is a sweet creature."

Move Heaven and Earth. Make a prodigious effort. Arthur Young, writing in 1792 on his travels in France, said: "Englishmen . . . would move heaven and earth to establish a better conveyance, at a higher price."

Movers and Shakers. Influential people; decision-makers. Used separately, mover and shaker (of heaven and earth) were words that alluded to God. George Chapman's translation of Homer's *Iliad* (1611) says: "Thou mightie shaker of the earth." Shakespeare, in *King Henry VI (Part II)* puts the king at the side of Cardinal Beaufort's deathbed. The king says: "O thou eternal mover of the heavens, look with a gentle eye upon this wretch!" When the two words were joined to intensify the thought is hard to say, but the term was known to the poet Arthur William Edgar O'Shaughnessy in the 19th century:

> We are the music-makers,
> And we are the dreamers of dreams . . .
> World-losers and world-forsakers,
> On whom the pale moon gleams:
> Yet we are the movers and shakers
> Of the world forever, it seems.

Moving Finger Writes. Time is passing; the record of your life is accumulating; your destiny is taking shape. It is from *The Rubáiyát of Omar Khayyám*, a translation by Edward Fitzgerald (in 1859) of the 12th-century Persian:

> The Moving Finger writes; and having writ,
> Moves on: Nor all your Piety nor Wit
> Shall lure it back to cancel half a Line,
> Nor all your Tears wash out a Word of it.

Much Ado About Nothing. Needless fuss; a tempest in a teapot. Although Shakespeare imprinted the saying on the language by using it as the title of a play in 1598, in one form or another it predated that. An example is in Richard Hyrde's translation (1529) of a work on the instruction of Christian women: "They make great ado about many small matters."

Mud In Your Eye, Here's. To your good health and success (a drinking toast). Strange; to get mud in the eye actually would make for discomfort and annoyance. One can only suppose the notion is that mud would blind one to the bad things nearby, as a series of drinks would. The toast was current by 1927, when H. V. Morton wrote, in his *In Search of England*: "'Here's mud in your eye!' said one of the modern pilgrims, tossing down his martini."

Muddy the Water. Confuse things; cause trouble. Most likely this phrase originated with a man fishing in a clear stream, only to have other people come wading clumsily along, so churning up the bottom that the water was no longer clear. The expression has been in vogue long enough to have appeared in *Blackwell's Magazine* in 1837.

173

My Heart Bleeds for You. I'm really not very interested in your trouble. The term is almost always said in irony, as in E.V. Cunningham's *Samantha* (1968): "My heart bleeds for the poverty of those who guard the wealthiest city in the world." Once the saying was a sincere if hyperbolic expression of sympathy; it took its ironic turn in the 1940's.

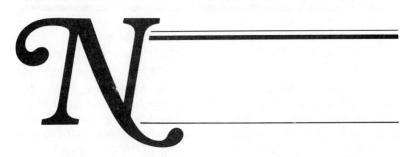

Naked Truth. Why naked? Well, an old fable has it that Truth and Falsehood went for a swim together, leaving their clothes on shore. Falsehood came out of the water first and put on Truth's clothes. Truth, refusing to don the clothes of Falsehood, went naked.

Naked as a Jaybird. Bare. It is a mystifying image, since none of the jays (the bluejay, for example) are bare or unadorned. Indeed, "jay" once meant a person who was flashily dressed. Still, "bare" it is, as in David Delman's *Sudden Death* (1973): "The corpus was naked as a jaybird." A British expression, "naked as a robin," dates to at least the 19th century and often meant without property.

Name is Legion, Their (My). There are many of them; I am part of a large group. The legion in the Roman army was a unit of as many as 6,000 troops, and the word came to represent a large number of people with a common purpose. In the Bible (Mark 5 : 9), when Jesus is talking with the "man with an unclean spirit" and asks his name, one reads the reply: "My name is Legion: for we are many."

Name of the Game, That's the. That's the crux of the matter, the issue we're really dealing with. This is what Eric Partridge calls a "catch phrase." It probably originated in sports journalism with an athlete or a writer defining the point of a game as, say, to put the puck in the net. By the 1960s it had been broadened to refer to the crux of virtually any matter.

Neat As a Pin. Particularly tidy, orderly or well arranged. Once it was "neat as a new pin," which sharpens the image of something trim and bright. Thus John Wolcot in 1796: "How neat was Ellen in her dress! As neat as a new pin!"

Necessity is the Mother of Invention. You often think better and come up with better ideas when you are sorely pressed to find a way out of a situation. This thought has appeared in many forms, including, "Nede taught hym wytte," which is how William Horman recorded it in his *Vulgaria* in 1519. Jonathan Swift had a vivid example of the modern version in *Gulliver's Travels* (1726):

"I sold [soled] my shoes with wood, which I cut from a tree. . . . No man could more verify the truth . . . 'That necessity is the mother of invention.' "

Neck of the Woods, This. Here; this region. An Americanism, defined by M. Schele De Vere in his *Americanisms; the English of the New World* (1871) as: "He will . . . find his neighborhood designated as a neck of the woods, that being the name applied to any settlement made in the well-wooded parts of the Southwest especially." Originally "neck" in this sense was a narrow stretch of land or water; "neck of the woods" suggests the limited area being described.

Needle in a Haystack. Something almost impossible to find; a forlorn quest. It is a vivid phrase, so old that the name of the first person to evoke it is lost. Once it was "needle in a bottle of hay," bottle meaning bundle. It has also been "a nedle in a medow" (1532) and "A pin's head in a cartload of hay" (1565). The haystack took over about the middle of the 19th century.

Needless to Say. You know this, but I'm going to tell you anyway. A space-filling and needless expression, always followed by the thing it is needless to say. "Nedelesse to speake" is the way it was put in 1530. Closer to the modern version is an entry from the journal *Kaleidoscope* in 1826: "The Squire was hard hit by this nonchalance, and [as the newspapers say] 'it is needless to add,' acted upon Sheridan's suggestion."

Neither Here Nor There. Irrelevant; of no significance. The Venetian scholar and printer Aldus Manutius (founder of the famous Aldine Press) was precise about this phrase in his *Phrases Linguae Latinus* (1581): "It is neither here nor there, or I passe not what you thinke of me."

Neither Rhyme Nor Reason. Not sensible; unsuitable for either entertainment or instruction. Henry More, writing on the "mystery of iniquity" in 1664, said: "Against all the Laws of Prophetick Interpretation, nay indeed against all rhyme and reason." There is a story that another More (Sir Thomas) told an author who had asked Sir Thomas's advice on a book, to turn it into rhyme. The author did so and brought it back. Sir Thomas said: "Ay! ay! That will do, that will do. 'Tis rhyme now, but before it was neither rhyme nor reason."

Net Result, The. The outcome; the basic meaning; the bottom line. "Net" as an adjective has several meanings, most of them now rare or obsolete (neat, pure, elegant among them); here it signifies whatever remains after all the deductions and allowances have been made. One sees the origins of the modern phrase in John Mellis's version of Hugh Oldcastle's *A Briefe Instruction* *and Maner How to Keepe Bookes of Accompts* (1588): "The remaine is the net rest, substance or capitall of the owner." C. J. Rolo offers this example of the broadened modern version: "The net result is a huge canvas of small-town life."

Never Darken My Door Again. Stay away; you've worn out your welcome here. It's a strange expression in its negativeness, and one not balanced by an affirmative equivalent that would mention brightening a door. Benjamin Franklin used it in a somewhat different context in *Busy-body* (1729): "I'm afraid she would resent it so as never to darken my door again." Tennyson put the modern meaning clearly in *Dora* (1842): "You shall pack / And never more darken my doors again."

Never-Never Land. An inaccessible or imaginary place or concept. James M. Barrie created this place in *Peter Pan* (1904); it was where the Lost Boys and the Red Indians lived. In Australia it once meant the entire unsettled area, but it now refers to the northern and western parts of Queensland. Mrs. Aeneas Gunn published a book about that region in 1908, *We of the Never Never*.

New Broom Sweeps Clean, A. A person new in a job (particularly in a political office) makes a lot of changes. The old proverb, which dates at least to the 16th century, referred literally to the efficacy of a new broom compared to an old one. It was recorded by John Heywood in 1546 as: "Some thereto said, the greene new brome swepith cleene."

Nick of Time, In the. Barely soon enough; at the crucial moment. It is asserted by some that the phrase grew from the practice of making nicks or notches in a stick to record scores, transactions and the like. This seems to be stretching it, as, for centuries, one of many meanings of "nick" has been, "at the crucial moment." Hence the old expression "in the nick," which appears as early as the 16th century in Meredith Hanmer's *Auncient Ecclesiasticall Histories* (1577): "The Romane navie . . . arrived at the very pinch, or as we commonly say, in the nicke." The modern expression is almost as old, appearing as "in this nick of time" in a declaration of the Lords and Commons in 1642.

Nine-Day Wonder. A passing fad; someone who achieves brief prominence or notoriety. An odd phrase, indeed. Why nine? Why not seven or 10 or 30, all more common measures of time? Probably to emphasize the oddness, freakishness or passing quality of the event. The expression is so old, however, that one can only guess at the reason for nine. Geoffrey Chaucer wrote in *Troilus and Criseyde* (1374): "For wonder last but nine night. . . . " In *Henry VI (Part 3)* Shakespeare has this exchange (after King Edward has said he might marry Lady Grey):

GLOUCESTER: "That would be ten days' wonder at the least."
CLARENCE: "That's a day longer than a wonder lasts."

Nip and Tuck. Dead even; neck and neck; in a close race or encounter. Each of the key words has so many meanings that dictionaries don't even attempt to specify which ones apply in this phrase. The *Oxford English Dictionary* contents itself with saying the expression is of U.S. origin. John Bartlett in his *Dictionary of Americanisms* (1859) offered this example: "Don't play that new game they've got where the jack takes the ace—'taint natural. I tried 'em at poker, and old sledge, and loo, but they couldn't get me down, it was nip and tuck between us; but by and by they fotched in that new game, and then I hollered."

Nip in the Bud. Kill off at an early stage. It is what a late spring frost will do to the buds of trees and flowers. In Richard Shacklock's translation (1565) of Jerome Osorius' *Pearl for a Prince* one reads: "Princes doe vnwisely which doo not nyp wickednes in the hed, / So sone as it doth begin."

No Business Like Show Business, There's. Actors and other entertainers are a unique lot, who are thought to do exotic things. Irving Berlin created and popularized the saying, making it the title of a song in his musical *Annie Get Your Gun* (1946).

No Defense Like a Good Offense, There's. Attack rather than wait for the enemy or the other team to attack you. It is mainly a sports phrase now, but it originated with the military. The Brackenridge *Gazette* recorded it in a slightly different form in 1790: "I say the best defence is offence."

No Earthly Business. Out of the question; an improper action. The implication is that the thing could be done only someplace other than earth. "Earthly" serves as an emphatic. A close parallel to the modern version was in *The Scots Magazine* in 1753: "What earthly purpose could the pannel serve by such a . . . piece of villany?"

No Flies On Me. I'm alert; I'm functioning vigorously; I'm taking advantage of my opportunities. It is a farmer's image, deriving from the fact that flies settle more on a standing horse or cow than on one that is moving briskly. The *Detroit Free Press* offered a definition in 1888: "There ain't no flies on him, signifies, that he is not quiet long enough for moss to grow on his heels, that he is wide awake." Even earlier there was the expression, "don't let flies stick to your heels," which appeared in an 1836 British publication.

No Fool Like an Old Fool, There's. One should act one's age; silliness or juvenile behavior is out of place in an old person. "But there is no foole to the olde foole, folke saie," was recorded by John Heywood as a proverb in 1546. In 1721 James Kelly, explaining Scottish proverbs to the English reader, wrote: "Spoken when

Men of advanc'd Age behave themselves, or talk youthfully, or wantonly."

No Great Shakes. Ordinary, mediocre. The *Oxford English Dictionary* speculates that the saying may have come from shakes of dice, which are usually not so great. Lord Broughton, writing in 1865 (*Recollections of a Long Life*) of an event in 1816, said: "W. said that a piece of sculpture there was '*nullae magnae quassationes*', and the others laughed heartily." (Try getting a laugh with a Latin phrase today.) Thomas Moore wrote in 1819 (*Tom Crib's Memorial to Congress*) of someone who was "no great shakes at learned chat."

No Love Lost. They don't like each other. For a while, several centuries ago, this phrase carried two opposing meanings: the one now current, and the thought of mutual affection. In the second, and defunct, sense of the phrase, the image was as of love shared in a common vessel; when affection was mutual, none of the love in the vessel was lost. An example is in *Faire Em*, a fraudulent Shakespeare published in 1592: "Nor was there any loue between vs lost, But I held the same in high regard." In the other sense, while love is possessed by two people, neither is losing any of it over the other. A translation in 1620 of *Don Quixote* offers this passage: "'There's no love lost,' quoth Sancho, 'for she speaks ill of me too when she list.' "

No News Is Good News. There's hope in a bad situation; if you are expecting bad news and it hasn't come, maybe the thing hasn't happened and maybe it won't happen. A forerunner of this thought can be found in 1574, in Edward Hellowes' *Guevara's Chronicle*: "Euil newes neuer come too late." Still closer, in 1616, is King James I, writing to Sir George More, lieutenant of the Tower, where the king's old favorite and confidant Robert Carr, Earl of Somerset, was imprisoned on a charge of poisoning. The king is urging More to persuade Carr to confess rather than come to trial: "Let none living know of this, and if it take good effect, move him to send in haste for the Commissioners and give them satisfaction; but if he remains obstinate I desire not that ye should trouble me with an answer, if it is no end; and no news is better than evil news." The modern version is at hand by 1645 in a book of letters gathered by James Howell: "I am of the Italians mind that said, *Nulla nuova, buona nuova*, no news, good news."

No Quarter Given. No leniency or clemency shown. The word "quarter" has many meanings, one of which is the ancient battlefield practice of sparing defeated enemies from death. That meaning may in turn have derived from one of two others, either a person's relationship with another (i.e., "to keep good quarter with" someone), or a place of residence and safety. In James

Howell's *Letters* (1645) one reads: "He suffered Tilly to take that great Town with so much effusion of blood, because they wood receiue no quarter."

No Respecter of Persons. Individuals aren't singled out or given special favor (by some authority or natural agency.) This figure of speech is directly from the Bible (Acts 10 : 34): "Then Peter opened his mouth, and said, Of a truth I perceive that God is no respecter of persons."

No Rest for the Wicked. Nothing ever lets up around me; things are always popping. In England it is often "no peace for the wicked." In any case, the saying derives from the Bible (Isaiah 48 : 22 and 57 : 21), where it appears without the modern irony: "There is no peace, saith the Lord, unto the wicked."

No Skin Off My Nose. No concern of mine; it doesn't affect me. The phrase, dating from the 1920s, seems to be of U. S. origin, perhaps in a transfer from boxing. The implication is that one has kept (or will keep) from sticking one's nose into a situation that could mean trouble.

No Slouch, He's. He is pretty good at it. Four hundred years ago "slouch" served as a noun to describe a lazy or clumsy person; today it serves only in the negative. The later usage started in the United States and was common by 1840, when Charles F. Hoffman wrote, in; *Greyslaer:* "You are no slouch of a woodsman to carry a yearling of such a heft as that."

No Sweat. Easily; without visible strain. Among other things, "sweat" has stood for hard work, which is likely to cause sweat. The notion that some things don't require hard work, or that the worker can do them without making them look hard, is also time-honored. Shakespeare uses it in *The Tempest* (1610), where Gonzalo says: "All things in common nature should produce without sweat or endeavour. . . ."

No Way. It's impossible; it won't happen. In statements such as "There is no way this bill will pass" the thought has been around for a long time. The abbreviated form became popular (and overworked) about 15 years ago. In 1971 *The New Yorker* offered an example: " . . . none of these conditions will ever get any better. 'No way,' as they keep saying. . . ."

No-Win Situation, A. No matter what you do or what happens, you can't expect to gain anything or to see any improvement. War-game activity may be the source of this label, which originated in the United States about 1962. There are plenty of "no-win situations" in war games and in real wars. Amitai Etzioni made use of the term in another context in the *New York Times Maga-*

zine in 1976: "The principal's main concern was that it was a no-win situation."

Non Compos. Out of it; of unsound mind; so seriously ill, injured or incapacitated one is unable to speak or act for oneself. It is two-thirds of a Latin phrase (*non compos mentis*), which for several centuries has served as a legal term meaning "not of sound mind." The broader meaning appears in *The Jacobite Conventicle* of 1692: "These men are sure *non compos mentis*, and Bedlam [the Hospital of St. Mary of Bethlehem in London, which served in the Middle Ages as a lunatic asylum] must sure be Enlarged."

Nose Out of Joint, Have Your. Be disgruntled, particularly when somebody seems to be taking your place. The nose is not a joint and so doesn't go out (unless it is broken), but the image of surprised displeasure is vivid. It is also of long standing. Barnaby Rich was familiar with it in 1581, when he wrote, in *His Farewell to the Militarie Profession*: "It could bee no other than his owne name, that had thrust his nose so far out of ioynte."

Nose to the Grindstone. Hard at work; held to a task. Another vivid nasal image. A nose put to a grindstone would quickly be abraded, but the picture of concentrated or compelled effort remains. Erasmus, in *A Merry Dialogue* (1557) wrote: "I would haue holden his nose to the grindstone."

Not On Your Life. No way; on no account. The suggestion is that you could wager your life (presumably your most important possession) on the truth or reliability of what is being said or proposed. The saying is perhaps 100 years old. It was picked up by the *New York Evening Post* in 1905: "The congressman was asked if there had been any gambling on the trip. 'Not on your life,' he said."

Not What It's Cracked Up to Be. Disappointing; less than one expected. It is largely unremembered today that one of the meanings of the verb "crack," is to boast, or to praise. That usage dates to at least the 15th century. Furthermore, "cracked up" was not always used as a negative; Charles Dickens wrote this passage in *Martin Chuzzlewit* (1844): "Our backs is easily ris. We must be cracked up or they rises, and we snarls. . . ." The negative version was in the language by 1884, when the *American* magazine reported "Mexico . . . is not all it has been cracked up to be."

Not Wisely But Too Well, Loved. Was deeply and uncritically enamored; acted more from emotion than with intellect. Othello says it in the final scene of Shakespeare's play, as he is about to kill himself:

> I have done that state some service, and they know't.
> No more of that. I pray you, in your letters,
> When you these unlucky deeds shall relate,
> Speak of me as I am; nothing extenuate,

Nor set down aught in malice: then must you speak
Of one that loved not wisely but too well. . . ."

Not Worth a Rap. Worth little or nothing. This rap was a counterfeit coin circulating as a halfpenny in Ireland in the 18th century. It succeeded because real money was in short supply. The expressions "not worth a rap," "without a rap," and "don't care a rap" date from the same period.

Not Worth the Powder to Blow It Up. Of little value. Originally said of military objectives that were not worth attacking or pursuing. The extended meaning turned up in *The Austin Papers* (1823): "All the government in the world would not make them worth the powder that it would take to blow them to Hell."

Not a Hope in Hell. Highly unlikely to succeed or be realized. It is the damned who go to hell, and presumably they have little to hope for. Oliver Onions wrote, in *Peace In Our Time* (1923): " 'I rather fancied Lovelightly.' 'Lovelightly? Not a hope in Hell!' "

Nothing New Under the Sun. Everything has happened before. In the Bible (Ecclesiastes 1 : 9) one reads the words of the Preacher, the son of David: "The thing that hath been, it is that which shall be; and that which is done, is that which shall be done: and there is no new thing under the sun."

Nothing to Write Home About. Ordinary, unexciting. The thought was put by Pliny the Younger in one of his letters almost 2,000 years ago: "There is nothing to write about, you say. Well then, write and let me know just this—that there is nothing to write about. . . ." The current version dates from the 19th century.

Now and Then. Intermittently; occasionally. In the past it was also heard as "now and again" and "now or then." In 1553, Lord Berners indicated the expression was then current when he wrote in his *Golden Boke:* "Sometyme on the daie, and nowe and than by nyght, they would walke abrode."

Now or Never. Here is one's last, or only, chance to do something. The phrase dates at least from Chaucer's time (the 14th century), since he used it in *Troilus and Criseyde.* The modern sense is clearer in John Daus's translation of *Sleidanes Commentaries* (1560): "Therefore thought they now, or els never, yt [that] God was on theyr side."

Nutty as (Nuttier Than) a Fruitcake. Highly eccentric; odd or mentally unbalanced. An inspired image putting together a figurative nut and a literally nutty dessert. The person who was thus inspired is unknown to me, but his or her phrase was current by 1935, when Graeme and Sarah Lorimer had it in *Heart Specialist:* " 'Listen, Alix, you're as nutty as a fruitcake,' I said."

Odd Man Out. Someone is excluded. An old gambling game was odd man wins. Three people tossed coins; the winner was the one who had heads when the others had tails, or vice versa, had tails when his opponents had heads. The same procedure often serves to decide who will be chosen (or left out) for some activity, such as playing on a pickup team. The extended meaning was in use by 1889, when the *Saturday Review* wrote of "the good luck which attends us in the political 'odd-man-out' game."

Odds and Ends. Miscellaneous things. Long ago it was "odd ends," an end being then, as now, a remnant or a half-piece of cloth. In 1567 Thomas Harmon had it in his *Caveat*: "There sekinge aboute for odde endes, [he] at length founde a lytle whystell of sylver." In 1746 John Collier, writing on the Lancashire dialect, defined "odds-on-eends" as "odd trifling things."

Off His Rocker. Insane or seriously muddled. It is the rocking chair that is central here, although why going off it should symbolize losing one's mind is hard to say. Perhaps it is the association of the rocker and the elderly, and the fact that many old people gradually drift into a state of mental confusion. A British newspaper (the *Daily News*) offered an example of the broader meaning in 1897: "When asked if he had swallowed the liniment, he said, 'Yes, I was off my rocker.' "

Off and Running. On the way; making good progress, at least at the beginning. It's a term from horse racing (redundant, really, since if the horses were not running, they wouldn't be off). The track announcer always says, "They're off!" at the start of a race, sometimes adding, "and running." The transfer to, say, politics is apparently rather recent, as witness the *Boston Herald* in 1967: "Although he has not announced it officially, Wallace appears to be off and running for the presidency."

Off the Beaten Track. Different; unusual. The phrase is a straightforward transfer from the well-worn path. Here is Francis Junius, Jr., in *The Painting of the Ancients* (1638): "They . . . propound unto us the right way, and not one usually beaten track onely."

Off the Deep End. Rashly or emotionally. It is the "deep end" of the swimming pool or the dock, and the implication is that it is rash and impulsive to jump or dive there unless you are sure of your swimming ability and can clearly see what is in the water. Here is Christopher Morley in *Kitty Foyle* (1939): "I wish there was some man she'd go off the deep end about."

Off the Wall. Unconventional, unusual, impromptu. One senses an origin in handball, squash or racquetball, where a ball coming off the wall can call for some nimble and unplanned maneuvers by a player. Since at least 1974 its meaning has extended beyond sports, as is evident in a sentence from the *National Review* that year: "[Denis] Brian knows how to startle the over-interviewed with off-the-wall questions that get surprising answers."

Old Coot. An elderly person (usually a man and usually somewhat dull-witted or eccentric). The coot is a waterfowl; some species were apparently thought to look rather stupid, hence the transfer to certain people. John Bartlett said in his *Dictionary of Americanisms* (1859): "It is often applied by us to a stupid person." Frances M. Whitcher, writing a few years earlier in *The Widow Bedott Papers*, said: "He's an amazin' ignorant old coot."

Old Customs (Habits) Die Hard. People don't change easily; they adhere to familiar practices. Thomas à Kempis worked the thought into his German translation of *The Imitation of Christ* in 1450; in the first English translation (1530) it appears as: "Olde custom is harde to breke."

Old Fuddy-Duddy. An old-fashioned person; someone who is set in his ways; a fogy (especially intellectually). The two nonwords "fuddy" and "duddy" go neatly together, but where they originated is unknown. William Dickinson recorded "duddy fuddiel" as meaning "a ragged fellow" in his glossary of the Cumberland dialect in England (1899), and the root may be there. The modern usage appeared in Donald Moffat's *Mott Family in France* (1938): "Mr. Mott wandered along the Promenade . . . looking at the damned old fuddy-duddies who cluttered it up."

Old Guard. The stalwarts of a political party, or another organization, and frequently members of long standing; often the implication is that they are the fossilized defenders of a tradition. The term is from Napoleon's Imperial Guard, which was conspicuously loyal to him. In *The Waterloo Campaign*, he wrote: "The Imperial Guard was composed of four regiments of the Young Guard, four of the Middle Guard, four of the Old Guard, four cavalry regiments and 96 pieces of artillery." It was the Old Guard that mounted the final charge of the French at Waterloo.

Old Hat. So familiar as to be dull or boring. Probably the rapid changes in hat fashions (particularly women's hats), gave rise to this figure of speech. The saying was in use by 1911, when Sir Arthur Quiller-Couch wrote (in *Brother Copas*): "So it has happened with Satan and his fork; they have become 'old hat.' "

Old Saw. A well-known saying or maxim. The meaning of "saw" (from the same root as "say") as a figure of speech is lost now except in the cliché. The cliché in former times was often, "said saw" or "old said saw." John Palsgrave, writing in 1530, defined "ould sayd sawe" as "prouerbe." Alexander Pope had these lines in *January and May* (1705): "We, Sirs, are fools, and must resign the cause / To heath'nish authors, proverbs, and old saws."

Old as Time. Ancient. The implication is that the tradition or person has been around forever. The Rev. Jacob Bailey is quoted in *The Frontier Missionary* (1853) as having said in 1754: "An old broken mug, almost as ancient as time."

Old-Boy Network. A body of men who through their common alliance with a group (school, college, the army, etc.), can be relied upon to do favors for one another, often to the exclusion of outsiders who might have an equal or better claim. "Old boy" began as a British expression and denoted someone who had attended a given private school or college; the "old-boy network" seems to have originated in relation to British officers in World War II. By 1959 the phrase had a broader meaning, as exemplified by the *Manchester Guardian*: "The party must show that the Old Boy network of the Left does not prevent its speaking out when necessary."

On Tenterhooks. In suspense; anxious about the outcome of something. "Tenter" today refers only to someone who is camping out, but its old meaning is a frame for stretching cloth. Indeed, what we now convey by saying "on tenterhooks" was once put as "on tenters," as in John Ford's *The Broken Heart* (1633): "My very heart-strings are on the tenters." The tenterhook was one of the hooks or bent nails that held the cloth on the tenter. The modern version of the cliché appears in Tobias Smollett's *The Adventures of Roderick Random* (1748): "I left him upon the tenter-hooks of impatient uncertainty."

On the Ball. With it; sharp and competent. The transfer seems to have been from baseball, where a pitcher who is able to get something on the ball (movement, not a foreign substance) is likely to have a good outing. *Collier's* had the expression in 1912: "He's got nothing on the ball—nothing at all." The positive and extended version turned up in *Mademoiselle* in 1935: "The lass has much on the ball."

On the Beam. Correct; following the right course. This is a fairly new phrase, arising from the practice of guiding airplanes by a radio beam, which began some 50 years ago.

On the Carpet. Being reprimanded by one's employer or boss. In England, an old definition of "carpet" was "table covering," and "on the carpet" meant "up for discussion." A related expression, in which the carpet is on the floor, was "walk on the carpet," meaning a servant had been summoned for a reprimand. Thus, John Galt in *The Entail* (1823): "Making . . . her servants 'walk the carpet.' "One can speculate that in many offices before the days of wall-to-wall carpeting, the boss's office was the only one with a carpet. An employee called in for a reprimand was most decidedly "on the carpet."

On the Fence. Neutral; undecided or uncommitted. A fence is a boundary, and if one is on it, one is on neither side. This pictorial image is especially appropriate for politics, as in the *Richmond Whig* (1828): "There are certain Administration Editors, Editors for a long time on the fence, who occasionally undertake . . . to sit as censors upon their fatigued and dusty brethren."

On the Fly. In motion; hastily. Originally this phrase meant only "on the wing," referring to a flying bird or insect. By 1850 it had been extended to the current meaning, as in Henry Mayhew's *London Labour and the London Poor* (1851): "Taking them on the fly; which means meeting the gentry on their walks, and beseeching them or sometimes menacing them until something is given."

On the Fritz. Out of order; broken. Fritz is the German nickname for Friedrich and, during World War I it came to stand for Germans in general. Considering America's distaste for Germany at that time, the expression may have sprung from the notion that if there was wrongdoing, the Germans must have had a hand in it. This is speculation, however, and one must note that *Webster's Third International Dictionary* says of the expression, "origin unknown."

On the Go. In action; briskly moving. The phrase has had other meanings, now forgotten; among them are, to be on the verge of destruction, to be in decline, and to be slightly intoxicated. The meaning given here was in use by 1843, when it appeared in Alexander Bethune's *The Scottish Peasant's Fire-side*: "But if you can only afford to wait until you get us on the go."

On the Lam. Fleeing (usually from the law). To "do a lam" was defined by *Appleton's Popular Science Monthly* in 1897 as meaning to run. A book on *Life in Sing Sing* by "No. 1500" in 1904 offered: "He plugged the main guy for keeps and I took it on the lam for mine."

On the Level. Dealing honestly or fairly with someone. In the Masonic organization the carpenter's level is a symbol of integrity, perhaps explaining the expression's derivation. In any case, it was a colloquialism in the United States by the end of the 19th century. Here is humorist George Ade in *Artie* (1896): "I see barrel-house boys goin around for hand-outs that was more on the level than you."

On the Make. Hot after financial, social or sexual gain. It started as an American slang expression more than 100 years ago; J. H. Beadle, in *The Undeveloped West* (1873) had, "They're all on the make." In England the *Pall Mall Gazette* offered this entry in 1890: "Suppose . . . that I am a man, as our American cousins say, 'on the make'—suppose that I have parliamentary ambitions."

On the Rampage. Storming (of a person); vigorously angry; spoiling for a fight or for revenge. "Ramp" is an ancient verb—dating to Chaucer's time at least—and means to act in a furious or threatening way. "Rampage" may come from that. The modern thought was known by 1861, when Charles Dickens wrote (in *Great Expectations*): "She's been on the Ram-page this last spell, about five minutes."

On the Rocks. Suffering physical, mental or financial troubles. The image is from seafaring and goes way back; a ship that has run on the rocks will quickly break up unless it is pulled or floated off. Use of the term to signify other disasters is more recent, as in Alexander G. Murdoch's *Scottish Readings* (1889): "Fork out, for I'm fair on the rocks."

On the Ropes. In great difficulty; on the brink of failure or defeat. The ropes delineate the boxing or wrestling ring, and the fighter who is on them is usually in trouble. Pierce Egan described the predicament in *Boxiana* (1829): "Lenny found himself hanging on the ropes, where he was milled down." Using the phrase to describe difficulties is equally old.

On the Spot. In difficulty; expected to explain some action, or to take some action. Today's meaning is milder than the original American slang expression, which meant to be marked for assassination. The "spot" is believed to be the ace of spades, which pirates showed to a traitor to indicate he was to be executed. In a sentence from a 1930 *Punch*, the less dire connotation can be seen developing: "You get rid of inconvenient subordinates . . . by 'putting them on the spot'—that is deliberately sending them to their death." In this case "death" is discharge, or transfer to a poorer job.

On the Spur of the Moment. Impulsively; with little or no fore-thought. Opportunity stimulates the beholder as the spur stimulates the horse. Archibald Duncan, describing the funeral of Admiral Nelson in 1806, wrote of "the contrivance of Mr. Wyatt, on the spur of the moment."

On the Up-and-Up. Honest, aboveboard, fair-dealing. It's hard to know which of the many meanings of "up" was originally appropriated for this expression; probably it was merely an intensifying form of saying that the person or proposition is up where you can see it clearly. The intensifier has been around for more than 100 years. In 1863 the *Humboldt Register* of Unionville, Nev., had this passage: "Now that would be business, on the dead up-and-up."

On the Wagon. Abstaining from drinking alcoholic beverages. This rather mysterious phrase becomes clear when one realizes it is short for "on the water wagon,"—a common piece of equipment in the days before paved roads—which was used to spray dirt roads to keep the dust down. The idea that someone forgoing hard liquor was on the water wagon was being expressed by 1904, when the *Dialect Notes* (a publication of the American Dialect Society) reported: " 'To be on the water wagon,' to abstain from hard drinks."

Once in a Blue Moon. Rarely; almost never. Supposedly the moon is never blue, although, on a clear night, some people perceive a faint blue cast to the part of the moon that is faintly visible when the bright part is in the shape of a fingernail. The rarity of the blue moon was suggested in a verse published in 1528 by William Roy and J. Barlow in *Rede Me and Be Nott Wrothe:* "Yf they say the mone is belewe, / We must beleve that it is true."

One Fell Swoop. A quick and often savage action. It's remarkable how many old words with multiple meanings survive in only a single phrase with just one meaning. Here it is "fell," which is from the same Latin root that produced "felon," and once meant (among other things) cruel, fierce, savage. So a fell swoop is a savage swoop, such as a hawk might make when seizing a chicken. In *Macbeth*, Shakespeare has Macduff say, on learning that his wife and children have been killed at Macbeth's order: "What, all my pretty chickens and their dam / at one fell swoop?"

One Foot in the Grave. In a bad way; seriously ill, or aged and infirm; on the point of death. Plutarch wrote 1,800 years ago of "an old dotard with one foot already in the grave." The image appeared in English no later than 1509, when Alexander Barclay used it in *The Shyp of Folys* [fools]: "Thy graue is open, thy one fote in the pyt."

One for the Road. Another drink before I leave. The expression probably dates from the 1930s, when long automobile trips had become fairly standard and Prohibition had ended. The traveler stopping in a bar might have (but would have been wiser not to have) one last drink before setting out again. In J. P. Donleavy's *Ginger Man* (1955) there was such a traveler: "You've had a few," observes one character. "Five for the road," boasts the traveler. "Never let it be said that I took to the highway or even byway without fuel for me little heart."

Onward and Upward. We must continue to advance, to improve. In *The Present Crisis* (1844), James Russell Lowell wrote:
> New occasions teach new duties: time makes ancient
> good uncouth;
> They must upward still, and onward, who would
> keep abreast of Truth.

Open Book, He's an. He's transparent; his motives are easily perceived. This transfer from the easy-to-read book to the easy-to-read person seems to have been made within the present century. P. G. Wodehouse wrote, in *Damsel in Distress* (1920): "There's no mystery about me. I'm an open book."

Open Question. An undecided issue. The phrase derives from a practice in the British Parliament; Homersham Cox described it in *The Institutions of the English Government* (1863): "Certain questions brought before Parliament are treated as 'open' questions; that is, questions on which [cabinet] Ministers in Parliament are allowed to take opposite sides without resigning."

Open Secret. Something widely known or easily discovered even though it isn't supposed to be. Here we have an oxymoron (a juxtaposition of opposites, such as "sweet sorrow"). Sir Frederick Pollock used it in an introduction to another man's book of lectures and essays in 1879: "It is an open secret to the few who know it, but a mystery . . . to the many, that Science and Poetry are own sisters."

Open and Aboveboard. Fair; conducting one's business without trickery. This is "board" in the sense of table; things done above the table were in the open and in view of everyone around it. The expression was common by the 17th century and then had a companion, "under board," meaning sneaky dealings. The modern usage is clear in Richard Carpenter's *The Conscionable Christian* (1620): "All his dealings are square and above-board."

Open-and-Shut Case. A straightforward matter that admits of no doubt as to the outcome. The "case" is a legal case, and the original concept was that the case was so clear-cut it could be closed almost as soon as it opened. However, the expression "open and shut" turns up earlier in other uses, as in the New Orleans *Picayune* in 1841: "The contest between *Humming Bird* and *Maria Collier* was considered all but a 'dead open and shut game.' "

Other Things Being Equal. Provided that nothing outweighs the matter you are considering or is changing in its effect on the matter. The phrase is a translation of the Latin *ceteris paribus*, which is occasionally still used to convey the thought. In 1889 the *Saturday Review* offered: "Other things being equal, the chances of any man being hit in action vary . . . with the rate of fire to which he is exposed." (If *The New Yorker* had been on the scene then, it might have run the sentence from *Saturday Review* under its heading, A Thought for This Week.)

Out and Out. Complete; extreme. This is "out" in its ancient adverbial sense of "to the conclusion." The phrase is equally ancient, appearing in Geoffrey Chaucer's *Troilus and Criseyde* (1374): "For out and out he is worthiest . . .."

Out of Sight, Out of Mind. You're likely to be overlooked if you don't make your presence visible. A similar figure of speech was a proverb in the 13th century: "For he that is not belooken is soon forgotten." (The virtually unreadable medieval English has been modernized.) A translation of *de Imitatione Christi* in 1450 offered this: "Whan man is out of sight, sone he passeth out of mynde."

Out of the Mouths of Babes. Kids say the damndest things. The phrase comes from the Bible, although the meaning has altered. Psalm 8, one of the Psalms of David (the one that asks, "What is man, that thou art mindful of him?"), says of the Lord (8 : 2): "Out of the mouth of babes and sucklings thou hast ordained strength . . .."

Out of the Woods. Clear of danger or difficulty. In England it is "out of the wood," which is the form that was in use 200 years ago when Mme. D'Arblay (Frances Burney) wrote, in her *Diary and Letters* (1792): "Mr. Windham says we are not yet out of the wood, though we can see the path through it." The developing image can be seen in an earlier remark by Henry More in one of his religious tracts (1664): "This wood is so wide, that I may easilier lose my self in it then get through it."

Out on a Limb. In an exposed or dangerous position. One can surmise that the literal origin of this saying was the treed animal, which was highly vulnerable to the hunter if it got out on a limb. The saying originated in the United States and by 1897 had acquired its figurative meaning, which is seen in *Wolfville*, by A. H. Louis: "Seven of us . . . seein' whatever we can tie down and brand, when some Mexicans gets us out on a limb."

Out the Window. Gone or lost all at once and suddenly (as one's hopes might be). We may see here an evolution of the older "throw the house out at the window," meaning to disrupt things, turn things upside down, stir up a commotion. Here it is in Philemon Holland's *Plutarch's Morals* (1603): "For such a fault as this, which of us here would not have cried out that the walles should have burst withall, and beene readie to have throwen the house out a window."

Over a Barrel. Helpless; at a disadvantage; in someone's power. The *Oxford English Dictionary* speculates plausibly that the expression comes from the practice of draping over a barrel someone who has been rescued from the water at the point of drowning, the idea being to empty his lungs of water. Raymond Chandler extended the thought in *The Big Sleep* (1939): "We keep a file on unidentified bullets nowadays. Someday you might use that gun again. Then you'd be over a barrel."

Over the Hill. Past one's prime. The "hill" here would seem to be the hill of life, from childhood to one's achievements as an adult. The time often comes when one is no longer achieving (particularly in a field where the person had achieved a lot) and is figuratively going downhill. The *New York Herald Tribune* gave a good example of the phrase in 1950: "He has lost his punch. . . . He's a lot farther over the hill than I was when I hung up the gloves in 1927."

Own Man (Master), To Be One's. Act independently; be free of control. "Own master" seems to be fairly recent, but "own man" has a long history, an example being found in John Gower's *Confessio Amantis* (1390, with the English modernized): "If I be not my own man, and dare not use what I can . . . .."

Own Worst Enemy, He's His. He brings most of his troubles on himself. This is an evolutionary development from the older "nobody's enemy but one's own." Robert Greene was close to that in *A Quip for an Upstart Courtier* (1592): "I thinke him an honest man if he would but liue within his compasse, and generally no mannes foe but his own."

Ox is Gored, Whose. One's viewpoint changes when it is his or her own interest that is affected. Martin Luther used the phrase in the 16th century: "It makes a difference whose ox is gored." The idea is also the moral of a fable ("The Partial Judge") recounted in Noah Webster's *American Spelling Book* (1802). A farmer says to a lawyer: "One of your Oxen has been gored by an unlucky Bull of mine, and I should like to know how I am to make you reparation." The lawyer says he expects one of the farmer's oxen. Then the farmer says he has made a mistake: it is the *lawyer's* bull that has killed the farmer's ox. "Indeed!" says the lawyer, "that alters the case. I must enquire into the affair; and if . . ." "And if!" said the farmer. "The business I find would have been concluded without an *if*, had you been as ready to do justice to others, as to exact it from them."

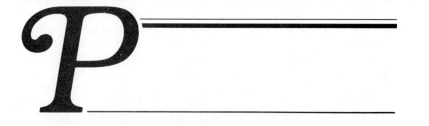

Pack It In. To retire; to quit. The phrase is taken from the notion of packing a suitcase in preparation for leaving. As "pack up" or "pack in," it seems to have originated as servicemen's slang during or soon after World War I, and to have meant to stop doing almost anything. *Soldier & Sailor Words* (1925) defined it as: "To stop [as opposed to 'carry on']. To give up. To finish. To die."

Pack a Wallop. Be able to strike a formidable blow, make a heavy impact (i.e., to wield authority or influence.) The saying was known by 1922, when Eugene O'Neill packed it into his play *The Hairy Ape*: "He packa da wallop, I tella you!"

Packed In Like Sardines. Jammed into a room or an enclosed space such as a bus. Those people who first put sardines in cans were marvels at making maximum use of the space (aided, to be sure, by the shape of the sardines, which, when laid head to tail, fit quite neatly). The phenomenon was observed by 1894, when George Du Maurier wrote in *Trilby*: "The guests were not packed together sardine-wise, as they are at most concerts."

Paddle Your Own Canoe. Be independent; take care of your own affairs. The canoe as an example of a device requiring skillful individual handling has appealed to white men since Columbus discovered it in use in the West Indies. "Paddle Your Own Canoe" was the title of a popular song in the 19th century, and in 1844 Frederick Marryat wrote, in *Settlers in Canada*: "Every man paddle his own canoe."

Pain in the Neck, A. A severe bother or annoyance. No doubt this figurative pain has been felt for millenniums, but it was only some 80 years ago that it appeared in the language (the written language, anyway). "You . . . folks give me a pain." was in R. E. Knowles' *Web of Time* in 1908, and P. G. Wodehouse had the fuller version in *Leave it to Psmith* (1924): "He got there first, damn him! Wouldn't that give you a pain in the neck!" As Charles E. Funk wrote in *Heavens to Betsy*, the expression is "a polite version of a pain previously associated with another part of the anatomy."

Paper Over, To. To deal with a problem by means of a temporary expedient; to conceal a blemish or defect. It's what you do with wallpaper; indeed, the phrase is sometimes expressed as "paper over the cracks." The literal meaning is as old as wallpaper, but the figurative meaning came later, as in *The* [London] *Times* in 1955: "This document was treated by the western Ministers as no more than an attempt to paper over the complete divergence in policy."

Paper Tiger. Something less tough or menacing than it appears. The phrase originated with Chairman Mao of the People's Republic of China in 1946; he was referring to "reactionaries," all of whom, he said, are "paper tigers." Since then it has been applied even to sports teams. A British writer said of a soccer team in 1976: "We were something of paper tigers when it came to the championship games."

Par For the Course. Normal (often implying that the standard of normality is low). Par in golf is what a good player should score on a hole; the calculation assumes two putts and takes into account the length of the hole and (sometimes) the special difficulties it presents. In the somewhat mistransferred sense that the performance is only so-so, the phrase appears in Muriel Beadle's *These Ruins Are Inhabited* (1961): "While waiting . . . I caught a fragment of another subscriber's telephone conversation. This is also par for the course in making an Oxford phone call."

Part and Parcel. A key component. With alliteration, redundancy and usage in the law going for it, this phrase was bound to be a veteran in the store of clichés. Indeed, it turned up as early as 1535 in the *Acts of Henry VIII*: "This present Act, and euery part and parcel thereof, shall extend . . . ."

Parting Shot. A riposte or thrust given as one leaves the scene of a contest or an exchange. Sometimes, among the very literary, it is "Parthian shot," a reference to the ancient Middle Eastern warriors who turned in flight to discharge arrows at their pursuers. Robert Greene offered a version of the term in *A Quip for an Upstart Courtier* (1592): "Thus much I must say for a parting blow."

Pass the Buck. To shift responsibility by shifting it (or trying to shift it) to someone else. The buck was an object (perhaps a piece of buckshot) passed from one card player to another to signify the recipient was to be the next dealer. In *The Innocents at Home* (1872), Mark Twain wrote: "Ante and pass the buck." President Harry S Truman kept on his desk a small sign that said, "The buck stops here."

Patience of Job. Willing to endure severe and prolonged hardship. Job, in the Old Testament book of that name, was a God-fearing man who became the victim of a contest between Satan and the Lord. Satan contended the Lord had favored Job; "put forth thine hand now," Satan said (Job 1 : 11), "and touch all that he hath, and he will curse thee to thy face." The Lord did, but Job (with some bolstering from his friends) held to his faith. The tale is recalled in the New Testament (James 5 : 11): "Ye have heard of the patience of Job . . . ."

Pave the Way. Prepare suitable conditions for some development; make matters smooth. Paving, even with cobblestones, is an improvement over mud. Thus, one finds this figurative expression used long before the development of asphalt and concrete, as in a note by Thomas Cartwright (1585): "The way will bee paued and plained for mutual entercourse."

Pay As You Go. Meet your obligations as they arise, rather than go into debt to do so. It is a philosophy that is often advocated for governments but rarely practiced by them. It is also quite old; the *Farmers' Cabinet* declared in 1840: "Pay as you go . . . is the truest economy."

Pay Through the Nose. Be charged an exorbitant price. Why nose? One supposition is that this kind of paying is as irksome as a nosebleed. Another tale has it that the Danes levied a tax on the Irish in the 9th century, and that anyone who failed to pay it was punished by having his nose slit. In any event, we find Andrew Marvell writing in 1672 (in *The Rehearsal Tranposed*): "Made them pay it most unconscionably and through the Nose."

Pay Your Money and Take Your Choice. You can have your own way as long as you are the buyer or have fulfilled some other obligation. Sometimes it is, "You pays your money and you takes your choice." Charles J. Lever expressed this thought in 1845: "You have paid your money, and you may take your choice."

Pay the Piper. Settle a bill or an obligation. The piper provided music in taverns and at ceremonies, and the listeners, or host, were expected to pay him. Hence, John Taylor in *Taylor's Feast* (1638): "Always those that dance must pay the musicke." From this came, in the 19th century, the thought that "he who pays the piper calls the tune."

Penny For Your Thoughts, A. What's on your mind? (Usually said to someone who is looking pensive.) The saying is from a time when the British penny was worth a significant sum. In 1522, Sir Thomas More wrote (in *Four Last Things*): "It often happeth, that the very face sheweth the mind walking a pilgrimage, in such wise that . . . other folk sodainly say to them: a peny for your thought."

Penny Wise and Pound Foolish. Overcareful about trivial things and undercareful about important ones. The literal image is of the person who fusses over small amounts of money to such an extent that he misses opportunities to save or make large amounts. But the figurative image goes way back; in *The Historie of Foure-footed Beastes* (1607) Edward Topsell wrote: "If by covetousnesse or negligence, one withdraw from them their ordinary foode, he shall be penny wise, and pound foolish."

Perk (Prick) Up One's Ears. Take notice; become alert or watchful. The horse does it, and so do many other animals when their attention is directed to a sound or an action. Shakespeare's *The Tempest* (1610) offers this from Ariel:

> Then I beat my tabor;
> At which, like unback'd colts, they prick'd their ears,
> Advanced their eyelids, lifted up their noses
> As they smelt music . . . .

Peter Out. To fail, give out, fade away. Some sources say "origin unknown." The *Oxford English Dictionary* asserts that it is a term from American mining. But why peter? Charles E. Funk thought it might derive from the apostle Peter, who, when Jesus was seized in the Garden of Gethsemane, "grasped a sword and rushed to his defense; but within the next few hours his enthusiasm had diminished to the extent that before the cock crowed he had thrice denied that he even knew Jesus." In any event, the expression was current by 1854, when H. H. Riley wrote (in *Puddleford and Its People*): "He hoped this 'spectable meeting warn't going to Peter-out.' "

Pick His Brain. Glean ideas from someone; draw on their experience. Sometimes, phrased inelegantly, it was "suck his brains." Nathaniel Willis, writing in 1850, said: "I . . . sat down to pick his brains of the little information I wanted."

Pick and Choose. Make a selection, usually with great care. Another redundancy rears its head. Once it was "pick and cull," which is somewhat less redundant, since "cull" implies careful or reasoned choice. When Sir Thomas Herbert wrote in 1665 about his travels in Africa and Asia, he said: "So little was the resistance he found as he had the liberty to pick and choose."

Picture Is Worth a Thousand Words, A. It's much easier to convey some ideas graphically than verbally, or in writing. It sounds like a dictum from the city editor of the New York *Daily News*, but, in fact, something quite similar ("One picture is worth more than ten thousand words.") was a Chinese proverb long ago. The

Russian writer Ivan Turgenev wrote (in *Fathers and Sons* in 1862): "A picture shows me at a glance what it takes dozens of pages of a book to expound."

Picture of Health. The image of well-being; ideally fit. It is sometimes used to flatter, or is said in mild surprise that the person described looks as good as he does. Thus *Punch* in 1871: "He looks the picture of health."

Pie in the Sky. Something unrealistic or unattainable; promised pleasures that will never come. The early 20th-century labor organizer and songwriter Joe Hill may have originated this arresting image in his parody (The Preacher and the Slave) of a hymn:

> You will eat, bye and bye,
> In the glorious land above the sky!
> Work and pray,
> Live on hay,
> You'll get pie in the sky when you die!

Piece of Cake, That's a. Something that can be done easily and pleasurably. The light-verse writer Ogden Nash had this line in *Primrose Path* (1936): "Her picture's in the papers now, and life's a piece of cake." The thought surely derives from the fact that for most people eating a piece of cake is easy and a pleasure.

Piece of My Mind, Gave Him a. I gave him my straightforward, unvarnished opinion; I rebuked or scolded him. Sir Henry Ellis's *Original Letters Illustrative of English History* (1824) has an example from 1572: "Thus am I bolde to unfolde a peece of my mynde."

Piece of the Action, A. A share in what is going on. To have a piece of this or that is a colloquialism that goes back some 50 years ("a piece of the show" 1929; "a piece of the cleaners' racket," 1930). The current phrase is more recent, as in this example (1976) from Charlie Frick: "They were . . . managers and agents and producers and all the others that had a piece of the action."

Pig in a Poke, Buy a. To buy something (or accept an idea) without having seen it or being sure of what it is. The poke was a small bag (the words "pouch" and "pocket" derive from the same roots), and the pig was a small pig. As related in Thomas Tusser's *Five Hundredth Good Pointes of Husbandrie* (1580), the game was to put a cat in the poke and try to palm it off in the market as a pig, persuading the buyer that it would be best not to open the poke because the pig might get away. If the buyer insisted on seeing what he was getting, and the seller opened the poke, he "let the cat out of the bag." The expression was around in the 14th century, when the *Douce Manuscript* offered: "When me proferreth ye pigge, opon the pogh."

Pile It On. Carry something (such as praise or ridicule) to excess; overdo. The sense is of heaping up needlessly. Thus, in Mark Twain's *Huckleberry Finn* (1884): "I reckon that was sort of piling it on maybe."

Pillar of Society (the Establishment, the Community). An important, or self-important person. The term is often used sarcastically to refer to those who think they are influential (or are thought to be in some circles) but, in fact, are not. They are being likened to a pillar that helps support a building. In 1888, Henrik Ibsen entitled his play, *The Pillars of Society.* In 1902 George Bernard Shaw wrote, in *Mrs. Warren's Profession:* "Dearer still . . . is that sense of the sudden earthquake shock to the foundations of morality which sends a pallid crowd of critics into the street shrieking that the pillars of society are cracking and the ruin of the State at hand."

Pinpoint Accuracy. Spectacular aim or achievement. The point of a pin is notably small and for some time has symbolized getting things in focus. The cliché dates from bombing attacks in World War II, but it was also applied to other weapons capable of precise aim. Thus, the *Baltimore Sun* (1949): " 'Kickless' guns, capable of pinpoint accuracy."

Pipe Down. Be quiet; stop making so much noise. The phrase is of naval origin, deriving from one of the signals the boatswain blew on his pipe or whistle. The signals meant such things as, "turn in" and "lights out." Thus, in Frederick Marryat's *Peter Simple* (1833): "The hammocks were piped down . . . and the ship was once more quiet."

Pitched Battle. A heavy fight (usually between evenly matched and well-prepared opposing sides). This is one of those phrases one uses without giving much thought to the meaning of the key words. Why "pitched"? Well, one of the meanings of "pitch," although not often used, is to set things out in an orderly fashion (fenceposts, for example). And a pitched battle was one in which the two sides were lined up in an orderly way and ready for the fight, as opposed to a skirmish or an unexpected battle. Since the past participle of "pitch" was once "pight," you find it that way in the early versions of the saying, as in a 16th-century translation of the 27th Psalm: "In battell pight if they will try I trust in God for ayde."

Place in the Sun, A. A situation in which one gets recognition and there is a favorable opportunity for advancement or development. Here is Basil Kennet, writing in 1727 on *Pascal's Thoughts*: "This Dog's *mine*, says the poor Child; this is *my* place, in the Sun. From so petty a Beginning, may we trace the Tyranny and Usurpation of the whole Earth." In 1911, as the tensions leading to World War I were building, Kaiser Wilhelm of Germany said of his country, (thus giving the phrase new currency): "No one can dispute with us the place in the sun that is our due."

Plain as Day. Obvious; perfectly clear. It is a crotchet of mine that words such as "obviously" and "of course" should be avoided, since they are a condescending response to the person who brought up the point. Presumably he wouldn't have done so if the point was obvious to him. The same is true of "plain as day," whch appeared in a slightly different form in James A. Froude's *Caesar* (1879): "It was plain as the sun at midday."

Plain as the Nose on Your Face, As. As evident as anything can be. At one time the saying had quite the opposite meaning: invisible, something one doesn't notice. Thus, Thomas Whythorne in his *Autobiography* (1525): "It shalnot be somuch seen as A noz in A mans fas." Apparently both meanings survived for a time; hence, William Congreve's *Love for Love* (1695): "As witness my hand... in great Letters. Why, 'tis as plain as the Nose in one's Face."

Play Fast and Loose. Fail to keep faith with someone to whom a promise was made or implied. Originally it was "to play at fast and loose," since "fast and loose" was a trick game that sharpsters played on the rubes at country fairs in times past. In 1847 James Halliwell, in a dictionary of words and phrases from the 14th century, described it this way: "A cheating game played with a stick and a belt or string, so arranged that a spectator would think he could make the latter fast by placing a stick through its intricate folds, whereas the operator could detach it at once." The saying was recorded in *Tottel's Miscellany* (1557): "Of a new married studient that plaied fast or loose."

Play It by Ear. Improvise; act according to what the situation suggests. The origin is made clear in John Playford's *A Brief Introduction to the Skill of Musicke* (1674): "To learn to play [a musical instrument] by rote or ear without a Book."

Play Musical Chairs. Compete for position; move people in and out of places of authority or responsibility. It is from a child's game (not always played only by children) in which the participants walk behind a circle of chairs (fewer chairs than people) to the accompaniment of music; when the music stops, everybody scrambles to get into an empty chair. *Trench Yarns*, by 'Peter' (1916), gave this anecdote: "We had to get the men through the danger zone by a sort of musical-chairs rush."

199

Play Possum. Feign innocence or unawareness. The origin and use of the term are concisely stated in *Notices of East Florida* by W. H. Simmons (1822): "After being severely wounded, they [possums] have been known to lie for several hours as if dead . . . . Hence, the expression of 'playing possum' is common among the inhabitants, being applied to those who act with cunning and duplicity."

Play With Fire. Deal irresponsibly with something that is dangerous; invite disaster. George Whetstone wrote in *Heptameron* (1582): "In doing of these three thinges is great daunger . . . to play with fire: to striue with water: and to giue a woman knowledge of our power."

Play Your Cards Right. Make good moves; deploy your resources and wits to the best advantage. It is of course from card games, but the meaning has been extended to any competitive activity. That meaning is also quite old; Samuel Foote's *Englishman in Paris* (1753) had it : "If Lucinda plays her Cards well, we have not much to fear from that Quarter."

Play a Trump Card. Make a move that should gain you victory or an advantage. In whist and bridge the suit of cards designated as "trumps" temporarily outranks all other suits and can be defeated only by a higher trump. (The word is derived from "triumph.") A "trump card" is usually, therefore, a devastating weapon. Thomas Hardy had the concept in *Tess of the D'Urbervilles* (1891): "She ought to make her way with 'en, if she plays her trump card aright."

Play on Words, A. A pun; a double meaning; a stretch of a meaning, often just for effect. David Hume found occasion, in *A Treatise on Human Nature* (1739), to "confess . . . that human reason is nothing but a play of words."

Pleased as Punch. Exuberantly satisfied. As Punch and Judy puppet shows aren't often seen today, it has to be alliteration that holds this expression in the language. The traditional Punch was given to strong emotions, and the audience knew when he was pleased or angry. Alliteration did the rest. In 1813 Thomas Moore wrote in a letter: "I was (as the poet says) as pleased as Punch."

Plugged Nickel, Not Worth a. Valueless. To plug a coin was to remove part of it and replace that portion with material of little value. You could still pass the coin off at its face value, and meanwhile you had the silver you had removed. If you did that often enough you would be well off. People were talking about plugged quarters 100 years ago; the plugged silver dollar and the plugged peso also received notice. The plugged nickel was probably more symbolic than real, since it would take a lot of plugging of nickels to make any money. Carl Sandburg wrote, in *People, Yes* (1936): "He seems to think he's the frog's tonsils but he looks to me like a plugged nickel."

Plumb the Depths. Get to the bottom of; reach the lowest (usually worst) point. It is literally what a sailor near the bow of a ship did with a plumb line when the vessel was in shallow or unknown waters. Arthur H. Clough gave an example of the extended meaning in *Amours de Voyage* (1849): "So I plumb the deeps of depression."

Point of No Return. The time or place when, or at which, it's too late to change your mind about what you're doing and alter your course of action. The term comes from flying, as explained in the *Journal of the Royal Aeronautical Society* in 1941:

> This three-engined operation data is used to determine our so-called 'Point of No Return.' Laymen are inevitably intrigued by this fatalistic expression. As a matter of fact it is merely a designation of that limit-point, before which any engine failure requires an immediate turn around and return to the point of departure, and beyond which such return is no longer practical."

The limiting factor is most likely to be the fuel supply, but it can also be whether the plane has gone more than half way on its projected journey.

Poker Face. An unreadable expression; a resolutely maintained expressionlessness. The 1885 *Encyclopedia Britannica* explained why the deadpan look is essential to the serious card player, particularly the betting poker player: "A good *poker face* is essential; the countenance should not betray the nature of the hand."

Poor As a Churchmouse. Genteel but hard up. The presumption was that a mouse living in a church had surroundings that were elegant enough but was unlikely to find much to eat, since a church usually had no pantry or larder. In the oldest version (James Howell's collection of proverbs in 1659), it was "hungry as a church mouse."

Possession Is Nine-Tenths of the Law. You are in a stronger position if you have something in hand or under your control than if you merely claim it. Once the expression was "possession is eleven points of the law," and it appears that way in *B. Discolliminium*, a book published in 1650. Whether eleven or nine, the idea is that nearly all (eleven of twelve, or nine of 10) of the points that may be raised in a legal action are in your favor.

Pot Calling the Kettle Black, The. An assertion that someone else has the very faults that can be attributed to you (the presumption being that the accuser is unaware of having such faults). The saying dates from centuries ago, when stoves ran on wood or coal. Presumably, after long use, both the pot and the kettle would be black. We can also surmise, however, that in many households the kettle (particularly if made of copper) was kept polished and hence, reflected the blackness of the pot. The pot, looking at the reflection, would see black, which would appear to be on the side of the kettle; the pot could then accuse the kettle of a fault it did not have. *Don Quixote*, written in the early 17th century, contains a sentence that can be translated: "You are like what is said that the frying-pan said to the Kettle, 'Avant, blacke-browes.' " A dictionary of cant published in 1699 recorded the saying in its present form and offered the definition, "when one accuses another of what he is as Deep in himself."

Pound of Flesh, A. An exaction, usually in retribution for something; the completion of a bargain. It is the payment demanded by Shylock, in Shakespeare's *Merchant of Venice*, for a loan of money to Antonio. Conditions arise in which Shylock is able to claim the payment. Portia, disguised as a judge, rules that he is entitled to it, but then says:

> Tarry a little; there is something else.
> This bond doth give thee here no jot of blood;
> The words expressly are 'a pound of flesh';
> Take then thy bond, take thou thy pound of flesh;
> But, in the cutting of it, if thou dost shed
> One drop of Christian blood, thy lands and goods
> Are, by the laws of Venice, confiscate
> Unto the state of Venice.

Pour Oil on Troubled Waters, To. To try to ease a turbulent or difficult situation. Mariners have known for centuries that oil on the surface of a heavy sea diminishes its waves. The Venerable Bede, in his *Ecclesiastical History* (A.D. 731), relates that St. Aidan gave a priest who was about to embark on an important sea journey, a cruse of oil, saying: "Remember to throw into the sea the oil which I give to you, when straightway the winds will abate, and a calm and smiling sea will accompany you throughout your voyage."

Power Behind the Throne, The. A person or group with substantial influence on the nominal leader. William Pitt (the elder) probably originated this image when he said (1770): "There is something behind the throne greater than the King himself."

Powers That Be, The. The people who are in authority or control. The phrase is directly from the Bible (Romans 13 : 1): "Let every soul be subject unto the higher powers. For there is no power but of God: the powers that be are ordained of God."

Powers of Darkness. The forces of evil; the realm of the devil. Satan was the prince of darkness, and the realm he controlled encompassed the powers of darkness. Saint Paul wrote (Colossians 1 : 13) of giving thanks to the Father, "Who hath delivered us from the power of darkness."

Practice What You Preach. Stop moralizing or being overfree with advice; do what you urge others to do. A version of the thought appears in William Langland's *Piers Plowman* (1377); in modern form it would be, "what he preaches he does not do." Sir Roger L'Estrange had the modern version in *Seneca's Morals* (1678): "We must practise what we preach."

Preach to the Converted. Propound an argument to people who already support it. Thus, in 1867 John Stuart Mill wrote in one of his many books: "Dr. McCosh is preaching not only to a person already converted, but to an actual missionary of the same doctrine."

Pretty as a Picture. Good looking. Since not all pictures are pretty, one must suppose the kind of picture meant was one that made the subject look his or her best. The (American) *Dialect Notes* said in 1909 that the phrase meant, "very pretty: often used of a fine specimen of fruit" (a common subject of still-life paintings). Eugene O'Neill wrote, in *Marco Millions* (1927): "Here! Let me get a good look at you! Why, you're still as pretty as a picture and you don't look a day older!"

Prime of Life. The best time; the years when one is at the peak of one's powers. Plato considered the matter more than 22 centuries ago in *The Republic*: "What is the prime of life? May it not be defined as a period of about twenty years in a woman's life, and thirty in a man's?"

Proof of the Pudding Is in the Eating. The way to test whether something came out as it was intended is to try it. The pudding may look good when it is put on the table, but the only way to know for certain is to taste it. As you might expect, it is an old proverb. One version of it dates to the 14th century. A translation in 1682 of Boileau's *Le Lutrin* offered this: "The proof of th' pudding's seen i' th' eating."

Prophet Without Honor. An unrecognized seer or predictor. The full saying is, "a prophet is not without honor save in his own country [or house]"; the implication is that the people close to the soothsayer don't want to hear what he says, or don't like what they hear. The phrase comes from the Bible (Matthew 13 : 57).

Jesus had been teaching the people of his own country, who were disbelieving and "offended in him." He says: "A prophet is not without honour, save in his own country, and in his own house."

Pull His Leg. To fool or tease someone, usually in a friendly spirit. In an earlier age it was sometimes "draw his leg." The image may be in gently tripping someone up, that is, fooling or confusing him. The *English Dialect Dictionary* offers the example of a Scottish rhyme from 1867: "He preached an' at last drew the auld body's leg, / Sae the kirk got the gatherins [the money] o' our Aunty Meg."

Pull It Off. Succeed; accomplish something (often by means of a stratagem). Exactly what analogy was being made originally is hard to say; there are too many meanings of "pull." The saying was familiar by 1887, when William Black included it in *Sabina Zembra*: "We haven't pulled it off this time, mother."

Pull Out All the Stops. Employ all the resources at hand; go all out in some effort. Organ stops are the source of the analogy. A "stop" in this sense is the knob by which the organist brings a pipe or a set of pipes into play or blocks it off. When he pulls out all the stops, all the pipes are in play. Matthew Arnold was close to the modern analogy in *Essays in Criticism* (1865), in a remark on knowing "how unpopular a task one is undertaking when one tries to pull out a few more stops in that . . . somewhat narrow-toned organ, the modern Englishman."

Pull Strings. Exert influence from behind or outside of the scene. It is what the puppeteer does to control the action of his docile characters. Bishop William Stubbs, lecturing in the 1860s on the history of Europe, spoke of "a king who pulled the strings of government so exclusively himself."

Pull Yourself Up By the Bootstraps. To improve one's position without help; to raise oneself socially, economically or culturally. The bootstrap is a loop of fabric sewn into the inside of a boot near the top rear, or sometimes two loops sewn into the sides near the top. One takes a device consisting of a handle with a perpendicular arm bearing a hook, inserts the hook in the strap and pulls up on the handle, thus easing the difficult job of getting the boot on. The bootstrap is so old (16th century) and the image of progressing from hoisting up boots to hoisting up oneself is so vivid you might expect the saying to be equally old. As a saying, perhaps it is, but in print it is recent. James Joyce came close to it in *Ulysses* (1922): "There were . . . others who had forced their way to the top from the lowest rung by the aid of their bootstraps." Stanley Kunitz and Howard Haycraft in *British Authors of the 19th Century* (1936) were closer still when they described "a poet who had lifted himself by his own bootstraps from an obscure versifier to the ranks of real poetry."

Pull a Rabbit Out of the Hat. Accomplish something unexpected; find a solution for a difficulty that seemed insurmountable. It is an old trick of the magician or conjurer to pull a rabbit (sometimes several rabbits) out of a hat he has made the audience believe is empty. As Edwin T. Sachs puts it in *Sleight of Hand* (1877): "The production of . . . rabbits from a hat is always very startling." The figurative meaning is apparently more recent. Del Shannon used it in *Death by Inches* (1967): "Well, you pulled the rabbit out of the hat."

Pull the Rug Out From Under. Sabotage someone's plans, expectations or activity; withdraw support. It must have originated with a flight of the imagination, since literally pulling the rug out from under somebody is not likely to have been a widely practiced activity. The phrase is of American origin and apparently not terribly old. *Time* magazine had it in 1946: "Strikes, for instance, would pull the rug out from under the best of prospects."

Pull the Wool Over His Eyes. Deceive him. Quite likely the literal origin of this phrase was in the wool wigs commonly worn by men well into the 19th century; if you pulled one of them over the wearer's eyes, he would be unable to see what was going on. Thomas C. Haliburton had a version of the saying ("draw the wool over his eyes") in *The Clockmaker* (1838).

Puppy Love. A childish infatuation. The thought probably comes from the affectionate nature of the typical puppy. It is usually said dismissively, as something that is unlikely to last. Thus, W. A. Caruthers, in *A Kentuckian in New York* (1834): "Oh! It is nothing more than puppy love."

Pure and Simple. Uncomplicated; straightforward; undiluted. The words reinforce each other, since what is "pure" is often "simple." George Eliot wrote (in one of her letters) in 1860: "But the most ignorant journalist in England would hardly think of calling me a rival of Miss [Dinah] Mulock—a writer who is read only by novel readers, pure and simple, never by people of high culture."

Push Comes to Shove, When. When the contest gets serious; words have to be backed up by action. The push and the shove are stages in the escalation of a quarrel, and usually the next stage is an all-out fight. The phrase is quite recent, certainly as a cliché, an example being in the *Calgary Herald* in 1970: "If push comes to shove, make good the threat."

Put (Take) Any Stock in It, I Don't. I have no regard for it; I don't believe it. The original edition of the *Oxford English Dictionary* lists 65 meanings for "stock" as a noun; number 52 is the subscribed capital of a company or some other organization. The broader meaning is that you wouldn't want to invest any confidence or moral support in a certain person or thing. In 1874 a report of the Vermont Board of Agriculture noted: "He . . . did not take stock in all the remarkable yields of butter reported on [cows fed on] grass and hay."

Put All Your Eggs in One Basket. To rely too much on one resource or one line of effort; to risk everything on a single venture. Actually it would be a rare person who, carrying a dozen eggs, would take the trouble to put them in more than one basket. Still, if one drops the basket, all the eggs are likely to break. The same thought was embodied in a proverb now forgotten: "Venture not all in one bottom." Giovanni Torriano, writing on popular phrases in 1666, used one expression to define the other: "To put all ones Eggs in a Paniard, viz. to hazard all in one bottom."

Put On the Dog. To put on airs or dress flashily. Taken literally, it makes no sense. How could you put on a dog? It does not help to learn that the phrase originated as college slang in the 1860s and was defined in Lyman H. Bagg's *Four Years at Yale* (1871) as meaning: "To put on dog is to make a flashy display, to cut a swell." One can guess that the phrase arose from the sight of people out walking a popular breed of dog.

Put That in Your Pipe and Smoke It. Take that; I've given you something to think about. The image derives from the general notion that pipe smoking and rumination go together, that the pipe smoker is a meditative person. Charles Dickens was close to the thought in the *Pickwick Papers* (1836): "Fill your pipe with that 'ere reflection."

Put Up Your Dukes. Get ready to fight. The connection between "duke" and "fist" is obscure. It may be that the word derives from the Latin *dux*, meaning leader; one leads with one's fists. Or perhaps "duke" grew out of the old Cockney habit of rhyming, which gave us "the Duke of York's forks." The forks are the fingers, which are part of the hands, etc. In either case, the expression began as British slang in the 1870s, and by 1879 *Macmillan's Magazine* was using the word (with a translation): "I said I would not go if he put his dukes (hands) on me."

Put Up or Shut Up. If your really believe your argument, you should be willing to bet on it; defend your position. The saying apparently comes from gambling (you bet on your hunches), although it has been argued that the origin is in the challenge, "put up your dukes" (be ready to fight). The saying appeared in the late 19th century, in F. H. Hart's *Sazerac Lying Club* (1878): "P. U. or S.U. means put up or shut up, doesn't it?"

Put Your Best Foot Forward. Make a good show; present your best case or performance. Where the idea of a best foot came from is uncertain. (It was also "best leg" sometimes.) Perhaps if one's trousers, stockings or shoes were a bit shabby, one would tend to stand or sit with the best one forward. Another possibility is that in such activities as jumping and dancing one is likely to do better in starting with one leg rather than the other. The saying is ancient. Henry Medwall's *A Goodly Interlude of Nature,* dating from around 1500, offers: "Com behynd and folow me. Set out the better legge I warne the [thee]."

Put Your Foot Down. Take a firm stand; resist or forbid some plan or action. It is from the placing of the foot (really the feet) when one intends to stand firm rather than move. You can see the usage developing in *The State Papers of Henry VIII* for the year 1526: "No man can or dare set his fote by ours in proving of the contrary." And here is James Payn, in *The Luck of the Darrells* (1886): "She . . . put her foot down . . . upon the least symptoms of an unpleasantry."

Put Your Money Where Your Mouth Is. Don't just brag or make assertions, show that what you say has some substance. The thought is that one should be willing to bet on what one is asserting. The saying, with its rather infelicitous image (presumably one's money and one's mouth would never occupy the same spot), was known in the United States by 1930 and perhaps sooner; in 1975 the British Government adopted it as an advertising slogan for the National Savings Bank Accounts Department.

Put Your Money on the Line. Back up your opinion with a bet or an investment. Perhaps this is the "line" that serves for side bets in shooting craps, or the imaginary line between you and the clerk when you put your money down at a betting window of a racetrack. John O'Hara has a character in *Pal Joey* (1940) who says, "You fellows always put it on the line for me every pay day." Damon Runyon was close to the cliché in 1929, writing in *Hearst's International*: "My rent is away overdue . . . and I have a hard-hearted landlady. She says she will give me the wind if I do not lay something on the line at once."

Put Your Shoulder To the Wheel. Pitch in; apply yourself vigorously to some task. It is what one had to do frequently with a horse-drawn vehicle when the going got heavy for the horse because of mud, a hill or the weight of the load. Here is Robert Burton in *The Anatomy of Melancholy* (1621): "Like him in Aesop, that, when his cart was stalled, lay flat on his back, and cryed, aloud, 'Help, Hercules!' but that was to little purpose, except, as his friend advised him. . . . he whipt his horses withal, and put his shoulder to the wheel."

Put a Good Face On It. Make the best of a bad situation. It is what one does when one keeps a stiff upper lip or smiles in a period of sadness or adversity. People have been doing it for centuries, long enough for *Higden's Polychronicon* to refer in 1387 to someone who "made good face."

Put in Mothballs. Lay up a piece of equipment or a program; put in storage. The strong-smelling ball of naphthalene is what you put in with your clothes or woolens when you store them because naphthalene is said to repel moths. The transfer arose after World War II, when all sorts of military equipment were being taken out of service and put in storage. *Notes and Queries* picked up the usage in 1946:" 'Mothball fleet': inactive U.S. Navy ships to be preserved for long periods by newly-developed techniques." An even more extended meaning showed up in *Football Record*, an Australian publication, in 1951: "And now for eight teams it's mothballs until 1952."

Put on Airs. Behave affectedly. "Airs" as affected or false behavior intended to impress someone seems to have come from the idea of the air that envelops all of us. Charlotte Brontë's novel *Villette* (1853) has a character say: "I hope you mean to behave prettily to her, and not show your airs."

Put on Hold. Postpone or delay something. It is a space-age term, arising from the countdowns before a launch. If something goes wrong, or there is a possibility that something might go wrong, the countdown is suspended: "put on hold." It also happens often with telephone calls; a busy secretary or operator puts the caller "on hold." Here is the *Observer* in 1961: "The long countdowns, checks and 'holds' possible at Cape Canaveral would be suicide on the moon."

Put on Ice. Set aside; stored; kept in reserve until needed. The ice house or ice box, filled with blocks of ice cut from a lake or a river, predates the gas or electric refrigerator. People were putting food on blocks of ice a century ago to preserve it. The idea transferred readily to things other than food. Paul L. Ford offered this version in *The Honorable Peter Stirling* (1894): "They say she's never been able to find a man good enough for her, and so she's keeping herself on ice."

Put on the Back Burner. Postponed; deferred as an item of relatively low priority; requiring less attention. A cook does it when one dish is done or is likely to be ready sooner than another. Still, it's surprising that this somewhat specialized activity should gain such wide currency as a figure of speech. *Science News* offered an example in 1974, just about the time the saying was becoming commonplace: "The first High Energy Astronomy Observatory satellites . . . resumed development this year after being put on the back burner by NASA in 1973."

Put the Arm on. Arrest. It is one of the gentler forms of arrest. Moreover, the policeman is often referred to as "an arm of the law." In *Lady in the Lake* (1943) Raymond Chandler wrote: "No hick cop is going to put the arm on me." Another meaning is to borrow money or to ask for a loan. John O'Hara recorded it in *Pal Joey* (1940): "I had a lot of fun out of it, writing a letter to my friend Ted without putting the arm on him for a couple of bucks."

Puts on His Pants One Leg at a Time. He's human, just like everyone else. This is probably a 20th-century expression, since at the beginning of the century the word "pants" was, as the *Oxford English Dictionary* said, "a vulgar abbreviation of *pantaloons*" and was chiefly heard in the United States. In those days people wore "trousers." If anybody ever said "he puts on his trousers one leg at a time" to indicate that a man was less than superhuman, I have not run across it.

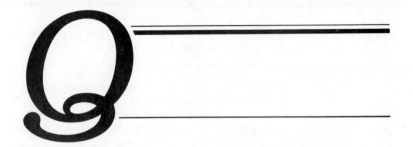

Q. E. D. That's how it is; thus it is demonstrated. The letters stand for *quod erat demonstrandum*, meaning, "that which was to be demonstrated." They are burned into the memory of anyone who has ever been exposed to Euclid's theorems in geometry, as Euclid appended them at the end of each theorem once he had demonstrated its solution to his satisfaction. (I puzzled once over Q.L.A.B. on the sign of a take-out restaurant in New York until it came to me that the letters stood for "quick like a bunny" and represented the management's claim for its service.)

Quaff a Brew. Drink a bottle, can, stein or glass of beer. "Quaff" is the mysterious word here, as is its origin. Probably it is onomatopoeic, meaning that it sounds like what it represents, namely someone swallowing. A forerunner of the modern phrase can be seen in Miles Coverdale's *A Worke Entytled of Ye Olde God and the New* (1523): "To quaft of two cannes or tankardes of wine."

Queer Duck (Fish). An odd person. Why the animal should be a "duck" or a "fish" rather than something else (such as a "bat," which many people regard as an animal of odd behavior) is hard to say. "Duck" has served to mean a person since the 19th century, starting in the United States as slang. Thus, Mark Twain in *Roughing It* (1872): "Are you the duck that runs the gospel-mill next door?"

Queer as a $3 Bill. Highly suspect; plainly phony; of dubious value. "Queer" as applied to counterfeit money goes back at least 250 years. Since there is no $3 bill, any one that turned up would be self-evidently counterfeit, or queer. John Habberton's *Jericho Road* (1877) offers this exchange: " 'Let's give him fifty [dollars] to send her.' 'Fifty queer?' asked Mr. Lodge. 'No, fifty straight,' said the little man."

Quick Study, He's a. He catches on to new ideas quickly; he absorbs the contents of briefing papers rapidly and easily. The phrase comes from learning parts for the theater, as Charles Dickens indicated in *Nicholas Nickleby* (1838): "I've got a part of twelve lengths here, which I must be up in tomorrow night . . . I'm a confounded quick study, that's one comfort."

Quick as a Cat. Swiftly, Alertly. The speed and agility of a cat in pouncing on a small moving object is legendary. In the early 19th century the thought was applied as "spry as a cat" to people who acted quickly or caught onto things fast. By 1855 Lyman Beecher was writing in his *Autobiography* of a Lambert who "was quick as a cat to see."

Quick as a Wink. Quite fast. The wink of an eye takes a fraction of a second—the deliberate wink, that is. A blink is even quicker, and the expression might just as well have been "quick as a blink." In 1825 *Brother Jonathan* offered: "Fire away as quick as a wink."

Quick on the Draw. Rapid in response to a challenge. "Draw" is what you do with your revolver or pistol if you intend to shoot or to give the impression that you are ready to shoot. The faster you do it, the more effective the gesture is likely to be. Cyrus T. Brady put the literal meaning in *The Bishop* (1903): "He had the reputation . . . of being the quickest man on the draw . . . in the Territory."

Quiet Before the Storm, The. Trouble is brewing. It is quiet in the eye of a hurricane, which will soon be upon you as a storm, and it is also often quiet just before a thunderstorm. The saying was current at least 100 years ago, as in *The Huguenots in France* by Samuel Smiles (1867): "It was only the quiet that preceded the outbreak of another storm."

Quiet as a Mouse. A silent or retiring person. There are plenty of quiet animals that could have qualified for recognition in this saying, but the "mouse" probably made it because it so commonly lives in association with people. Today's version of the expression is cut down from "quiet as a mouse in cheese," which one sees in *The Pleasant History of Two Angry Women of Abington* by Henry Porter (1599): "Mum, mouse in cheese, cat is neare." George Eliot had the modern version in *Adam Bede* (1859): "She looks as quiet as a mouse."

Race is Not to the Swift, The. Anybody can win; a likely winner is not a sure winner. It is part of a memorable passage from the Bible (Ecclesiastes 9 : 11): "I returned, and saw under the sun, that the race is not to the swift, nor the battle to the strong, neither yet bread to the wise, nor yet riches to men of understanding, nor yet favour to men of skill; but time and chance happeneth to them all."

Rack My Brain. Strain to remember or solve something. The rack was an instrument of torture on which the body was stretched. At times one seems to do that to one's brain to get it to function as desired. William Beveridge said in a sermon in 1680: "They rack their brains . . . they hazard their lives for it."

Rags to Riches. Success achieved from an unpromising or dis-advantaged start; from poverty to wealth. It doesn't happen often, and the poor are seldom literally dressed in rags, but alliteration is there to give impetus to this phrase. An example from 1947 is in Ralph de Toledano's *Frontiers of Jazz:* "Goodman was the first real rags-to-riches success in the swing-jazz field."

Ragtag and Bobtail. The common herd; riffraff. This expression has passed through a variety of forms: tag and rag; rag and tag; tag, rag and bobtail, and the modern version. The rag and tag were inconsiderable objects or people; bobtail is a transfer from what one did to the tail of a horse. In the transferred meaning a bobtail was a contemptible fellow. Here is Samuel Pepys in his *Diary* (1660): "They all went into the dining-room, where it was full of tag, rag, and bobtail, dancing, singing, and drinking." One can see the expression evolving in Robert Laneham's *Letter* (1575), where he writes of, "tag and rag, cut and long tail."

Rain Cats and Dogs. To pour; to rain heavily. One explanation that has been offered for this strange saying is that thunder and light-ning suggest a cat-and-dog fight. Another is that in ancient my-thology the cat was thought to influence the weather and the dog was a symbol, or signal, of wind. Although Jonathan Swift used the expression in *Polite Conversation* in 1783, it is probably older. Swift's version was: "I know Sir John will go, though he was sure it would rain cats and dogs; but pray stay, Sir John."

Rain or Shine. Come what may; under all conditions. George Wither was picking up this meteorological allusion 300 years ago in *Philarette* (1622): "Or shine, or raine, or Blow, I, my Resolutions know."

Raincheck, Take a. Accept a promise of future delivery; arrange to take a certain item or opportunity later. The raincheck is part of the ticket issued for a professional baseball game; if the game is rained out, you can present the check to get a ticket for a later game. The practice of issuing rainchecks was started in professional baseball in the 1880s. So it has come to mean deferral in a variety of forms. Jack Lait's *The Big House* (1930) says: "A parole is a 'rain check.'"

Raise His Hackles. Make him angry or fearful. The hackles of a rooster are erect when he is angry or frightened, as are the hairs on the back of a dog's neck when the dog is frightened or excited. One sees it in hounds as they are about to close in on their quarry, and this was apparently the sense intended by Edward Pennell in *Elmhirst—The Cream of Leicestershire* (1883): "I almost saw the hackles of a good old squire rise as he waved his hat and cheered."

Raise the Roof. Vent one's spleen; show anger; stir up an uproar. The image is of sound and action being so vigorous as to lift the roof of the room in which things are happening. Mark Twain wrote in the *Century Magazine* of June 1894 about a black woman watching a court trial: "When dat verdic' comes, I'se gwine to lif' dat *roof*, now, I *tell* you."

Rake Over the Coals. To chastise or reprimand, often severely. It was once the punishment of heretics to be burned to death—to be "fetched over the coals." The saying turns up in various forms, including haul, fetch, and bring over the coals. William Fulke's *A Confutation* (1565) has this passage: "S. Augustine, that knewe best how to fetche an heretike over the coles."

Rally 'Round the Flag. Show support for a cause or a beleaguered person. It is what one presumably does in war or in a national emergency. The origin is in the Civil War song *Battle Cry of Freedom* by G. F. Root: "Yes, we'll rally round the flag, boys, we'll rally once again. Shouting the battle cry of freedom."

Rank and File. The ordinary people. "Rank" and "file" are military terms: A rank is a line of men side by side, and a file is a line of men one behind the other. Arranged as a platoon or a company in a formal setting, the enlisted men line up in ranks and files; the officers are separate. As Robert Burns wrote in 1784: "The words come skelpan [galloping], rank and file."

Rat Race. A tough job; a situation in which one is struggling to stay ahead of one's competitors. The rat race is not a common sporting event; indeed, I suspect there's never been an organized one. Nevertheless, the rat has such a reputation for ferocity and assertively looking after its interests that the notion of a rat race as symbolic of fierce struggle is a natural one. The expression originated in the United States perhaps 50 years ago. By 1939 Christopher Morley was using it in *Kitty Foyle:* "Their own private life gets to be a rat-race."

Rats Abandon a Sinking Ship. A failing enterprise (often bearing the connotation that it is scurrilous to leave, even if it is failing). The saying comes from an old superstition among sailors that if rats were seen leaving a ship before the start of a voyage, the voyage would be ill-fated. The forms have varied: rats are said to desert, forsake, leave or abandon a sinking ship or a falling house. Here is a 16th century version by Thomas Lupton in *A Thousand Notable Things of Sundrie Sorts:* "Rats and dormice will forsake old and ruinous houses, three months before they fall."

Read Between the Lines. To surmise that what is really meant is something other than, or is only suggested by, what is written. There have been forms of cryptography in which one literally read between the lines; the text was written to make sense when read line by line, but the reader knew that the real message was contained in every second line. The figurative meaning appears in one of James Martineau's essays (1866): "No writer . . . was ever more read between the lines."

Read Him Like an Open Book. He's transparent, guileless. No secrets in an open book, or in a closed book either if you have it in your hands. Indeed, the image used to be rendered without the "open," as in *The Hinderers* by "Edna Lyall" (Ada E. Bayley), in 1909: "We ordinary mortals are at the mercy of you artists. . . . You read us like books."

Read Something Into It. Attach significance to something that may not be significant; make an interpretation. It is equivalent to "reading between the lines." We are close with an entry in the *Westminster Gazette* in 1903: "The learned counsel argued that his lordship must read in a negative."

Read the Riot Act. Issue a severe warning; scold. A Riot Act was actually decreed by George I of England in 1716. It was explained as follows in the 11th edition of the *Encyclopaedia Britannica:*
[The act] makes it the duty of a justice, sheriff, mayor or other authority, wherever twelve persons or more are unlawfully, riotously and tumultuously assembled together, to the disturbance of the public peace,

to resort to the place of public assembly and read the following proclamation: 'Our Sovereign Lord the King chargeth and commandeth all persons being assembled immediately to disperse themselves, and peaceably to depart to their habitations or to their lawful business, upon the pains contained in the act made in the first year of King George for preventing tumultuous and riotous assemblies. God save the King.'

Read the Tea Leaves. Claim to foretell the future or ascertain the auguries. In some forms of making tea (rarer now than they used to be) leaves get into the teacup. When the tea has been drunk, the leaves remain on the bottom of the cup in various orientations. Some people claim to be able to read the pattern as a portent of future events. Louis Golding touches on the practice in *Magnolia Street* (1932): "In the little town in . . . Lancashire where she was born quite as many people read tea-leaves as read their ABC."

Real McCoy, The. The genuine article. Take your pick. One real McCoy was a late 19th-century boxer who fought under the name of Kid McCoy and was so good that other fighters adopted the name, whereupon he had to bill himself as "the real McCoy." Or it was a Scotch whisky made by A. & M. MacKay of Glasgow (in the United Kingdom the saying is "the real MacKay"). Yet another idea is that the expression came from heroin originating in Macao. It would be nice if the real McCoy could be asked to stand up, but it is apparently too late.

Really and Truly. For sure; I'm being honest; it's genuine. This is mainly a children's locution, doubtless said without realization that the saying is a redundancy. But it turns up in adult sayings and writings, too, as in L. M. Montgomery's *Anne of Green Gables* (1908): "They all had puffed sleeves. . . . It was awfully hard there among the others who had really truly puffs."

Reamed Him Out. Upbraided him; reprimanded him, with at least a show of anger. Army and Marine sergeants in World War II were regarded as experts in the art. Ernest Hemingway, who served as a war correspondent in that conflict, recorded the phrase in *Across the River and into the Trees* (1950): "You ream out people you respect, to make them do what is fairly impossible, but is ordered."

Red Flag to a Bull, Like a. An inflammatory action or statement that is likely to provoke retaliation. Although the bullfighter traditionally waves a red flag in front of the bull, I suspect the color doesn't matter, and perhaps the flag doesn't either; the bull probably would be just as fired up by simply seeing the bullfighter. Still, the thought that bulls particularly dislike red is ingrained in the language. Here is John Lyly, in *Euphues and His England* (1580): "He that commeth before an Elephant will not wear bright colors, nor he that commeth to a Bul red."

Red Herring. Something used to disguise a trail or an event in order to throw searchers off the track; a diversionary issue. A herring that is cured by smoking turns red. It also has a strong odor, and hunting dogs were often trained to follow a scent by means of a red herring that had been dragged along the ground. On the other side of the coin, people who opposed fox hunting sometimes drew a red herring across the path of the fox; the dogs would give up on the fox and follow the scent of the herring. The figurative meaning has been common since the 19th century. President Harry S. Truman provided an example of the modern usage in 1948 when he assailed charges of Communist influence over the Government as "just a red herring to get the minds of the voters off the sins of the 80th Congress."

Red-Carpet Treatment. A lavish reception; first-class hospitality. The red carpet is laid down at airports and official buildings to accommodate the steps of important personages. As a description of treatment, with or without an actual carpet, it can be found in Sinclair Lewis's *Work of Art* (1934): "He's got to be a certified public accountant . . . or one-night-stand lecturer that blows in and expects to have the red carpet already hauled out for him."

Red-Letter Day. A memorable day or date. It comes from the custom, which has endured since the 15th century, of signifying holy days or days otherwise important to the church by printing the numbers in red or purple on the calendar. In the extended meaning it is an important or happy day for anybody. Fanny Burney picked it up in *Cecelia* (1782): "To-day is a red-letter day, so that's the reason for it."

Rest in Peace. Let that be an end to it; don't dig up old scandal about him or her. Doubtless the saying derives from the RIP found on old tombstones; the letters stand for *requiescat in pace*, meaning may he (or she) rest in peace. The extended sense is seen in Charles Kingsley's *Westward Ho!* (1855): "Into her merits or demerits I do not enter deeply here. Let her rest in peace."

Rests on His Laurels. Is satisfied with what he has achieved, so that he stops striving for success or decides that further effort isn't needed. The Greeks awarded wreaths of laurel leaves to the winners of the Pythian Games, and the Romans gave similar awards to distinguished citizens. For some winners, as with winners of gold medals in modern Olympic games, the award is enough; they have reached the pinnacle. Emanuel Deutsch's *Literary Remains* (1874) carries the suggestion: "Let them rest on their laurels for a while."

Return to the Fold. Come back to a place where one once lived or worked or was involved in an enterprise (the suggestion being that one left in anger or disgrace). This "fold" is an enclosure for domestic animals, a safe place, and it occurs figuratively in religious literature. Thus Robert Harnes in 1541: "You come into the fold of Christ without him."

Ride Roughshod Over. Treat harshly without regard for the recipient's physical or mental feeling; show no consideration. In a "roughshod" horse the nails of the horseshoes stuck out so far as to keep the horse from slipping. Robert Burns wrote in 1790 of "a rough-shod troop o'Hell." Thomas Moore's *Intercepted Letters* (1813) offers: " 'Tis a scheme of the Romanists, so help me God! To ride over Your Most Royal Highness roughshod."

Right as Rain. Definitely correct; just the way it should be. It could just as well be "right as clouds" or any number of other things, but "rain" it is, doubtless because of the allure of alliteration. The expression has had heavy work since the late 19th century, but an example from 1909 (in Max Beerbohm's *Yet Again*) has the virtue of offering two clichés in one sentence: "He looked . . . 'fit as a fiddle', or 'right as rain'."

Right on! Keep going; you're doing OK; you've got it. It was in black English in the United States as long ago as 1925, when Howard W. Odum and Guy B. Johnson recorded it in *The Negro and His Songs*: "Railroad Bill was a mighty sport, Shot all buttons off high sheriff's coat Den hollered 'Right on, Desperado Bill!'."

Ring Down the Curtain. Bring an end to something. One does not often see now the kind of theater curtain that goes up and down rather than being drawn horizontally, but the ringing down of the vertical kind signified the end of a play. At one time the signal to raise or lower a theatrical curtain was actually a bell rung backstage. Sheila Kaye-Smith had the figurative meaning in *John Galsworthy* (1916): "Thus the curtain rings down on Irene Forsyte, crushed under the heel of prosperity."

Ring the Changes. Go through the variations or permutations of something; try different ways of doing a thing. It is from the practice (almost exclusively British) of ringing the bells of a peal (or set) in every possible combination. In a proper peal of bells each bell gives off a different musical note in the major scale. E. Cobham Brewer's *Dictionary of Phrase and Fable* offers a means of calculating how many changes are possible on a given set of bells: "Multiply the number of bells in the peal by the number of changes that can be rung on a peal consisting of one bell less, thus: 1 bell, no change; 2 bells, 1 by 2 = 2 changes; 3 bells, 2 by 3 = 6 changes; 4 bells, 6 by 4 = 24 changes" and so on. By the time you are

217

up to six bells you have the possibility of 720 changes. The thought transfers easily to running through the variations of other things, as in Thomas Adams's *The Divells Banket* [Devil's Banquet] (1614): "Some ring the Changes of opinions."

Rings a Bell. Sounds familiar; stirs a memory; reminds you of something you can't recall precisely. Presumably the "bell" is in the recesses of one's mind and is reminiscent of a bell heard ringing deep inside a house when one pushes the doorbell.

Riotous Living. Revelry to excess. College students and young blades are thought to be partial to it, and indeed some of them are. The term is exceedingly old and was originally used in disapprobation. Riotous living was viewed as immoral and scandalous, as suggested by a passage in *English Gilds* (1389): "Nat be his owne folye ne ryotous lyuyng."

Rip (Tear) to Shreds. Destroy; make mincemeat of. It is what you literally do with fabric, paper or (if it is rippable) plastic. Thomas Carlyle wrote in *The French Revolution* (1837) of "A Townhall torn to shreds."

Rise and Shine. Get up (out of bed) and show some verve. It is what you say to someone who is more likely to get up yawning and moving groggily. Your advice is to be like the sun. This one seems to have originated with hearty noncommissioned officers waking up the privates at the usual military hour of 5 or 6 A.M., as suggested by the *Recruiters' Bulletin* of the U.S. Marine Corps in 1916: "He rapped at the door and in stentorian tones cried, 'Rise and shine. . . . Wiggle a toe.' "

Rising Tide. A strong trend, as in support for a political candidate. This is the sea "tide," as opposed to the time "tide" (as in "tide over"). Each rising tide is matched by an ebbing tide, but for some reason (probably because it carries a negative connotation) one doesn't hear much figurative use of the latter. An ebbing tide of support for Louis XVI? No, even though there was one that ended with his execution in 1793. Joseph Priestley wrote, in *Disquisitions Relating to Matter and Spirit* (1777): "The tide of popular prejudice may rise still higher."

Risk Life and Limb. Take a grave chance; embark on a dangerous enterprise. It is a strange ordering of risk. If one puts one's life at stake and loses, it doesn't much matter what happens to one's limbs. It would be a more logical expression as "risk limb and life." At some times in the past it was "life and member." Thus, Thomas Burton's *Diary* for 1658: "It is not enough to serve in those offices, unless they venture life and member."

Road to Perdition. On the way to ruin; following a course that will lead from one disaster to another. "Perdition" has served mainly as a theological term meaning spiritual ruin or damnation. Sir Walter Raleigh wrote in *The History of the World* (1658): "[They] daylie trauaile towards their eternall perdition."

Rob Peter to Pay Paul. Take an undesirable or unwise action to accomplish a desired one (particularly borrowing money from one fund to replenish another); take money intended for one purpose and use it for another. John Heywood recorded it in his *Proverbs* in 1546, but it is older. John Wycliffe had it in the 14th century: "How should God approve that you rob Peter, and give this robbery to Paul in the name of Christ?"

Rock and a Hard Place, Between a. In difficulty no matter which way you turn; without an attractive alternative. The modern phrase was noted and defined by *Dialect Notes* in 1921: "to be bankrupt. Common in Arizona in recent panics; sporadic in California." Now it is common everywhere, and it means facing any hard choice, including bankruptcy.

Rock the Boat, Don't. Don't disturb the equilibrium here; don't do anything to disrupt a stable situation. People who move around in a small boat or a canoe always make the other passengers nervous for fear the movement will capsize the craft. In *Only Yesterday* by Frederick Lewis Allen (1931), one finds: "Unfortunate publicity had a tendency to rock the boat."

Rocks in His Head, He Has. He is acting stupidly or bizarrely; what he is doing or proposing doesn't make sense. Rocks in the head would certainly make you dense, and that is probably the thought that gave rise to the figure. It seems to be a 20th-century creation. Here is Max Shulman, in *The Many Loves of Dobie Gillis* (1951): "Kid, you got rocks in your head?"

Roll With the Punch(es). Adjust to adversity; take things as they come. A good boxer rolls with a punch by shifting his body to avoid the full force of a blow. The extended meaning is seen in Harry Kurnitz's *Invasion of Privacy* (1956): "He had mastered the trick of rolling with the punches, rendering himself invisible when a crisis darkened the neighboring skies."

Rolling Stone. A footloose person; one who moves from job to job or place to place. The old proverb, dating back at least 600 years, is "A rolling stone gathers no moss." In those days it was thought to be a bad thing; if you kept moving around, you were unlikely to accumulate much in the way of money or position. This view appears in Thomas Tusser's *Fiue Hundredth Pointes of Good Husbandrie* (1573):

> The stone that is rolling can gather no moss,
> For master and servant oft changing is loss.

Rolling in Money. Rich; thought to be well-fixed financially. The picture is of a person with so much money (presumably paper, since "rolling in coins" would be uncomfortable) that he can lie down in it and roll around. The thought is often put as simply "rolling." In 1905 H. A. Vachell wrote, in *The Hill* "He's going to marry a girl who's simply rolling."

Rotten Apple Spoils the Barrel, A. One bad thing or person may spoil or corrupt the good ones nearby. Rot does seem to spread from one stored apple to another, and the thought transfers easily to other bad things and to people who are thought to have a bad influence. The thought is old enough to have a Latin equivalent. And here is John Northebrooke, in *A Treatise wherein Dicing, Dauncing* [etc.]*Are Reproved* (1577): "A penny naughtily gotten, sayth Chrysostoms, is like a rotten apple laid among sounde apples, which will rot all the rest."

Rotten to the Core. Thoroughly corrupt or untrustworthy. The image is from the apple that is spoiled all the way through, not just a little spoiled. The periodical *The Free-thinker* ventured this diatribe in 1718: "He is Rotten at the Core, and his Soul is dishonest."

Rough and Ready. Makeshift; unfinished but adequate to the purpose; an unpolished person who functions effectively. One wonders why it isn't "rough but ready," which is really the sense being conveyed. It has been "rough and ready," however, for a long time. F. J. Jackson, assembling the diaries and letters of Sir George Jackson in 1810, found this remark: "A more rough and ready state of things . . . than we had before been accustomed to."

Rough and Tumble. The vicissitudes of life; a contest in which the rules are not scrupulously observed. Long ago it was a boxing term; if you fought "rough," you might "tumble" your opponent. Joel Palmer's *Journal of Travels over the Rocky Mountains* (1810) says: "I understand the question is generally asked, will you fight fair or take it rough and tumble?"

Rub Elbows. Associate with, usually referring to strangers in a public place. It could just as well be "rub shoulders," and in England it usually is. The "rubbed elbow" is more an American usage. Thomas Carlyle, though, had the elbow version more than 100 years ago in Great Britain (in *The Life of John Sterling*): where he wrote of "one right peal of concrete laughter at some convicted flesh-and-blood absurdity, one burst of noble indignation at some injustice or depravity, rubbing elbows with us on this solid Earth."

Rub Salt In the Wound. Exacerbate an affront or a defeat; add insult to injury. To literally rub salt in a wound is quite painful physically; to do it figuratively is painful mentally. In *Company for Henry* (1967) P. G. Wodehouse offered: "He could see that Henry was deeply stirred, and he had no wish to rub salt in his wounds."

Rubber Check, A. A check that "bounces" (is returned) because it is unsupported or insufficiently supported by money in the account on which it was drawn. The analogy is to the bounce of a rubber ball. *Mouthpiece* (1936) by Edgar Wallace and Robert Curtis, describes the typical situation: "By now the woman has exhausted her credit in Vienna, issued a few rubber checks and passed on to Budapest or somewhere."

Rubs Me the Wrong Way. Annoys me; I don't agree with what is being said or done. It is what happens when one's hair is rubbed backward (it may feel good at first, but it can become annoying and uncomfortable) or when you rub a plane against the grain of wood. Charles Hamilton Aïdé offered the figurative meaning in *Carr of Carrlyon* (1862): "Don't rub her prejudices up the wrong way . . . if you can help it."

Rule with an Iron Hand (Rod). Be stern, strict and perhaps harsh. It is the kind of image that comes to the mind rather than the eyes, since hands of iron and rulers wielding iron rods are uncommon. "To rule with a rod of iron" was the way Raphael Holinshed recorded it in his *Chronicles of England (1577)*.

Rule of Thumb. A rough measure or guide. The part of the thumb from the knuckle to the end is approximately one inch and has often served as a measure when a more precise one was not at hand. Probably the "rule " originated here. Sir William Hope told his readers in *The Compleat Fencing-Master* (1692): "What he doth, he doth by rule of Thumb, and not by art."

Rule the Roost. Dominate; be in charge. In the days when many families kept chickens, which lived in a coop of fairly good size and often were able to go in and out of it so that they could scrounge around in the yard, the presence of a rooster provided a demonstration of what is meant by "ruling the roost." The rooster was in charge. As "rule the roast," with "roast" or "roste" probably meaning "roost," the saying goes back to the 15th century, as cited by W. C. Hazlitt in *English Proverbs:* "What so euer ye brage ore boste, My mayster yet shall reule the roste."

Run Amok. Behave wildly or strangely. It was once spelled more often as "amuck" and sometimes still is, but in either form it rarely stands alone. At one time it did, however, as in Charles

Brooke's *Ten Years in Sarawak* (1866): "On our return to Sarawak, we found a boy only sixteen years old had amoked in the town." The key word is from the Malay *amoq*, which is defined in William Marsden's 18th-century *Malay Dictionary* as "engaging furiously in battle, attacking with desperate resolution, rushing in a state of frenzy to the commission of indiscriminate murder."

Run Circles (Rings) Around. Vastly outdo, outmaneuver or exceed in skill. The picture is probably of a competitor (such as the tortoise) who plods steadily along in a straight line while his opponent (the hare) is so much faster that he might be expected to run in circles around the tortoise and still win (although in the fable he didn't because he "nonchalanted," as the sports broadcasters say today, and took a nap). In 1891 the *Melbourne Argus* told its readers that "Considine could run rings around the lot of them."

Run Its Course. Go to completion; finish a more or less established route or action. The original reference was to a racecourse, but the broader meaning is very old too. Abraham Fleming had it in *A Panoplie of Epistles* (1576): "The yeare hath runne his course."

Run Off at the Mouth. Talk excessively, particularly in a situation where it would be better if one said little or nothing. The picture is of someone talking so much that the words flow out of his mouth like a liquid. *Dialect Notes* recorded the saying in 1909: "Loquacity; talking too much. Used of one excessively loquacious. 'He's got a bad case of runnin' off at the mouth.' "

Run With the Hare, Hunt With the Hounds. Try to stay in favor with both sides at the same time; play a double game. It is what some people do in touchy political situations or as traitors. The image from hunting is clear enough, but what is arresting is that someone should have thought of it—of a person who puts himself now hunting with the hounds and now eluding the hounds with the hare. It was thought of long ago, for it appears in *Jacob's Well* (1440) as: "Thou hast a crokyd tunge heldyng wyth hownd and wyth hare."

Run of the Mill. Ordinary; normal; routine. Sometimes (more in the past than now) it is "run of the mine." In either case it refers to the product of the gristmill, knitting mill or mine as it emerges from the machines, before it has been graded according to quality. The *Century Dictionary* in 1909 looked into "run of the kiln" and "run of the mine," defining them respectively as "bricks of all kinds and qualities just as they happen to come from the kiln" and "coal just as it comes from the mine, large and small sizes and all qualities together." The broader meaning appeared in *Hearst's International* in 1930; describing a woman as "level-headed as a wife and a darned sight better-looking than the run of the mill wives."

Run the Gauntlet. Go through a series of trials or tests. The "gauntlet" started out in the Thirty Years War (1618–1648) as "gantlope." It was a form of military punishment in which the soldier or seaman being punished had to run through two parallel rows of men, each of whom had a stick or a knotted cord that he was supposed to swing at the passing victim. The saying had acquired a broader meaning by 1649, as in Thomas Forde's *Lusus Fortunae*: "Being now exposed to run the Gantelope of the Worlds censure." The saying is sometimes confused with "run the gamut," which comes from what was once a name for a musical scale. And sometimes "run the gamut" is not confused with "running the gauntlet," as in John Hill Burton's *The Scot Abroad* (1864): "He ran over the gamut of Latin metre." Or Dorothy Parker's memorable line on an actress who "ran the gamut of emotions from A to B."

Run to Earth. Track down; find a person, animal or concept that has been elusive; get to the bottom of something. This is "earth" in its now rather rare meaning of the den or burrow of an animal such as a fox. Indeed, the term comes from fox hunting, but it had been extended by 1857, as one sees in Charles Kingsley's *Two Years Ago*: "Frightened—beat—run to earth myself, although I talked so bravely of running others to earth just now."

Run to Seed. Become a little too old or decayed. In growing vegetables it is often what you do not want; if the plant goes to seed, it is no longer edible or at least is less tasty than it would have been if you had picked it earlier. As a metaphor it means anything that has continued somewhat past its prime. Henry Fielding had it in an article published in 1740: "For Virtue itself by growing too exuberant, and (if I may be allowed the Metaphor) by running to Seed changes its very Nature."

Runs In the Blood. Is characteristic of a family, a race or a nationality. The concept is of inherited traits. Once it was "a blood," as in a sermon by Bishop Robert Sanderson in 1621: "Tempers of the mind and affections become hereditary, and (as we say) run in a blood."

Russian Roulette. Any foolhardy activity so dangerous as to be potentially fatal. It is from a practice, said to have originated among Russian Army officers in World War I, in which a foolhardy fellow puts a single bullet in a revolver and then points the weapon toward his head and pulls the trigger. With a six-shooter he has one chance in six of killing himself. Sometimes it was played even more dangerously: The officer would remove one of the six bullets and then put the gun to his head. The *Manchester Guardian* gave this example of the extended meaning in 1960: "This party . . . had 'played Russian roulette with American strength and American progress.' "

Sackcloth and Ashes, To Wear. To be contrite, penitent or chagrined over something one has done. It was an ancient Hebrew custom to wear sackcloth dusted with or accompanied by ashes as a sign of humbleness in religious ceremonies. It is alluded to in the Bible (Daniel 9 : 3): "And I set my face unto the Lord God, to seek by prayer and supplications, with fasting, and sackcloth, and ashes . . . ."

Sacred Cow. A thing, idea or event that is immune to criticism for no better reason than that a person in authority forbids it or would be angered by it. The cow is sacred to Hindus; as a symbol of something beyond criticism it arose in American journalism around 1910. In that year the *Atlantic Monthly* had this passage: "In the office these corporations were jocularly referred to as 'sacred cows'."

Sad Sack. A weak, ineffective, incompetent person; a misfit. Sergeant George Baker created Private Sad Sack as the central figure of an extremely popular comic strip that appeared in *Yank*, a magazine published for U.S. troops in World War II. The Baltimore *Sun* took note, in 1943, of a soldier who described himself as fitting the type: "A forlorn look, a G.I. haircut, an oversized fatigue uniform and all the paraphernalia that goes with them branded me as a typical 'sad sack.' " The underlying idea is that the person looks and acts limp and shapeless, like an empty or ill-filled sack.

Sadder and (But) Wiser. Having learned from experience (usually a difficult or unpleasant one). "Sad and wise" was an expression of the 16th century, carrying the suggestion that experience makes one sad or sober. These lines appear in *The Rime of the Ancient Mariner* by Samuel Taylor Coleridge (1798):

> He went like one that hath been stunned,
> And is of sense forlorn:
> A sadder and a wiser man,
> He rose the morrow morn.

Safe and Sound. Out of a dangerous predicament. Alliteration and redundancy again. If one is "safe," one is probably "sound," and vice versa. It has appealed to people since at least 1529, when it appeared in Thomas Lupset's *An Exhortation to Yonge Men*. Shakespeare records it in *Comedy of Errors* (1592), where Antipholus of Syracuse says: "I long that we were safe and sound aboard."

Salad Days. One's youth; the time when one was at a peak of vigor or most exuberant; also the time when one was inexperienced and green. The analogy is to the greens commonly used to make a salad. In *Antony and Cleopatra* Shakespeare has Cleopatra speak of:

> My salad days,
> When I was green in judgement: cold in blood,
> To say as I said then!"

Sales Pitch. A line of patter; a presentation intended to persuade someone or a group of people to do something or buy something. This sense of "pitch" goes back at least 100 years and was often associated with salesmen, particularly high-pressure salesmen. A hint of the phrase was in Charles Hindley's *The Life and Adventures of a Cheap Jack* (1876): "When I had done my 'pitch' and got down from the stage."

Salt of the Earth. A valuable person or group of people; people on whom one can rely. Salt has always been one of the most basic and essential of human needs. The saying is in the Bible (Matthew 5 : 13) where Jesus says to his disciples; "Ye are the salt of the earth . . . ."

Sand in His Craw, He Has. He is determined, plucky, gutsy. A bird or fowl breaks up its food with sand or grit in the gizzard. To have a good supply there is to be better able to cope with whatever comes along, and this is the source of the transferred meaning, which was shown in *Sut Lovingood* by G. W. Harris, in 1867: "I tell yu he hes lots ove san' in his gizzard; he is the best pluck I ever seed."

Sands of Time. The passing of the hours or years. It wasn't too many centuries ago that the main means of measuring periods of time was a sandglass or an hourglass, in which grains of sand flowed through a narrow aperture into a receptacle at a predetermined rate, so that all of them would have passed from top to bottom in, say, an hour. These are the "sands of time," which are recorded in *Tottel's Miscellany* (1557) in this way: "I saw, my tyme how it did runne, as sand out of the glasse."

Saturday-Night Special. A cheap handgun. Since Saturday night is a traditional time for revelry and revelry often progresses to violence or crime, the pistol frequently used in holdups (quite likely bought a short time earlier) came to acquire this name. The *New York Times* explained matters in 1968: "Title IV of that law bans the importation of the cheap, small-caliber 'Saturday night specials' that are a favorite of holdup men."

Sauce For the Goose is Sauce For the Gander, What's. What's good or fitting for one person or situation is equally good for another. Strictly speaking, the goose is the female of the family and the gander is the male, but in terms of the sauce put on them after they are cooked it doesn't matter which is which. John Ray recorded the saying this way in *A Collection of English Proverbs* (1670): "That that's good sawce for a goose, is good for a gander."

Save Face. Avoid embarrassment or disgrace; retrieve or preserve one's reputation at a time of a challenge to it. "Face" here is figuratively the aspect that one presents to the world or one's associates. "Saving face" is said to be of great importance to Chinese, Japanese and other Oriental people, but it is equally practiced in other parts of the world. Here is *Chambers's Journal* in 1917: "The civilian native staff had bolted at the first sign of trouble, 'going to report to the authorities' being their 'save face' for it!"

Save For a Rainy Day. Put something aside against a time of need or adversity. The maxim was around in 1580, when it was put as follows in *The Bugbears:* "Wold he haue me kepe nothyng agaynst a raynye day?"

Saving Grace. A manner or a deed that relieves a difficult situation. In works on theology the phrase goes back 400 years, but its modern implication is perhaps clearest in C. Day Lewis's autobiography, *The Buried Day* (1960): "Tchekhov . . . has indeed said, but with all the saving grace of his felicitous compassion, that we are not put on the earth to be happy."

Say (Cry) Uncle. Acknowledge defeat or demand that an opponent do so. It is boys' lingo, originating apparently in the United States early in this century, and its origins are obscure. Charles E. Funk wrote in *Heavens to Betsy* (1956) that he and his contemporaries in southern Ohio said, "cavy" to mean the same thing and that later in life he was astounded to learn that it came from the Latin *peccavi*, meaning "I have sinned." Perhaps "uncle" in this sense derived from Uncle Sam as representative of the supreme authority.

Scarce As Hen's Teeth. Nonexistent or extremely rare. The hen has no teeth, grinding up its food in the gizzard, so hen's teeth are scarce indeed. The saying appeared in print in 1862 in *My Southern Friends* by "Edmund Kirke" (the pen name of James R. Gilmore), but since it is a barnyard phrase it was probably known much earlier.

Scared (Frightened) Out of His Wits. Thoroughly alarmed or up-set; badly shaken by an experience or gravely worried in anticipa-tion of one. It seems more often said hyperbolically than as a statement of a fact. Either way it is quite old. Thomas Babington Macauley reflected it in his *Essay on Clive* (1840): "The governor . . . was frightened out of his wits."

Scratch the Surface. Do something superficially or in a prelimi-nary way; come nowhere near getting to the bottom of some-thing. Sometimes it is all one wants to do, but in farming, archae-ology and stone carving it is not enough. The literal meaning appears in Reginald Bosworth Smith's *Carthage and the Carthaginians* (1878), where he writes of "its cultivators—if those who just scratch the surface of the earth may be so called." The *New Republic* offered an example of the figurative meaning in 1915: "With all his earnest intention Amherst merely scratches the surface of the immense field of American social en-deavor."

Screw Loose, Have a. Be a bit unsound or irregular; have some-thing wrong. A machine with a screw loose is likely to sound odd and may not work right; in any case, it probably will get worse unless it is put right. The saying goes back farther than one might expect, having turned up in *Sporting Magazine* in 1810: "The others . . . had got a screw loose."

Scylla and Charybdis, Between. To be or move between perils. Sometimes it is "to steer (sail) between Scylla and Charybdis." In Greek legend Scylla was a six-headed monster that lived on the rock of Scylla (opposite Charybdis in the Straits of Messina) and seized passing sailors. Charybdis was a whirlpool. The Roman poet Horace wrote of the likelihood that anyone in a tight spot might drift into Charybdis while seeking to avoid Scylla. In the sense of confronting twin perils of any kind it was a common saying in English by the 16th century, as in Shakespeare's *The Merchant of Venice* (1596), where Launcelot Gobbo says:

> Truly then I fear you are damned both
> by father and mother: thus when I shun
> Scylla, your father, I fall into Charybdis,
> your mother: well, you are gone both ways.

Seat of His Pants, By the. By instinct or experience. The first aviators had little else to go by in sensing what their planes were doing, and the phrase originated among them. By 1942 things had improved, as indicated in *Harper's* magazine: "When you check your instruments you find it [the airplane] is doing a cor-rect job of flying and that the seat of your pants and your eyes would have tricked you had you been allowed to do the 'co-ordinating.'"

Second to None. As good as any competitor. It is a rather limp kind of praise, often carrying the implication that the person or thing under discussion may in fact not be such a paragon. Latin has a similar thought (*nulli secundus*), and Chaucer wrote in c. 1374 (*Troilus and Criseyde*): "Troilus was neuere vnto no wight As in his tyme in no degre secounde." In *The Comedy of Errors* (1590) Shakespeare has Angelo say, when a merchant asks him about Antipholus of Syracuse:

> Of very reverent reputation, sir,
> Of credit infinite, highly beloved,
> Second to none that lives here in the city . . . .

See Eye to Eye. Be of the same mind; agree. The picture is of two people standing side by side and looking at the same thing (although even in that literal scene they don't necessarily see the thing the same way). Christopher Isherwood gave a negative version of the cliché in *Mr. Norris Changes Trains* (1935): "I'm afraid Schmidt and I don't see eye to eye on the subject just at present."

See How the Land Lies. Size things up; reconnoiter a situation. This is a variation on "the lie of the land," an old term by which surveyors, reconnaissance officers and the like allude to the physical characteristics of a region or a plot of ground. A paper of 1697 in the collections of the Connecticut Historical Society states an objective as "nott to alter the proper lye of the Land."

See It Through. Stick with a matter to the end. Thus, Henry Kingsley, in *Hornby Mills* (1872): "O'Flaherty told him that he would see the bonfire through and the captain to bed, and take the consequences."

See Light At the End of the Tunnel. Begin to think one will emerge safely or successfully from a time or situation of difficulty. People have been seeing light at the end of a tunnel ever since they began making tunnels for mining, which was in prehistoric times, but the figurative extension of the idea seems to be fairly recent. Bartlett's *Familiar Quotations* identified it as a "current phrase" when President John F. Kennedy used it at a press conference in 1962: "We don't see the end of the tunnel, but I must say I don't think it is darker than it was a year ago, and in some ways lighter."

See Red. Become quickly (and perhaps violently) angry. Probably the origin of this thought is the belief that a red flag enrages a bull. In 1901 Mary Harrison, writing under the name of Lucas Malet, picked up the expression in *The History of Sir Richard Calmody:* "Happily violence is shortlived, only for a very little while do even the gentlest persons 'see red.' "

See the Light. Get the idea; grasp the meaning or significance of something. It is the kind of "light" one sees after a period of darkness or disorientation: sunlight, moonlight, a lighthouse and so on. The expression seems to have been fairly new in 1812, when *Niles' Register* found need to put it in quotation marks: "It is indispensably necessary that every man should 'see the light'."

Sell Like Hotcakes. Go over big. The hotcake, or pancake, isn't a notably big seller in modern times, but the phrase dates from the 19th century—before the hot dog and the ice-cream cone and other tasty items were available in public places such as fairs. Presumably the hotcake then had much less competition. O. J. Victor offered the broader meaning in *The History of the Southern Rebellion* (1860): "Revolvers and patent fire-arms are selling like hot cakes."

Send Shivers Down One's Spine. Make one nervous, apprehensive or frightened; give one a thrill of pleasure. The poet Robert Graves discussed the sensation in *The White Goddess* (1948):

> The reason why the hairs stand on end, the eyes water, the throat is constricted, the skin crawls and a shiver runs down the spine when one writes or reads a true poem is that a true poem is necessarily an invocation of the White Goddess, or Muse, the Mother of All Living, the ancient power of fright and lust—the female spider or the queen bee whose embrace is death.

Separate the Men From the Boys. Distinguish which people in a group are mature, tough and capable of dealing with the job at hand. John Braine put it clearly in *Life at the Top* (1962): "Every day one was tested, the men were separated from the boys."

Separate the Sheep From the Goats. Distinguish one thing from another and segregate them. It was something shepherds did long ago, a practice recorded in the Bible (Matthew 25 : 31–34), where Jesus says:

> When the Son of man shall come in his glory, and all the holy angels with him, then shall he sit upon the throne of his glory: And before him shall be gathered all nations; and he shall separate them one from another, as a shepherd divideth his sheep from the goats: And he shall set the sheep on his right hand, but the goats on the left. Then shall the King say to them on his right hand, Come, ye blessed of my Father, inherit the kingdom prepared for you . . .

Separate the Wheat From the Chaff. Distinguish the wanted from the unwanted, the valuable from the relatively valueless. It is what one did literally in the ancient agricultural practice of winnowing, one form of which was to expose, say, wheat to the wind so that the chaff blew away and the grains remained. Peter Walkden recorded in his diary in 1729 that he had "Winnowed my wheat the chaff out of it." The thought appears metaphorically in the Bible, where John the Baptist, speaking of the one "that cometh after me," continues (Matthew 3 : 12), "Whose fan is in his hand, and he will thoroughly purge his floor, and gather his wheat into the garner; but he will burn up the chaff with unquenchable fire." Paraphrasing this passage in 1685, Richard Baxter said: "He will winnow and thoroughly separate the wheat from the Chaff, the Faithful from the Rebellious."

Sets Your Teeth on Edge. Is severely annoying or unnerving. It is a vivid image of how one feels on biting a lemon, or hearing a piece of chalk squeal as it moves across a blackboard or the wheels of a subway car shriek on a curve. The thought appears twice in the Bible. In Jeremiah 31 : 29 it is: "In those days they shall say no more. The fathers have eaten a sour grape; and the children's teeth are set on edge." In Ezekiel 18 : 2 it is: "What mean ye, that ye use this proverb concerning the land of Israel, saying, the fathers have eaten sour grapes, and the children's teeth are set on edge?" Jeremiah is asserting that the children suffer from the afflictions of or the wrongs done by the father; Ezekiel denies it (18 : 20), saying, "The son shall not bear the iniquity of the father . . . ."

Settle Old Scores. Get even; clear up an obligation. The "score" is what you owe an innkeeper, a shopkeeper or someone else. As "rub out" or "pay off" or "clear" the score, the saying was known in the 17th century. It can be seen developing in John Dryden's *The Conquest of Granada by the Spaniards* (1672): "Yet, forced by need, ere I can clear that score, I like all debtors, come to borrow more."

Settle Your Hash. Deal with you; make sure you no longer present a problem. This "hash" is something that you have messed up, at least in the eyes of the observer, so he is going to put it right. John T. Brockett took note of the saying in *A Glossary of North Country Words* (1825), remarking that it appeared in a song: "The hash of the Yankees he'll settle."

Seventh Heaven, In. Extremely happy; thoroughly pleased with one's situation. Among the ancient Jews the seventh heaven was the highest: the "heaven of heavens," the abode of God and the most exalted angels. Muhammad also recognized seven heavens.

In the modern sense of a pinnacle of joy or ecstasy it shows up in Sir Walter Scott's *St. Ronan's Well* (1824): "He looked upon himself as approaching to the seventh heaven."

Share and Share Alike. Apportion things equally; participate equally in some venture. Randle Cotgrave defined it in his dictionary of 1611: "Whereat euerie guest payes his part, or share and share like." It was old then, appearing in Richard Edwards's *Damon and Pythias* (1571): "Ley vs into the Courte to parte the spoyle, share and share like."

She's No Chicken. She (sometimes he) is not young; she's older than she looks. "Chick" (less often "chicken") has meant a young person since the 13th century. Now "chick" applied to a person means an adult woman, but "chicken" (the adult chick) means youthful and almost always appears as a negative. G. D. Prentice drew the picture neatly in *Prenticeana* (1860): "Call a lady 'a chicken,' and ten to one she is angry. Tell her she is 'no chicken,' and twenty to one she is still angrier."

Ship of State. The nation. Probably the metaphor was irresistible: a great vessel, manned by a human crew, sailing the seas of diplomacy. It is old enough for Niccolò Machiavelli to have employed it in *The Prince* (1532): "But when times are tempestuous, and the ship of State has need of the help . . . of the Subject . . . ."

Ships That Pass In the Night. Casual acquaintances or relationships; people you encounter only once. Henry Wadsworth Longfellow devised this felicitous image in *Tales of a Wayside Inn* (1863):

> Ships that pass in the night, and speak each other in passing,
> Only a signal shown and a distant voice in the darkness;
> So on the ocean of life we pass and speak one another,
> Only a look and a voice; then darkness again and a silence.

Shoe Is On the Other Foot, The. Conditions have been reversed; the complexion of the situation has changed; now things are in my favor instead of yours. Sometimes in the past the same idea was expressed as "the boot is on the other leg." Nowadays it would not be easy to shift a boot from one leg to the other or a shoe from one foot to the other, but until the 19th century boots and shoes weren't made expressly for left and right feet; a boot or a shoe would go on either side and could be swapped from one side to the other. Winston Churchill gave a good example of the extended meaning in *My African Journey* (1908): "Here . . . the boot is on the other leg, and Civilization is ashamed of her arrangements in the presence of a savage." As "boot" the saying was in use by the early 19th century.

Shoot the Bull. Converse discursively, perhaps touching subjects one knows little about. "Bull" here is a euphemism for what Charles E. Funk described in *Heavens to Betsy* as "the end product of the domestic bull, used chiefly as fertilizer." Perhaps one hears, too, an echo of the now obsolete meaning of "shoot" as to discharge the bowels. "Shooting the bull" is what one does in "a bull session." Both expressions are of 20th-century American origin.

Short End of the Stick, Have the. To be at a disadvantage or to be treated unfairly. A variation, which can mean the same thing or can mean to size up a situation erroneously, is to have "the wrong end of the stick." In any case, the "stick" is the staff once used for fighting; if your opponent controls most of it and you have a hold on only a short piece of it, you are in trouble. People haven't regularly fought with staffs for a long time, and yet the expression seems to be fairly recent, which suggests that it began life as a figure of speech alluding to the earlier custom. Rolf Boldrewood (the pen name of T. A. Browne) advised his readers in *A Colonial Reformer* (1890): "If you happen to have the arrangement of a bargain with the rural Australian, you will rarely find that the impassive countryman has 'got the wrong end of the stick.' "

Short Leash, On a. Closely controlled; given little room for maneuver. It is what wives are often alleged to do to husbands, husbands to wives, parents to children and employers to employees. A forerunner of the modern saying can be found in *A New Catechisme* by Thomas Becon (1560): "For God hathe them in lease. Yea . . . they are his slaues."

Short and Sweet. Pleasant, satisfying (often because something you thought would be disagreeable doesn't last as long or turn out to be as bad as you thought it would). The ironical flavor can be found in Sir Thomas More's *The Deballacyon of Salem and Bizance* (1533): "It is a good swete sermon and a short." A variant no longer heard is "short and sweet, like a donkey's gallop," which also suggests relief of mind that something wasn't as unpleasant as one had thought it might be.

Shot His Bolt. Made his attempt (usually with the implication that he doesn't have the resources or strength to try again). This "bolt" was a special kind of arrow (short and thick, with a blunt head) shot from a crossbow. Once you had shot it, you were vulnerable to attack until you could load up another one. The expression dates from at least the 13th century, appearing in *The*

Legend of St. Katherine (c. 1225) as "Ouwer bolt is sone ischote." An equally old variant is "a fool's bolt is soon shot."

Shot His Wad. Spent all his money; had his chance. People were literally shooting wads in the earliest days of guns, since the "wad" was what held the powder and shot in position for firing. "Wad" has also meant something rolled up tightly, such as paper money, for more than 100 years. The current cliché, however, apparently dates from about 1925.

Shot in the Arm, A. A boost; something that renews one's energy or spirits. Probably from the hypodermic shot, either one administered by a doctor to make a patient feel better or one that a person gives himself to get a "high." The expression seems not more than about 50 years old.

Shot in the Dark, A. A guess or conjecture (the implication usually is that it is a wild one, made without much to go on). A shot made at night with a bow or a gun is a poor proposition with small chance of success. The image is more vivid than "a leap in the dark," which is nonetheless much older. It appeared as long ago as 1698 in Sir John Vanbrugh's *The Provok'd Wife:* "Go, now I am in for Hobbe's Voyage: a great Leap in the Dark."

Shot to Hell. Badly damaged or fatigued; destroyed. The idea is old but the wording is not, doubtless because h——l was not an acceptable word in print until rather recently. The age of the idea is suggested by Edward Ward's *The Wooden World Dissected* (1706): "He will . . . fix ye a Couple of new [ship's] Knees, when the old ones are shot to the Devil."

Show Must Go On, The. Don't let calamity interrupt the proceedings; we mustn't stop what we are doing, even if something unfortunate has happened; it would make us look bad or worry the spectators. The saying and the principle are traditional in the theater, but apparently they both originated in the 19th century with circuses. If an animal got loose or a performer was injured, the ringmaster and the band tried to keep things going so that the crowd would not panic.

Show the Flag. Make your presence known; represent your organization. President Theodore Roosevelt did it when he sent the Great White Fleet to visit several foreign ports in a demonstration of America's presence and determination to make its weight felt. Other countries, notably Great Britain, have sent naval vessels on similar missions. So the phrase came to mean broader things. *The* London *Times* said in 1963: "This was a genuine effort on the bank's part to show the flag at a time when they thought it should be showed. A series of six British products would be advertised."

Sick As a Dog. Miserable; really laid low. Every creature is sick occasionally, so why a dog? Apparently because of the Bible (Proverbs 26 : 11 and 2 Peter 2 : 22). In Proverbs it is: "As a dog returneth to his vomit, so a fool returneth to his folly." In 2 Peter it is: "The dog is turned to his own vomit again."

Sight For Sore Eyes. A person or thing one is particularly pleased to see, usually because one is beleaguered in some way and is relieved by the sight. Jonathan Swift used the phrase in *Polite Conversation* (1738), when it was probably already popular: "The sight of you is good for sore eyes."

Sight Unseen. Without previous inspection of something bought or bargained for. Long ago it was "unsight unseen" or "unsighted, unseen," as in *The Old Law*, a comedy by Thomas Middleton and William Rowley (1622): " 'Take that at hazard, sir' . . . 'Unsighted, unseen, I take 3 to one.' " *Dialect Notes* gave an example of the modern phrase in 1892: "To trade knives sight unseen is to swap without seeing each other's knife."

Sign of the Times. Something that is characteristic of a particular period (often with reference to the present). This is another phrase deriving from the Bible (Matthew 3 : 16). The Pharisees are asking Jesus to show them a sign from heaven. He points out that they are able to predict the weather by the evening and the morning sky and says; "O ye hypocrites! ye can discern the face of the sky; but can ye not discern the signs of the times?"

Signed, Sealed and Delivered. Completed, with attention having been paid to the details. It has the redundant ring of a legal phrase, particularly with the reference to the wax seal, and indeed it so originated, indicating the complete execution of a property deed. Sir Walter Scott, who was a lawyer as well as a novelist and a poet, picked up the phrase in *Rob Roy* (1818): "How does Farmer Rutledge? . . . I hope you found him able to sign, seal and deliver?"

Silver-Tongued Orator. An eloquent speaker. One wonders why not "gold-tongued." Probably because silver objects have been commoner cherished possessions than gold ones. The term has been applied to many public figures who are now forgotten; it may not be applied again, because not many public figures really speak now; they read from prompting devices or talk into a microphone, which does not encourage oration. The appellation has been in the language since at least the 16th century, when it was applied to the English preacher Henry Smith. In the United States the description was often applied to William Jennings Bryan, "the silver-tongued orator of the River Platte."

235

Simon Pure. The genuine article. "Pure" is really an absolute and shouldn't need qualifying, so one wonders why "Simon." Well, Simon Pure was a character in an 18th-century play by Susannah Centlivre. The play was *A Bold Stroke for a Wife.* Pure had a letter of introduction that was supposed to get him an heiress for his bride. Colonel Feignwell stole the letter and married the heiress. In the end Pure is able to establish himself as "the real Simon Pure."

Sink or Swim. Succeed or fail, mainly according to the competence and diligence of your own effort. In the 14th century and for some time thereafter it was "float or sink," probably reflecting the fact that few people learned to swim then and also reflecting a stronger role for fate in one's success or failure. Chaucer had "flete or sinke" in *The Compleynte unto Pite* (c. 1368). Thomas Starkey's *England in the Reign of Henry the Eighth* (1538) says: "They care not (as hyt ys commynly sayd) 'whether they synke or swyme.'"

Sit Tight. Hold your ground; wait. It is a poker expression. If you don't want to bet further but don't want to throw in your hand either, you "sit tight." Violet Hunt described the saying as slang in 1897, in her *Unkist, Unkind*: "'Sit tight!' she exclaimed, pinching my arm violently. She always talks slang when she is excited."

Sitting Duck. An easy mark or target. *Reader's Digest* had the phrase as part of a title in 1944: "Why Tankers Are No Longer Sitting Ducks." I. Willis Russell, writing in *American Speech* in 1949, said the expression is "probably derived from the fact that marksmanship in duck hunting is determined by the ability to hit ducks in flight and not while they are sitting."

Sitting Pretty. Well situated; in an advantageous position; raking in good things. The phrase was the title of two musical comedies (*Sittin' Pretty* and *Sitting Pretty*) in the 1920s. P. G. Wodehouse helped cement it into the language in *Sam the Sudden* (1925): "If you are American, we're sitting pretty, because it's only us Americans that's got real sentiment in them."

Six of One, Half a Dozen of the Other. It's all the same. A play on numbers, similar to, "A cold lasts a week if you treat it and seven days if you don't." An early appearance of the saying was in Frederick Marryat's *The Pirate and the Three Cutters* (1836): "I knows the women, but I never knows the children. It's just six of one and half-a-dozen of the other, ain't it, Bill?"

Sixes and Sevens, To Be At. In disarray; uncertain how to proceed; indifferent to the consequence. Long ago it was "set all on six and seven," apparently from a kind of dice game played in the 15th century. By 1631 it was "at six and at sevens," and by 1712 it was "sixes and sevens." A passage in the Bible (Job 5 : 19) may have been the origin: "He shall deliver thee in six troubles; yea, in seven there shall no evil touch thee."

Sixth Sense. An uncanny ability to be aware of things that most other people miss. Today humans are credited with five senses: sight, hearing, taste, smell and touch. (In ancient times it was seven, with animation and speech added to the modern five.) Someone with a "sixth sense" is unusually endowed. In 1903 *Science Siftings* wrote of the " 'sixth sense' by which blind persons perceive certain objects."

Skate on Thin Ice. Risk danger; argue from a weak position. At one time daring folk did literally skate on thin ice; if you went fast enough and didn't stop, ice that was too thin to hold you otherwise would hold you up as long as you were moving. The risk was plain: if you stopped or slowed down too much or got on ice that was really thin, you wound up in the cold water. The broader meaning was reflected in *Church Times,* in 1897: "Cardinal Vaughan is an adept at skating over thin ice. In his address . . . - there were many points which every one knows were weak, but he glided over them with surprising deftness."

Skeleton in the Closet. Something you don't want known; a family secret. *Brewer's Dictionary of Phrase and Fable* (1870 and subsequent editions) tells without attribution a tale of an effort to find someone who had not a single care. A woman was found who seemed to qualify, but she showed the inquirers a closet containing a human skeleton, telling them that it was a rival her husband had killed in a duel. "I try to keep my trouble to myself," she said, "but every night my husband compels me to kiss that skeleton." William Makepiece Thackeray was making use of the phrase by 1845, in *Punch in the East.*

Skin and Bones. Thin; emaciated. One step removed from skeletal, either because of starvation, illness or anorexia nervosa. The result of starvation is probably the picture being conveyed in *Hymns to the Virgin and Christ* (1430): "Me is left but skyn & boon."

Skin of the Teeth, By the. Narrowly; just barely. The teeth have no skin, so that if you achieve something by that slim a margin, it is close indeed. It is a biblical phrase, somewhat modified since the 18th century. In the Bible (Job 19 : 20) it is: "My bone cleaveth to my skin and to my flesh, and I am escaped with the skin of my teeth."

Sky's the Limit, The. There is no limit; do what you want to do. How high is the sky? It's immeasurable, so it sets no limit. Cervantes was close to the modern saying in *Don Quixote* (1605): "No limits but the sky."

Sleep Like a Log. Sleep soundly. A log is notably inert, and so is a sound sleeper. You can see the phrase evolving in John Withals's dictionary, published in the 16th century: "Thou liest like a logge without life or soule."

Slender Reed. A weak or unreliable support. The reed is hardly a symbol of strength to begin with, although houses and other structures have been built of grouped reeds. So the image of relying on a reed for support as being a poor idea is very old. Thus, the first English translation (in about 1450) of *De Imitatione Christi:* "Truste not ner leene not upon a windy rede." Over the centuries the unreliable reed has been described not only as "slender" but also as "broken," "rotten" and "bruised."

Slice (Cut) the Melon. Share the profits or proceeds. "Melon" probably won this position because it is of good size, is juicy and is usually served in slices. The *New York Evening Post* picked up the expression in 1909: "A purse of $25,000 will be distributed among employees. About 8,000 men will participate in cutting the melon." (If the melon was cut in equal slices, each man got about $3.12.)

Slim Pickings. Not much there; a poor reward for one's efforts. The harvest is the source of this saying, which is now extended to anything where one gets little (and usually less than one had hoped for) in return for one's quest. John Milton put it this way in a work of long title (the key word is *Smectymnuus*) in 1642: "The Vulturs had then but small pickings."

Slings and Arrows of Outrageous Fortune, The. The hard things that life brings one's way; the miseries that one has to put up with or feels one has to put up with. Shakespeare probably created this line; at any rate it appears in Hamlet's famous soliloquy:

> To be, or not to be: that is the question:
> Whether 'tis nobler in the mind to suffer
> The slings and arrows of outrageous fortune,
> Or to take arms against a sea of troubles,
> And by opposing end them.

Slippery As an Eel. Elusive; hard to hold. An eel is long, thin and wet and thus hard to hold with one's bare hands. Nevertheless, in past centuries many people went out and caught eels with their bare hands; now it is a rare experience. Variants of the saying date from the 14th century. By 1412 Thomas Hoccleve was writing, in *The Regement of Princes:* "Mi wit is also slippir as an eel."

Slouch, He's No. He's pretty good (at some particular activity); his abilities should be respected. It's odd that one rarely hears the opposite thought: "he is a slouch." The popularity of the negative may arise from a need for polite means of giving faint praise. This version was in Charles F. Hoffman's *Greyslaer* (1840): "You are no slouch of a woodsman to carry a yearling of such a heft as that."

Slow (Quick) Off the Mark. A slow or fast starter, either in some activity or in thinking through a problem. This is the "mark" made at track meets to identify the starting point of a race or the jumping-off point of a broad jump. In 1931 the *Oxford Mail* could be seen beginning to extend the meaning (in describing a cricket match): "G. Fisher and L. Rogers were quickly off the mark, 20 runs being scored in the first ten minutes."

Slow to Anger. Normally calm and even tempered. The advice is in the Bible (James 1 : 19–20): "Wherefore, my beloved brethren, let every man be swift to hear, slow to speak, slow to wrath: For the wrath of man worketh not the righteousness of God." Thomas Nashe offered a gloss on the advice in *Christ's Teares Over Jerusalem* (1593): "There is a certaine kind of good sloth, as to be slowe to anger, slowe to iudgement, slow to reuenge."

Small Beer. Something unimportant or insignificant. In England "small beer" originally meant beer with a low content of alcohol and therefore something beneath the notice of a serious drinker. By Shakespeare's time it had come to signify any unimportant thing. In *Othello* Iago uses it that way in his talk of a hypothetical woman who would "suckle fools and chronicle small beer."

Small World, It's a. You keep encountering the same people or events. In a large world and an active life you wouldn't expect to bump into those people or go through that event again; the world therefore seems to have shrunk. Here is Weedon Grossmith, in *The Diary of a Nobody* (1919): "I . . . recognized her as a woman who used to work years ago for my aunt at Clapham. It only shows how small the world is."

Smart As a Whip. Bright, clever, alert. A whip "smarts" and operates with snap. In the days of horse-drawn vehicles one was often able to urge on the horse merely by flicking or cracking a whip near the animal, and if that failed, you could be sure of results by seeing that the flick or crack touched him lightly. The transfer must have arisen from that widespread exercise. An expression in use early in the 19th century was "smart as a steel trap," which does indeed operate smartly too, but by 1860 the *Mountaineer* in Salt Lake City was printing: "Mr. A—— was a prompt and successful businessman, 'smart as a whip,' as the Yankees say."

Smart Cookie. A bright and perhaps wily person. How the "cookie" (originally "cock cake") came to represent a person is a question the dictionaries leave unanswered. In the 19th century a "cookee" was a cook's assistant in an American lumbering camp, and perhaps one should look there for the first "smart" or "tough" cookie. Fredric Brown's *Murder Can Be Fun* (1948) says: "A smart cookie, that Wilkins."

Smell a Rat. Have suspicions about something; suspect that something is wrong. The allusion is to the cat's reaction when it smells a hidden rat. John Skelton was employing the broadened meaning in 1550 in his *Image of Hypocrisy:* "Yf they smell a ratt, / They grisely chide and chatt." "Grisely," a cousin of "grisly," is a word that has gone out of the language; it meant fearfully.

Smells Fishy. Is suspect or of doubtful worth. It seems probable that "fishy" took on this meaning either because the fish is slippery (as the proposition seems to be) or because a meat dish extended or modified with fish did not smell quite like a proper meat dish. The meaning is reflected in Benjamin Disraeli's *Coningsby* (1844): "The most fishy thing I ever saw."

Smells to Heaven. Is a thoroughly bad or contemptible proposition or deed. It's presumably a long way to heaven and thus a powerful smell. Shakespeare may have originated this phrase; at least he made it famous by having Hamlet's uncle, the king of Denmark, say:

> O, my offence is rank, it smells to heaven;
> It hath the primal eldest curse upon 't,
> A brother's murder.

Smite Them Hip and Thigh. Lay about oneself with vigor; attack one's foes fiercely. To hit them "hip and thigh" suggests that you are flailing about, hitting your opponents wherever you can. The phrase is from the Bible (Judges 15 : 8), relating what Samson does to the Philistines: "And he smote them hip and thigh with a great slaughter . . . ."

Smoke It Out. Ascertain a fact by some wile. The transfer is from hunting, when the hunter forced a fox or some other animal out of its den by blowing smoke into it. The figurative meaning appeared long ago, as suggested by Thomas Nashe's reference, in *Christ's Teares over Jerusalem* (1593), to "smoking this . . . tracte out of his startingholes."

Smoke-Filled Room. The place where important political decisions are alleged to be made. It is a newspaper cliché that originated in 1920 when the *New York Times* attributed the saying to Harry M. Daugherty, the manager of Senator Warren G. Harding's campaign for the Republican presidential nomination. According to the *Times,* Daugherty predicted a deadlock in the convention and said the nomination would be decided by a group of men who "will sit down about two o'clock in the morning around a table in a smoke-filled room." Daugherty always insisted that he had not said "smoke-filled."

Smooth (Soft) As Silk. Done in a felicitous, highly slick way. Today one might think of fabrics softer and smoother than silk, but when the simile originated many centuries ago, silk was the softest and smoothest fabric. In *Specimans of Lyric Poetry* (1842) Thomas Wright cited this specimen from 1310:

> Body ant brest wel mad al, . . .
> Eyther side soft ase sylk.

Snake in the Grass. A treacherous or unexpectedly threatening person. The literal thing, a snake that one comes on lying in or slithering through the grass, can be quite unnerving. Vergil evoked the image in Latin in his *Eclogues: Latet anguis in herba* [a snake lurks in the grass]. A 13th-century political song in England also went in for Latin but showed the transferred meaning: *Cum totem fecisse putas, latet anguis in herba* [though all appears clean, a snake lurks in the grass].

Snap To (Into) It. Get smartly into action. Of American origin, dating from early in the 20th century. F. A. Pottle picked it up in *Stretchers* (1918): "Oh, snap into it! We want to get this done." Perhaps it was the "snap" of the whip that gave rise to this exhortation to action.

Snare and a Delusion, A. A false hope. The "snare" is the noose-like device that one uses to catch small animals. By transfer it is the trap one gets caught in when one has succumbed to a delusion. The British justice Lord Denman put it this way in *O'Connell* v. *The Crown* (1844): "Trial by jury . . . will be a delusion, a mockery and a snare."

Snow Job. An effort to flatter someone or to distract his or her attention from the reality of a matter. Morroe Berger, writing in *American Speech* in 1945, gave what I think is the place and time of origin of this saying. His subject was "Army Language" in World War II. "Snow job," he wrote, "comes from the phrase 'to snow someone under,' and means a concerted effort to convince a girl, a superior or a fellow soldier of something that takes a lot of convincing."

Snowball in Hell, Chance of a. No chance; foredoomed. Hell is invariably portrayed as a hot place, where homemade snowballs would be unheard of, and imported snowballs would quickly melt. *American Speech* recorded the metaphor in 1931: "As much chance as a snowball in hell."

Snug as a Bug in a Rug. Safe; comfortable. The saying doesn't have much going for it except the appeal of similar sounds. Probably the only bug that would find a rug snug is a carpet beetle. The others would soon have to go out and forage for something edible. *The Stratford Jubilee,* a play of 1769, carries this line: "If she [a rich widow] has the mopus's, I'll have her, as snug as a bug in a rug." "Mopus" is a lost word meaning money.

So Far, So Good. Nothing bad has happened yet; the project is moving along satisfactorily. The phrase appears in Samuel Richardson's *The History of Sir Charles Grandison* (1753).

Soft Soap. Flattery; persiflage. Real soft soap is smeary and unctuous. The resemblance to flattery is plain. As a verb the idea turns up in Frances M. Whitcher's *The Widow Bedott Papers* (1840): "Ye don't ketch me a slanderin' folks behind their backs and then sof-soapin' 'em to their faces."

Son of a Gun. You don't say; oh, him. The phrase equally serves as a mild expression of dislike, an affectionate response and an exclamation of surprise. A source for it was given by the British admiral William Henry Smyth in *The Sailor's Word-Book* (1865): "An epithet applied to boys born afloat, when women were permitted to accompany their husbands to sea; one admiral declared he literally was thus cradled, under the breast of a gun-carriage."

Sooner or Later. Sometime (almost always with the implication that the event will certainly come to pass). Barnaby Googe in 1577 translated a book that came to be known as *Heresbach's Husbandry* and included this advice: "The stones, stickes, and such baggage . . . are to be throwen out sooner or later."

Sound and Fury. A lot of clamor, usually empty and leading to no result. It is hard to know with Shakespeare whether he is originating a phrase or has picked it up from the speech of his time, but this one (from *Macbeth*) has the ring of originality. Macbeth, informed that Lady Macbeth is dead, delivers a moving requiem, part of which is:

> Life's but a walking shadow, a poor player
> That struts and frets his hour upon the stage
> And then is heard no more: it is a tale
> Told by an idiot, full of sound and fury,
> Signifying nothing.

Sound as a Dollar. In good health; a reliable proposition. The dollar has been a symbol of sound currency both nationally and internationally for some 200 years. By 1852 Charles Casey was offering this blurb in *Two Years on the Farm of Uncle Sam:* "May be ridden or drove by man, woman, or boy—sound as a dollar, or no sale!—as good a horse, gen'lem, as ever wore hair!"

Sour Grapes. A claim that something desirable but unattainable wouldn't be very good anyway; a negative attitude. Aesop's fable, "The Fox and the Grapes," is the source of this idea. In one translation it reads: "A hungry fox one day saw some tempting grapes hanging at a good height from the ground. He made many attempts to reach them, but all in vain. Tired out by his failures, he walked off, grumbling to himself, 'Nasty, sour things I know you are, and not at all fit for a gentleman's eating.' "

Sow Wild Oats. Do (usually as a young man) some zany or foolish things. The wild oat, *Avena fatua,* is actually a tall grass—a weed—resembling the cultivated oat. If you sow that, you are being foolish and wasting your time. Thomas Newton's translation (from Latin) of *Lemnie's Touchstone of Complexions* (1576) defines the saying: "That wilfull and vnruly age, which lacketh rypenes and discretion, and (as wee saye) hath not sowed all theyr wyeld Oates."

Speak Off the Cuff. Make more or less impromptu remarks. A formal speech is usually written out in advance, but sometimes the speaker doesn't spend much time preparing or is told on short notice that he will be asked to speak. Then he may hastily assemble some thoughts, scribbling on his shirt cuff if nothing else is available.

Speak for Yourself. State your own opinion, not somebody else's. In the Bible's tale of Festus hearing the accusations of the Jews against Paul, Festus tells King Agrippa that the case seems weak and should be appealed to Caesar. The king says he wants to hear the man himself. Paul is brought before him, and Agrippa says (Acts 26 : 1): "Thou art permitted to speak for thyself." The line was also made memorable by Henry Wadsworth Longfellow in *The Courtship of Miles Standish* (1858). Standish, a strong but apparently bashful captain, has sent his friend and aide John Alden to pay court to the maiden Priscilla. Alden loves her himself, but he does his duty, becoming quite eloquent and "full of the praise of his rival." Whereupon:

> Archly the maiden smiled, and, with eyes overrunning with laughter,
>
> Said, in a tremulous voice, "Why don't you speak for yourself, John?"

Speak of the Devil. Somebody or something recently mentioned has just turned up. In older times it was thought to be unwise to speak of the devil, since if you did, some sign of his works was likely to appear soon. Giovanni Torriano, publishing a collection of Italian proverbs in 1666, included a few observations on English sayings. In this case he wrote: "The English say, Talk of the Devil, and he's presently at your elbow."

Spic and Span. Tidy; clean; in good order. Did you ever hear "spic" in any other connection? Or "span" having to do wtih neatness? They are ancient words, "spic" or "spick" meaning a spike and "span" meaning a chip. And the saying was once "spick and span new," meaning with bright spikes or nails and freshly shaped wood. Sir Thomas North's version of *Plutarch's Lives* in 1579 reads: "They were all in goodly gilt armours, and brave purple cassocks upon them, spicke, and spanne newe."

Spill the Beans. Reveal something that was supposed to be kept secret; give away information or a plan prematurely. "Spill" meaning to talk and "beans" meaning what you know are individually quite old, the one dating to the 16th century and the other to the 13th. They seem to have been put together, however, early in the 20th century, as in Eric Linklater's *Poet's Pub* (1929): "'Tell me the truth,' she says. 'Spill the beans, Holly, old man!' "

Spirit is Willing but the Flesh is Weak, The. I can't do this even though I would like to. The saying is from the Bible (Matthew 26 : 41), where Jesus says to his disciples, "Watch, and pray, that ye enter not into temptation: the spirit indeed is willing, but the flesh is weak."

Spit and Polish. The smart and natty appearance that is insisted on in armies, navies and air forces; extreme attention to ceremonial and to smartness of appearance, sometimes at the expense of operational efficiency. One ploy that soldiers, sailors and airmen have used to get a quick shine on a pair of shoes is to spit on them and then polish them with a cloth. Admiral Lord Charles Beresford wrote in his *Memoirs* of his views on the subject. When he assumed his first command in 1873, he said, he at first had the crew work on the decks until they were "as clean as a hound's tooth," but later "I set myself against bright-work and spit-and-polish. Under the spit-and-polish system no doubt the men take a pride in keeping the ship bright, but such a process involves perpetual extra bother and worry, which are quite unnecessary."

Spitting Image. An exact likeness (usually said of a child's resemblance to one of its parents). In most of its long life the phrase has been "spit and image," which in fact is a redundancy, since "spit" means, or once meant, likeness. An old saying was that a boy resembling his father was as much like him as if he had been "spit out of the father's mouth." The two words seem to have been put together in the 19th century. Egerton Castle's *The Light of Scarthey* (1895) has the line: "She's like the poor lady that's dead and gone, the spit an' image she is."

Split Hairs. Argue extensively over trifles or fine distinctions; quibble. A hair can be split today without much trouble, but once it was thought to be so fine that an effort to split it would be a waste of time. The same was true of trifling points, and the analogy between the one and the other was made long ago. A translation in 1691 of Gabriel D'Emillianne's *Observations on a Journey to Naples* offered: "Shewing himself very inventive and dexterous at splitting a Hair in his way of handling Scholastick matter." Gabriel D'Emillianne was the pseudonym of Antonio Gauin.

Sport of Kings. Horse racing in modern times; the chase (another form of horse racing) in older times. The phrase is a sports page cliché today. In 1735 William Somerville wrote, in *The Chase:*

> The chase, the sport of kings,
> Image of war, without its guilt.

Somerville is the man of whom Samuel Johnson said, "He writes very well for a gentleman."

Square Deal. Fair treatment; an honorable arrangement. The phrase has been in the language for some three centuries; it became a cliché after President Theodore Roosevelt made it one of his administration's slogans. Gerard's *Description of Somerset* (1633) speaks of "square dealing."

Square Meal. A full and satisfying repast (particularly to someone who has not had a meal for a while). This is "square" in the sense of solid, right. It began to be applied to meals by people in the United States about the middle of the 19th century and had become commonplace by about 1880. In 1864 *All the Year Round* wrote of "roadside hotel-keepers . . . calling the miners' attention to their 'square meals': by which is meant full meals."

Square Peg in a Round Hole, A. A misfit; a person mismatched or unfitted for the task at hand. It has also been "a round peg in a square hole." Either way, the fit is poor. Sydney Smith said, in one of his lectures early in the 19th century: "We shall generally find that the triangular person has got into the square hole, the oblong into the triangular, and a square person has squeezed himself into the round hole."

Squeaking Wheel Gets the Grease, The. Attention is usually paid to the person who complains the most, or to the problem that is most evident. The wagon wheel needed to be greased regularly or it would begin to squeak and run stiffly. The prudent owner applied the grease before those things happened, but others would put off the job until a squeak forced them to act. In his poem, "The Kicker," the 19th-century American humorist Josh Billings (whose real name was Henry Wheeler Shaw) wrote:

The wheel that squeaks the loudest
Is the one that gets the grease.

Staff of Life, The. Bread. Any number of food items could be called "the staff of life," but bread won the label because it is such a basic item. A hint of the idea is in the Bible (Isaiah 3 : 1): "For, behold, the Lord, the Lord of hosts, doth take away from Jerusalem, and from Judah, the stay and the staff, the whole stay of bread, and the whole stay of water." Matthew Henry drew a similar lesson from Psalm 104, of which he wrote (in his commentaries on the Bible early in the 18th century): "Here is bread, which strengthens man's heart, and therefore called the staff of life."

Stalking Horse. A front for some scheme or maneuver; a means of causing an opponent to reveal his strategy. The literal origin is in the hunter, who, approaching his quarry, would get off his horse and, using the horse as a blind, stalk step by step until he got within shooting distance of the game. The practice was old by Shakespeare's time, and he showed, in *As You Like It*, how the meaning had been broadened. The Duke and Jaques have been conversing with the clown Touchstone; Jaques says, "Is not this a rare fellow, my lord? he's as good at anything and yet a fool." The Duke replies, "He uses his folly like a stalking-horse and under the presentation of that he shoots his wit."

Stand Pat. Adhere to an existing policy or state of affairs. It is a term from poker, where it means to play the hand as it was dealt to you and not to draw additional cards. The phrase is of American origin and has been part of the game for at least 100 years. Its extended meaning was employed by Senator Marcus A. Hanna of Ohio in 1903: "Now I say, Stand pat; you are not on the defensive." This is "pat" in the sense of exactly suitable. John S. Farmer's *Americanisms* (1889) defined the "pat hand" in poker as "an original hand not likely to be improved by drawing."

Stand the Gaff. Hold up under pressure or adversity. "Gaff" is a word with an astonishing number of meanings, but mostly is used now only to refer to the type of rigging of a sail known as the "gaff rig." The "gaff" of the familiar saying was loud, rude talk. When "stand the gaff" arose in the United States around 1900, it meant to accept blame or reproach for something one had done. You see this in W. M. Raine's *B. O'Connor* (1910): "Neil has got to stand the gaff for what he's done."

Stark Raving Mad. Out of his mind; acting bizarrely; putting forward a strange proposal. You could call this a triple intensifier, since any one of the words would suffice to suggest that something strange is afoot. Gabriel Harvey drew a distinction, though, in *Pierces Supererogation* (1593): "I wis hee mought haue spied a difference . . . betwene raging, and starke-madde." At one time the thought was put as "stark staring madness." Thus Nicholas Udall in 1548 paraphrased the passage in the Bible (Luke 6 : 6–11), where the Pharisees were "filled with madness" when Jesus in their opinion violated the Sabbath by healing the man with the withered hand: "Thei are turned into stercke staryng madness." Henry Fielding had the modern version in *The Intriguing Chambermaid* (1734): "I find I am distracted! I am stark raving mad!"

Start From Scratch. Begin with nothing, without advantage. In racing the "scratch" is the starting line, sometimes literally scratched on the ground. Horses or people racing with a handicap start ahead of the line; the ones thought not to need a handicap "start from scratch." James Joyce, in *Ulysses* (1922), wrote of "A poor foreign immigrant who started scratch as a stowaway and is now trying to turn an honest penny."

Steal His Thunder. Take away the effect of someone's remarks or actions; appropriate someone's idea or claim to fame. The playwright John Dennis wrote *Appius and Virginia* and presented it in 1709. It was a failure, but it had one distinction: Dennis had devised a way of creating the sound of thunder as part of the staging. Later he heard his thunder at a presentation of *Macbeth*. "My God," he said, "the villains will play my thunder but not my plays!" The story is related in Brewer's *Dictionary of Phrase and Fable*.

Steal a March on. Gain an advantage, often by stealth. It was a military maneuver in which a commander moved troops in such a way that the enemy was unaware of the change and was put at a disadvantage by it. Thus, the *London Gazette* in 1716: "We saw him . . . steal a March for our Preservation."

Steer Clear of. Avoid. As you might expect, it is a nautical phrase, as is made clear in *My Novel* by Edward Bulwer-Lytton (1853): "He is safest from shoals who steers clearest of his relations." In 1723 Daniel Defoe wrote, in *The History and Remarkable Life of Colonel Jacque*: "We would have steered clear of them, and cared not to have them see us, if we could help it, but they did see us, and cried, Who comes there?"

Stem the Tide. Arrest or divert a trend that is running against one's interests. The literal tide of the sea is not to be stemmed. It can only be diverted or its effect locally mitigated by breakwaters and jetties; but one can hope to do better with a trend less irresistible than a tide. Fred A. Paley, writing in 1855 on the tragedies of Aeschylus, said: "Aristophanes evidently saw the trend that was setting in favour of the new candidate for scenic supremacy, and he vainly tried to stem the tide by the barrier of his ridicule."

Step on It. Hurry. The advent of the automobile and the accelerator ("step on the gas") brought this exhortation into favor. Frank L. Packard was on it in 1930, in *Jimmie Dale and the Blue Envelope Murder*: "Then for heaven's sake step on it, old man!"

Stew in His Own Juice. Be in a difficulty of one's own making. Once it was "fry in one's own grease," said inelegantly of someone being burned at the stake. In that form it can be found in Chaucer's *Canterbury Tales* of the 14th century. Later variations included "stew in their own water" (1656) and "stew all Night in my own grease" (1664). Sir William Harcourt is the first recorded to have used the modern version; in a speech in 1885 he said, "Liberals must not be in a hurry to turn the Tories out. He would let them for a few months stew in their own Parnellite juice."

Stewed to the Gills. Very drunk. Several things reach the gills, meaning that if you got any more of the thing, you would suffocate, as a fish would if anything blocked its gills. Thus one hears "loaded to the gills" for rich and "stuffed to the gills" for I ate too much. The version meaning drunk is evidently of the 20th century. Nelson Algren has it, in *The Man with the Golden Arm* (1949): "He came in stewed to the gills, with Sparrow holding him up by the belt. . . ." "Stewed" meaning drunk derives from cooking by stewing; in this case alcohol supplies the heat.

Stick Your Neck Out. Take a risk; expose oneself to criticism. In the present form the saying originated as American slang some 60 years ago, probably based on the barnyard or backyard chicken that was laid on a chopping block with its neck stretched out and was then beheaded with an ax. A closely related form goes back at least to Shakespeare's time. In *Henry V* Fluellen, thinking the soldier Williams has done a traitorous thing, says, "Let his neck answer for it . . .."

Stick in One's Craw, To. To be unacceptable or repugnant. It has also been "crop" and "gizzard," all three expressions referring to the place in a bird's digestive tract where food is ground up. In the *Vindication of Sir Thomas Player* (1679) one finds: "'Tis the Matter, not the Manner, that sticks in our Unworthy Respondents Gizzard."

Stick in the Mud. Ignore or have no part in what others regard as progress; to be content with one's situation. The horse-drawn wagon, once bogged down in mud, was as difficult to move as a self-satisfied person and probably gave rise to the image. The same thought has been put as "sticking in the clay," "the mire" and "the briers." In one or another of those forms it goes back more than 500 years.

Stick to Your Guns. Hang in there; hold your position in the face of argument or adversity. The origin is military and probably naval, since a gunner on a besieged ship might well need such an exhortation. In the figurative sense it appeared in Samuel Warren's novel *Ten Thousand a Year* (1839): "Titmouse, though greatly alarmed, stood to his gun pretty steadily." This is the first recorded literary use of the saying, but one suspects that it was applied verbally by military officers to wavering soldiers and sailors soon after guns replaced bows and battering rams.

Stick to Your Last. Do or comment on only the things you know well. The full version, no longer heard, is: "A cobbler should stick to his last." The "last" is the foot-shaped form that the cobbler, or shoemaker, uses to make or repair a shoe. In Shakespeare's *Romeo and Juliet* a servant who has been given what he regards as ambiguous instructions to find some people and invite them to a Capulet feast makes a play on the saying:

> Find them out whose names are written here!
> It is written that the shoemaker should meddle with
> his yard and the tailor with his last, the fisher with
> his pencil and the painter with his nets. . ..

Stickler for the Rules. Someone who adheres scrupulously, even fussily, to established procedure. The "stickler," a word never heard now in any other context, was an umpire or moderator in a sporting event or a dispute. It also came to mean someone who insists on a certain procedure, as in Daniel Featley's *Levites Scourge* (1644): "A Great stickler for the new Reformation."

Sticks to (by) the Ribs. It's filling and nourishing food. So you suggest that it is causing you to put on weight. John Ray recorded this standard way of saying you're enjoying what you're eating as a proverb in 1670.

Sticky Wicket. A touchy or difficult situation. In cricket the wicket ($27'' \times 8''$) is not only the structure the bowler aims at and the batsman defends, but is also a general term for the playing field. A "sticky wicket" is wet or soft and so changes the pace of the bowler's ball (which usually reaches the batsman on one bounce). The condition makes things tougher for the bowler, the batsman or the fielder, depending on who adapts least well to the situation. Thus this exchange in *Pall Mall Magazine* in 1888: " 'Do you think the bowler suffers much under the present law?' 'Well, he does somewhat; but only on sticky wickets.' "

Still Waters Run Deep. Quiet people are often found to have profound insights. The shallow water in a brook or river runs fast; the deep water seems calmer. The *Cursor Mundi* of about 1400 notes that where "the flode is deppist the water standis stillist." In Shakespeare's *Henry VI, Part 2*, the Duke of Suffolk, talking of the Duke of Gloucester, says:

> Smooth runs the water where the brook is deep;
> And in his simple show he harbours treason.

Stir Up a Hornet's Nest. Provoke (usually unintentionally) an angry reaction; let oneself in for trouble; run into opposition. One can feel in this phrase the pain of a person who has blundered into a hornet's nest and been thoroughly stung for it. Samuel Richardson recorded the image in *Pamela* (1739): "I rais'd a Hornet's Nest about my Ears, that . . . may have stung to Death my Reputation."

Stitch in Time Saves Nine, A. Preventive action is wise. It was doubtless a woman faced with a pile of mending who first thought of or was given this advice. In earlier days the thought was expressed a bit less firmly, as in Thomas Fuller's *Gnomologia*, a collection of proverbs (1732): "A stitch in time may save nine." The extended meaning was evident in Charles Reade's *Foul Play* (1869): "Repairing the ship. Found a crack or two in her inner skin. . . . A stitch in time saves nine."

Stone-deaf. Unhearing or unable to hear. The stone as a symbol of hardness, deadness or insensibility turns up in many associations, including blind, cold and dead. "Stone" intensifies the description, indicating that the condition is severe. Thomas Hood's *Tale of a Trumpet* (1841) says of a woman: "She was deaf as a stone."

Stonewall It. Be obstructive or obdurate. Although the origin is in building or taking refuge behind a stone wall, the meaning of obstructionism arose as a political term in Australia, where it was applied to parliamentary groups. It also is a term from cricket, where it refers to a batsman who plays defensively by blocking the ball away from the wicket. The political meaning appeared in the *Victorian Hansard* in 1876: "Mr. G. Paton Smith wished to ask . . . whether the six members . . . constituted the 'stone wall' . . . which was to oppose all progress?" The cricket version was in *Played On* (1889): "A brother professional began to stonewall in a distracting manner. 'Take care of your wicket and let the runs take care of themselves,' was his motto."

Stop the Music. Hold up; suspend the action. The musical accompaniment that is common in the theater and many radio and television programs and formerly the silent motion pictures is probably the source of the saying, which became a trademark of the comedian Jimmy Durante. He would cry, "Stop da music!" whenever (which was often) he was portraying someone who was confused or thought things were getting ahead of him.

Straight From the Shoulder. Directly; without sham or deception. The saying comes from boxing, as one sees from Charles Reade's *It Is Never Too Late To Mend* (1856): "No! give me a chap that hits out straight from the shoulder."

Strain at a Gnat and Swallow a Camel. Fret over small wrongs but commit or accept big ones. It is in the Bible (Matthew 23 : 24), where Jesus says, "Ye blind guides! which strain at a gnat, and swallow a camel." In some versions it has been "strain out," suggesting that the original reference was to straining small impurities from wine or water but ignoring or accepting big ones.

Strange Bedfellows. Odd or unlikely couplings or groupings of people. Today the phenomenon is usually attributed to politics. In *The Tempest,* however, Shakespeare has Trinculo say, looking at Caliban as a storm approaches, "Alas, the storm is come again! best way is to creep under his gaberdine; there is no other shelter hereabout: misery acquaints a man with strange bedfellows."

Stray (Go) Off the Reservation. Go beyond the limits. The Indian reservation is the source of the phrase, but now one can go off a nonphysical reservation, that is, beyond the limits imposed by or understood to exist in a situation. An example was in the *Saturday Evening Post* in 1949: "[President] Truman's sweeping demand for civil-rights legislation . . . stampeded the Southerners right off the reservation."

Stream of Consciousness. One's running and more or less random thoughts. William James discussed it in *The Principles of Psychology* (1890): "Consciousness. . . . does not appear to itself chopped up in bits. . . . A 'river' or 'stream' are the metaphors by which it is most naturally described. In talking of it hereafter, let us call it the stream of thought, of consciousness, or of subjective life."

Street Smarts. Urban wisdom; the ability to make one's way in a big city. The phrase, quite possibly of black origin, began to be popular about 1972. By 1976 the *New York Times* had picked it up: "To be free [of trouble or fear] in New York requires street smarts, the cunning of the survivor."

Stretch the Truth. Exaggerate. It is possible that Mark Twain originated this image. It appears in *Huckleberry Finn* (1884): "There was things which he stretched, but mainly he told the truth."

Strike While the Iron is Hot. Act at a time when conditions are favorable; take advantage of an opportunity. The iron was on the anvil, and the striker was the blacksmith. If he didn't strike while the iron was hot, the metal could not be worked properly and he would have to reheat it. As a figure of speech the expression goes back at least to Chaucer's time. As he put it c. 1386: "Whil that iren is hoot, men shoulden smyte."

String Along. Deceive, gull or josh someone. Probably the image is of a line pulling an object along behind a horse or a boat. "String" in this sense originated in the United States around 1900. *Munsey's Magazine* recorded it in 1901: " 'Someone has been stringin' those reporters!' thought Dan."

Stubborn (Obstinate) as a Mule. Ornery. "With no good reason, the mule is a proverbial type of obstinacy," the *Oxford English Dictionary* says. Many a mule driver would dispute the statement. If a mule does not want to go, it takes a considerable effort to get it going. At any rate, the impression of mulish obstinacy is of long standing. Maria Edgeworth's *Absentee* (1809) says: "She was as obstinate as a mule on that point."

Stuff and Nonsense. Foolishness; something not to be believed or credited. It could just as well be "nonsense and stuff," and in years past it sometimes was put that way. Henry Fielding used it in *Tom Jones* (1749) as: "Pooh, all stuff and nonsense, I tell thee, she shall ha' thee to-morrow."

Stuffed Shirt. A pompous man (usually with the implication that he is not as important or capable as he thinks he is). A look at a mannikin in a men's-clothing store, well dressed but lifeless, might have inspired the anonymous creator of this inspired term. It's probably a 20th-century invention. Willa Cather was using it familiarly in 1913 in *O Pioneers!*: "He characterized Frank Shabata by a Bohemian expression which is the equivalent of stuffed shirt."

Stung to the Quick. Gravely affronted, insulted or wounded in pride. The "quick" is the sensitive part of the flesh below the skin, and one can literally be stung there by, say, a hornet. It is painful indeed. In the figurative sense one finds Daniel Defoe writing, in *Moll Flanders* (1722): "This stung the elder brother to the quick."

Suffer Fools Gladly, He Doesn't. He's impatient with people who don't think as quickly as he does or who act in a way he regards as unintelligent. It's almost invariably in the negative now, but in the original version in the Bible (Corinthians 11 : 19) it was positive: "For ye suffer fools gladly, seeing ye yourselves are wise."

252

Survival of the Fittest. The strongest or best adapted succeed. It is essentially what Charles Darwin saw as the governing principle of natural selection, but he did not originate the four-word encapsulation of the thought. Herbert Spencer did. Discussing evolution in *The Principles of Biology"* (1867), he wrote: "By the continual survival of the fittest, such structures must become established."

Swallow Your Pride. Accept what's happening or what is being offered even though you find it humiliating or at least beneath your dignity. If you let pride stand in the way, you'll miss an opportunity. An example from 1821 appears in *Letters from John Pintard to His Daughter*: "How much pride have I to swallow?"

Swan Song. A farewell; one's last appearance. The swan in fact does not sing, but ancient legend has it that the dying swan does manage at last to give voice to something like a song. The legend appears in Chaucer's *Anelida and Arcite* (c.1374): "The swane . . . Ageynist his dethe shall sing his penavnse [penance]."

Sweat Blood. To do agonizing physical work or worry agonizingly over a situation. The idea is from the Bible (Luke 22 : 44), referring to the agony of Jesus on the Mount of Olives: "And being in agony he prayed more earnestly: and his sweat was as it were great drops of blood falling down to the ground."

Sweetness and Light. False or overdone good cheer. It is not always applied ironically; sometimes people or situations are said to embody genuine sweetness and light. Jonathan Swift, in his "Battle of the Books" (1697), wrote an imaginary fable in the Aesop mode; it concerned the merits of the bee, representing the old, and the spider, representing the new. Swift concluded: "The difference is that instead of dirt and poison, we have rather chosen to fill our hives with honey and wax, thus furnishing mankind with the two noblest of things, which are sweetness and light." ("Light" because the wax could be made into candles.)

Swept (Carried) Off His Feet. Overwhelmed by the impact of something; highly impressed. Probably the image is of the ocean wave upending someone who is walking along a beach. Elizabeth Cleghorn Gaskell, the novelist and biographer who in the Victorian tradition wrote as "Mrs. Gaskell," said in a letter in 1854: "I'll enclose you two pieces of Mr. S. Gaskell to show how *he's* carried off his feet."

Sword of Damocles. Impending danger. The original sword, according to legend, was suspended by a thread over the chair where Damocles sat at a banquet given by King Dionysius of ancient

Syracuse. Damocles had carried on about the ease of kingly life, and Dionysius chose the dangling sword as a way of showing him that life (including the life of kings) also entails perils and responsibilities.

T

Tail Between His Legs, Went Off With His. Departed in defeat, embarrassment or discouragement; retreated in a cowardly way. It is what a dog does when he encounters something that is too much for him. *Lanfrank's Science of Cirurgie*, dating from about 1400, speaks of "a wood hound" that goes off with "his tail bitwene hise leggis."

Take Him Down a Peg. Deflate a pompous person; show up a boaster. "Pegs" have served in various ways to indicate rankings or quantities; ships' colors, for example, were put on pegs at a height reflecting the honor the ship had gained. The expression is very old, an early example being in John Lyly's *Pappe with an Hatchet* (1589): "Now haue at you all my gaffers of the rayling religion, tis I that must take you a peg lower."

Take It With a Grain of Salt. Be skeptical; examine it (a statement or an idea) carefully before you accept it. The thought seems to be that a bit of salt makes food easier to swallow. It is old enough to have a Latin version: *cum grano salis*. One of John Trapp's commentaries on the Bible in 1647 carried the line: "This is to be taken with a grain of salt."

Take It or Leave It. Make up your mind; the offer stands as is and won't be changed. A version of this phrase can be found in the *Cursor Mundi* as early as 1300. Shakespeare was closer to the modern usage in *King Lear*. Lear has decided to disinherit his youngest daughter, Cordelia, who is sought in marriage by the king of France. Lear says to the French king and the Duke of Burgundy:

> Will you, with these infirmities she owes,
> Unfriended, new adopted to our hate,
> Dower'd with our curse and stranger'd with
> our oath,
> Take her, or leave her?

The king of France takes her.

Take Pen in Hand. Write. It is a florid way of saying that you are about to communicate. Samuel Johnson was close to the phrase in one of his pithy witticisms, as recorded by James Boswell. Speaking of Oliver Goldsmith, Johnson said: "No man was more foolish when he had not a pen in his hand, or more wise when he had."

Take Potluck. Take one's chances (usually at what one will get to eat if one arrives unexpectedly at someone's house). It is literally the luck of the pot—whatever is cooking when you arrive—that you are apt to get on an unannounced visit. In *The Spiritual Quixote* (1773) Richard Graves wrote: "The Gentleman said . . . he should be very welcome to take potluck with him."

Take Umbrage. Feel resentment or suspicion at what someone has done or said. "Umbrage" started out to mean shade or shadow; it still means that, although you seldom find the word in that context. The transfer implies that the person against whom you "take umbrage" is in some kind of shade in your mind. Lord Fountainhall recorded in 1680 that "the Bishop . . . took umbrage at his [a priest's] freedom of speech in the pulpit anent the government."

Take Up the Cudgels. Prepare to do battle. "Cudgel" survives in the language only as a verb, and mainly in the sense of cudgeling one's brain. The cudgel was a short, stout stick used as a weapon. Richard Whitlock wrote in his *Zootomia* of 1654 (a work on English manners) of writers "taking up the Cudgels on one side or other."

Take a Bow. Acknowledge applause or commendation for something one has done; retire from a scene. It is traditionally the last moment at the theater: the actors are onstage as a group, the audience applauds, the actors bow and the curtain is closed. The other sense appears in J. Thomson's *Life of W. Thomson* (1875): "The old farmer is making his bow—passing off the stage never again to return."

Take a Leaf (Page) Out of Your Book. Follow your example. As a couth person you wouldn't literally do this, but you might do it figuratively in plagiarism or in admiration. Here is Benjamin H. Malkin in *Gil Blas* (1809): "I took a leaf out of their book."

Take a Load Off Your Feet. Sit down (or lie down). An informal welcome. This casual greeting was common by 1945, when Arthur Kober wrote in *Parm Me*: "How's about taking a load off your feet?"

Take a Powder. Depart (usually in haste). One can only speculate about the kind of powder. An earlier phrase was "dust out of here," and the "dust" may have turned into the "powder." There is also the possibility that the "powder" was a laxative, as suggested by the phrase from the 1930s: "take a run-out powder." In any case, the saying became a cliché in about 1925.

Take a Shine to. Find that one likes a person or an idea (usually one newly met with). In the 1880s the expression "shine up" to someone, probably meaning to put on a shining face and the appropriate accompanying behavior, was quite popular, and it may indicate the origin of the older "take a shine to." James Russell Lowell used that one rather oddly in his *Bigelow Papers* (1848): "My gracious! it's a scorpion that's took a shine to play with't."

Take by Storm. Gain quick (perhaps unexpected) entry or popularity. The "storm" here was a military term, in common use by the 17th century, meaning to attack a fortified place with great force. Charlotte Brontë showed the figurative meaning in *Jane Eyre* (1847): "How I looked when these ideas were taking my spirit by storm, I cannot tell."

Take the Bit in His Teeth. Proceed resolutely; push aside restraints and forge ahead. When a horse takes the bit in his teeth, he is a good deal less subject to control, since he does not feel so sensitively the pull of the reins. The notion had been extended to people by the 16th century. *Pappe with an Hatchet*, thought to have been written by John Lyly in 1589, contains this line: "But if like a resty iade thou wilt take the bit in thy mouth, and then run over hedge and ditch, thou shalt be broken as Prosper broke his horses."

Take the Rough and (with) the Smooth. Handle things as they come, the bad with the good, the difficult with the easy. The advice was being given as early as 1400 in *The Tale of Beryn*: "Take your part as it comyth, of roughe and eke of smooth."

Take the Veil. Become a nun; retire from everyday concerns. The "veil" here is the outer covering of the nun's headdress and is symbolic of the modesty and innocence the nun is expected to display. The expression is doubtless as old as the establishment of religious orders, but its first appearance in English writing seems to have been in *English Metrical Homilies* (1325); "maydens . . . toke thaire uayles."

Take the Wind Out of His Sails. Cramp his style; impede his momentum; deflate his ego. It is what one literally does in sailing (sometimes deliberately in a race) by sailing close to and upwind of another vessel, so that your sails rob the other boat's sails of the wind. Sir Walter Scott shows the transferred meaning in *Nigel* (1822): "He would take the wind out of the sail of every gallant."

Taken to the Cleaners. Relieved of one's money or aspirations, perhaps by flimflam; easily bested. The advent of professional dry cleaners not so many decades ago brought about this modernization of the earlier phrase "cleaned out." James H. Vaux, in his *New* *and Comprehensive Vocabulary of the Flash [slang] Language* (1812) defined the older phrase as follows: "Said of a gambler who has lost his stake at play; also of a flat [dupe] who has been stript of all his money."

Takes the Cake, That. It wins the prize (perhaps an imaginary prize and quite likely something in the booby-prize category). Giving a cake as a prize for some achievement is an ancient practice. The application of the expression to situations where there was actually no cake seems to date to the 19th century. In 1884 the *Lisbon Star*, in what is now North Dakota, told its readers: "Sheriff Moore takes the cake for the first wheat-harvesting in Ransom County."

Tale of Woe. A lament; a recital of real or imaginary troubles. In some versions of Shakespeare's *Romeo and Juliet* it is "tale of woe" and in others "story of woe." In any case, it is in the next to last line of the play, where Escalus, the Prince of Verona, says:

>For never was a story of more woe
>Than this of Juliet and her Romeo.

In 1790 Samuel Taylor Coleridge put it this way in *Genevieve*:

>Within your soul a voice there lives!
>It bids you hear the tale of Woe.

Talk (Argue) in Circles. Make an assertion that is unsupported or doesn't prove anything; come back to one's starting point. In formal logic to argue in a circle is to set forth a proposition, use it to reach a conclusion and then use the conclusion to prove the proposition. Henry More wrote, in *A Platonicall Song of Soul* (1647): "You dispute in a Circle as all Logicians know."

Talk It Up. Boost something; say things that will advance the cause. Daniel Defoe was fond of the phrase, using it in several of his works, among them *The History and Remarkable Life of Colonel Jacque* (1722): "I failed not to talk up the gallantry . . . of his . . . majesty."

Talk Through Your Hat. Say something without really knowing your subject matter; make an unsupported assertion; talk nonsense. The origin must be in the thought that a person talking through his hat would look ridiculous; in the transfer, what he is saying is ridiculous. The phrase must have been current by 1884, since the *New York World* offered it then without explanation. A reporter was interviewing a streetcar man about the transit company's effort to get its operators to wear white shirts. The man said (and was quoted in a way that would get a reporter reprimanded or fired today); "Dis is only a bluff dey're makin'. Dey're talkin' tru deir hats."

Talk Turkey. Get serious; get down to business. Until perhaps a century ago the expression meant merely to talk pleasantly, making harmless noises like the gobble of the turkey. A tale of the 19th century shows the change. The tale had a white man and an Indian hunting, catching among other things some turkeys. The white man began dividing the catch in such a way that he got all the turkeys. The Indian finally said: "All time you talk turkey. Now I talk turkey to you."

Talk Your Ear Off. Talk too much, to the point of boredom. The ear doesn't fall off when a bore is at hand; it just feels as though it has or is about to. What is actually getting numb is the mind. The *New York Daily News* used the expression in 1952 ("Donna talked his ear off"), but it is probably much older.

Tan Your Hide (Britches). Physically chastise someone or threaten to. The human skin has been contemptuously or jocularly referred to as a "hide" since the 17th century. In tanning a real hide one converts it into leather by curing it in a solution of tannin or some other preservative material. J.W. Orderson's *Creolana* (1842) speaks of "one who . . . tanned the hide of a poor pigmy." Presumably he gave the pigmy a thrashing.

Tarred With the Same Brush. Made a victim of the same punishment, indignity or treatment visited on someone else; equally involved in some bad or out-of-favor activity. It could come from the practice of tarring and feathering someone who had fallen into disgrace, but more likely the origin is in treating the sores of sheep with a brush dipped in tar. They all got the same brush. In a slightly different version the thought goes back at least 400 years, as is reflected in Stefano Guazzo's *The Civile Conversation* (1581): "Of one selfe pitch, we all have a touch."

Tear Your Hair. Express anger, grief or worry. I suppose some people have actually torn out hair in such an extremity of emotion, but in most cases the description is symbolic. William Caxton had it vividly in *The Foure Sonnes of Aymon* (1489): "He . . . wrange his handes and pulled his berde and tear alle his heres."

Tell It (That) to the Marines. It's an unlikely story. I had supposed (I suspect along with many other people) that this piece of advice originated in World War I or II and applied to the United States Marine Corps, but it is much older, coming from a time when sailors regarded marines as of little use. Indeed, the saying was old in 1824, when Lord Byron offered this footnote to his *The Island:* " 'That will do for the marines, but the sailors won't believe it,' is an old saying." In the same year Sir Walter Scott wrote, in *Redgauntlet:* "Tell that to the marines—the sailors won't believe it."

Tell Tales Out of School. Betray confidences. It was originally said only of children, apparently children who let drop at home things they had heard from schoolmates in the nature of gossip or happenings within a family. Now it applies to anyone who reveals confidences (usually not very weighty) he has received. The saying is old enough to have been picked up by William Tyndale in *The Practyse of Prelates* (1530): "So that what cometh once in may never out, for fear of telling tales out of school."

Tempest in a Teapot. A squabble or an outburst over a trifle. A similar expression (*excitare fluctus in simpluo*: to stir up a tempest in a ladle) goes back to Roman times. Other versions include "storm in a cream bowl" (1678) and "storm in a tea-cup" (1872). The "storm" seems to have become a "tempest" and the "teacup" a "teapot" within the past 100 years.

That Does the Trick. It meets the requirement or achieves what was desired. "Trick" is a word with many meanings; here it is essentially "accomplishment." In 1872 *Punch* put it this way: "Pail of whitewash and box o' paints will do the trick."

Then and There. At that time and place; right away. The phrase used to be expressed as "there then," as in an item from 1428 published in the *Miscellanea* of the Surtees Society in 1861: "And there then he was asked." The *Rolls of Parliament* for 1436 record a harrowing tale including the modern phrase: "Ye said William . . . put hir in a stronge chaumbre till nyght; and yen yere . . . felonousely . . . ravysshed ye said Isabell."

There But for the Grace of God Go I. It could have happened to me; I could be in the position of that unfortunate. A biographical notice in the Parker Society edition of *The Writings of John Bradford* (1853) says: "The familiar story, that on seeing evildoers taken to the place of execution, he was wont to exclaim, 'But for the grace of God there goes John Bradford,' is a universal tradition, which has overcome the lapse of time." (Bradford eventually went to the place of execution; he was an English Protestant burned as a heretic in 1555.) A related line, "there but for the grace of God goes God," has been attributed to several people, among them Orson Welles.

There's the Rub. That's where the difficulty is; that's the problem. "Rub" as a noun has several meanings, among them an obstruction or impediment, including at one time anything that interfered with the ball (or bowl) in the game of bowls. That meaning gave rise to a play on the word in John Hooker's continuation in 1586 of Raphael Holinshed's *Chronicle of Ireland*: "Whereby it appeareth how dangerous it is to be a rub, when a king is disposed to sweepe an alleie." But the expression has stuck in the language because of Shakespeare, who has Hamlet say (in his renowned soliloquy):

To die, to sleep;
To sleep: perchance to dream: ay, there's the rub;
For in that sleep of death what dreams may come,
When we have shuffled off this mortal coil,
Must give us pause. . . .

Thereby Hangs a Tale. What has just been said suggests another story. John Skelton's *A Ryght Delectable Treatyse upon a Goodly Garlande or Chapelet of Laurell* (1523) puts it as: "Yet, thoughe I say it, therby lyeth a tale." Shakespeare put it as "thereby hangs a tale" in several plays, thereby making it a cliché.

Thick and Fast. In close and rapid succession. It's hard to think of a better way to describe something that's coming at you quickly and in dense numbers. A chronicle of the reign of Henry VIII records this item for 1548: "When mo newe Testamentes were Imprinted thei came thick and threfold into Englande." That was an older way of putting the thought. The current way appears in *The Wooden World Dissected*, by Edward Ward (1706): "He and his Brother-Jacks . . . toss Jests and Oaths about as thick and fast as Boys do Squibs."

Thick as Thieves. Intimate; conspiratorially close. Since it could have been "close as thieves" or "intimate as thieves," one again has to look to the appeal of alliteration for the birth and persistence of this phrase, which nonetheless reflects the conspiratorial framework required when two or more thieves work together. As it is put in *The Parson's Daughter* by Theodore E. Hook (1833): "She and my wife are thick as thieves, as the proverb goes"

Thin (Small) Edge of the Wedge, The. The beginning of a venture that is expected to expand; the leading edge of a program or activity. This "wedge" is the metal one, about six inches long, employed to split logs. Once you get the leading edge started you have a good chance of splitting the wood (unless it is unseasoned or has the kind of grain that does not split readily). Anthony Trollope had the image in *Doctor Thorne* (1858), both as a chapter heading (The Small End of the Wedge) and as a description of a ploy by a woman against the doctor (there Trollope wrote "the little edge"). In 1884 *The Graphic* offered: "Cremation advocates have managed to get in the thin edge of the wedge in France."

Thin Red Line. A small group (perhaps the remnant of a much larger one) dealing with a difficult problem. It is a phrase from the Crimean War and was introduced by the British reporter William Howard Russell in *The British Expedition to the Crimea* (1877): "The Russians . . . dashed on towards that thin red line tipped with steel." The phrase came to symbolize the British army and then to represent any group dealing heroically or mock-heroically with an adversary.

Thing of Beauty is a Joy Forever, A. The impact of something truly beautiful is strong and lasting. The line is from John Keats's poem, *Endymion* (1818):

> A thing of beauty is a joy forever:
> Its loveliness increases; it will never
> Pass into nothingness; but still will keep
> A bower quiet for us, and a sleep
> Full of sweet dreams, and health, and quiet
> breathing.

Third Degree, The. Rough physical treatment by the authorities, designed to make a prisoner talk. In the Masonic organization one advanced to the third degree (Master Mason) only after an examination of one's qualifications. Perhaps this is the source of the name of the police tactic. In any case the police tactic had the name by 1904, as recorded in the *New York Times*: "He was at first arrested merely as a suspicious person, but when put through the 'third degree' at the station admitted that he entered the house last night."

Thorn in the Side. An annoyance; a bothersome person or problem. As "a thorn in the flesh," which makes more sense because a thorn anywhere in the body is an annoyance, it is from the Bible (2 Corinthians 12 : 7) "And lest I should be exalted above measure through the abundance of the revelations, there was given to me a thorn in the flesh, the messenger of Satan to buffet me. . . ." The "side" version was in print by 1822, when John Galt wrote (in *The Provost*) of the "perverse views . . . of that Yankee thorn-in-the-side, Mr. Hickery."

Three Sheets to (in) the Wind. Drunk. In a sailing vessel a "sheet" is a rope that controls a sail; if it is allowed to go slack, it is said to be "in the wind," and as a result the sail is ineffective. If several sheets are in the wind, the ship goes erratically, like a drunkard. Pierce Egan offered the metaphorical meaning in *Real Life in London* (1821): "Old Wax and Bristles is about three sheets in the wind."

Threescore and Ten. The allotted span of human life (70 years) according to the Bible. It is set forth in Psalms (90 : 10): "The days of our years are threescore years and ten; and if by reason of strength they be fourscore years, yet it is their strength, labour and sorrow: for it is soon cut off, and we fly away."

Through Thick and Thin. Persistence in a task or in support of someone through both easy and difficult periods; overcoming everything that is in the way. The "thick" and the "thin" seem to have referred originally to the conditions encountered by a rider on a horse, who passes now through thickets of wood and now through areas where the growth is sparse or thin. The phrase is ancient enough to have appeared in *The Exeter Book*, which is nearly 1,000 years old. Chaucer had it in his *Canterbury Tales* c.1386. Edmund Spenser's *The Faerie Queene* (1590) suggests the origin:

> His tyreling Jade he fiersely forth did push
> Through thicke and thin, both over banck and bush.

Throw (Empty, Pour) the Baby Out With the Bathwater. Discard the essential with the waste; disregard the important thing. Here is George Bernard Shaw, in *Pen Portraits & Reviews* (1909): "Like all reactionists, he usually empties the baby out with the bath." Shaw used the saying on several occasions and may have originated it.

Throw Caution (Modesty) to the Winds. Decide on a bold (or brazen) course. The image of the wind or winds as a means of dispersal is old enough to appear in John Milton's *Paradise Lost* (1677): "Fear of Death deliver to the winds."

Throw Light On. Clarify; augment what you know about a matter. One looks for a theatrical origin here, an allusion to the spotlight being cast onto the stage, but similar sayings go back so far (at least to the 15th century) as to suggest that the dark subject was illuminated with sunlight or candlelight. The old form was to "give," "bring" or "carry" light. The modern form is to "throw," "cast" or "shed" light, and was current by 1841, when Thomas Carlyle offered in *On Heroes, Hero-worship and the Heroic in History*: "When he did speak, it was to throw new light on the matter."

Throw a (Monkey) Wrench in the Machinery (Works). Interfere with or sabotage a plan or an operation. Doubtless some disgruntled employee has literally done this, with devastating effects if the machine was running or was started up with the wrench still in it. One need only imagine the effects to see the basis for the figurative expression, which was offered in 1929 by Garry Allighan in *The Romance of the Talkies*: "The Talkies [the first name for the motion pictures in which the voices of the actors could be heard] threw several kinds of monkey-wrenches into the machinery of production."

Throw the Book at. File all possible criminal charges or give the maximum penalty. The "book" is imaginary but based on books containing laws and establishing punishments for crimes. This version appeared in *Flynn's Weekly* (1932): "The prosecuting attorney [is] determined to try to get the trial judge to 'throw the book' at him (which means give him the limit)."

Thump the Tub. Strongly promote an idea or a program. In the 17th century the pulpit of nonconformist preachers came to be called the "tub," and the preachers were called "tub-thumpers." Henry Foulis explained matters in *The History of the Wicked Plots and Conspiracies of Our Pretended Saints* (1662): "Tub-Thumpers . . . a sort of people more antick in their Devotions than Don Buscos Fencing-Master."

Tickle Your Fancy. Please, divert or amuse you. It is a more delicate image than the companion phrase "strike your fancy." Yet in 1774 Abraham Tucker characterized the thought as vulgar. In *The Light of Nature Pursued* he wrote of animals "whose play had a quality of striking the joyous perception, or, as we vulgarly say, tickling the fancy."

Tie the Knot. Marry or get married. It would be interesting to know whether it was a man or a woman who first envisioned marriage as a knot. Matthew Prior had heard the expression by 1717, when he wrote (in *Alma*): "So to the priest their case they tell: He ties the knot."

Tied to the Apron Strings. Unusually influenced or ruled by a woman (usually said of an adult male in relation to his mother or wife). The apron seems not to be as common now as it was until perhaps 40 years ago, but then it was virtually part of the uniform for a woman working in her kitchen, and it was always tied behind the waist with what could be (and were) called strings. Here is Anne Brontë, in *The Tenant of Wildfell Hall* (1848): "Even at *his* age, he ought not to be always tied to his mother's apron-strings."

Tiger by the Tail, Have a. Cope with an obsession; pursue an idea, a talent or even a vice obsessively; face a trying problem. I doubt that anybody ever literally had a tiger by the tail, but the image is vivid. You wouldn't want to hold on, but you wouldn't dare let go. You would be, as other sayings go, in a pickle or a bind. The saying has also served to describe the lowest hand one can draw in poker: a 7 high, a 2 low, with no pair, straight or flush. Alan Lomax was referring to the other meaning in his biography of the jazz pianist and composer Jelly Roll Morton (*Mr. Jelly Roll*, 1950): "And all his life Jelly Roll held a tiger by the tail."

Tight as a Drum. Snug; close-fitting; overtight. The skin that forms the drumhead is the part that has to be tightened to tune the drum. It was human skin that was tightened in the analogy used by Thomas Hughes in *Tom Brown's School Days* (1857): "Tom has eaten, and imbibed coffee, till his little skin is as tight as a drum."

Tight as a Tick. Extremely close with one's money. If you have ever tried to separate a tick from an animal or some person's skin, you know what "tight" is. Sometimes the phrase has served to mean "drunk," but there it is merely alliterative and reinforcing, since drunken ticks are unknown. That meaning was popular some 30 years ago, appearing in *Collier's* this way: "At lunch you have two cocktails and feel tight as a tick."

Tighten Your Belt. Cope with or prepare for a time of economic difficulty; economize. If you are so beset financially as to be going hungry, you tighten your belt as you get thinner. The image transferred easily to any economic pinch. In 1927 *The Observer* wrote of "a travelling troupe who quoted Corneille while tightening their belts."

Tilt at Windmills. Take on impossible or ridiculous challenges. It is what Don Quixote was famous for. Here is how Cervantes puts it in his 17th-century classic:

> At this point they came in sight of thirty or forty windmills . . . and as soon as Don Quixote saw them he said to his squire, 'Fortune is arranging matters for us better than we could have shaped our desires ourselves, for look there, friend Sancho Panza, where thirty or more monstrous giants present themselves, all of whom I mean to engage in battle and slay, and with whose spoils we shall begin to make our fortunes; for . . . it is God's good service to sweep so evil a breed off the face of the earth.' The "tilt" here is the medieval contest in which two combatants tried to unhorse each other with lances.

Time Immemorial, From. Going way back; of ancient origin (sometimes said of things that aren't all that old but just seem to have been going on for a long time). It's a rather elaborate way of describing something that predates living memory. In English law the term has meant beyond legal memory, meaning earlier than the reign of Richard I (1189–1199) ; the law decreed that certain kinds of actions could not be brought in relation to events antedating that reign. William Fulbecke's *The Pandectes of the Law of Nations* (1602) speaks of "making title by prescription and continuance of time immemoriall."

Time Out of Mind. A long time; something going back beyond living memory. The *Rolls of Parliament* for 1414 record that the people of Lymington had asserted that since "tyme oute of mynde . . . . - there were wont many diverse Shippes . . . to come . . . yn to the saide Havenes."

Time and Again. Repeatedly. Once it was "times and again," which is closer to the meaning of the thought. The plural seems to have been dropped by 1864, when Donald G. Mitchell wrote *Seven Stories*: "Time and again I looked over the way."

Time and Tide Wait for No Man. It is foolish to procrastinate; there is no stopping either time or the tide, so you'd best do now what has to be done. When similar expressions were first recorded in the 15th century, "tide" meant time, but since the 16th century it has referred to the tide of the sea. An earlier verson was "tide nor time tarrieth no man."

Time is Ripe, The. The moment has come to do something or for something to happen. One cannot watch a plant or a whole crop ripen without thinking there is an opportune moment for almost everything. In *Henry IV, Part 1*, Shakespeare has Hotspur, his father and his uncle (the Earl of Worcester) planning a rebellion against the king. Hotspur and Worcester are departing; Worcester says:

> Cousin, farewell: no further go in this
> Than I by letters shall direct your course.
> When time is ripe, which will be suddenly. . . .

Time of Your Life, The. A thrilling or memorable experience. "Time" here is an episode, a usually all-too-brief period. William Saroyan made the phrase the title of a memorable play he wrote in 1939. Anne Sullivan, the teacher of Helen Keller, wrote in a letter in 1887: "We took Helen to the circus, and had 'the time of our lives.' " The fact that Miss Sullivan put the phrase in quotation marks suggests it was a colloquialism.

Time on My Hands. I'm bored; I haven't enough to do. It could have been "on my mind" or "on my nerves," but perhaps because of the religious ethic that idleness is bad it came out as "time on the hands," right out where others can see it. Thomas Brown's translation of *Fresny's Amusements Serious and Comical* (1700) refers succinctly to "Persons . . . that have a great deal of Idle Time lying upon their Hands."

Time to Kill. A period when one is unable to do what one had planned and must look for a diversion. The thought of killing time usually carries with it the notion that one will spend the time doing something frivolous or entertaining. That thought is reflected in *The Provok'd Husband*, a play by Sir John Vanbrugh and Colley Cibber (1728): "What think you, if we three sat soberly down to kill an hour at ombre?" (Ombre was a three-person card game that was quite popular in the 17th and 18th centuries.)

266

Times Are (Time Is) Out of Joint, The. Things aren't going right; this body of human affairs doesn't hang together properly. The transfer is from the elbow, hip or shoulder that goes out of joint, leaving the person unable to function normally. Shakespeare made unjointed time memorable, and may indeed have originated the phrase, in *Hamlet*. Hamlet has seen his father's ghost and has learned that his father was murdered by Hamlet's uncle, the new king. Planning vengeance at the ghost's bidding, Hamlet says:

> The time is out of joint: O cursed spite,
> That ever I was born to set it right.

Tinker's Dam (Damn), I Don't Give a. I don't care; it's worthless. "Tinker" as a noun is virtually out of the language now except in this cliché; a tinker was an itinerant mender of metal objects such as pots and pans. If you prefer "dam," the reference is to a piece of clay or dough that the tinker spotted to keep solder in place; when the solder hardened, he threw the "dam" away. If you like "damn," it is suggestive of the language reputedly used by tinkers and alluded to in print as early as 1611. Since an earlier version of the saying was "a tinker's curse," the weight of the evidence seems to be in favor of "damn."

Tip of One's Tongue, At the. Ready to be spoken; in the memory, although one can't quite fetch it out and put it into words. In the case of searching the memory, one literally feels in this situation that the words are at the tip of the tongue and could be formulated with some slight further effort of mind. Daniel Defoe seems to have been thinking of the first meaning in *Moll Flanders* (1722): "She had arguments at the tip of her tongue."

Tip of the Iceberg. A small part of a large problem or phenomenon. It is an invariable characteristic of icebergs that by far the greater part of the monster is below water; all you see is the tip. Michael Gilbert explained the metaphor neatly in *The Etruscan Net* (1969): "I believe that Broke's been made the victim of an elaborate frame-up. I think, to employ a well-known metaphor, that all we can see is the tip of the iceberg, and that there is depth beyond depth below it."

Tit for Tat. A blow for a blow; an insult for an insult; an equalization of some kind. An ancient and now forgotten meaning of "tit" was a tug or a jerk. "Tat" has no modern meaning aside from this expression, in which it is apparently a variant of "tap." Although "tit for tat" can be traced as far as the 16th century, "tip for tap" goes back a century farther. John Heywood's *The Spider and the Flie* (1556) has: "That is tit for tat in this altricacion [altercation]."

To All Intents and Purposes. The way it is; practically speaking; the thrust of the matter. It sounds like one of those legal tautologies, since an "intent" is a "purpose" and vice versa, and so it was originally. An act adopted under Henry VIII in 1547 was said to apply "to all intents, constructions and purposes," thereby creating a triple tautology.

To Hell and Gone. A great or endless distance or time. Hell is presumably a long way off, and if one has got that far and gone beyond, one is far away indeed. S. J. Perelman made it one word in *The New Yorker (1938):* "Sarah Trenwick just got blasted to hellangone in her tepee at the Gayboy."

To a T. This idea or garment is a perfect fit. Several of the people who have looked into the origin of this saying attribute it to the T square of the architect and the carpenter, but the idea seems not to hold up, since "to a tittle," meaning the same thing, is much older. The earliest recorded use of "to a T" is in 1693, whereas "to a tittle," meaning a small stroke in printing or writing (such as the dot over the *i*), can be traced to 1607, in Francis Beaumont and John Fletcher's *Woman Hater:* "I'll quote him to a tittle."

Toe the Line. Meet a standard; be up to snuff. The "line" is the mark that appears in the incantation, "On your mark, get set, go!" It is the starting point for a foot race. In the broader sense the term appeared in the *Westminster Gazette* in 1895: "The phrase 'toeing the line' is very much in favour with some Liberals."

Tom, Dick and Harry, Every. The common herd; hoi polloi. They were popular names 200 years ago. Similar expressions have been Tom, Dick and Francis (in Shakespeare's *Henry IV Part 1*) and "Jack, and Tom, and Will, and Dick" (by King James I in 1604). The present array turned up in *The Vocal Miscellany* (1734): "Farewell, Tom, Dick, and Harry, Farewell, Moll, Nell, and Sue." What would it be today? Kevin, Keith and Bruce?

Tongue-in-Cheek. Speaking facetiously or insincerely. Try saying something with your tongue in your cheek. The origin here is probably the way you say something and *then* put your tongue in your cheek, as you might wink, to show that you are not being serious. Richard Barham recorded the expression in 1845, in *The Ingoldsby Legends:* "He . . . cried 'Superbe!–Magnifique!' (With his tongue in his cheek)."

Too Clever by Half. Too crafty for one's own best interest; outwitting oneself. In William Westfall's *Birch Dene* (1889) one encounters this bit of dialogue: " 'He's a good scholar, and nodody can deny as he's clever.' 'Ay, too clever by half.' "

Too Good to Be True. Implausible; not readily believable. The mind of the pessimist is evident: if a thing looks or sounds good, something must be wrong with it. Thomas Lupton made the phrase part of a title in 1580: *Sivqila: Too Good to Be True.*

Too Many Cooks Spoil the Broth. The greater the number of people working on a thing, the worse it's apt to turn out to be. Doubtless if you had several cooks preparing a broth, each with his own ideas about seasoning, length of simmering and so on, the broth wouldn't be very tasty. George Gascoigne, writing on John Hooker's *Life of Sir Peter Carew* (1575) has: "There is the proverb, the more cooks the worse potage." An 18th-century version had it as "too many Cooks spoil the Meat."

Too Many Irons in the Fire. Taking on more projects or work than you can handle efficiently. The picture is straight from the smithy; a blacksmith with too many irons in the fire is likely to spoil some of his work through overheating the pieces. A letter written by Sir Paget in 1549 offers this advice: "Put no more so many yrons in the fyre at ones."

Too Much of a Good Thing. Pleasure in such amounts as to become tiresome. Something quite close to this thought appears in Geoffrey Chaucer's 14th-century *Canterbury Tales*: "That that is overdoon, it wol nat preeve Aright, as clerkes seyn; it is a vice." A 16th-century version was "too much is naught." Shakespeare looks at the other side of the coin in *As You Like It*: "Why then, can one desire too much of a good thing?"

Took the Words (Right) Out of My Mouth, You. You finished my thought for me; we are thinking alike. Here is one of those images that is entirely figurative, since you can't literally take words out of anyone's mouth; but it is certainly vivid. John Palsgrave, writing on the French language in 1530, didn't think much of the practice: "It is no good maner to take the worde out of my mouthe, or I have made an ende of my tale."

Top-Drawer People. The best (most capable) people available; of high social standing. The top drawer of a dresser usually contains one's jewelry and other valuable things, and herein probably lies the origin of this 20th-century phrase. Rose Macaulay wrote, in *Potterism* (1920): "The Potter family, however respectable now, wasn't really top-drawer."

Touch and Go. Precarious; a situation that could result either in disaster or in a narrow escape from disaster. Admiral William H. Smyth offered a plausible thought about the origin in *The Sailor's Word-book* (1865): "Said of anything within an ace of ruin; as in rounding a ship very narrowly to escape rocks, &c, or when, under sail, she rubs against the ground with her keel, without much diminution of her velocity." The term seems to have originated early in the 19th century.

Tough (Hard, Long) Row to Hoe. A difficult or unappealing task. Once the hoe was about the only tool available for weeding a row of plants in a garden that was too small for a horse-drawn rig, and working one's way down such a row (or more likely several of them) was a tedious business. The image transferred readily to any unpleasant and time-consuming job. David Crockett was using the expression in that way in his *Tour of the North and Down East*(1835): "I never opposed Andrew Jackson for popularity. I knew it was a hard row to hoe."

Tough It Out. Face difficulty or danger resolutely. It is an expression of American origin, probably early in the 19th century. Seba Smith had an example in *Major Jack Downing* (1834): "We little fellows had to tough it out as well as we could."

Tough Nut to Crack, A. A difficult problem or a person who cannot easily be persuaded to do something. The packaged nut, cracked open, cooked and salted, is a modern invention. In older times one had to crack nuts open by hand, and some of them did not crack easily. The broader meaning was in use by 1739, when William Stephens offered an example in *Journal of the Proceedings in Georgia*: "Wherefore that Nut was a little hard for us to crack."

Tower of Strength. Someone you can rely on to provide help, support or guidance in a difficult time. It's a poet's image: you might speak of a strong tower or a person of strength, but it took (in this case) a Tennyson to combine them. He did it in his *Ode on the Death of the Duke of Wellington* (1852):

> O iron nerve to true occasion true,
> O fallen at length, that tower of strength
> Which stood four-square to all the winds that blew.

One senses that Tennyson was laboring to equal the occasion.

Track Record. One's accomplishments in a particular field of activity. The track record of a racehorse is closely studied by any serious bettor thinking of putting money on the horse. By 1971 the phrase had been extended in meaning to include human activity, as shown in *The Atlantic*: "A modern university president is expected to have practical vision, a good track record in administration, and national prominence as a scholar."

Train of Thought. The line or trend of one's mental processes. The expression was carefully defined by Thomas Hobbes in 1651, suggesting that he originated it. In *Leviathan* he wrote: "By

Consequence, or TRAIN of thoughts, I understand that succession of one thought to another, which is called, to distinguish it from discourse in words, *mental discourse.*"

Trim One's Sails. To adapt (usually to something that isn't going quite right); to modify one's position. When you trim your sails literally, you are merely adjusting them to take maximum advantage of the wind. The sense of adapting to a situation is what has been transferred to the larger meaning. Sir Walter Scott carried the metaphor even farther in *Kenilworth* (1821): "He could scarce have missed shipwreck, knowing . . . so little how to trim his sails to a court gale."

Trip the Light Fantastic. Dance. This is a creation owed to John Milton, who transferred "fantastic" into "dance" because of the fantastic movements often made in dancing. It is in *L'Allegro* (1632):
> Come, and trip it as ye go
> On the light fantastick toe.

True Blue. A loyal adherent of a group. The phrase was applied in the 17th century to the Scottish Covenanters (Presbyterians who wore blue as their badge) and to the Whig party in England. Later it came to designate Tories in England (blue was the official color of the Conservative party) and members of the varsity (crew, cricket and so on) at Oxford and Cambridge universities. The origin is evident in Samuel Butler's *Hudibras* (1663):
> For his Religion it was Fit
> To match his learning and his Wit;
> 'Twas Presbyterian true blue.

The literal origin of the phrase is in the blue thread made in Coventry in the Middle Ages; it was prized for holding its color. John Ray wrote in 1670: "Coventry had formerly the reputation for dying of blues; insomuch that true blue became a Proverb to signifie one that was always the same and like himself."

Truth Is Stranger Than Fiction. Some things are quite remarkable and indeed hard to believe. Byron may have said it first. In *Don Juan* (1823) he wrote: "Truth is always strange; Stranger than fiction."

Truth Will Out, The. A secret or a deception will be discovered or reveal itself sooner or later. Other ways of putting the thought have been that truth will "come to light" or "break out." In one way or another the saying was current by the 16th century. Thus Richard Taverner in *Publius* (1539): "The thyng that good is (as trouth and iustice) thoughe it be suppressed and kept and under for a time, yet is it not quenched utterly, but at length wyll breake out agayne." Shakespeare had it, in the modern form, in *The Merchant of Venice* (1596). It is the scene where old Gobbo is

271

unable to recognize his son, Launcelot, who says: "Nay, indeed, if you had your eyes, you might fail of the knowing me: it is a wise father that knows his own child. Well, old man, I will tell you news of your son: give me your blessing: truth will come to light; murder cannot be hid long; a man's son may; but, at the length, truth will out."

Turn Back the Clock. Go or wish one could go to a past state of affairs; take a backward step; change things so as to restore an earlier situation. James Russell Lowell offered the image in *The Bigelow Papers* (1862): " 'T would put the clock back all o' fifty years."

Turn Over a New Leaf. Take a fresh start; reform one's conduct or attitude. The "leaf" is a page in a book of precepts or in a diary. Several hundred years ago the saying was more often, "turn a leaf," as in Raphael Holinshed's *Chronicles of England, Scotlande, and Ireland* (1577): "He must turne the leafe, and take out a new lesson, by changing his former trade of liuing into better."

Turn Turtle. Capsize; surrender. One way to catch a turtle or a tortoise is to flip it onto its back, rendering it helpless. When turtle soup and other dishes based on the turtle were commoner comestibles than they are now, that was a standard way of obtaining the basic ingredient. The similarity between the flipped turtle and the capsized ship brought about the extended meaning, which was in use at least 150 years ago.

Turn Up One's Nose. Show disdain or scorn. I'm not sure if literally turning up the nose is natural body language or an inheritance from the theater. Whichever, the saying was in use by 1562, when Johann Wigand included it in *De Neutralibus*: "The Papistes caste vp the nose into the wynde and crake, that the churche is tyed to the Byshoppe of Rome and hys College."

Turn Your Head, That Will. It will get your attention; it will make you feel conceited. Both meanings are figurative, but in one the head is imagined as actually turning and in the other it is one's mind that is turned. *The Wrecker*, written by Robert Louis Stevenson and Lloyd Osbourne in 1893, has this line: "I looked at the handbill and my head turned."

Turn a Deaf Ear. Ignore someone; refuse to acknowledge a statement or request. The image of the ear that has suddenly become deaf fits this situation well. So well that it served as long ago as 1440, when Walter Hylton wrote in *Scala Perfeccionis*: "Make deef ere to hem as though thou herde haue not [have not heard]."

272

Turn of the Tide. A change of fortune (almost always with the meaning that it is for the better). The natural tide of the sea turns every six hours or so, usually without significance in terms of being good or bad, but it does so definitely represent a change as to have taken on a larger, symbolic meaning. Lord Macaulay used it in his *History of England* (1849) as: "From that moment the tide of battle turned."

Turn the Corner. Improve; begin to recover from a difficult situation (as an illness). The image is of taking a new and better direction. Charles Dickens employed it in a letter in 1837: "I hope to find on Monday at 12 o'Clock, that you have turned the corner and come back again."

Turn the Other Cheek. Refuse to retaliate; permit or encourage another blow. The advice appears twice in the Bible, each time reporting teachings of Jesus. In Matthew 5 : 39 it is: "But I say unto you, That ye resist not evil: but whosoever shall smite thee on thy right cheek, turn to him the other also." And in Luke 6 : 29 it is: "And unto him that smiteth thee on the one cheek offer also the other; and him that taketh away thy cloke forbid not to take thy coat also." Oliver Wendell Holmes's poem *Astraea* (1850) offers this:

> Wisdom has taught us to be calm and meek,
> To take one blow, and turn the other cheek.

Turn the Tables. Reverse the situation or the relationship. Literally it is what one did in some games, such as chess, checkers and backgammon, played on a board or table. Doubtless, in the long history of those games there have been boards or tables of the lazy-Susan type that one could turn to reverse positions instead of physically reversing the players. The saying is so old, however, that the precise origin is lost. A line in George Chapman's play, *The Widdowes Teares* (1612), is: "I may turn the tables with you ere long."

Turnabout Is Fair Play. We should do this by turns; each of us should have some time in this good or bad situation. "Turnabout" is an old noun meaning for two people to do something alternately or by turns, and the saying dates at least to 1755, when it appeared in *The Life of Capt. Dudley Bradstreet.*

Turning Point. A critical juncture; the place where or time when a situation changes for better or worse. It is based upon the situation of not being sure which fork in the path or road to follow, and therefore being uncertain where you will end up. One sees the figurative meaning clearly in John Ruskin's *Arrows of the Chace* (1851): "I believe these young artists to be . . . at a turn-

273

ing point, from which they may either sink into nothingness or rise to very real greatness."

20/20 Hindsight. A clear view, once a problem has been dealt with, of what should or could have been done to handle it better. The term is a play upon the ophthalmologist's and optometrist's measure of desirable or optimal vision. A standard assessment of that level of vision is the ability to distinguish letters and numbers one-third of an inch high at a distance of 20 feet; 20/20 means you see at 20 feet what you should see at 20 feet. With, say, 20/40 vision, you have to be within 20 feet to see something you should be able to see at 40 feet (or the object has to be twice as large as an object that a person with good vision would see clearly at 40 feet.)

Twinkling of an Eye, In a. Quickly. The reference is to the time it takes to wink an eye. The phrase is from St. Paul (1 Corinthians 15 : 51–52): "Behold, I shew you a mystery: We shall not all sleep, but we shall all be changed, In a moment, in the twinkling of an eye, at the last trump: for the trumpet shall sound, and the dead shall be raised incorruptible, and we shall be changed."

Two Sides to Every Question, There are. An argument can be made about this issue; I'm not necessarily right. James Ralph seemed to have had this saw in mind when he chose *The Other Side of the Question* as a title for a book in 1742. Charles Kingsley wrote, in *The Water Babies* (1863): "Let them recollect this, that there are two sides to every question."

Two's Company, Three's a Crowd. Leave lovers to themselves. Until perhaps 100 years ago the thought was more often put as "two's company, three is none," and in that form it is old enough to have been recorded in John Heywood's book of proverbs in 1546. The saying also once had a broader meaning, which is seen in John Stevens's Spanish-English dictionary of 1706: "A Company consisting of three is worth nothing. It is the Spanish Opinion, who say that to keep a Secret three are too many, and to be Merry they are too few."

Two-Faced. Deceitful; looking and dealing both ways. The Roman deity Janus was portrayed as having two faces for his duties as keeper of the gate of heaven, the idea being that he could keep a thorough watch. In older times the modern thought was expressed as "double-faced." By 1619 it was in its present form, at least in *The Queene of Corinth*, a play by John Fletcher and others: "Who can trust the gentle looks and words of two-faced man?"

U

Ugly Duckling. An unpromising child, project or idea that turns out well. The original ugly duckling was a cygnet that, in one of Hans Christian Andersen's tales, was hatched with a brood of ducklings and was ridiculed for its clumsiness until it grew into a swan. "The Ugly Duckling" was the title, and not long after Andersen wrote it the phrase was well lodged in the language. In 1883 *Harper's* magazine reported: "The mother's fears about her 'ugly duckling' . . . took another turn."

Ugly as Sin. Repellently unattractive. Sin wore a grimmer face in past times than it does generally now, which is not to say that it is widely approved. Sin was ugly. Similar phrases now no longer current were "ugly as the devil" and "ugly as hell." The current phrase was well known more than 300 years ago, when Giovanni Torriano recorded it in a book of Italian proverbs that was translated into English: "To be uglier than sin, viz. most ugly."

Unalloyed Delight. Pure pleasure. One wonders how it came to be "unalloyed delight" and "unadulterated pleasure" when it could just as well have been the other way around, "alloying" being to alter the purity of metal or adulterating to alter the purity of food (among other things). Or why not just "delight" and "pleasure?" Apparently they needed intensifying, which in the case of "delight" came at least 125 years ago. In John Lothrop Motley's *History of the United Netherlands* (1860) one reads: "There is hardly a character in history upon which the imagination can dwell with more unalloyed delight."

Under a Cloud. In disfavor; in trouble or difficulty; under suspicion. It is almost a photographic image; most of the subjects standing in the sunshine but one unfortunate looking gray in the shadow of a cloud. The figurative meaning was in use by the 16th century, but the meaning is clearest in Thomas Fuller's *The History of the Worthies of England* (1662): "He was under a cloud at court."

Under the Counter. Sold or done surreptitiously; a transaction done somewhat on the sly. The expression arose in World War II when so many storekeepers kept items under the counter for friends or good customers, since so many things were rationed or in short supply.

Under the Thumb. Subservient to or under the control of. "Under the hand" has served to say the same thing, but the subservience seems to be emphasized by "thumb," which is the controlling finger of the controlling hand. The expression was around in the 18th century, as is shown in Samuel Richardson's *The History of Sir Charles Grandison*(1754): "She . . . is obliged to be silent. I have her under my thumb."

Under the Weather. Sick; indisposed. That's how one is likely to feel if one is more or less exposed in bad weather, so the transfer is natural and easy. It was made originally in the United States some 200 years ago. D.G. Mitchell, writing *The Lorgnette* in 1850, penned a passage that begins: "As for the Frenchman, though now, between the valorous Poussin and the long-faced Bonaparte, a little under the weather. . . ."

Unkindest Cut of All. The worst treachery, insult, affront or show of scorn. Shakespeare fixed it in the language (and probably originated it) in the passage in *Julius Caesar* where Antony eulogizes the assassinated Caesar:

> Through this the well-beloved Brutus stabb'd;
> And as he plucked his cursed steel away,
> Mark how the blood of Caesar followed it,
> As rushing out of doors, to be resolved
> If Brutus so unkindly knocked, or no:
> For Brutus, as you know, was Caesar's angel:
> Judge, O you gods, how dearly Caesar loved him!
> This was the most unkindest cut of all. . . .

Until Hell Freezes Over. Never, or at least not for a very long time; forever. "Hell" figures in so many familiar expressions of great age that one would expect this one to be old, too. Perhaps it is as a vivid oral image, but it seems not to have been recorded in print until this century. In 1919 Admiral J. A. Fisher, former first sea lord of the British Admiralty, signed off a letter saying, "Yours till hell freezes."

Unvarnished Truth. The plain facts; told like it is. Is truth an absolute? Philosophically it may be, but in the minds and words of many people it receives embellishment, so much so that truth in the absence of embellishment has come to be noted by this cliché. Matilda Betham-Edwards recorded a typical progression in *Disarmed* (1883): "Valerian . . . had set out with the intention of adhering to the unvarnished truth, but finally ended in romancing." Shakespeare had a somewhat different version in *Othello*, showing that the thought itself is quite old. Othello says to the Duke and others in the council chamber:

> I will a round, unvarnish'd tale deliver
> Of my whole course of love. . . .

Unwept, Unhonored and Unsung. Truly unnoticed and insignificant; a good riddance (usually applied to a menacing or disagreeable person after he has died). Sir Walter Scott probably formulated this bleak eulogy, which he presented in *The Lay of the Last Minstrel* (1805) : "The wretch . . . shall go down, To the vile dust . . . Unwept, unhonour'd, and unsung."

Unwritten Law. A precept or restriction observed as a matter of custom. John Milton, always eloquent, may be the source of this expression, which he employed in *The Reason of Church-government Urg'd Against Prelaty* (1641), referring to "those unwritten lawes and Ideas which nature hath ingraven in us."

Up Against It. In difficulty; in a tight spot. "It" is a you-fill-in-the-blank word. The saying became popular in the United States and Canada in the late 19th century. The humorist and dramatist George Ade, who made much use of slang, wrote this slangy sentence in *Artie* (1896): "I saw I was up against it." Today we frequently use "the wall" to fill in the blank, from the practice of policemen and gunmen of standing a suspect or a victim against a wall to reduce his chance of getting away.

Up a Tree. In a quandary or a difficulty. The image is from the hunted animal that has been trapped up a tree. The expression started as an American colloquialism and was current by 1825, when John Neal used it in *Brother Jonathan*: "I'm up a tree—that's a fact."

Up and About (Doing). Moving into action; resuming activity after an illness. It doesn't sound like a poetic phrase, but Henry Wadsworth Longfellow employed it in "A Psalm of Life" (1838), which also includes the familiar "Life is real! Life is earnest!" and "Art is long, and Time is fleeting." The last verse is:

> Let us, then, be up and doing,
> With a heart for any fate;
> Still achieving, still pursuing,
> Learn to labor and to wait.

Up for Grabs. Available if one makes the effort to get it; open to competition; easily obtained. The "grabbing" was somewhat more restricted when the saying appeared some 40 years ago; Lou Shelly defined it in *Hepcats Jive Talk Dictionary* (1945) as an "easy to make gal." The broader meaning was recorded in the *Boston Globe* in 1967: "Right now every position is up for grabs. Every player is going to get a shot."

Up in Arms. Ready to fight; rebelling. The picture of people so provoked as to take up weapons is at least as old as Shakespeare, who evokes it in *King Henry VI, Part 2*, where the sea captain

277

says to the Duke of Suffolk:
> The princely Warwick, and the Nevils all,
> Whose dreadful swords were never drawn in vain,
> As hating thee, are rising up in arms."

Up to Par. Normal. One associates "par" with golf now, but the word is far older than the game. The meaning is the same, a standard or a norm. Laurence Sterne was writing in *Tristram Shandyj* (1767) of "the livre or two above par for your supper and bed."

Up to Scratch. Satisfactory; meeting a standard. The "scratch" was a line drawn as a starting or meeting point in several sports. In boxing, for example, it was the line where the two fighters met before the start of the match. One sees the origin of the term in a piece written by Thomas De Quincey 150 years ago: "No prudent champion, however game, would have chosen to offer himself to the scratch for the second round." The same sort of "scratch," serving as the starting point for a race, gave rise to the term "start from scratch" meaning without a handicap.

Up to Snuff. Matching the desired or usual level of quality, performance or health. Tobacco snuff gave rise to the saying because it is sharp and not easily taken in. Snuff-taking is almost a lost vice now, but at one time it was quite the thing. It was in those days that John Poole picked up the broader meaning in *Hamlet Travestie* (1811): "He knows well enough the game we're after: Zooks, he's up to snuff."

Up to the Hilt. All the way; to the utmost. If you plunge a sword or dagger in up to the hilt, you have plunged it as far as it will go. It is a gruesome image of support or totality, but it comes from a passionate act and bespeaks a passionate feeling. Sir Roger L'Estrange employed it in his *An Answer to a Letter to a Dissenter* (1687): "He is All, Politiques here, up to the Hilts." A related expression is "back him to the hilt," meaning to give him the utmost support.

Uphill Battle. A difficult struggle. When battles were fought by men on foot or mounted, the top of a hill was a favorable place to be because it commanded a view of a considerable area and was easy to defend. Conversely, the people trying to fight up the hill to capture it were at a disadvantage. That kind of struggle against adverse odds is what "uphill battle" stands for now. The British statesman Richard Cobden showed the enlarged meaning in a speech in 1849: "We had an uphill battle, but we succeeded."

Upper Crust. The aristocracy; the élite. Nothing more glamorous than the top crust of bread provided the inspiration for this label; the upper crust is, though, the most visible part and the mark by which you can judge the quality of the bread before you buy it or taste it. The phrase has also referred to the toffs for quite a while. Thomas C. Haliburton, in *The Clockmaker* (1835), wrote: "I want you to see Peel . . . Macaulay, old Joe, and so on. These men are all upper crust here."

Upset the Applecart. Interfere with or thwart someone's plan or program. The Romans had a similar phrase that referred only to a cart. The "applecart" probably got into the image because of the mess that results if one is upset and the amount of work the farmer must do to collect the apples and continue on to market. Francis Grose defined the term in his *Classical Dictionary of the Vulgar Tongue* (1796): "Down with his apple-cart; knock or throw him down." Thomas G. Fessenden employed the phrase around 1800 in one of his poems attacking Thomas Jefferson: "He talketh big words to congress and threateneth to overturn their apple-cart."

Use Your Head. Think; consider what you're doing or planning to do. It could just as well have been "use your brain," but the head as the seat of the brain seems to serve better because it also is the seat of such senses as sight and hearing, which can help one in reasoning. A similar expression is "use your noodle," which refers not to a stringlike pasta but to "noddle," an ancient word for "head." The Associated Press columnist Hal Boyle, quoting an American soldier in 1950, wrote: "The Army also teaches a man to use his head and to do the best he can."

Utility Infielder. Someone who is useful in an enterprise because he can take on a variety of jobs. The saying is from baseball and started out as "utility fielder." Apparently in former days a utility man could play any position. Indeed, the term was defined in Webster's dictionary in 1911 as "a substitute capable of taking any position in a baseball team."

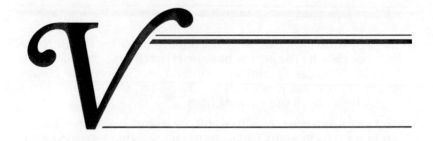

Vale of Tears. Life or the world (as seen in a time of adversity). "Vale" is a poetic word meaning valley, and by 1400 it was symbolic of the world as a place of woe and misery. The various usages have included "vale of trowbull" in 1400, "vale of wepynge" in 1435, "vale of mysery" in 1497 and "wail of teiris" in 1554.

Vanish Into Thin Air. Disappear or fail (said usually of a plan, an idea or money). It used to be merely "air." Shakespeare, in a different context, envisioned "thin Ayre" in *The Tempest*. The notion of "thin air" seems to emphasize the total disappearance of whatever it is that one is talking about. Thomas Dekker wrote, in *The Guls Horne-book* (1609), of "Plaudities, and the Breath of the great Beast, which (like the threatnings of two Cowards) vanish all into aire."

Vent One's Spleen. Air one's anger or opinions. The spleen is a fairly obscure abdominal organ of which little is heard or thought unless it is ruptured. Nevertheless, it has over the centuries been regarded as the seat of morose feelings, mirth, temper and other things. What one vents has come to mean only bad temper or ill feelings. George Rawlinson's *Egypt and Babylon* (1885) has this passage: "This time he . . . vented his spleen on the Jews by renewed attacks and oppressions."

Vested Interest. A cohesive political or economic group that often undertakes to make its weight felt. "Vested" is a legal term meaning to have an established or secured right to something, usually property. One sees this meaning in William Cruise's *Digest of the Laws of England* (1818): "The limitation . . . gave him a vested interest in the surplus of the estate." Edward S. Abdy offered the extended meaning not much later, in *The Water Cure* (1842), where he wrote of "finding the new truths have not as many vested interests to recommend them as old fallacies."

Vicious Circle. A disagreeable situation that keeps repeating itself; a chain of events in which dealing with one problem creates another problem. The term is from formal logic and refers to proving one statement with a second one that relies on the first one for proof. The 1792 edition of the *Encyclopaedia Britannica* described it: "He runs into what is termed by logicians a *vicious circle* (failure to make connection between premise and conclusion.)"

Vote With Your Feet. Leave a place or a situation you don't like; show disapproval by leaving. It is probably the flow of refugees from political oppression since World War II that accounts for this term. It was sufficiently familiar by 1966 to be picked up by the *New York Times*, which, however, thought it was novel enough to be put between quotation marks: "Some [East Berliners] continue to 'vote with their feet' by climbing over, digging under or slipping through the Wall."

W

Wages of Sin. The consequences of a mistake or a moral lapse. The Bible is uncompromising (Romans 6 : 23): "The wages of sin is death."

Wait With Bated Breath. Be expectant or apprehensive. "Bate" is one of those words that once had several meanings but now is seldom heard except in relation to the breath. There the meaning is to restrain or lessen in intensity, which suggests slightly less of a crisis than would cause one to hold one's breath. George Eliot put it this way in *Adam Bede* (1859): "To his dying day he bated his breath a little when he told the story."

Waited On Hand and Foot. Assiduously (and perhaps obsequiously) served. Usually a servant directs his attention either to the hands (as in bringing food) or to the feet (as in bringing slippers), so to wait on a person hand *and* foot is an extra measure of subservience. The *Assumption of Our Lady,* dating from the 14th century, has this version: "Sche . . . serueded hem to hande & fote."

Walk On Air. Be happy or exultant. You can't really walk on air unless you have found the way to heaven, but that image may well be the source of the saying: You feel as though you were in heaven. Robert Louis Stevenson recorded the feeling in *Memories and Portraits* (1887): "I went home that morning walking upon air."

Walk On Eggs. Proceed warily and with great caution. It's what you would have to do if you literally walked on eggs, since otherwise you would break them and be in for some messy footing. Sir John Harington, translating Ariosto's *Orlando Furioso* from Italian in 1591, wrote: "So soft he treds . . . As though to tread on eggs he were afraid."

Walk the Plank. Go to one's doom; be fired from one's job or ousted from a group. It was a popular form of execution among pirates at sea, particularly during the 17th century: A plank was put out from the deck, rather like a diving board, and the captive or the untrustworthy associate was made to walk to the end and keep going. It soon became a popular literary image. Sir Walter Scott used it in *The Pirate* (1822): "They should be made to walk the plank for their impudence."

Walking Encyclopedia (Dictionary, Library). Someone with a vast store of knowledge. The "walking library" was abroad as early as 1691, when Anthony Wood, writing about the University of Oxford in *Athenae Oxoniensis,* said: "Mathew Slade . . . was . . . a walking Library."

Warm Heart. Compassion; empathy. Robert Henryson employed the term ironically in his version of Aesop's fables (*The Morall Fabillis of Esope*) in 1480. In his rendering of "The Cock and the Fox" the fox tries to persuade the cock that a proclamation of universal peace and harmony among all kinds of beasts and birds has been put into effect, and he urges the cock to come down off his perch and talk about it, asserting: "My hart is warme." The cock did not fall for the line.

Warm Welcome. A hearty greeting. This term and "warm reception," which sounds like the same thing, have reached quite opposite meanings. The "warm reception" is what one gets when he falls into hostile hands. It was in the language in the early 18th century. The "warm welcome" seems to have arisen somewhat later. Byron had a version of it in *Lara* (1814): "Warm was his welcome to the haunts of man."

Warms the Cockles of Your Heart. Pleases you; makes you feel good. The ancient anatomical name for the ventricles of the heart (which was thought to be the seat of the feelings) is *cochleae cordis,* whence came the otherwise strange modern word "cockles." John Eachard's *Observations* (it's actually a much longer title) in 1671 was close to the modern saying: "This Contrivance of his did inwardly . . . rejoice the Cockles of his heart."

Wash Dirty Linen in Public. Talk openly about the problems or scandals of one's family or business. The allusion is to the fact that one usually does the laundry in a more or less private setting and would think it bad taste to do so publicly. Napoleon, in a speech on his return from Elba, made a remark that translates as: "It is in the family, not in public, that one washes one's dirty linen."

Wash One's Hands Of. Rid oneself of a problem. It is what Pontius Pilate did when he "saw that he could prevail nothing" in saving Jesus (Matthew 27 : 24): "When Pilate saw that he could prevail nothing, but that rather a tumult was made, he took water, and washed his hands before the multitude, saying, I am innocent of the blood of this just person: see ye to it."

283

Waste of Breath. Not worth saying; an unavailing plea or argument. The concept is old enough to have been in Vergil's *Aeneid*. In John Dryden's translation of 1697 it appears as:

> Why these insulting Words, this waste of Breath,
> To Souls undaunted, and secure of Death?

Watchful Eye, Keep a. Be wary or protective. Probably the most watchful eyes were those of Argus, the many-eyed monster of Greek mythology who was set to guard Io. It is he who is supposed to have been the source of the "eyes" in the tail of the peacock, as recounted in Timothy Kendall's *Flowers of Epigrammes*: "Of the Peacock . . . , then Iuno took his [Argus's] watchfull eyes, and bravely by and by, She plast them in my traine."

Water Over the Dam. Something that's done with; an irretrievable situation. An alternative was "water under the bridge," as one sees in Richard Sale's *Passing Strange* (1942): " 'That's water under the dam.' 'Bridge,' I said. 'Or water over the dam.' " Either way, the flowing water has passed by and will not return.

Wave of the Future. A strong trend; an idea or a program that looks as though it is going to make a substantial impact. The analogy is to the force of an ocean wave. Anne Morrow Lindbergh gave the phrase currency by making it the title of a book (1940) in which she wrote: "The wave of the future is coming and there is no fighting it."

Wax Wroth. Become angry. This meaning of "wax" is to show an increasing movement or feeling. Except for the alliterative pull the saying could just as well have been "wax angry." Charles Dickens was making use of the expression in 1840, in *The Old Curiosity Shop:* "Mr. Chuckster waxed wroth at this answer." One is reminded of the Marx Brothers movie in which Groucho, appearing as a college president, is told by his secretary that Mr. Smith and Mr. Jones are still waiting to see him, "and they are waxing wroth." Groucho says: "Send Roth in and tell the other two to wait."

Way of All Flesh. Death; a common path through life. Two phrases in the Bible apparently gave rise to this ancient expression, which actually does not get the Bible quite right. In Joshua 24 : 13 one reads: "And, behold, this day I am going the way of all the earth." . . . In 1 Kings 2 : 2 it is: "I go the way of all the earth . . . ."King Edward III of England is quoted as saying in 1337: "And so also for his own soule the day that hee shall goe the way of all flesh."

Ways and Means. Revenue for a government; the approach to the solution of a problem. The two words are synonymous, but they have been yoked together in tautology for a long time. The Rolls of Parliament for 1430 speak of "menes and wyes." The thought was also put, in the distant past, as "ways and grounds."

Wear Two Hats. Have two job titles or responsibilities; hold two appointments at the same time. The "hat" often reveals one's occupation, as with policemen, trainmen, military people and so on. If you take off one and put on another, you appear in two guises. The figure of speech seems to be quite recent, having been recorded by *The Times* of London in 1963: "They . . . - would perform that precarious feat known in the Whitehall idiom as wearing two hats."

Wear Your Heart on Your Sleeve. Show your emotions or feelings plainly. It was once a custom for a young man to attach to his sleeve a gift from a young lady he loved, thus displaying his feelings. Shakespeare alludes to the practice in *Othello*, where Iago says:

> For when my outward action doth demonstrate
> The native act and figure of my heart
> In compliment extern, 'tis not long after
> But I will wear my heart upon my sleeve."

Wears the Pants, She. She dominates a man or a household. In the days before the word "pants" stopped being regarded as a vulgar curtailment of "pantaloons," the saying was "she wears the breeches." In that form it is old enough to have appeared in *Choice, Chance and Change* (1606): "She that is master of her husband must weare the breeches."

Weasel Words. Ambiguities; a statement that the speaker or writer hopes will enable him to wriggle out of a difficult situation. The phrase was probably originated by Stewart Chaplin in the *Century Magazine* (1900): "Why, weasel words are words that suck the life out of the words next to them, just as a weasel sucks the eggs and leaves the shell." The phrase was popularized by Theodore Roosevelt in 1916, when he was criticizing President Wilson:

> "In connection with the word 'training,' the words 'universal voluntary' have exactly the same effect as an acid has on an alkali—a neutralizing effect. One of our defects as a nation has been a tendency to use what have been called '*weasel words*'. . . . If you use a *weasel word* after another there is nothing left of the other. Now you can have universal training or you can have voluntary training, but when

you use 'voluntary' to qualify 'universal,' you are using a *weasel word*; it has sucked all the meaning
out of 'universal.' The two words flatly contradict
each other."

Weighed In the Balance and Found Wanting. Shown after a test
to be inadequate; deficient in ability to do the task. The phrase
comes from the same biblical passage that speaks of handwriting on the wall and of days being numbered. Daniel is interpreting for King Belshazzar the message that was written on the wall
(MENE, MENE, TEKEL, UPHARSIN) and says (Daniel 5 : 27),
"TEKEL; Thou art weighed in the balances, and art found wanting."

Welcome With Open Arms. Receive a person or an idea with great
enthusiasm. The "arms" are "open" in order to form an embrace,
as one does in welcoming some people. Alexander Pope offered a
slightly different version of the modern saying in the prologue to
his *Satires and Epistles of Horace Imitated* (1735): "And St.
John's self . . . with open arms received one Poet more."

Well Nigh. Nearly; almost entirely. "Nigh" means "near" but nigh
has dropped out of the language except for this expression and a
few others, such as "nigh onto midnight." Richard Farews
(1581) shows how it was used long ago: "There was alreadie a
whole yeare and a halfe welnie paste [past]."

Well and Good. OK; what you say is all right, but something else is
more to the point. It could just as plausibly be "good and well,"
and at one time it was. Here is Tobias Smollett's translation of
Gil Blas in 1749: "My mother's predictions were always
favourable to those who solicited them; if they proved true, good
and well. . . ."

Well's Run Dry. Nothing is left; the opportunity has ended (often
because of excessive use). Not so many households rely on a well
now, and so they don't know the inconvenience of having one dry
up (sometimes only temporarily). One of Benjamin Franklin's
maxims in *Poor Richard's Almanack* was: "Then as Poor Dick
says, When the Well's dry, they know the Worth of Water." A cousin of this saying is, "He went to the well once too often."

Wend One's Way. Go. Mainly a literary cliché, included here because it makes the point that some words mysteriously shrivel in
meaning. "Wend" as a verb has had enough meanings to take up
five and a half columns in the *Oxford English Dictionary*, with
16 different definitions. Now it remains only in the cliché, and
even that had died out before 1800 but was then revived. It
appears in the 14th-century work *Cursor Mundi*: "I haue my
ways for to weynde, For to speke with a frynde."

Wet Behind the Ears. Innocent; naive. The allusion is to the newborn farm animal—a colt or a calf, say—that starts out being wet all over and dries last in the small indentation behind the ears. If you're young enough to be still wet behind the ears, you have had little experience in life.

Wet Blanket. A spoilsport; someone who dampens a social occasion. You can imagine what it would be like to sleep under a wet blanket: disagreeable. So is the sour, carping, humorless person in a social gathering. John Galt was using the phrase in his novel of 1830, *Lawrie Todd, or the Settlers in the Woods*: "I have never felt such a wet blanket before or syne."

Wet One's Whistle. Take a drink. One cannot whistle easily without at least licking one's lips. Since any liquid serves the purpose, it is a good excuse for having a drink. The term appears in Chaucer's *Canterbury Tales* ('The Reeve's Tale"): "So was hir ioly [jolly] whistle well y-wet."

Wet to the Skin. Thoroughly and (usually) unpleasantly soaked. In John Lyly's use of the saying in 1589 there is a suggestion that in some circumstances, such as a hot day, one might enjoy the sensation, but not in the situation he describes: "We care not for a Scottish mist, though it wet vs to the skin."

What's New? Tell me what's going on? How are things with you? A conversation-starter and a form of greeting. Put thus, it is fairly recent, but in a slightly different form one finds the thought in John Milton's *Paradise Regained* (1671): "Where ought we hear, and curious are to hear, what happ'ns new."

Wheels Within Wheels. The complexities of thought or action that are not always apparent. The allusion is to the story in the Bible (Ezekiel 1 : 16), where Ezekiel tells of "four living creatures" who heralded his vision of God: "The appearance of the wheels and their work was like unto the color of a beryl; and they four had one likeness: and their appearance and their work was as it were a wheel within a wheel."

When All Is Said and Done. At the end; when the matter is finished; nevertheless. People were voicing this rather wordy thought 400 years ago, as is evident in *The Disobedient Child* by Thomas Ingelend (1560): "Whan all is saide and all is done, Concernynge all thynges both more and lesse . . . ."

When In Rome, Do As the Romans Do. Go along; follow the local customs. St. Augustine tells in one of his letters (*Epistle XXXVI*) how his mother, Saint Monica, once asked Saint Ambrose: "At Rome they fast on Saturday, but not at Milan; which practice ought to be observed?" Saint Ambrose replied: "When I am at

Milan, I do as they do at Milan; but when I go to Rome, I do as Rome does!"

When It Rains, It Pours. If something happens at all, it is likely to show up in excess, to be too much of a good thing (as a heavy rain can be). The phrase was once the advertising slogan of a company in the United States that makes table salt, which has a tendency to coagulate in humid conditions; the company claimed its salt would continue to flow freely in those conditions. But the phrase is old enough to have served as part of a title of a work by John Arbuthnot in 1726: *It Cannot Rain but It Pours; or London Strow'd with Rarities.*

When My Ship Comes In. When I get rich; when I achieve success, thereby making a pile of money. Many investors ashore were likely to have a financial interest in the cargo carried by a merchant ship in the days of sail, when travel and communication were slow. Since it was uncertain when such a ship would arrive, the people with a financial interest had to wait quite anxiously and to worry about "when the ship comes in." Henry Mayhew picked up the extended meaning of the phrase in his *London Labour and the London Poor (1851):* "One [customer] always says he'll give me a ton of taties [potatoes] when his ship comes home."

Where There's Smoke There's Fire. Some clues are highly suggestive or revealing. Certainly the smoke of a fire must often have given away people who did not want to be discovered. The saying has had many forms, including "there is no fyre without some smoke" (1546) and "there can no greate smoke aryse, but there must be some fire, no great reporte without great suspition" (1579). Publilius Syrus had the thought in Latin in *Sententiae* (43 B.C.); the Latin translates: "Nor, when a fire is made, will smoke be lacking."

Whisper (Sweet) Nothings. Talk in an intimate situation without saying much that is weighty. Benjamin Disraeli described the art neatly in *Sybil* (1845): "Whisper nothings that sound like something."

Whistle in the Dark. Be cheerful or optimistic in a situation that doesn't warrant cheer or optimism. It is a great temptation to try to cheer oneself up by whistling or singing in a dark and lonely place. Sigmund Freud, in *The Problem of Anxiety* (1925), had a thought on the practice: "When the wayfarer whistles in the dark, he may be disavowing his timidity, but he does not see any the more clearly for doing so." The notion that one should whistle in difficult circumstances to show that one is not concerned or frightened can be found in Robert Blair's *The Grave* (1742): "The Schoolboy . . . Whistling aloud to bear his Courage up."

White Elephant. A possession that is more of a problem than a pleasure; a useless possession (perhaps quite valuable) that one cannot easily get rid of. Legend has it that rare albino elephants in ancient Siam automatically became the property of the king. At least one such king had the custom of giving a white elephant to any courtier who had fallen out of favor. The courtier was soon ruined by the cost of keeping the elephant. One sees the broadened meaning in a work of 1883 on Sir Thomas Elyot's book *The Gouernour*, of 1531: "Elyot regarded the new dignity much as the gift of a white elephant."

Whole New Ball Game, A. The situation has changed; we're in a different field of action. Here is how *The New Yorker* put it in 1971, which was probably not long after the phrase entered the language:

> If this were to happen [Chinese entry into the Vietnam War], some official of our government would no doubt announce that we were in a "whole new ballgame," which would mean that none of the policies or promises made in the past were binding any longer, including the prohibition against the use of nuclear weapons.

Whys and Wherefores. The questions and answers; the reasons. "Why" implies a question and "wherefore" an answer. The term smacks of ancient usage, and indeed it turns up as "quarfor and qui" in the *Metrical Homilies* of 1325. John Fletcher's play *Rule a Wife and Have a Wife* (1624) puts it thus:

> Such as are understanding in their draughts,
> And dispute learnedly the whyes and wherefores.

Wild and Woolly. Lively and unstructured; raucous. Adair Welcker's *Tales of the 'Wild and Woolly West'* (1891) had a publisher's note that sought to explain the term: "Woolly . . . seems to refer to the uncivilized—untamed—hair-outside, wool-still-in-the-sheepskin-coat—condition of the Western Pioneers."

Wild-Goose Chase. A pointless quest; a harebrained scheme. The saying comes from the notion that the pursuit of a wild goose is (or was in the days before guns) quite unlikely to succeed. (It is hard enough to catch a tame goose.) In the Middle Ages the name was given to a kind of horse race in which all the horses had to follow the course of the leader at a definite distance—akin to the flight of wild geese in a V formation. Sometimes the same kind of race was done with people as the participants. In *Romeo and Juliet*, Shakespeare has Mercutio say to Romeo: "Nay, if thy wits run the wild-goose chase, I have done; for thou has more of the wild goose in one of thy wits than, I am sure, I have in my whole five. . . ."

Will Wonders Never Cease. That's a marvel, a surprise. The question is often asked ironically, provoked by a statement or an event that isn't particularly remarkable although the originator of it appears to think it is. The expression was current by 1776, when Sir Henry Bate Dudley put it this way in a letter: "Wonders will never cease."

Win Hands Down. Triumph easily; finish way ahead of the field. The saying derives from the custom among jockeys of letting down the hands, thereby relaxing the tension on the reins, when victory seems assured. Here is an entry in *Lyrics and Lays* (1867): "There were good horses in those days, as he can well recall, / But Barker upon Elepoo, hands down, shot by them all."

Win One's Spurs. Achieve something difficult; gain admission to a group as a result of such an achievement. In medieval times it was often the custom for a knight to be awarded gilded spurs as a result of some heroic feat, and the aim of winning such a prize was a motivation for many knights. John Lydgate suggests the pull of the prize in *Assembly of Gods* (1425): "These xiii knyghtes made Vyce [voice] that day; / To wynne theyre spores they seyde they wold asay."

Wing It. Improvise. The image is that you are unexpectedly airborne (in a figurative sense) and will have to think or act imaginatively if you are going to get back to the ground safely. The phrase has been in vogue since around 1970, a year in which *Time* offered it this way: "You mean you've got to wing it."

Wintry Blast. A chilling or angry remark or attitude. The "wintry blast" is a staple of newspaper writers and television people talking about a winter storm with high winds. It is in that sense that the image first turns up in print, when Robert Burns wrote on *Winter* in 1781: "The wintry west extends his blast."

Wishful Thinking. An unrealistic attitude; an ill-founded hope. One is not supposed to let one's reason be directed by one's wishes. The expression has been current since about 1930 and was probably derived from the much older "the wish is father to the thought." Shakespeare had that one, in *Henry IV, Part 2*. Prince Henry says to the king, "I never thought to hear you speak again." The King replies: "Thy wish was father, Harry, to the thought. . . ."

Withering Glance (look, scowl). An expression of reproach, disdain or disgust (usually from a boss or one's spouse). Nobody ever "withered" under such a stare, but it is what you feel like doing, as if you were an unwatered plant left too long in the sun or the cold. The concept has been around for a long time; William

Collins (in his "Ode to the Passions," 1747) wrote of a person "with a with'ring Look"; and Samuel Rogers, writing *The Pleasures of Memory* in 1792, said: "A withering scowl she wore."

Within An Ace of. Close; a near success or disaster. The "ace" is the single pip on a single die; "ambsace," an archaic term, was the lowest throw possible with a pair of dice: two single pips. To be "within an ace" is to be close to the lowest possible point. The figurative meaning was in use by 1704, when Thomas Brown wrote in a letter: "I was within an ace of being talked to death."

Without Further Ado. Let's finish this; let's proceed to the next stage. Usually there is further "ado" after the speaker utters this formal rubric, but sometimes the phrase serves to move things along or quicken the pace. "Ado" was originally "at do" and in the 14th century was curtailed to "a-do." The modern form turns up in Edward A. Freeman's *History of the Norman Conquest* (1876): "William wanted a wife, and they were married without more ado."

Wits' End, At. Unable to think of what to do next; so vexed or harried as to be unable to think clearly. At the end of one's wits one has no thinking power left. Chaucer has a character say in *Troilus and Criseyde* (c. 1373): "At dulcarnon [in a dilemma], right at my wittes end."

Wolf In Sheep's Clothing. A person (usually of evil intent) who purports to be someone he isn't; a person in disguise (usually bent on evil deeds). It is the title of one of Aesop's fables (the wolf comes to a bad end), and the thought appears in the Bible (Matthew 7 : 15), where Jesus says; "Beware of false prophets, which come to you in sheep's clothing, but inwardly they are ravening wolves."

Word To the Wise, A. A hint of trouble or of pitfalls ahead should be all an intelligent person needs to be ready for it; it shouldn't take much, if you have your wits about you, to make you realize you've embarked on a dangerous or imprudent course. Variants include "a word to a wise man is enough," "few words to the wise suffice" and "a word to the wise is sufficient." A Latin expression carried the same advice: *Verbum satis sapienti* [a word is enough to the wise]. Versions of the saying in English go back to the 13th century. By 1546 John Heywood was recording something close to the modern version: "Fewe woord is to the wise suffice to be spoken."

Work One's Fingers to the Bone. Work very hard, to the point of exhaustion. People and animals have been worked to death, but it is doubtful that any fingers have been worked to the bone. It is just a vivid image. Edward Bulwer-Lytton had it in *My Novel* (1853): "I'll work my fingers to the bone till I pay back the other five."

Worked (Done) to Death. Overdone; repeated too often. H. D. Traill told his readers in *Recaptured Rhymes* (1882): "I am also called Played-out and Done-to-death, and It-will-wash-no-more." He seems to have been using expressions that were already well known.

Works His Butt Off. Labors long and hard. "Butt," as you might guess, is short for "buttock." In 1869 John Bartlett was telling the readers of his *Dictionary of Americanisms* that "the word is used in the West in such phrases as, 'I fell on my butt,' 'He kicked my butt.' "

World Is My Oyster, The. Things are going well; I have a lot of favorable opportunities. You get something of value from an oyster: a pearl. A bright and energetic person figures to get something of value from his circumstances, his world. Shakespeare popularized the phrase in *The Merry Wives of Windsor*. Falstaff has asked his brash young associate Pistol for a favor and has been refused. Later Pistol asks Falstaff for a loan and is refused. Pistol says:
> Why then, the world's mine oyster,
> Which I with sword will open.

World of Good, A. Something that will help you. Among other things, "world" has meant a large amount since the 15th century. Stephen Crane shows the current usage in *The Third Violet* (1897): "These long walks in the clear mountain air are doing you a world of good."

Worm Turns, The. Someone previously downtrodden gets his revenge; an unfavorable situation is reversed. The saying represents an evolution of the old proverb, "Tread on a worm and it will turn." The meaning was that even the most humble creature tries to counteract rough treatment. Shakespeare picked up the thought in *Henry VI, Part 3*, where Lord Clifford urges the king against "lenity and harmful pity," saying:
> To whom do lions cast their gentle looks?
> Not to the beast that would usurp their den . . .
> The smallest worm will turn being trodden on,
> And doves will peck in safeguard of their brood.

Worn Threadbare. Overworked or overused, like a cliché. Even the best of clothes meet this fate eventually, and the look of such a garment prompted the transfer to ideas, sayings and programs. John Skelton was making the transfer in 1518, when he wrote *Magnfycence*: "Welth and Wyt, I say, be so threde bare worne."

Worn to a Frazzle. Extremely tired or nervously exhausted from hard physical effort or mental strain. "Frazzle," a word now seldom met except in this context, started as a verb meaning to fray or to tear to ribbons. Then came "frazzled" and finally, in the middle of the 19th century, "frazzle" as a noun with such accompanying words as beaten, fought and worked. The modern form appears in J. C. Harris's *Uncle Remus* (1881): "Brer Fox dun know Brer Rabbit uv ole, en he know dat sorter game done wo' ter a frazzle."

Worth His (Its) Weight in Gold. A person (or a thing) that is extremely valuable or useful. The weight of a person, even a child, in gold would always have been convertible into a considerable sum of money. A 15th-century tale in verse (*Sir Eger, Sir Graham, Sir Graysteel*) has a character say: "A bed then I would rather, / Than my weight of gold and silver." Henry Medwall's *A Goodly Interlude of Nature* (1500) has the line: "Nay ye ar worth thy weyght of gold."

Worthy of (Worth) His Salt. He's proved himself; he is a good worker. At one time the Romans paid part of the wages of their soldiers in salt, then a rare commodity. Later the soldiers got money for buying salt (*salarium*, of salt, is the root of "salary"). Oddly, the modern expression dates only from the 19th century, probably originated by a classicist who was recalling the Roman practice. Thus, in Frederick Marryat's *The King's Own* (1830): "The captain . . . is not worth his salt."

Wrack and Ruin. Destruction or disaster. Do you ever see or hear "wrack" except in this phrase? It is an old variant of "wreck." In 1599 Thomas Fowler, writing *The History of Corpus Christi College*, spelled it "rack," a version that is still seen and that is sometimes thought to refer to the torture rack. Most likely the image was maritime: A wrecked ship was ruined. What Fowler wrote was: "In the mean season the College shall goe to rack and ruin."

Wreak Havoc. Destroy; devastate something. Long ago the cry "Havoc!" was a signal or order to soldiers to seize spoils or to pillage. Gradually the meaning shifted toward destructive devastation in general, not necessarily by soldiers, but even by inanimate things, such as a storm. "Wreak," incidentally, has gone out of the language except for its association with "havoc" and "vengeance." In 1480 William Caxton, writing *The Cronicles of Englond*, said: "They slowe [slew] al alyens and despoilled all hir goodes and made hauoke."

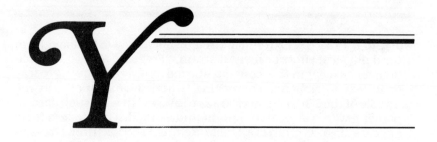

Yawning Gulf. A formidable obstacle or hazard. The physical "gulf" that is deep and wide can be said to resemble a yawn, and the idea transfers easily to a nonphysical gulf. St. Luke was close to the modern phrase in the New Testament (Luke 16 : 26): "And beside all this, between you and us there is a great gulf fixed. . . . ." Edmund Spenser had the modern phrase in *The Faerie Queene* (1590): "They . . . brought the heavy corse . . . To yawning gulf of deepe Avernus hole."

Year In and Year Out. Repeatedly or continuously over a long period of time. The year comes in, the year goes out, and the thing is still happening. Here is Louisa May Alcott, in *Little Women* (1868): "You see other girls having splendid times, while you grind, grind, year in and year out."

You Can Bet Your Bottom Dollar. You can be sure of it. The "bottom dollar" is the last one in a hypothetical (or perhaps real) stack; if you are prepared to stake that on something, it must be a good bet. In 1866 the *Congressional Globe* described a man who, the recent Civil War over the issue notwithstanding, believed "that a State can go out of the Union and he is willing to bet his bottom dollar on his judgement."

You Can Lead a Horse to Water But You Can't Make Him Drink. You can get only so far trying to persuade a stubborn or independent person to do something or to agree with a proposition. Time was when practically everybody had occasion to water a horse and would sometimes find, after going to that trouble, that the horse was not interested. John Heywood recorded the saying as a proverb in 1546: "A man may well bryng a horse to the water, But he can not make hym drynke without he will." One can't bring up this old saw without recalling a modern variant by the witty Dorothy Parker, who was asked to use the word "horticulture" in a sentence. She said: "You can lead a whore to culture but you can't make her think."

You Can't Make A Silk Purse Out of a Sow's Ear. You have to have the right starting material to make something or generate a useful idea; you can't make something good from inferior or inappropriate raw material. It's plain enough that the ear of a female pig cannot be passed off as silk; the question is how this particular way of putting the thought arose. Probably because the parts of the pig, including the skin, are put to many uses (including some splendid products), but there are some things you just can't make them into. In the 16th century Alexander Barclay put the thought this way in *Certayne Eglogues*: "None can . . . make goodly silke of a gotes fleece." In 1579 Stephen Gosson wrote (in his *Ephemerides*) of "seekinge . . . too make a silke purse of a Sowes eare."

You Can't Teach an Old Dog New Tricks. Old people or people with long experience in a task find it difficult to learn new ways. I wonder if it's really true about the dog. Probably an old dog that has been learning tricks all his life could keep right on in old age. The same with people. Still, the perception of the oldster as unable or unwilling to change is prevalent enough for versions of today's cliché to be very old. In 1523 John Fitzherbert told the readers of his *Newe Tracte or Treatyse Moost Profytable for Husbande Men:* "The dogge must lerne when he is a whelpe, or els it wyl not be; for it is harde to make an olde dogge to stoupe." In 1670 John Ray recorded this version in his collection of proverbs: "An old dog will learn no tricks. It's all one to physick the dead, as to instruct old men."

You Can't Win 'Em All. You won't always succeed (said often by or about people who usually do succeed). As a bit of self-deprecation, which may have originated among poker players, this line has been popular in the United States since about 1940 and in the United Kingdom since about 1955. Here is James Munro, in *The Innocent Bystanders* (1969): "He hesitated just a split second too long, and was already starting to turn when Craig's voice spoke behind him. 'Be sensible,' said Craig. 'You can't win them all. Guns on the bed, please.' "

You Get What You Pay For. If you buy things on the cheap, you probably won't get much that is of value or good quality. The lesson was learned a long time ago and reflected (in Latin) in Gabriel Biel's 15th-century *Expositio Canonis Missae: Pro tali numismate tales merces.*

You Said a Mouthful. What you have said is pithy, pertinent or sums up the situation. H. L. Mencken recorded the remark in *The American Language* (4th edition, 1936); it probably dates from just after World War I. Ring Lardner's *First and Last* (1934) has: " 'Well Lardy we will have to make it some other time,' said Gerry. 'You said a mouthful Gerry' was my smiling reply."

Young Man's Fancy, A. What is likely to be on the mind of a youthful male. It can be almost anything, but in the classic and original version it is love in the spring. The line is from Tennyson's poem "Locksley Hall" (1842): "In the spring a young man's fancy lightly turns to thoughts of love."

Your Guess is as Good as Mine. Neither of us knows enough about this to make a reliable judgment. The expression seems to be fairly new, having first turned up in print a bit less than 50 years ago, in Irene Baird's *Waste Heritage* (1939).

A

About-face, Do An. *See* Do An About-face.
Acres, Ancestral. *See* Ancestral Acres.
Adam, I Don't Know Him From. *See* Know Him From Adam, I Don't.
Against the Grain, Go. *See* Go Against the Grain.
Alack, Alas and. *See* Alas and Alack.
Along for the Ride, Go. *See* Go Along for the Ride.
At First Blush. *See* First Blush, At.
At Your Beck and Call. *See* Beck and Call, at Your.

B

Bacon, Bring Home the. *See* Bring Home the Bacon.
Baggage, Bag and. *See* Bag and Baggage.
Bananas, Go. *See* Go Bananas.
Band, Beats the. *See* Beats the Band.
Be All Things to All Men. *See* All Things to All Men, Be.
Beauties, Bevy of. *See* Bevy of Beauties.
Bed, and So to. *See* And So to Bed.
Belfry, Bats in the. *See* Bats in the Belfry.
Believe, You'd Better. *See* Better Believe, You'd.
Best Foot Forward, Put Your. *See* Put Your Best Foot Forward.
Between a Rock and a Hard Place. *See* Rock and a Hard Place, Between a.
Bib and Tucker, Best. *See* Best Bib and Tucker.
Boat, All in the Same. *See* All in the Same Boat.
Bone to Pick, Have a. *See* Have a Bone to Pick.
Bones, Bag of. *See* Bag of Bones.
Bonnet, He has a Bee in His. *See* Bee in His Bonnet, He Has a.
Book, By the. *See* By the Book.
Boots, You Can Bet Your. *See* Bet Your Boots, You Can.
Bottom of One's Heart, From the. *See* From the Bottom of One's Heart.
Breath, With Bated. *See* Bated Breath.
Britches, Too Big For His. *See* Big For His Britches, Too.
Broad Side of a Barn, Can't Hit the. *See* Can't Hit the Broad Side of a Barn.
Brook, Babble Like a. *See* Babble Like a Brook.
Brother's Keeper, I Am Not My. *See* I Am Not My Brother's Keeper.
Brunt, Bear the. *See* Bear the Brunt.
Buffaloed, To Be. *See* Be Buffaloed, To.

297

Bullet, Bite the. *See* Bite the Bullet.
Bush, Beat Around the. *See* Beat Around the Bush.
Button, Bright as a. *See* Bright as a Button.
By Hook or By Crook. *See* Hook or By Crook, By.
By the Board, Go. *See* Go By the Board.

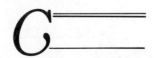

Cake and Eat It, You Can't Have Your. *See* Have Your Cake and Eat It, You Can't.
Can't See the Forest for the Trees. *See* Forest for the Trees, Can't See the.
Cards On the Table, Lay Your. *See* Lay Your Cards On the Table.
Cat, Who'll Bell the. *See* Who'll Bell the Cat.
Cats and Dogs, Rain. *See* Rain Cats and Dogs.
Chew, Bit Off More Than You Can. *See* Bit Off More Than You Can Chew.
Choosers, Beggars Can't Be. *See* Beggars Can't Be Choosers.
Circles, Going Around in. *See* Going Around in Circles.
Coat According to the Cloth, Cut the. *See* Cut the Coat According to the Cloth.
Comb, A Fine-tooth. *See* Fine-tooth Comb, A.
Compliment, Back-Handed. *See* Back-Handed Compliment.
Conditions of Men, All Sorts and. *See* All Sorts and Conditions of Men.
Cradle to Grave, From. *See* From Cradle to Grave.
Cropper, Come a. *See* Come a Cropper.
Crow Flies, As the. *See* As the Crow Flies.
Crystal Ball, A Clouded. *See* Clouded Crystal Ball, A.

Daggers At, Look. *See* Look Daggers At.
Day's Work, All in a. *See* All in a Day's Work.
Deep Blue Sea, Between the Devil and the. *See* Between the Devil and the Deep Blue Sea.
Devil and the Deep Blue Sea, Between the. *See* Between the Devil and the Deep Blue Sea.
Discord, Apple of. *See* Apple of Discord.
Dishwater, Dull as. *See* Dull as Dishwater.
Dogs, Go to the. *See* Go to the Dogs.
Dollar, The Almighty. *See* Almighty Dollar, The.
Don't Care a Rap For. *See* Care a Rap For, Don't.
Don't Count Your Chickens Before They're Hatched. *See* Count Your Chickens Before They're Hatched, Don't.
Drawing Board, Back to the. *See* Back to the Drawing Board.
Driver, Back-Seat Driver. *See* Back-Seat Driver.
Dust, Bite the. *See* Bite the Dust.

E

Ear, Let Me Bend Your. *See* Bend Your Ear, Let Me.
8-Ball, Behind the. *See* Behind the 8-Ball.
Element, In His. *See* In His Element.
End-All, Be-All and. *See* Be-All and End-All.
Excusions, Alarums and. *See* Alarums and Excursions.
Eye, Apple of His. *See* Apple of His Eye.

F

Fair in Love and War, All's. *See* All's Fair in Love and War.
Fast and Loose, Play. *See* Play Fast and Loose.
Fate Would Have It, As. *See* As Fate (Luck) Would Have It.
Fill, Back and. *See* Back and Fill.
Fingers to the Bone, Work One's. *See* Work One's Fingers to the Bone.
Fingertips, At His. *See* At His Fingertips.
Fire, Baptism of (by). *See* Baptism of (by) Fire.
Fox, Crazy (Dumb, Sly) Like a. *See* Crazy (Dumb, Sly) Like a Fox.
Frying Pan into the Fire, From (Out of). *See* From (Out of) the Frying Pan
    into the Fire.
Full Circle, Go (Come). *See* Go (Come) Full Circle.

G

Gangbusters, Come on Like. *See* Come on Like Gangbusters.
Get Down to Brass Tacks. *See* Brass Tacks, Get Down to.
Gifts, Beware of Greeks Bearing. *See* Beware of Greeks Bearing Gifts.
Gilead, Balm in. *See* Balm in Gilead.
Good Cheer, Be of. *See* Be of Good Cheer.
Good, All to the. *See* All to the Good.
Goods, All His Worldly. *See* All His Worldly Goods.
Grapevine, By the. *See* By the Grapevine.
Grass Grow Under His Feet, Lets No. *See* Lets No Grass Grow Under His
    Feet.
Grave, Enough to Make Him Turn in His. *See* Enough to Make Him Turn
    in His Grave.
Greek to Me, All. *See* All Greek to Me.
Grind, Have an Ax To. *See* Ax to Grind, Have An.
Ground, Have Both Feet on the. *See* Both Feet On the Ground, Have.

H

Half-Cocked, Go Off. *See* Go Off Half-Cocked.
Halt, Grind to a. *See* Grind to a Halt.

Hand That Feeds You, Bite the. *See* Bite the Hand That Feeds You.
Hand to Mouth, Live. *See* Live Hand to Mouth.
Hand, Give Him the Back of the. *See* Back of the Hand, Give Him the.
Harder They Fall, The Bigger They Come, the. *See* Bigger They Come, the Harder They Fall, The.
Hat in Hand, Go. *See* Go Hat in Hand.
Hatches, Batten Down the. *See* Batten Down the Hatches.
Haywire, Go. *See* Go Haywire.
Head Over Heels, Fall. *See* Fall Head Over Heels.
Head to Heels, From. *See* From Head to Heels.
Heart in Your Mouth, Have Your. *See* Have Your Heart in Your Mouth.
Heat of the Day, Bear the Burden and the. *See* Bear the Burden and the Heat of the Day.
Heels, Close on the Heels of. *See* Close on the Heels of.
Heels, Show a Clean Pair of Heels. *See* Clean Pair of Heels, Show a.
Hell in a Handbasket, Going to. *See* Going to Hell in a Handbasket.
Hell, Like a Bat Out of. *See* Bat Out of Hell, Like a.
High Hopes, Entertain. *See* Entertain High Hopes.
Hindsight, 20/20. *See* 20/20 Hindsight.
Hog on Ice, Independent as. *See* Independent as a Hog on Ice.
Hole, Ace in the. *See* Ace in the Hole.
Hollow, Beat Them All. *See* Beat Them All Hollow.
Honcho, Big. *See* Big Honcho.
Horse's Mouth, From the. *See* From the Horse's Mouth.
Horse, Beat a Dead. *See* Beat a Dead Horse.
Hot Water, In. *See* In Hot Water.
Hoyle, According to. *See* According to Hoyle.
Humble Pie, Eat. *See* Eat Humble Pie.

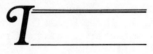

In on the Ground Floor, Get. *See* Get in on the Ground Floor.
Injury, Add Insult to. *See* Add Insult to Injury.
Insult to Injury, Add. *See* Add Insult to Injury.

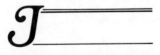

Jib, I Don't like the Cut of his. *See* Cut of his Jib, I Don't like the.

Kettle of Fish, A Fine. *See* Fine Kettle of Fish, A.

L

Leg Up On, Get a. *See* Get a Leg Up On.
Legion, Their (My) Name is. *See* Name is Legion, Their (My).
Life is Just a Bowl of Cherries. *See* Bowl of Cherries, Life is Just a.
Light At the End of the Tunnel, See. *See* See Light at the End of the Tunnel.
Light of Day, First Saw the. *See* First Saw the Light of Day.
Like an Open Book, Read Him. *See* Read Him Like an Open Book.
Lion in His Den, Beard the. *See* Beard the Lion in His Den.
Loggerheads, At. *See* At Loggerheads.
Love and War, All's Fair in. *See* All's Fair in Love and War.
Luck Would Have It, As. *See* As Fate (Luck) Would Have It.
Lucre, Filthy. *See* Filthy Lucre.
Luxury, Cradled in the Lap of. *See* Cradled in the Lap of Luxury

M

Madding Crowd, Far From the. *See* Far From the Madding Crowd.
Magnitude, of the First. *See* First Magnitude, of the.
Make Head or Tail of It, Not Able to. *See* Able to Make Head or Tail of It, Not.
Make the Fur Fly. *See* Fur Fly, Make the.
Man, As One. *See* As One Man.
Mean Maybe, And I Don't. *See* And I Don't Mean Maybe.
Medicine, Give Him a Dose of His Own. *See* Dose of His Own Medicine, Give Him a.
Men, Be All Things to All Men. *See* All Things to All Men, Be.
Morpheus, In the Arms of. *See* In the Arms of Morpheus.
Mother of Invention, Necessity is the. *See* Necessity is the Mother of Invention.
Musical Chairs, Play. *See* Play Musical Chairs.

N

Nail on the Head, Hit the. *See* Hit the Nail on the Head.
Neither Hide nor Hair. *See* Hide nor Hair, Neither.
Nickel, Not Worth a Plugged. *See* Plugged Nickel, Not Worth a.
Nines, Dressed to the. *See* Dressed to the Nines.
Nose, Can't See Beyond the End of His. *See* Can't See Beyond the End of His Nose.
Nose, Looked Down His. *See* Looked Down His Nose.

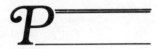

Off the Cuff, Speak. *See* Speak Off the Cuff.
Oil on Troubled Waters, To Pour. *See* Pour Oil on Troubled Waters, To.
Omega, Alpha and. *See* Alpha and Omega.
On the Brink of Disaster. *See* Brink of Disaster, On the.
Open the Floodgates. *See* Floodgates, Open the.
Out in the Cold, Leave. *See* Leave Out in the Could.
Over His Head, In. *See* In Over His Head.

Pale, Beyond the. *See* Beyond the Pale.
Pants, Ants in His. *See* Ants in His Pants.
Pay Dirt, Hit. *See* Hit Pay Dirt.
Penny, Costs a Pretty. *See* Costs a Pretty Penny.
Pie, Have a Finger in Every Pie. *See* Finger in Every Pie, Have a.
Pillar to Post, From. *See* From Pillar to Post.
Pin Drop, You Could Hear a. *See* Hear a Pin Drop, You Could.
Plague, Avoid Like the. *See* Avoid Like the Plague.
Port in a Storm, Any. *See* Any Port in a Storm.
Pot, Go to. *See* Go to Pot.
Power, Balance of. *See* Balance of Power.
Purple, Born to the. *See* Born to the Purple.

Question, Beg the. *See* Beg the Question.

Rap, Beat the. *See* Beat the Rap.
Respect, With All Due. *See* All Due Respect, With.
Retreat, Beat a. *See* Beat a Retreat.
Reward, Go to His. *See* Go to His Reward.
Right Arm, He'd Give (or Cut off) His Right Arm. *See* Give (or Cut off) His
    Right Arm.
Roses, Bed of. *See* Bed of Roses.
Route, Go the. *See* Go the Route.
Row to Hoe, Tough (Hard, Long). *See* Tough (Hard, Long) Row to Hoe.
Rut, In a. *See* In a Rut.

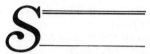

Salt Mine, Back to the. *See* Back to the Salt Mine.
Salt in the Wound, Rub. *See* Rub Salt in the Wound.
Same Boat, All in the. *See* All in the Same Boat.
Sardines, Packed In Like. *See* Packed In Like Sardines.
Schemes, The Best-laid. *See* Best-laid Schemes, The.
Schoolboy Knows, As Every. *See* As Every Schoolboy Knows.
Scot-free, Go. *See* Go Scot-free.
Sea, All at. *See* All at Sea.
Seize the Bull By the Horns. *See* Bull By the Horns, Seize the.
Shadow, Afraid of His Own. *See* Afraid of His Own Shadow.
Shirt Off His Back, He'd Give You the. *See* Give You the Shirt Off His Back, He'd.
Sigh of Relief, Heave a. *See* Heave a Sigh of Relief.
Silver Lining, Every Cloud Has a. *See* Every Cloud Has a Silver Lining.
Silver Spoon in His Mouth, Born With a. *See* Born With a Silver Spoon in His Mouth.
Sinking Ship, Rats Abandon a. *See* Rats Abandon a Sinking Ship.
Skin Deep, Beauty is Only. *See* Beauty is Only Skin Deep.
Skittles, Not All Beer and. *See* Beer and Skittles, Not All.
Sleeve, Ace Up His. *See* Ace Up His Sleeve.
Sorts and Conditions of Men, All. *See* All Sorts and Conditions of Men.
Soul Your Own, Can't Call Your. *See* Can't Call Your Soul Your Own.
Square One, Back to. *See* Back to Square One.
Start to Finish, From. *See* From Start to Finish.
Stiff Upper Lip, Keep a. *See* Keep a Stiff Upper Lip.
Stone, No Getting Blood From a. *See* Blood From a Turnip (Stone), No Getting.
Storm, Any Port in a. *See* Any Port in a Storm.
Stumped, Had Me. *See* Had Me Stumped.
Sublime to the Ridiculous, From the. *See* From the Sublime to the Ridiculous.
Sundry, All and. *See* All and Sundry.
Swing of It (Things), Get into the. *See* Get into the Swing of It (Things).
Swords into Plowshares, Beat. *See* Beat Swords into Plowshares.

Take the Bitter with the Sweet. *See* Bitter with the Sweet, Take the.
Teeth, Armed to the. *See* Armed to the Teeth.
Ten-foot Pole, I Wouldn't Touch It with a. *See* I Wouldn't Touch It with a Ten-foot Pole.
That's Not Cricket. *See* Cricket, That's Not.
There's No Fool Like an Old Fool. *See* No Fool Like an Old Fool, There's.
Thieves, Den of. *See* Den of Thieves.

Things to All Men, Be All. *See* All Things to All Men, Be.
Thumbs, All. *See* All Thumbs.
Time, At This (Particular) Point in. *See* At This (Particular) Point in Time.
Time, Bide Your. *See* Bide Your Time.
Tip of My Tongue, At the. *See* At the Tip of My Tongue.
Token, By the Same. *See* By the Same Token.
Tongue, At the Tip of My. *See* At the Tip of My Tongue.
Tooth and Nail, Fight. *See* Fight Tooth and Nail.
Town, Go to. *See* Go to Town.
Tricks, Bag of. *See* Bag of Tricks.
Truck With, Have No. *See* Have No Truck With.
Tucker, Best Bib and. *See* Best Bib and Tucker.
Turn in His Grave, Enough to Make Him. *See* Enough to Make Him Turn in His Grave.
Twinkling of an Eye, In the. *See* In the Twinkling of an Eye.

Velvet Glove, Iron Hand in a. *See* Iron Hand in a Velvet Glove.
Verities, The Eternal. *See* The Eternal Verities.

Wall, Have Your Back to the. *See* Back to the Wall, Have Your.
War, All's Fair in Love and. *See* All's Fair in Love and War.
War, All-Out. *See* All-Out War.
Warpath, Go on the. *See* Go on the Warpath.
Wax, A Whole New Ball of. *See* Ball of Wax, A Whole New.
Way the Ball Bounces, That's. *See* Ball Bounces, That's the Way the.
Wet, All. *See* All Wet.
Whole Cloth, Cut from. *See* Cut from Whole Cloth.
Whole Hog, Go. *See* Go Whole Hog.
With All Due Respect. *See* All Due Respect, With.
With Bated Breath. *See* Bated Breath, With.
With Malice Aforethought. *See* Malice Aforethought, With.
Woman Scorned, Hell has No Fury Like a. *See* Hell has No Fury Like a Woman Scorned.
Wonders Never Cease, Will. *See* Will Wonders Never Cease.
Woods, Babe in the. *See* Babe in the Woods.
Wool and a Yard Wide, All. *See* All Wool and a Yard Wide.
Words, Actions Speak Louder Than. *See* Actions Speak Louder Than Words.
Work, All in a Day's. *See* All in a Day's Work.
Worldly Goods, All His. *See* All His Worldly Goods.
Worlds, The Best of All Possible. *See* Best of All Possible Worlds, The.
Worst Enemy, He's His Own. *See* Own Worst Enemy, He's His.

Yard Wide, All Wool and a. *See* All Wool and a Yard Wide.